How to Do *Everything* with

Adobe InDesign CS

...rgsland

McGraw-Hill/Osborne

New York Chicago San Francisco Lisbon
London Madrid Mexico City Milan New Delhi
San Juan Seoul Singapore Sydney Toronto

686 2254 BERG

The **McGraw·Hill** Companies

McGraw-Hill/Osborne
2100 Powell Street, 10th Floor
Emeryville, California 94608
U.S.A.

To arrange bulk purchase discounts for sales promotions, premiums, or fund-raisers, please contact **McGraw-Hill**/Osborne at the above address. For information on translations or book distributors outside the U.S.A., please see the International Contact Information page immediately following the index of this book.

How to Do Everything with Adobe® InDesign® CS

34567890 CUS CUS 01987654

ISBN 0-07-223153-X

Publisher	Brandon A. Nordin
Vice President &	
Associate Publisher	Scott Rogers
Acquisitions Editor	Megg Morin
Acquisitions Coordinator	Athena Honore
Technical Editor	Marcia Best, Owner Best Graphics
Copy Editor	Marilyn Smith
Proofreaders	Paul Tyler and Beatrice Wikander
Indexer	Claire Splan
Composition	Apollo Publishing Services
Illustrators	Kathleen Edwards, Melinda Lytle
Series Design	Mickey Galicia
Cover Series Design	Dodie Shoemaker
Cover Illustration	John Sledd

Dedication

I dedicate this to the women in my life:
Pastor Pat, Elizabeth, Ann, Lauren, and Taylor. What a joy they are.
(And I'm sure Kevin, Jacob, and Dylan are not jealous.)

About the Author

David Bergsland has been working in printing and publishing since 1967. With a B.F.A. from the University of Minnesota in 1971, he has built a career as a graphic designer, an author, and a teacher. Since 1991, he has taught at the Albuquerque Technical Vocational Institute. He was hired to take over and revitalize the commercial printing program—bringing it into the digital age. In 1996, he developed the school's Business Graphics and Communication program, which combines print, Web, and multimedia training into a single degree. He designs the class materials for the program and teaches about 300 students a year.

David has written seven books on digital publishing, including *Introduction to Digital Publishing*, *Publishing with InDesign*, *Publishing with Illustrator and FreeHand*, and *Publishing with Photoshop*. He has been on the alpha team for InDesign since 1999. For relaxation, he designs and sells fonts through MyFonts.com and fonts.com.

Contents

Acknowledgments

First and foremost, I acknowledge my wife, Rev. Patricia H. Bergsland. I assure you that she has earned the title merely by putting up with me. Her wisdom and love are my strength and joy.

My agent, Jawahara Saidullah, did a marvelous job of getting me this book and has been a strong support throughout its production. Megg Morin has been a wonderful acquisitions editor as we roamed through the capabilities of InDesign and the production department at Osborne. Athena Honore kept me in the loop and managed the huge pile of files I was throwing at Osborne. Madhu Prasher straightened out all production problems. And, I can't say enough about Marilyn Smith's editorial abilities. She made this book coherent. This was the first book I have ever been required to fit into a preexisting format. In fact, this is the first book I have not written, designed, and formatted (including creating the fonts and graphics), and then produced the final digital documents. I had a lot to learn. I have a new appreciation for book production as a team sport, instead of a fine-art experience.

It was a difficult book. Not only were we dealing with the vagaries of alpha software, but I lost two hard drives in the midst of production. With one, I lost everything. In addition, I had to install and learn Windows XP Professional. That was an experience! I have a new appreciation for the ability of my PC students to bear pain.

Introduction

This book covers the software that has given us the largest step forward in page layout capabilities since QuarkXPress 3 delivered the knockout punch to PageMaker 4. You could be reading this book for a variety of reasons. You may have realized that what you are doing cannot really be done in Word or is too clumsy to do in QuarkXPress. Or perhaps you are finally ready for the upgrade from PageMaker. Of course, if you are upgrading from an earlier version of InDesign, you've already proved your wisdom.

InDesign CS is the page layout application for people who need to make their documents look professional. As you will come to understand from this book, InDesign has far surpassed the capabilities of QuarkXPress, the page layout application of the last millennium.

InDesign has many powerful capabilities, including some that are completely unavailable outside Adobe:

- Full transparency
- Tables that can be formatted and flow like text from column to column and page to page
- Unlimited undo of almost everything
- Paragraph-level justification of copy for greatly improved type color
- Optical margin alignment
- Automatic optical kerning
- OpenType support for automatic features like true small caps, oldstyle figures, fractions, swashes, and ligatures
- Nested master pages
- Completely customizable shortcuts and workspace arrangements
- A built-in word processor
- Mixed spot-color swatch sets
- Custom-drawn screen previews of exceptional quality
- Separation and overprint previews
- Direct PSD import with transparency (we no longer need clipping paths)

- Direct export of prepress-quality PDFs, as well as interactive PDFs with movies and sound
- Solid scripting, tagging, and XML support

And this list is by no means complete. The only downside is the current lack of competition. It's an exciting new world for page layout.

A Brief History of Digital Page Layout Design

For the past decade, we have been watching the world of professional graphic design convert entirely to digital output. This transition has already occurred in the business office environment, but the world of professional printing is much more complex than the world of the office. The entire process has been a challenge, to say the least. Let me give you a quick, nonscholarly history of events.

In the beginning, with the Mac in 1984, desktop publishing was just a gleam in the eye of many people. The Mac would have died except for desktop publishing. Aldus, in the form of PageMaker, along with Adobe's PostScript and the Apple LaserWriter, saved the day. In fact, Paul Brainerd, the head of Aldus, is credited with coining the phrase *desktop publishing*.

By 1990, PageMaker, and PostScript (fonts, laser printers, and imagesetters) were absolutely dominant. PageMaker's interface was designed by and for designers. People like the McWades and Ole Kvern were in on the beginnings. Aldus itself was named after the publisher of the original italic font (created in northern Italy during the Renaissance).

However, as great as PageMaker was, it had some serious flaws. One of its competitors gave it a roundhouse in 1991, with the release of QuarkXPress 3, which actually supported CMYK and separations. It didn't matter that PageMaker caught up with version 4.2 in a matter of months. Quark was the buzz, and PageMaker was the old thing. You could hardly run Quark without hundreds, if not thousands, of dollars of Xtensions, but it didn't matter. The graphic designers switched to digital about that time, and they would not be caught dead using the old software. They all wanted Quark. When printer companies and service bureaus started converting to digital production, all they received were Quark files.

There were a few other applications. Letraset's ReadySetGo made a little run. FrameMaker developed a following in the bureaucratic, scientific community because it could set equations, footnotes, and other technical necessities. On the PC side, Ventura Publisher gained industrial muscle, but it was never a serious contender, because Windows wasn't. Windows didn't fully support PostScript until Windows 2000. (That should give you an idea of why Macs dominate desktop publishing, although with Windows XP Professional, the PC side finally has a mainstream operating system that can compete head to head.)

By the mid-1990s, PageMaker, QuarkXPress, Freehand, Illustrator, and Photoshop were producing virtually all the professional output sent to printers. But after Adobe purchased Aldus in the late 1990s, it basically pulled the plug on PageMaker. Ole Kvern has said that Adobe purchased Aldus because of that company's developments, which ended up with InDesign. Rumors started floating around about the new Quark Killer, K2, that Adobe had in the works. Fantastic capabilities were whispered about. InDesign was supposed to be a simple plug-in manager that could be updated radically very quickly. There was a lot of truth to the rumors.

In the new millennium, a new tool for professional page layout has become available. I mentioned what QuarkXPress did to PageMaker in the early 1990s. What Quark did then, InDesign is now doing to Quark. Forget the earlier rumors you heard of versions 1 and 1.5. By InDesign 2, Quark was of historical interest, used by those unable to keep up (for whatever reason). InDesign CS is yet another huge upgrade, as major as the leap from InDesign 1.5 to 2.

From the outset, InDesign has been completely cross-platform. In fact, it is the only application that can read either PC or Mac fonts (just drop them into the Fonts folder in the InDesign application folder). We haven't had type and page layout this good—ever.

Who Is This Book For?

An InDesign CS book must serve a wide variety of readers. Some of you are coming from the business world, having been told that you are now doing the newsletter and you are doing it with InDesign. This book will tell you everything you need to know to get started in the production of printable professional documents. The explanations of features will assume some background knowledge in typography and printing history. For that, I recommend my earlier book, *Introduction to Digital Publishing*.

Most of you are graphic designers with various levels of experience in digital production using QuarkXPress, PageMaker, or earlier versions of InDesign. This book is designed for you. You might be tempted to skip some of the basic stuff, but you need to be careful, because a lot of the basics have been radically improved. For example, the New Document dialog box now allows you to set custom preset page sizes, plus you can set bleeds, slugs, and margin locks in the presets.

I think you will find this book an excellent resource. My goal was to answer all your questions about the software, while providing guidance to those new to the industry. I will show you the most efficient and productive ways to use InDesign, so you can compete in our deadline-driven and budget-conscious industry. I will not only point out what works and how I think it is best used, but what doesn't work and why you should avoid it.

How Is This Book Organized?

This book includes 18 chapters, organized into 6 parts, to take you from starting up the software through producing your final publication.

Part I, Get Started with InDesign CS   This part covers the InDesign interface—what it contains, how to control it, and how to customize it. It also explains how to open documents, including those from QuarkXPress and PageMaker.

Part II, Add Typography   The five chapters in this part are devoted to the core of graphic design: typesetting. Along with the basics of adding and editing type, you'll learn about InDesign's superior typography features, including OpenType, paragraph-level justification, and optical margin alignment. OpenType is going to change your whole approach to setting type, with true small caps, oldstyle figures, true fractions, superiors, inferiors, superscript, subscript, discretionary ligatures, swashes, multiple languages, and more. InDesign's powerful Story Editor, paragraph styles, and table features are also covered in this part.

Part III, Add Graphics   Most designers are used to importing graphics made in other applications into a page layout program. Although InDesign makes it easy to bring in art from Photoshop, Illustrator, FreeHand, and other applications, it also provides some very useful graphics-creation capabilities, based on the same PostScript drawing techniques as FreeHand and Illustrator. This part describes how to use InDesign's drawing and graphic-editing tools, as well as how to import and export graphics.

Part IV, Add Color   The two chapters in this part focus on the complexities of designing with color. It describes InDesign's masterful ability to apply color, primarily controlled by the Swatches palette, which is unprecedented in power—in any application. You'll also find solutions for common problems with color printing, ranging from handling separations and duotones to ensuring proper registration and trapping.

Part V, Design Web and Multimedia Documents   This part concentrates on InDesign's Web and interactive PDF features. It explains how to add hyperlinks, buttons, movies, and sound clips to your documents. There are also plenty of tips on designing for the Web.

Part VI, Produce Finished Documents   This part takes you through the process of using InDesign's page layout capabilities and your knowledge of design to assemble the pieces, prepare the document for production, and produce your final output. These chapters include information to help you design your document to suit the capabilities of its output device, whether it's an in-house laser printer, a high-end imagesetter or platesetter, or anything in between. You'll also learn how to export PDFs and use InDesign's printing options.

Throughout the book, you'll see several different types of sidebars:

- *How to…* sidebars provide step-by-step instructions for tasks.

- *Did you know?* sidebars give you extra information about a variety of related topics.

- *For Newcomers* sidebars explain page design fundamentals that people new to page design may find enlightening.

- Note icons point out additional information.

- Tip icons point out tips to help you work more quickly and efficiently.

- Caution icons point out some areas that could cause problems.

- Shortcut icons point out shortcut keys.

- Unique to InDesign icons point out features that you won't find in other page layout programs.

- Tips for Quark Users icons point out features that help Quark users make the transition to InDesign.

- New to InDesign CS icons point out new additions to this version of InDesign.

You'll find exercises to practice your skills throughout the book. Additionally, I am offering the tutorials from the book on my web site at http://kumo.swcp.com/graphics, so that you can download the pieces. E-mail me at graphics@swcp.com if you have any questions.

Part I

Get Started with InDesign CS

Chapter 1

Understand the InDesign Interface

How to…

- Know the palettes
- Learn the tools of InDesign
- Locate menu options

InDesign really is a brand-new program. It is not a step up from PageMaker. It is not Adobe's version of QuarkXPress. It is not a multipage Illustrator. It uses pieces and concepts from all of those programs, but the feel of the application is very different. It is a very comfortable program to work in, once you become used to it. Most of us find it nearly addictive.

The first thing you need to know is that InDesign CS has the normal Adobe interface. Keyboard shortcuts and palettes drive this interface. What is unique about InDesign CS is that its entire focus is on assembling pages into documents. InDesign CS is the premier page layout program currently available. It has far outstripped Quark and other competitive products. InDesign CS can produce page layouts and typography with a quality that was previously unavailable to digital designers.

InDesign's interface is really well thought-out. After a few tweaks to customize it (described in Chapter 4), you will see a very different program from Illustrator, GoLive, Photoshop, or Acrobat. However, these applications work together very well, with many similar internal pieces.

The goal of this chapter is to introduce you to the InDesign interface. We'll go over each palette, tool, and menu.

Know the Palettes

The main workhorses of the InDesign interface are its palettes. In the original version, there were 18 palettes, and I thought that was a lot. In InDesign CS, there are 34 palettes (I think—I keep getting different counts). However, there are around a dozen or so that are geared toward programmers and script writers. Most of us will not use those palettes much, if at all.

You will need to spend some time organizing the palettes you do find useful. Thankfully, with InDesign's new side-docking palettes and saved workspaces, the control you need is easily available. I will spend an entire chapter describing how to customize the interface (Chapter 4).

Here, we will go through the list of palettes. I will give you a brief description of what each palette is used for and tell you which chapters in the book describe the palette in detail. I will also give you my opinion about the relative importance of the palette and how it might help you get your job done.

The Control Palette

The Control palette looks similar to Photoshop's Options palette, but it is actually much more powerful than that. It includes everything from the Measurement palette in Quark and the Control palette from PageMaker, plus quite a bit more functionality.

The Control palette is context-sensitive, changing its appearance and functions depending on which tool you are using and what you have selected. Basically, it includes most of the InDesign Character, Paragraph, and Transform palettes. We will examine the Control palette in Chapter 2.

TIP   *You will want to keep the Control palette open at all times. I recommend docking it to the top of the window, directly below the menu bar.*

The Character Palette

The Character palette is comparable to Quark's Character Specifications dialog box. The only mildly disconcerting aspect is the lack of a dialog box for these specifications. However, it has many more options, solves many problems caused by those applications from the last millennium, and offers features unheard of to most designers coming from Quark or PageMaker.

Some of you will access this palette using the same keyboard shortcut you used in PageMaker or Quark. However, most of the fields in the Character palette are also available in the Control palette, so you won't need to keep this palette open very often. In fact, this palette should not be used much at all. The choices in this palette are primarily for local formatting. As I will discuss in Chapter 8, you should do all your general formatting with character and paragraph styles. Then you might be forced to use local formatting to clean up widows, orphans, and the like.

UNIQUE TO
InDesign
CS
Chapter 5 covers the Character palette in detail. As a little tease of Chapter 5, one feature InDesign adds that has not been available before is optical kerning. Optical kerning analyzes the spaces between letters to determine what looks best. My experience suggests that optical kerning is an amazing option. As a test, I made a simple font in Fontographer, with no built-in kerning and purposely poor spacing, and watched InDesign do a very good job of spacing that font.

The Paragraph Palette

The Paragraph palette is much like PageMaker's Paragraph dialog box or Quark's Formats dialog box. The normal options of this type of dialog box are here: left indent, right indent, first-line indent, space before paragraph, and space after paragraph.

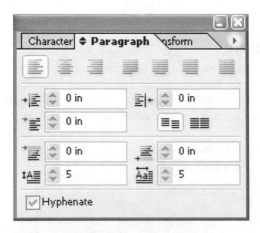

InDesign's Paragraph palette also includes drop cap controls and a surprising number of alignment choices. The details of using the Paragraph palette are in Chapter 5.

Like all professional design programs other than Quark, InDesign considers leading to be a character attribute, rather than a paragraph attribute. When placing inline (or anchored) graphics, the copy automatically adjusts to the size of the graphic, for example. If you prefer, you can make the entire paragraph use one leading very easily. But do note that the leading settings are found in the Character palette and the Character and Paragraph Styles palettes.

Paragraph Alignment

UNIQUE TO
**InDesign
CS**

Here, you begin to see the benefits of InDesign's paragraph justification options, which represent a major advance in digital typography. InDesign was the first to add justified left, justified center, justified right, and fully justified to the designer's repertoire. Basically, it offers the old controls we had with phototypesetters (quad left, quad right, and so on). InDesign's justification is so good that it is no longer true that you must use flush-left copy for professional typesetting. You will be using justified copy much more often than you have in the past.

Drop Caps

Another one of InDesign's strengths is evident in the Paragraph palette: It offers a lot of control over drop caps. All you need to do is type in how many lines you want the letters to drop and how many letters you want to drop. If you change your mind, change the numbers. More than that, you can drop inline graphics.

The Glyphs Palette

InDesign was the first professional application to support OpenType. All current programs can use OpenType, but they use only the first 256 characters. These are the same characters available in TrueType and PostScript fonts. InDesign can use *all* of the characters in a font. For example, the Adobe Jenson Pro Light Italic font has 770 characters and glyphs. (I'll cover OpenType fonts in detail in Chapter 5.)

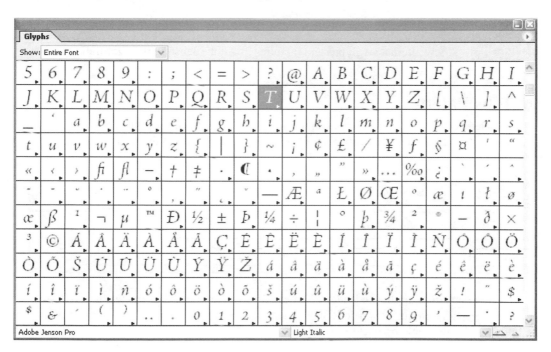

A *glyph* is an alternate form of a character. Open type fonts have automatic small caps, dozens of ligatures, and many special glyphs. You can use the Glyphs palette to add any glyph found in the font. More than that, you can place many of them automatically. Figure 1-1 shows some examples of Adobe Jenson Pro Light Italic glyphs in a document. The little swash at the end of the word *ligature* in Figure 1-1 surprised me—it just appeared. Also notice the two variants of *y, g, d,* and other characters. The Glyphs palette is covered in Chapter 6.

Special glyphs of Jenson Pro Light Italic

dD *and the alternate glyphs* $D^d dD D$

Ligature glyphs:

st *and* *sty; sp* *and* *spry; ct* *and* *ct; ft* *and* *soft*

A few alternative glyphs and ligatures of Adobe Jenson Pro Light Italic

The Tabs Palette

The Tabs palette offers all of the features you would expect. It has the normal three tabs: left, right, and centered. But it also includes a special-character tab, which you can use to line up a tab on any character you choose.

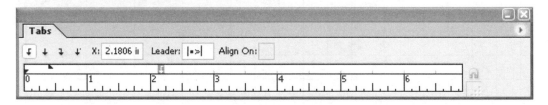

The same versatility applies to leaders. You can now use up to eight characters to make your leaders. For example, in the Tabs palette shown here, the leader is a combination of a vertical line, bullet, and right-angle bracket (|●>).

NOTE   *The ability to combine characters in leaders is wonderful. Why? You can make decorative rules with dingbats. Yes, it's true that this capability has no common use, but that is because it's not yet common. I am certain that I will use it, now that the capability is available. That is the nature of this new paradigm of digital publishing. We are software-driven. (Now, if only we were all driven by good taste.)*

One additional feature is the vertical line that appears in the text block when you move a tab. This is very handy. In fact, I recommend that complicated tabs be adjusted this way in a sample paragraph before you make a new paragraph style. I'll show you how to use the Tab palette features in Chapter 7.

The Transform Palette

The Transform palette includes all of the functionality of Quark's Measurement palette, plus the handle proxy feature that makes PageMaker's Control palette so useful. Everything can be measured from the handle of your choice, plus you have Illustrator's option of dragging the transformation center to whatever location you need.

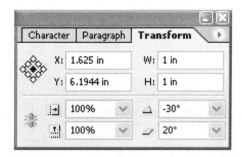

The XY numbers measure the location of the handle selected in the proxy on the left side of the palette. Probably the most useful aspect of the Transform palette is the ability to accurately locate any object on a page, measured from any point, the center, or the transformation point. The Transform palette is covered in Chapter 11.

The Info Palette

NEW TO
InDesign
CS

The Info palette, new to InDesign CS, gives information about whatever is selected. As you can see in the palette shown here, the insertion point is in a frame that has 543 characters, 95 words, 8 lines, and 2 paragraphs.

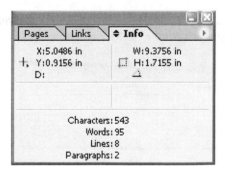

The Info palette also gives the size and location of the text frame. For graphics, it gives type, format, resolution (if any), and so on.

The Layers Palette

The Layers palette has the full functionality of Illustrator's Layers palette. It's missing several of FreeHand's abilities, but then, this is a page layout program. The example here illustrates the use most often touted by Adobe: the ability to work on a document in multiple languages. This is certainly a good use of layers. The Layers palette is covered in Chapter 11.

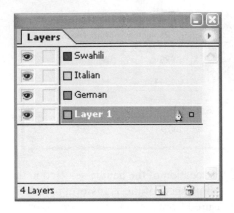

 Personally, I find little use for this type of layers organization in a page layout program. In fact, I find that most designers grossly overuse this capability and end up needlessly complicating their design and slowing their production speed. In most cases, you can do what is needed with the simple shortcuts used to move selections up or down through the creation order (using the Object | Arrange command).

The Story Palette

UNIQUE TO
**InDesign
CS**   *The Story palette is really a preference or command masquerading as a palette. It controls the optical margin alignment feature, which takes hanging punctuation to new levels.*

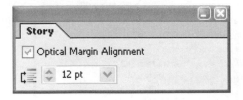

Optical margin alignment hangs punctuation and the edges of letters over the margins to give a more accurate optical alignment. This is similar to the idea of hanging bowls and angles of type characters below the baseline so that they look properly aligned. Optical margin alignment now enables us to eliminate the optical illusion that the edges of our columns do not line up. Figure 1-2 shows an example. Using optical margin alignment makes the edges of the type look much cleaner and the type color much smoother.

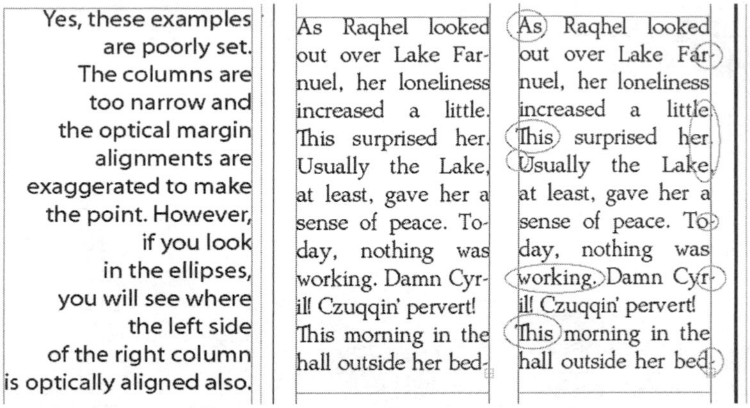

Yes, these examples are poorly set. The columns are too narrow and the optical margin alignments are exaggerated to make the point. However, if you look in the ellipses, you will see where the left side of the right column is optically aligned also.

As Raqhel looked out over Lake Farnuel, her loneliness increased a little. This surprised her. Usually the Lake, at least, gave her a sense of peace. Today, nothing was working. Damn Cyrill Czuqqin' pervert! This morning in the hall outside her bed-

As Raqhel looked out over Lake Farnuel, her loneliness increased a little. This surprised her. Usually the Lake, at least, gave her a sense of peace. Today, nothing was working. Damn Cyrill Czuqqin' pervert! This morning in the hall outside her bed-

FIGURE 1-2   Optical margin alignment hangs punctuation and the edges of letters over the margins.

Type characters are widely varied, and lining them up visually has always been one of the signs of a pro. InDesign has now automated that process with remarkably good results. In general, optical margin alignment is a wonderful feature that has been missing ever since we went digital. Chapter 5 covers the Story palette and optical margin alignment.

The Pages Palette

The Pages palette adds PageMaker's Master Pages palette to Quark's Document Layout palette, with very impressive capabilities and a far more useful layout. The unique feature of nesting master pages with parent-child relationships just gives you a hint of the additional possibilities. It is a very customizable interface. As shown in Figure 1-3, you can choose to set up the Pages palette in InDesign style or in Quark style. I will cover its capabilities in Chapter 3.

The Paragraph Styles Palette

In general, the Paragraph Styles palette provides the best global document control I have ever used—better than PageMaker, Quark, and FreeHand. Part of this is simply because

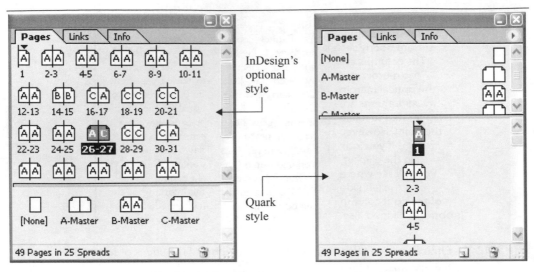

As you can see, with InDesign's optional setup, you can easily manage many more pages without the need for constant scrolling, viewing up to 100 pages at the same time without any problems. You can shuffle pages around by dragging the icons.

FIGURE 1-3   The Pages palette set up the new way and in Quark style

InDesign has so many unique features the other programs are still missing. But a large portion of it is due to the interface itself.

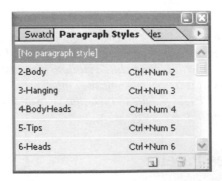

The Paragraph Styles palette is easy to use and very complete, as you'll see in the coverage of styles in Chapter 8.

The Character Styles Palette

The Character Styles palette basically completes the tool set needed for document formatting. Quark 4 implemented it first, but InDesign's version is more powerful and extremely elegant.

The Character Styles palette basically gives you global control over local formatting. Character styles are covered in Chapter 8.

The Swatches Palette

I did a lot of whining about the Swatches palette in the first InDesign version. It was very much like Illustrator's version, with all of its weaknesses. There was no drag-and-drop color; no tint slider; and no control over the stroke, fill, text, or frame in the original Swatches palette. That is no longer true. The Swatches palette is now incredible. It gives the same sort of global control over color as the Paragraph Styles and Character Styles palettes provide for type. Plus, it makes colors easy to set up and easy to apply.

Basically, nothing should be done, when using color, unless you have added the color, tint, or gradient to the Swatches palette. In Chapter 13, you will see that this is done with commands that open actual dialog boxes (gasp!) to produce these colors, tints, and gradients.

The Stroke Palette

The Stroke palette allows you to control stroke options. It is very much like Illustrator's version, using Illustrator's superior stroke-generation capabilities, but InDesign's palette is better laid out. These capabilities are normal for PostScript drawing programs. There are now some fairly impressive stroke style options.

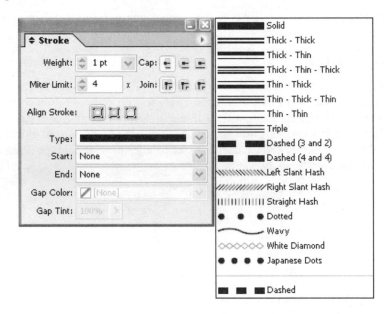

The new custom stroke options are over the top. In addition, you can now align the stroke to the path by the inside edge, the outside edge, or the center of the stroke. You'll learn how to use the Stroke palette in Chapter 10.

The Align Palette

The Align palette contains all of the capabilities of Quark's Space/Align dialog box, all of FreeHand's Align panel's options, plus more. InDesign allows you to align multiple selected objects in any manner, including by specifying a certain space between the objects.

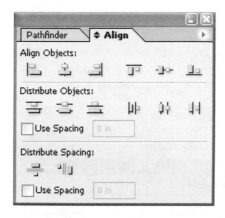

Using the Align palette is simple: All you need to do is select the objects you want to align and click the appropriate button. The ability to align perfectly (mathematically) can save you a great deal of time. This palette's use is covered in Chapter 11.

The Text Wrap Palette

The Text Wrap palette is very powerful, and the wraps work exceedingly well. You can wrap text around the frame or around the object shape, and make the text jump the object or cause it to jump to the next column.

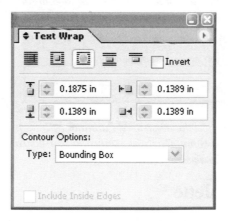

The outline wrap can be around the object's clipping or outline path, bounding box, or graphic frame. You can even have it detect edges (although computers are too dumb to do that well). There is also an Invert check box that lets you wrap text inside a wrapping path. The Text Wrap palette is covered in Chapter 11.

The Links Palette

The Links palette provides all of the functionality of PageMaker's Links dialog box and Quark's Picture Usage dialog box. You can edit the original graphic or relink to a different graphic. Plus, you can select multiple items to update many graphics at the same time.

The question mark and exclamation point icons that appear in the Links palette shown here indicate there are linking problems with these graphics files. As you'll learn in Chapter 12, up-to-date links are crucial for document production. The Links palette provides an easy way to discover and fix linking problems.

The Pathfinder Palette

The buttons on the Pathfinder palette enable you to combine paths in very useful ways.

This is where you will find the most-used Pathfinder filters from Illustrator. They are not all here, but the palette is not nearly as confusing as Illustrator' version, either. The Pathfinder palette is discussed in Chapter 11.

The Transparency Palette

Transparency abilities are certainly unique to page layout, and InDesign's Transparency palette is uniquely powerful. The transparency options are basically the same as Illustrator's capabilities (but, of course, Illustrator cannot do pages).

The Transparency palette has an opacity slider, as you would expect. But equally as important, it has most of the blending modes of Photoshop. The Transparency palette is covered in Chapter 11.

NOTE

When I first heard about InDesign's blending mode capability, I was not impressed. It was so far outside my paradigm, I just didn't see any use for it. I've changed my mind, and now I sometimes apply blending modes in my designs.

The Table Palette

The Table palette is not your normal little dedicated table tool or application. InDesign completely integrates tables within page layout as part of the normal text flow.

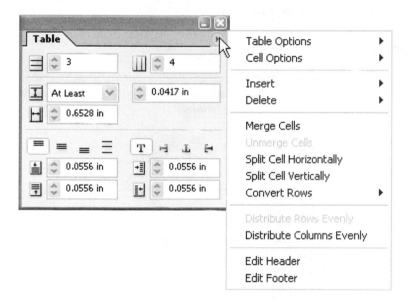

A table can flow from page to page. The copy can be formatted with normal paragraph and character styles. Any cell can hold text, graphics, or both. Any border can use any stroke style. Cells can be merged, unmerged, remerged, or whatever your heart desires. You can have automatic headers and footers that travel from page to page with the table.

There are enough new and unique features that I've dedicated an entire chapter to a discussion of tables (Chapter 9). Imagine a price list with pictures, flowing throughout a 48-page catalog. Two cell tables can be used for hanging headers. The list goes on. You'll be amazed at how often these features can solve all types of layout problems.

The Attributes Palette

The Attributes palette simply allows you to set overprint characteristics, both stroke and fill, of selected objects.

You'll rarely use this palette. If you are forced to hand-construct traps, you'll need it. If you are working with coarse registration duplicators, you may need to eliminate knockouts. I'll cover the Attributes palette's uses in Chapter 14.

The Separations Preview Palette

NEW TO
InDesign
CS

Here is a new and unique capability that lets you see exactly what will be on each plate when you print your project. The Separations Preview palette provides an excellent way to check for overprint problems and solutions.

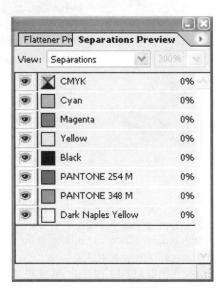

At a glance, this palette lets you know if you are using more colors than you think you are using. Chapter 14 describes the uses of this palette.

1

The Flattener Preview Palette

NEW TO
InDesign
CS

The Flattener Preview palette is not nearly as powerful or useful as the Separations Preview palette, but it does show you where you have applied transparency, what will be rasterized when you print, and so on.

Keep in mind that PostScript printing does not support transparency, so things must be flattened before they can be printed. This palette is useful for getting information about the flattening, but I do wish it gave a preview of the flattened image.

The Trap Presets Palette

The Trap Presets palette is where you choose trapping presets you have created.

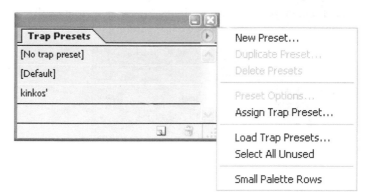

These are top-end, full-color printing options that you normally do not need to worry about. If you do, follow the instructions of your printing company precisely. I discuss the options in Chapter 14.

The Color Palette

The Color palette allows you to create colors using the RGB, CMYK, or LAB model. The colorized sliders are a great help when working in normally foreign color spaces, like RGB and LAB.

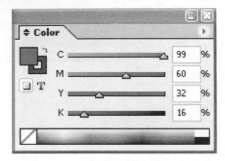

You should just forget about the Color palette. The New Color Swatch command on the Swatches palette's option menu is far more powerful and intuitive. The Color palette changes the color of whichever is active: stroke or fill. It does not add the color to the Swatches palette. Having unspecified colors roaming around your document is asking for disaster. You need the global control of color that the Swatches palette offers. I explain why in Chapter 13.

The Gradient Palette

The Gradient palette, like the Color palette, uses Illustrator's model. It works well enough, and even contains a reverse direction button, but it's crippled by the need to pick the colors from the Color palette. It also has other limitations that make it frustrating to use.

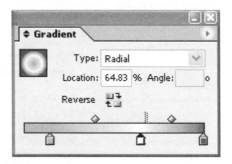

As you will learn in Chapter 13, using the New Gradient Swatch command from the Swatches palette's option menu is the easiest way to add gradients.

The Interactive Group of Palettes

The Hyperlinks, Bookmarks, and States palettes are used to add interactivity to Portable Document Format (PDF) files or Web sites that are exported from InDesign.

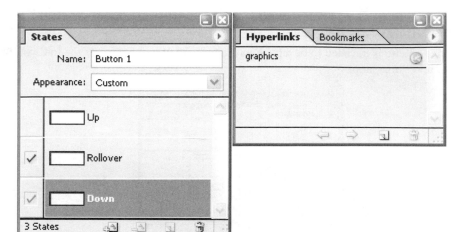

If you need the features offered on these palettes, you already know what they are. (If you do not, you need to learn more about Acrobat and GoLive.) These features are covered in Chapter 15.

The Scripting Set of Palettes

By all reports, no page layout program comes close to offering the scripting power of InDesign CS. Scripting offers you an interface to make plug-ins and mini-applications to add to your software. You can use AppleScript, Visual Basic, or JavaScript to write your scripts. There are many free scripts available online, including from InDesign's section of www.adobe.com.

Scripting is for power users in rigidly controlled production environments. If you work for a company like that, you probably have a full-time script writer on staff to solve all your production problems. For most of us, the scripting palettes are of little help. The variety of our projects means that scripts have little use, because they work only for high-volume, repetitive tasks. Scripting is not for the faint of heart.

The Tags Palette

The Tags palette stores pieces of power-user commands. These are not Quark tags, but the concept is the same. The basic idea is to write commands into raw text, so that when the text is imported into InDesign, the formatting is automatic.

What you might want to know about tags is that exporting your copy in Adobe Tagged Text format keeps all the formatting. It works better than Rich Text Format (RTF) for this purpose. The resulting text file is very small and easy to attach to an e-mail message. All the recipient needs to do is import the file, and the copy portions of the document are completely re-created (assuming the person receiving the file has the fonts you used, of course). The Tags palette is covered in Chapter 6.

The Navigator Palette

The Navigator palette is intended to be a page-navigation aid. It is the same as the tool you find in Illustrator and Photoshop.

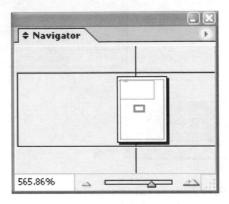

Using this palette is a very slow way to work. I do know people who love this palette (people who do everything with the mouse, mostly in Photoshop). I will talk about the Navigator palette in Chapter 2, where I will explain why you should not use it.

The Library Palette

The Library palette is for graphic storage. The local newspaper uses a library of images for clients to store their repetitive graphics and client logos. If you use libraries, this palette works very intuitively. The ease with which you can save multiple libraries, which can be tabbed into a common palette, makes it easy to organize your graphics.

Palette Wrap-up

By now, it's obvious that InDesign has opted to eliminate most dialog boxes in favor of palettes. I can see where this is a good thing, but it might be disconcerting at the beginning. My simple solution is to make the keyboard shortcut that opens the palette the same one as I used to open the corresponding dialog boxes in other programs. InDesign has already done this in several cases. The Character palette, for example, is opened with the same keyboard shortcut as the one used for the Character Specifications dialog box in PageMaker and Quark.

The new palettes work so well, and I can locate them so comfortably, that I use shortcuts to access palettes far less than I did in the past. As I result, I don't need to remember as many shortcuts.

If you are accustomed to Adobe's interface in Photoshop and Illustrator, the proliferation of palettes will be no problem at all (other than the fact that you will begin complaining about those two because InDesign does its interface so much better than they do). For those of you coming from Quark, there are methods you can use to make yourself more comfortable. I'll offer tips for Quark users throughout the book.

Keyboard Shortcuts Are a Production Necessity

With the production speed required by our industry, there is no way you can keep up without the fluid use of keyboard shortcuts. My students know how crucial I consider shortcuts. In fact, one of my students—a retired programmer, in the industry since the 1950s—accused me, "After rejecting DOS because of its code and turning to a GUI, you are now advocating code again!"

There is no way you can memorize all the shortcuts, nor do you need to know every one of them. However, you do need a set of memorized shortcuts. InDesign offers real help here, because every command in InDesign is available for shortcuts. Thus, you can create the shortcuts you need for your workflow. You can change the predefined shortcuts to match what you're already using in other applications.

Throughout this book, I will suggest defaults you might find useful and custom shortcuts that might help you. However, all I can do is share my opinions. There is no right or wrong method. Shortcuts are very personal. You will need to understand all of the options, and then set up shortcuts so they work for you.

No matter how you're used to working, organizing your InDesign palettes in not an option—it's a necessity. Without palette organization, it's impossible to work effectively. In Chapter 4, I will give you many options to help you get a handle on palette control.

Learn the Tools of InDesign

After the lengthy discussion of the palettes of InDesign, it's time to turn to the tools of the software. For those of you coming from Illustrator, PageMaker, or Photoshop, the InDesign toolbox will look very familiar. In fact, if you consider this toolbox as a finally functional version of a PageMaker/ Illustrator hybrid, you are close.

InDesign does have all of the relevant Illustrator tools, but they are laid out in a way that makes them instantly recognizable as page layout functions. Strange tools like the Graphing tool, Gradient Mesh tool, Blending tool, and so forth are missing, as they should be. It does not have Illustrator's incredible Brush tool or FreeHand's Perspective Grid and Envelope tools. This is a page layout program, not a graphics creation program.

If you have been working in an exclusively Quark/FreeHand environment, the look and feel of these tools will be a little disconcerting. The InDesign toolbox contains everything from Quark, but these tools are much easier to use, as well as more powerful.

Figure 1-4 shows the InDesign toolbox, with each tool labeled. Now, I will take you on a quick tour of these tools.

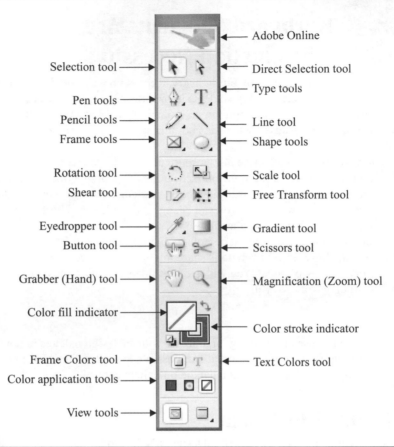

Adobe Online

Selection tool ⟶

Direct Selection tool

Type tools

Pen tools ⟶

Pencil tools ⟶

Line tool

Frame tools ⟶

Shape tools

Rotation tool ⟶

Scale tool

Shear tool ⟶

Free Transform tool

Eyedropper tool ⟶

Gradient tool

Button tool ⟶

Scissors tool

Grabber (Hand) tool ⟶

Magnification (Zoom) tool

Color fill indicator ⟶

Color stroke indicator

Frame Colors tool ⟶

Text Colors tool

Color application tools ⟶

View tools ⟶

FIGURE 1-4 The InDesign toolbox contains all of the tools you need for page layout.

The Selection Tools

The Selection and Direct Selection tools are similar to Illustrator's selection tools in appearance. They are also much like Quark's selection tools in function. The solid arrow on the left is Quark's Item tool, and the hollow-pointed arrow to the right is similar to the Content tool in Quark.

I make shortcuts to convert back and forth between the two tools. I suggest you do the same. Being left-handed I use COMMAND-*' for the Selection tool and* COMMAND-\ *for the Direct Selection tool (*CTRL-*' and* CTRL-\ *for PC users). Right-handed people should find something on the right side of the keyboard that is not already in use.*

If you want to move a frame or resize it, you need the Selection tool. If you want to modify the shape in any way, you need the Direct Selection tool's capabilities. You can tell which tool you are using by the look of the paths and points of the frame. These tools are covered in Chapters 10 and 11.

NOTE *One of the most important advantages of InDesign's approach is the simplicity of the various forms of frames. The frame changes according to which tool is selected. You can make any frame a text frame by simply clicking it with the Text tool. Any frame can hold text, pictures, or both. For those coming from Quark, this straightforward approach should be a breath of fresh air.*

The Type Tools

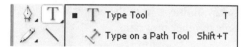

Basically, the Type tool works like any other Type tool you have used. I will talk about adding type in Chapter 5.

The Type on a Path tool lets you type on any path you want to create. You will see how this works in Chapter 11.

The Pen Tools

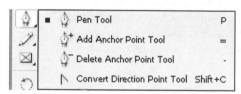

InDesign's Pen tool is the same as Illustrator's four-part Pen tool, with all of its advantages and disadvantages. For those coming from FreeHand's single Pen tool, this may be a shock.

The nice thing is that you do not need to worry about choosing from the four tools. It's completely automatic. You simply need to watch the tool closely when working with a path to find out what is happening. If you see a little plus next to the tool, you will add a point by clicking. If you see a little minus, you will subtract a point by clicking. If you see the little open pointer, you will change the point from smooth to corner or vice versa. (There are shortcuts to access any of the tools individually, which are the same as Illustrator's shortcuts.)

TIP *One of the things you will pick up quickly as you are learning to use InDesign is that it gives you many visual clues. Carefully watch the graphic signals on the screen.*

Holding down the ALT/OPTION key switches you to the Convert Point tool. The most disconcerting aspect is that there is no way to drag out handles on a corner point. All you can do is drag out the handles with the Convert Point tool, and then move the tool over the handles that result (while still holding down the ALT/OPTION key). This changes the pointer to a Change Point icon that allows you to drag the handles individually. You'll learn how to use the Pen tools in Chapters 10 and 11.

The Frame Tools and Shape Tools

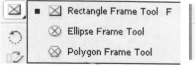 

The next six tools are a little confusing, because Adobe has divided them on two separate menus: the frame tools and the shape tools, as shown here. But, it doesn't make any difference which one you are using. If you have a graphic frame and click in it with the Type tool, it becomes a text frame. If you have a text frame with no type in it and place a graphic, it becomes a graphic frame. Graphics placed into a text frame become inline graphics (Quark calls them anchored).

The only other difference is the default fill and stroke when frames and shapes are created. The frame tools have no stroke or fill. There is an X through the frame. If you click the frame, it moves. The shape tools use the stroke and fill currently chosen in the Swatches palette.

The shape and frame tools work as follows:

■ **Ellipse**   This is a normal Ellipse tool. If you hold down the SHIFT key, the shape is constrained to a circle. If you hold down the ALT/OPTION key, it draws from the center out. It also draws from handle to handle, as do Ellipse tools in other programs.

■ **Rectangle**   This is a normal Rectangle tool that works similarly to the Ellipse tool. Hold down the SHIFT key to constrain the shape to a square. If you hold down the ALT/OPTION key, it draws from the center out.

■ **Polygon and Star**   This is a severely limited version of the Polygon tool (when compared to FreeHand). Star drawing is an option that you see when you double-click the Polygon tool. Because you need to guess the shape of the points of the star, and there is no preview, this tool is difficult to use to make star shapes. Of course, it does polygons well.

The frame and shape tools are covered in Chapter 10.

The Pencil Tools

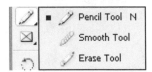

The Pencil tool is a typical Illustrator triple tool: Pencil, Smoother, and Eraser. It works the way you would expect. The Pencil tool draws freehand. The Smoother tool progressively smoothes out the line (without much control, although it often does a nice job) by converting corner points to curve points and by moving curve points. The Eraser tool does what you would like it to: erases sections of a line.

A nice capability is that the Smoother and Eraser tools work on any path you draw, with any tool. The Smoother tool, for example, will convert a star into a polygon with concave sides (it changes the entire shape). These tools even work on type converted to paths, but the effects are rather unpredictable. In general, however, these are very elegant freehand drawing tools. They are discussed in Chapters 10 and 11.

The Line Tool

What can I say? The Line tool draws lines. When you hold down the SHIFT key, it draws horizontal, vertical, and 45-degree lines. The only difference in InDesign is that it is possible to assign a gradient to a line. Add an arrowhead to the end, and you have a great tool for drawing callout arrows.

The Transformation Tools

The four transformation tools are the Rotation tool, Shear tool, Scale tool, and Free Transform tool. These are, for the most part, similar to their Illustrator counterparts.

- **Rotation**   InDesign's Rotation tool works like Illustrator's Rotation tool. A little target indicates the rotational center of the selected shape or shapes. When you move the cursor over the target, it changes to a black pointer, which allows you to drag the center to wherever you desire. This is very handy, but it is disconcerting to FreeHand users, who are accustomed to click-drag rotation (where the center is determined by where you click). For more precise rotation, use the Transform palette, where the center shows up in the X/Y field.

- **Scale and Shear**   These tools work as expected, once you take the transformation center target into account. The previews while transforming are exceptional, and both of these tools are much easier to control than either their Macromedia counterparts or the Illustrator tools (perhaps because InDesign has brand-new code).

- **Free Transform**   This tool is the same as its counterpart in Illustrator and Photoshop. If the tool is over a handle, you can scale. If it is outside the selected shape, you can rotate. If you drag a side handle on the side of the bounding box (not a corner), and then hold down CONTROL-ALT/COMMAND-OPTION as you drag, the shape will be sheared—seemingly in perspective, but not really. To reflect, simply drag a handle across to the other side. To constrain the tool, SHIFT-drag with it.

NOTE   *The only thing missing from the Free Transform tool is the ability to drag out a corner handle separately. For simple shapes like rectangles, you can accomplish that with the Direct Selection tool.*

The transformation tools are covered in Chapter 11.

The Eyedropper and Measure Tools

The Eyedropper tool copies typographic settings or graphic settings from one object to another. It works with imported graphics. It copies from one document to another. Double-click to set options determining what is copied. It can copy any attribute: stroke, fill, paragraph, character, or transparency.

The Measure tool will measure from anywhere on a pasteboard to anywhere else on a pasteboard. The results are shown in the Info palette.

The Gradient Tool

The Gradient tool works exactly like its counterparts in Photoshop and Illustrator. It allows you to apply a gradient across multiple selected shapes, controlling the angle of the gradient by the direction of the click-drag. The distance between the click and the release controls the length of

How to ... Measure Angles

You can also measure angles with the Measure tool, as follows:

1. Measure a line in one direction.

2. Double-click or ALT-click/OPTION-click the starting point or ending point of the measure line.

3. Drag to create the second line of the angle.

The second line's measurement will appear in the D2 section of the Info palette.

the gradient. (This is a gradient tool that FreeHand should have, but the interactivity of drag-and-drop gradients found in FreeHand is completely missing.)

In InDesign (as with all Adobe products), producing the gradient and saving it into the Swatches palette is the clumsy part of the operation. The only functional method is to add a gradient swatch using the Swatches palette's option menu. Once you have the gradient on the Swatches palette, the Gradient tool applies that gradient very elegantly. Creating gradients is discussed in Chapter 13.

The Button Tool

You can use the Button tool to create buttons for interactive PDF files and Web sites. You can add the states needed and set the graphic parameters. But InDesign is not like ImageReady or Fireworks, so your options are limited. I'll cover the use of the Button tool in Chapter 15.

The Scissors Tool

The Scissors tool cuts any editable PostScript paths. It is a single-function tool, without any of the fancy options found in FreeHand or Illustrator. All you do is click on a path to break it at that point.

The Hand Tool

The Hand tool works as expected: It grabs the image on the screen so you can move it around. However, this is one of the areas of greatest complaint about InDesign. (The mere fact that this is a "major" complaint shows clearly how well InDesign works, in general.) Many people do not like the fact that, in earlier versions, the Hand tool was accessed with the SPACEBAR unless you were working with the Type tool. If you had an insertion point in a text frame, this tool was accessed with the ALT/OPTION key. Now, to make no one happy, the shortcut is ALT-SPACEBAR/OPTION-SPACEBAR.

The Zoom Tool

You will use the Zoom tool constantly, but you will rarely access it through the toolbox. Here is a keyboard shortcut you must learn immediately: CTRL-SPACEBAR/COMMAND-SPACEBAR. This selects the Zoom tool for magnifying. Adding the ALT/OPTION key makes it a Zoom-Out tool.

The Fill and Stroke Tools

The fill and stroke indicators work exactly like those found in Illustrator. These controls are very obvious and extremely handy if you have any Adobe experience.

- ■ Pressing the D key gives you the default stroke and fill (set up with the rest of your defaults).

- ■ Pressing the X key switches the colors.

- ■ Pressing the SHIFT-X combination switches which tool is active. (It is a little clumsy keeping track of which is active.)

Single-letter shortcuts do not work while the Type tool is active. If you need one, create the shortcut with the CTRL/COMMAND *or* ALT/OPTION *key. Chapter 4 describes how to customize keyboard shortcuts.*

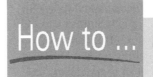 **Control the Percent View of a Document**

There is only one truly efficient method of controlling the percentage (%) view of your document. First, press CTRL-0 (zero)/COMMAND-0 to zoom out to the Fit Spread in Window view. Then hold down CTRL-SPACEBAR/COMMAND-SPACEBAR (the Zoom tool shortcut) and draw a marquee around the area you want enlarged and centered on your monitor. The area marqueed will then be enlarged as much as possible and centered on the monitor. You will soon find that the Zoom-marquee shortcut is essential for your financial health in graphic design.

If you can already see the object you need enlarged, you can simply hold down the Zoom shortcut keys and click. However, in this instance, you will not be able to control how much it is enlarged. The enlargement will just be to the next step shown in the pop-up menu in the lower-left corner of your document window.

The Color Application Tools

The color application tools include Apply Color, Apply Gradient, and Apply None. These three tools are extremely useful ways to apply color without slowing the creative process. In earlier versions of InDesign, which did not have stroke and fill boxes at the top of the Swatches palette, these tools were the only way to quickly apply color. In InDesign CS, you can just use the Swatches palette to apply color.

The only confusing (and often frustrating) aspect of using the toolbox buttons is that where the color or gradient is applied (or removed) is determined by whether the fill or the stroke box is active. It is relatively common to apply a color, and then discover that the stroke is active when you meant to change the fill.

The color application tools work as follows:

- **Apply Color**   Clicking the left button changes the color of the object(s) selected to the color of the swatch currently selected in the Swatches palette.

- **Apply Gradient**   Clicking the center button changes the fill or stroke color of the object(s) selected to the last-used gradient swatch in the Swatches palette. InDesign is the first software application (at least, that I am aware of) that can apply a gradient to a stroke (and it is still the only one of the Big Seven: PageMaker, Quark, InDesign, FreeHand, Illustrator, Photoshop, and Acrobat—even with the Creative Suite).

UNIQUE TO
InDesign CS

- **Apply None**   Clicking the right button changes the fill or stroke color of the object(s) selected to None, depending on which is selected in the toolbox.

The View Modes

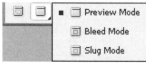

In the view mode set, the button on the left is the default. This is the Normal View mode. The button on the right switches to the Preview View mode. This turns off all nonprinting items like rulers, frame edges, and guides. The default shortcut is W.

NEW TO
InDesign CS

InDesign has two new preview modes: Bleed mode and Slug mode. If you want to see the bleed, select the Bleed mode. If you want to see the area set aside for a slug, choose Slug mode. While it is chosen, you can easily add any notes such as signature lines, a list of fonts, or whatever you want to appear on every page. I'll cover bleeds and slugs in Chapter 3.

Toolbox Wrap-up

This completes our overview of the tools in the toolbox. As you have seen, InDesign has a reasonably full set of PostScript drawing tools in a powerful page layout package. Naturally, these tools are slanted toward an Adobe Illustrator view of graphic construction. In some areas, this helps; in other areas, this hinders. What is really important is that all the tools you need are readily available.

Locate Menu Commands

Now we will take a quick look at each menu on the menu bar at the top of the InDesign window. I'll explain how the specific menu commands work in the chapters about their functions.

The File Menu

The File menu is for documents as a whole. It contains the New, Open, Close, Save (in all its variants), Import, Export, Document Setup, Preflight, Package, and Print commands. You will use most of these so regularly that you will memorize their shortcuts.

The Edit Menu

This well-named Edit menu is for the editing commands, including the ones that work with the Clipboard: Cut, Copy, and Paste and its variants. Undo and Redo are here as well. The Find/Change, Check Spelling, and other text-editing commands are also on the Edit menu.

The Edit menu also contains the very important Color Settings, Transparency, and Keyboard Shortcuts commands. On a PC, the Preferences command is found here. On Mac OSX, the Preferences command is on the InDesign menu.

The Layout Menu

On the Layout menu, you will find the controls for margins, columns, guides, and automatic layout adjustment.

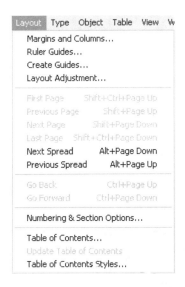

All of the page and spread navigation commands are also here. My advice is to learn these shortcuts early and well. If it helps, change them to keystrokes that are easy for you to remember (see Chapter 4 for details on customizing shortcuts).

The Layout menu is also where you find the numbering and section options and the table of contents controls.

The Type Menu

All the typographic commands and controls are on the Type menu in command form. You will rarely use them here. Most of the time, you will choose these options from the palettes, by using styles, or from the context menu.

The Object Menu

The Object menu is all about what you can do to objects: transform, arrange, group, and lock them. It has the Text Frame Options command, which allows you to pick how your text frames fit with their content. It includes the transparency functions, such as Drop Shadow and Feather.

The interactivity commands are on the Object menu. InDesign can add movies, sounds, buttons, forms, and anything you need for interactive PDFs, Web sites, and eBooks. The Object menu is also where the commands for path operations are found. Finally, this is where you can set the individual display performance of selected objects.

The Table Menu

The Table menu contains all of the commands you need to make incredible tables. All of Chapter 9 is about this capability.

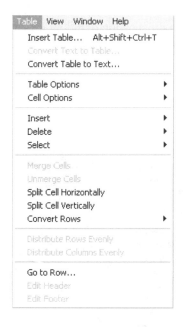

The View Menu

The View menu has the monitor-viewing commands: previews, proof color space, display quality, page size, fit in window, and so on. It also lets you turn on guides, frame edges, and grids of all kinds, and then turn them off when you do not want to see them.

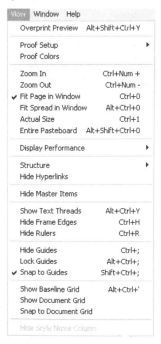

This is also where the command for showing or hiding master pages is located. You will use these commands a lot. Memorize the shortcuts for them.

The Window Menu

The Window menu is where you find the commands to open your palettes. All of this will be taken care of by setting up a functional workspace, as you'll learn in Chapter 4.

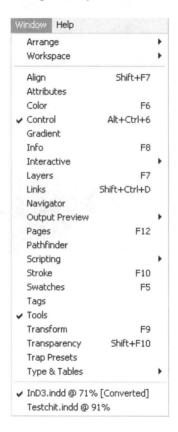

The Help Menu

HELP!!! That should cover it, I guess. InDesign comes with excellent HTML documentation. Open this documentation from the Help menu, and it comes up in your default browser. This is also where all the legalese is available for those of you who cannot do without it.

Now that you've been introduced to the InDesign interface, the next step is learning how to control it. That is the topic of the next chapter.

Chapter 2

Control the Interface

How to...

- Set your preferences
- Create fractions
- Set application defaults
- Set document defaults
- Navigate in your documents

As you know, the first step to take when you're starting to use an application is to set up the preferences and default settings. Although you'll modify this setup over time, as you adapt the software to your personal needs, you need a starting place.

InDesign doesn't have many preferences settings, and this is a good thing. In this paradigm, defaults are the major method of setting up your program for your personal use. Preferences are simply long-term choices concerning the application's interface. This approach is practical, because preferences are changed so rarely that it's hard to remember what the options are. In InDesign, those preferences that you use regularly can be set up to toggle on and off with a keyboard shortcut. On the other hand, defaults are settings you change regularly (often several times a day), so they need to be readily accessible in familiar locations.

In this chapter, we will first go through the preference options quickly (some of them are reasonably important), and then talk about defaults. Finally, you'll learn about some easy ways to navigate through your documents. By the end of this chapter, you'll be ready to open your first documents and take a look at them. And that's what you'll learn how to do in the next chapter.

Set Your Preferences

Setting preferences is not a long, drawn-out affair. You don't need to make crucial decisions (like whether or not you are going to use a real em space). The Preferences command is on the Edit menu in Windows XP Professional and on the InDesign menu in Mac OSX. We'll work our way through the list on the left side of the Preferences dialog box, from top to bottom.

General Preferences

In the General page of the Preferences dialog box, shown in Figure 2-1, are options for page numbering, tool tips, and the toolbox display, as well as overprinting and font handling.

Page Numbering

For Page Numbering, your choices are Section Numbering and Absolute Numbering. If you are using section numbering (as was done with the front matter of this book), it is really helpful to show

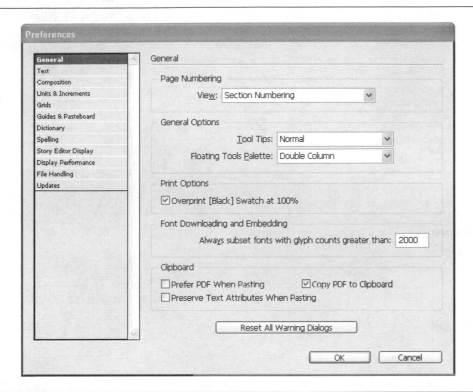

FIGURE 2-1   The General page of the Preferences dialog box

that in the page-turning controls at the bottom of the document window and in the Pages palette. Absolute numbering simply counts all of the pages from the first to the last, even though the section numbers show up on the pages themselves with the automatic numbering markers.

General Options

The first choice under General Options is Tool Tips. The choices are Normal, None, and Fast. *Tool tips* are those little boxes that pop up to show you the name of the tool and its keyboard shortcut. This is usually the easiest way to learn the keyboard shortcuts for the tools you use all the time. InDesign lets you set up your tool tips to appear quickly (Fast), in around one second. With the Normal setting, there is a two- to three-second delay. When you are sick of the little pop-ups, you can turn them off (None).

The Floating Tools Palette option lets you customize the appearance of your floating toolbox. You can keep it in its normal format (double column), or you can make it a single row or a single column. I normally use the single row, because it gives me more width for two-page spreads. It fits under the ruler in the margin of the document, where I rarely place anything of interest.

Once you are working, you can easily reset the toolbox appearance at any time by double-clicking its title bar. This will cycle you through the three arrangements.

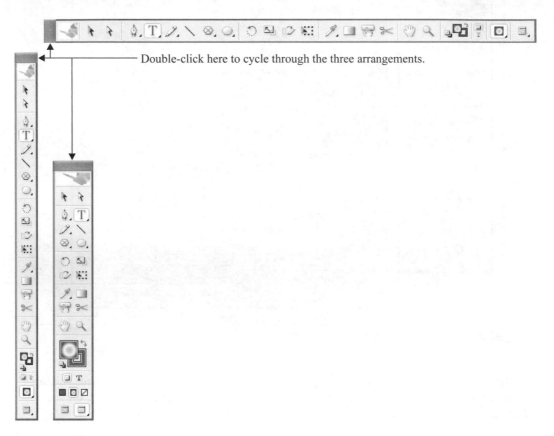

Double-click here to cycle through the three arrangements.

Print Options

The check box for Overprint [Black] Swatch at 100% lets you decide about overprinting the default [Black] swatch. The default is to always overprint black. However, for those times when this causes a problem, you can turn that default off.

CAUTION *The Overprint [Black] Swatch at 100% option affects only solid-black swatches, picked from the Swatches palette. Any tints of [Black] will knock out. This is a radical departure from previous behaviors. Also, any created blacks or rich blacks will knock out. You will need to watch this in the Separations Preview palette. Overprinting and knockouts are covered in Chapter 14.*

Font Downloading and Embedding

The Font Downloading and Embedding preference protects your file sizes, if you are using OpenType fonts with extremely large numbers of characters. If you use the default to always subset fonts with glyph counts greater than 2,000, InDesign will download only the actual characters you use when printing. This means that the font will not be included; just a subset of that font will be used.

It is rare to find a font with more than 2,000 glyphs. The fonts I create are larger than most of Adobe's fonts, and my largest font contains only about 900 glyphs. Most fonts have fewer than 600 glyphs. However, OpenType fonts can contain over 60,000 characters. Asian fonts commonly reach the tens of thousands. The problem with subset fonts is that you cannot fix exported PDFs if the font is subset. You will need to fix any problems in the original document.

Clipboard

There are rumors about Clipboard problems with PDFs, so you might want to uncheck the Copy PDF To Clipboard option. If you select the Preserve Text Attributes When Pasting option, Rich Text Format (RTF) is used with all the paragraph styles and so forth.

Reset All Warnings

The Reset All Warning Dialogs choice must be important (the button is big enough), but few of us constantly change our minds when we turn off a warning. If you think of a warning you turned off and now want back on, click here.

Text Preferences

The Text page of the Preferences dialog box, shown in Figure 2-2, includes some settings that may be important to you. Whether you will want to adjust these preferences depends on the types of documents you design and how you are used to working.

Character Settings

You may wonder why you might need to change the default settings for superscript, subscript, and small caps. InDesign's defaults are typical. They are based on the idea of using superscript and subscript for exponents, footnotes, and chemical formulas: a^2b^3 or $H_2O + CO_3$. However, very few of us spend much time thinking about, writing about, or typesetting these scientific constructions. In this industry, superscript and subscript are primarily used for constructing fractions.

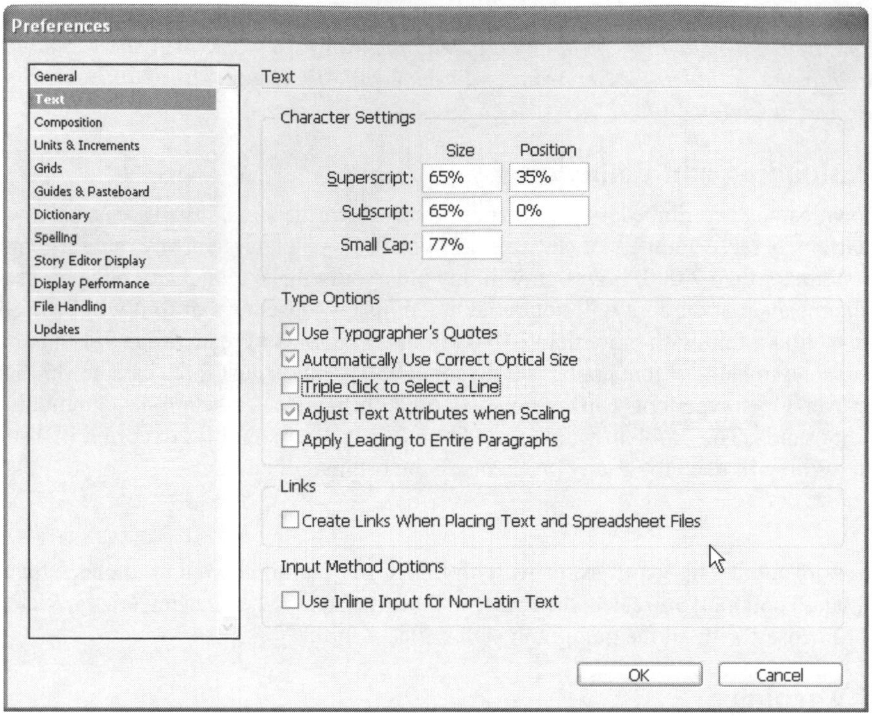

FIGURE 2-2   The Text page of the Preferences dialog box

The real problem is that normal superscripts and subscripts are merely proportionally reduced characters. This makes them much thinner and lighter. If you look at the Times New Roman samples shown here, you can clearly see what I am talking about. So, for better-looking equations, you need to reduce the size of superscripts and subscripts as little as possible.

Times New Roman: $7^1/_2$, $^5/_8$, $^4/_5$, $^{23}/_{32}$, $^{139}/_{144}$
An Unmodified TrueType font, very light numbers and needs kerning.

DiaconiaPro: $7^1/_2$, $^5/_8$, $^4/_5$, $^{23}/_{32}$, $^{139}/_{144}$
The half and five-eighths are built-in, the rest need kerning
$7^1/_2$, $^5/_8$, $^4/_5$, $^{23}/_{32}$, $^{139}/_{144}$

Minion Pro: what about fractions like $\frac{3}{4}$ or $\frac{11}{14}$?

How to ... **Create Fractions**

A couple of years ago, there was a flurry of recommendations in the InDesign BlueWorld list about setting fractions. Many recommended getting special math fonts, but the problem is these math fonts are not available in the fonts you will be using.

Several others suggested using the fractions that come with some fonts, but the fonts that come with fractions are limited, as is the choice of fractions that do come with fonts. Even if you have a font that includes fractions for one-half, one-quarter, three-quarters, one-third, two-thirds, one-eighth, and so on, it is still almost useless. You discover that almost as soon as you let fractions onto your page, sooner or later you need 4/5 or 127/256. No standard font covers these fractions. More than that, you will quickly find that you cannot match your fractions to the ones in the font. And I haven't even mentioned the use of the fraction slash instead of the normal keyboard slash. It's a little more vertical and has very tight spacing built in—if your font has one.

OpenType Pro fonts now offer a good solution to this dilemma. Some of the new OpenType Pro fonts contain many fractions, plus a complete set of true numerators and denominators. This method still requires manual intervention, but its results are remarkable.

Another option might be to construct the fractions in FreeHand or Illustrator and import them. Stylistically, the choice is yours. Formerly, there were strict standards. Now these vary by situation.

Most typically, if you don't have OpenType Pro fonts, you'll need to construct your fractions manually. The normal procedure for this is to type the fraction, select the numerator and make it a superscript, select the denominator and make it a subscript, and then kern everything precisely. Even with InDesign's excellent optical kerning option, hand-kerning will still be required. (And actually, for some of the styles, even kerning won't do you any good.)

Some of you will immediately think, "Ah, ha! I can write a little script!" This was the next most common suggestion in the InDesign BlueWorld list. However, scripts are useless unless they work perfectly every time. So, this is a lot of work for something that is used so seldom, and for something that changes with every font. Another suggestion is to set up paragraph styles. You can certainly do these things, but you will still need to manually build your fractions.

If you don't want to purchase a good OpenType Pro font (or use the ones that come with the software), it is far better to simply set the superscript and subscript options in the Text page of the Preferences dialog box to work when you need fractions. The same changes also work for setting prices in newspaper ads and similar projects.

For my Superscript and Subscript preferences, I usually raise the percent of point size to around 65%. Then I make the Superscript Position value enough to equal around 100% when the two are added together—in this case, 35%. Settings such as 60% and 40% or 70% and 30% also work for the Superscript Size and Position values.

As soon as you pick the fonts for a long project, you will need to make sure that the percentages you have set here work with the font you will be using. For example, 65% and 35% do not work with lowercase numbers. In that case, you'll need to make special adjustments.

Another place you might use superscripts is with ad pricing, as in $^{\$}147^{\underline{93}}$. As you can see in the example, the cents are often underlined. However, using the underline style is almost always too heavy. You will probably need to draw the line to get the weight right.

The small caps default is 70% of the point size. This makes the small caps look noticeably thinner than the caps. I recommend going to 77% to minimize that weight difference. Of course, this makes the cap/small cap distinction harder to see. It is a compromise at best (and one of the reasons I always try to use an OpenType font with true small caps).

Remember that true small caps are specifically drawn so the strokes of the small caps are the same weight as the strokes of the uppercase and lowercase characters. You will need a small caps font or an OpenType Pro font to get true small caps.

Type Options

The five Type Options choices are check boxes that you can toggle on and off. A couple of these may be useful for those of you coming from Quark.

Use Typographer's Quotes   Turn this option on to automatically add curly quotes (quotation marks) in the appropriate places. Of course, you'll need to turn it off when you're working with copy that actually has inch and foot marks in it, or other text that requires straight quotes. One of the really nice features of InDesign is that you can use a keyboard shortcut to toggle the curly quotes on and off. The default shortcut is CTRL-ALT-SHIFT-'/COMMAND-OPTION-SHIFT-'. Just remember to toggle before you type the character.

Automatically Use Correct Optical Size   This option matters only if you are using a Multiple Master (MM) font with an optical axis. If you have one, you know why. However, these are no longer for sale. As far as I can tell, this preference only affects MM fonts. (However, you can leave this option checked in hope.)

For those without MM fonts, I suggest using a font like Adobe Jenson Pro with opticals. These fonts mimic the old letterpress cold type that was thinner and more elegant at very large sizes, and heavier and stronger at very tiny sizes. Here are three examples of Jenson Pro optical weights:

The large *g* to the left is a regular 14-point character. The center one is a caption 8-point *g*. The character on the right is a display 36-point *g*. Below these three characters, the three weights are shown at their true size. As you can see, the baselines shift a little, and the weight of the characters changes a lot. However, when they are at their true size, they look correct.

Triple-Click to Select a Line

This is a Quark norm. It means that you need to quadruple-click to select a paragraph and to quintuple-click (yes, five rapid clicks) to select a story. Personally, I am relieved that I am not forced to use these super-clicks. However, if you are used to working in Quark, you may want to select this preference.

Adjust Text Attributes When Scaling   This determines how the changes appear in palettes when you scale a text frame. Here, we run into one of InDesign's quirks. Adobe makes a distinction between scaling and resizing. Resizing is when you drag a corner handle of a frame. Scaling uses the Control palette, Transform palette, or Scaling tool. When you resize a text frame, the text is not scaled. If you scale a text frame, the type is scaled.

If this option is turned on when you double the scale, the values in the Control palette and Character palette double, while the scaling values remain at 100% in the Transform palette. If this option is turned off, the Transform palette will indicate 200% scaling, but numbers in the point size field of the Control palette or Character palette appear as 12pt (24). Other palette fields, such as leading and kerning, keep the original values, even though they have really been scaled. (Maybe *quirk* is not the right word; maybe *stupid* is a better choice.)

The Adjust Text Attributes When Scaling preference applies to text frames scaled after the option is turned on. It will not affect existing frames. To add to the confusion, if you scale a group of text frames, text attributes are not scaled in the palettes, even if this preference is checked.

If you edit the text or resize the frame when the Adjust Text Attributes When Scaling option is checked, the scaled text remains in 24-point type, even if it moves to a different frame. However, if this option is not checked, any text that flows to a different frame as a result of editing returns to its original size.

Apply Leading to Entire Paragraphs

This option addresses another Quark quirk. Somehow, Quarksters have the idea that leading is a paragraph attribute instead of a character attribute. If you must, check this one.

Links

The option in the Links section, Create Links When Placing Text And Spreadsheet Files, addresses a real problem. In previous versions of InDesign, placed text files were automatically linked. This caused a problem when you edited the type. If you accidentally updated the link in the Links palette, you could eliminate all of the changes you made in the document.

On the other hand, large projects commonly do not allow editing in the document. All editing takes place in the editing group, often with an application like InCopy that lets the layout people adjust the layout, while the editorial staff is editing the copy.

If you uncheck the Links preference, no link is made. Most of us will want to leave this unchecked.

Input Method Options

The Input Method Options section also has only one check box: Use Inline Input for Non-Latin Text. This is used to add 2-byte and 4-byte characters to your text. Asian characters are 2 bytes and 4 bytes.

Composition Preferences

The settings on the Composition page of the Preferences dialog box, shown in Figure 2-3, are usually left at the factory defaults. This page of preferences is concerned with letting you be aware of certain typographic problems. There are many automatic things taking place when you set type. These options can warn you when something is not quite as you hoped.

Highlight

The Highlight options can be helpful, but they also can be visually irritating. The only one I leave checked is Substituted Fonts. This puts a pink slug behind all places where font substitution has occurred.

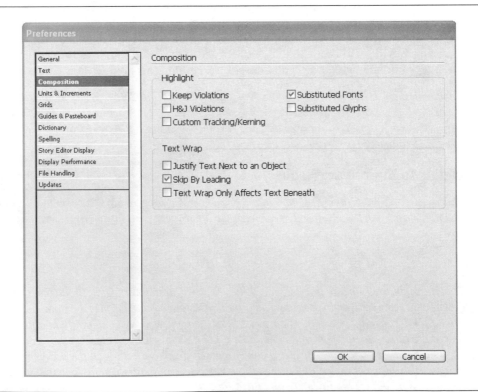

FIGURE 2-3   The Composition page of the Preferences dialog box

2

One of the real benefits of InDesign is that it is impossible to spec fonts that do not exist because of the way its Character palette works. This virtually eliminates substituted fonts in your final printed documents. However, when you spec fonts, adding them to your Paragraph Styles and Character Styles palettes, InDesign sometimes generates font possibilities that do not exist. For example, if you are working in Papyrus and apply a bold character style to some of the copy, a pink slug will appear behind the copy, because there is no such font as Papyrus Bold. InDesign's visual flags will enable you to quickly eliminate these problems. This feature is unique to page layout programs, although now it is normal behavior in the Adobe Creative Studio (CS) suite.

The most common place this pink bar appears is in documents from another computer or from an older version. Often, you will have changed the fonts you use or simply not have the fonts the other designer used. As a result, many paragraph styles and locally formatted copy will show up in a pink slug. When you open such a document, you will get a chance to fix it through the Missing Fonts dialog box (discussed in Chapter 3).

You can choose to turn on or off the following Highlight options:

- **Keep Violations**   This will flag places where InDesign was unable to stay within your decisions for widows, orphans, column breaks, and page breaks (discussed in Chapter 5). Because InDesign has still not figured out what a widow is and the rest are all automatic things that are obvious visually, this option is merely irritating and useless from a practical viewpoint.

- **H&J Violations**   This will flag lines that are outside the desired specs for hyphenation and justification. If you get a project for an old account executive accustomed to premium typography, this may become necessary. For 99.8% of your projects, this is yet another visual irritant in an interface already littered with guides, frames, and paths. If you set your defaults well, InDesign's type passes muster. More than that, it is beautiful with a good-looking, well-spaced font.

- **Substituted Fonts**   This flags all fonts that are missing and therefore substituted. As I noted earlier, this is the one I leave checked.

- **Substituted Glyphs**   This shows you where InDesign has automatically substituted ligatures, swashes, true small caps, and so on when using OpenType capabilities. It will also show ligature substitutions for the older 256-character fonts. Because these glyphs are almost always substituted on purpose (at your request), this is yet another visual irritant.

- **Custom Tracking/Kerning**   This shows where you have made tracking and kerning changes. You might find this useful when looking for places that others may have made these changes. However, in most cases, you made these local changes on purpose, by hand, and you do not need the interface cluttered with yet another set of colored bars.

Text Wrap

The three settings in the Text Wrap section are fairly obvious choices:

- **Justify Text Next to an Object** This is useful when you are using flush-left copy and wrap your text around the left side of a graphic. If the wrapped copy is flush left on either side of a graphic, the wrap looks very clumsy. The default is unchecked. I check this one.

- **Skip by Leading** This affects only wrapped copy that skips over an object. With this preference unchecked (which is what I use), the copy under the wrapped graphic will tuck up as close to the graphic as possible. However, some designers require that all copy line up sideways, from column to column. If you are one of them, you need to check this (the default). That way, your carefully crafted leading will not be disturbed.

- **Text Wrap Only Affects Text Beneath** This is another preference to make Quark converters more comfortable. I want text wrap to affect all type. Evidently, this drives Quarksters crazy. If you need this, check it.

Units and Increments Preferences

The Units & Increments page of the Preferences dialog box, shown in Figure 2-4, is important. These options are so fundamental that you'll usually set them once, and then never touch them again.

If you work globally (in different cultures), you may need to consider these settings more often. For example, I used to need to come here regularly because my overseas students usually work in metric, many of my students who are upgrading their skills work in points, and all of my students in the United States work in inches. But this was before I found that right-clicking the ruler of the document lets me change the measurement units with the context menu.

Another time you will need to set these preferences is when you are working on a newspaper ad. Most newspaper work is set up with picas horizontally and inches vertically. Also, there are quite a few designers who use inches horizontally and the leading in points vertically, so they can align their type to the leading grid. For that system, you will usually want your type to snap to a grid to keep the horizontal alignments rigidly accurate.

Ruler Units

The Horizontal and Vertical options are obvious. InDesign has more measurement unit options than most: centimeters, picas, and custom, in addition to inches, decimal inches, points, millimeters, and ciceros. You can set these differently for the horizontal ruler and the vertical ruler.

The Origin option allows you to choose the location of the zero points for your pages. The *zero points* are where the zero locations on the horizontal and vertical rulers intersect. By default, each spread has one zero point at the upper-left corner of the first page, but you can also locate it at the binding spine or specify that each page in a spread has its own zero point. You get the choice of setting the zero point of your rulers to the Spread, Page, or Spine. I use Spine.

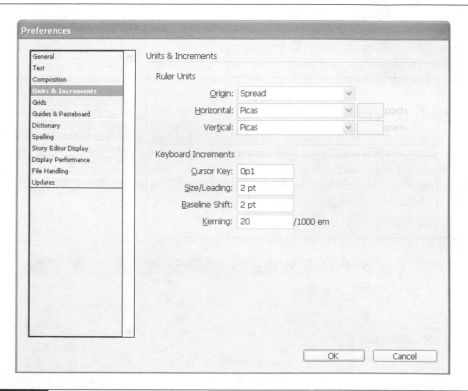

FIGURE 2-4   The Units & Increments page of the Preferences dialog box

Keyboard Increments

The Keyboard Increments options affect what happens when you change sizes and locations with keyboard shortcuts or the arrow keys. I find the factory defaults to be too large. Large movements should be done with tabs and the fixed spaces. You will want to set these options to suit the way that you work.

- ■ **Cursor Key**   This option changes how far selected objects will move when you press an arrow key. The default is 1 point, which is far too large for how I work. I use the arrow keys to gently nudge things into place (I don't use snap-to guides). I set this to 0p.25, or one-quarter point.

- ■ **Size/Leading and Baseline Shift**   The next two options control how much change occurs when you use the keyboard shortcuts to increase or decrease leading, point size, and baseline shift. The factory defaults are 2 points. Again, I use these shortcuts to nudge pieces into position. I reset my increments to 1 point, and now I am thinking about going to one-half point.

■ **Kerning:** The default for this option is 0.020 em, which is very large. Kerning requires nudging into place and delicate adjustments, not big movements. I reset this option to 0.007 em. The shortcut is ALT/OPTION-LEFT ARROW or RIGHT ARROW. If you add the CTRL/COMMAND key, you adjust five times as much. In my case, this is 0.035 em. With the factory defaults, this would be one-tenth of an em, which is far too large to be useful.

Grids Preferences

Some designers use grids for everything. Others (like me) almost never use them. If grids are important to you, the Grids page of the Preferences dialog box, shown in Figure 2-5, offers options for their appearance and placement.

InDesign has two grids built into the program: Baseline and Document. The defaults are a good starting place for both of these grids.

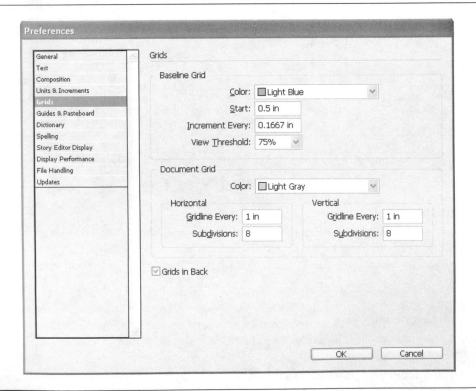

FIGURE 2-5   The Grids page of the Preferences dialog box

NOTE   *The use of too many guides and grids can result in a rigidity that is boring, at best. However, for designers that are too loose, a grid can be a real help. Many designers use what is called the Swiss system, a large grid with uniformly spaced lines.*

Guides and Pasteboard Preferences

The Guides & Pasteboard page of the Preferences dialog box, shown in Figure 2-6, is where you have some control over the color of all the lines needed for page layout. You can set the color of margins, columns, bleed area, and slug area. If you are color-blind to one of the defaults, change it. If the colors are upsetting your design judgment, use grays.

NEW TO
**InDesign
CS**   *Notice that you can pick colors for the bleed size lines and the slug size lines. I'll discuss those options in Chapter 3. They are a major improvement to the software.*

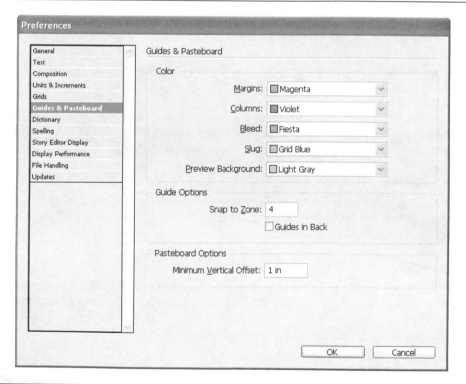

FIGURE 2-6   The Guides & Pasteboard page of the Preferences dialog box

On a lighter note, you can now set the color of the preview background. Normally, you will want the default light gray. You need a light, neutral color in most cases to make design judgments. However, for those times when you are designing a piece that will be seen on a colored background, this could be very helpful. Maybe you want to try a black background.

The Guide Options choices matter if you are using snap-to guides a lot. And you may want to move your guides to the front or back.

In the Pasteboard Options section, you now have the opportunity to make the pasteboard behind each spread taller by typing in a larger number for the minimum vertical offset. This could help if you want to do something like make a large slug area for an art-proof signature block.

Dictionary Preferences

Dictionary preferences might seem to be a simple set of choices that you do not need to worry about, but that is true only if you are an Ugly American—one of those who believes that everyone ou't'speak'Merican.

Language

As you can see in Figure 2-7, InDesign comes with 20 languages installed by default. This is not a minor thing. If you have a phrase or paragraph in French or Swedish in the midst of your copy, you can spell check in that language.

More than just the simple choice of language, you need to choose the type of single or double quote you want to use. Every language is a little different. United Kingdom English is the reverse of United States usage, for example. In the UK, they put double quotes inside single quotes.

Hyphenation Exceptions

Hyphenation exceptions can be composed using your user dictionary, the document, or both. For a detailed explanation, use InDesign Help. In most cases, User Dictionary and Document is the best choice.

User Dictionary

Here, you have two more choices that matter. You really want to merge the user dictionary into the document dictionary if you are going to send your document to another computer for additional work.

The second choice makes sure that when you add a word to the user dictionary, it is applied to the entire document. That sure sounds like a good idea to me.

Spelling Preferences

As you can see in Figure 2-8, there are not too many choices in the Spelling page of the Preferences dialog box. All you need to do is decide if you want to check for misspelled words, repeated words, uncapitalized words, and uncapitalized sentences.

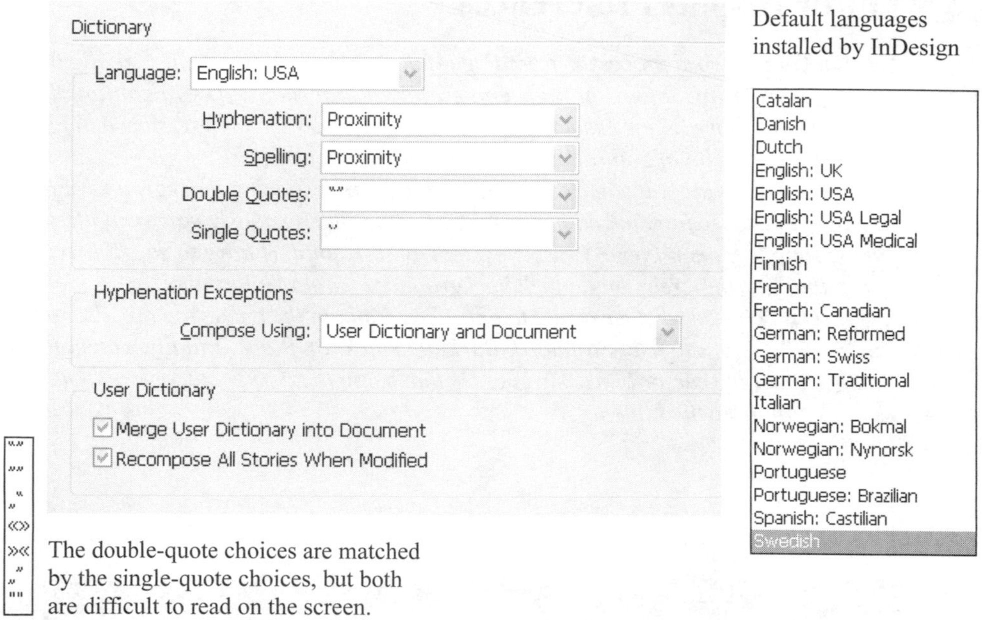

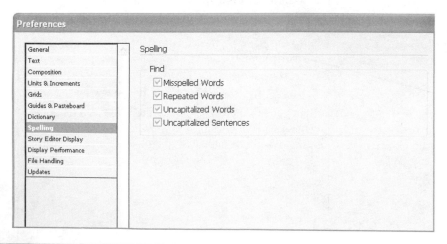

Dictionary

Language: English: USA

Hyphenation: Proximity

Spelling: Proximity

Double Quotes: ""

Single Quotes: ''

Hyphenation Exceptions

Compose Using: User Dictionary and Document

User Dictionary

☑ Merge User Dictionary into Document
☑ Recompose All Stories When Modified

Default languages
installed by InDesign

Catalan
Danish
Dutch
English: UK
English: USA
English: USA Legal
English: USA Medical
Finnish
French
French: Canadian
German: Reformed
German: Swiss
German: Traditional
Italian
Norwegian: Bokmal
Norwegian: Nynorsk
Portuguese
Portuguese: Brazilian
Spanish: Castilian
Swedish

The double-quote choices are matched
by the single-quote choices, but both
are difficult to read on the screen.

FIGURE 2-7   The Dictionary Preferences, showing the languages and double-quote
choices available

Preferences

General
Text
Composition
Units & Increments
Grids
Guides & Pasteboard
Dictionary
Spelling
Story Editor Display
Display Performance
File Handling
Updates

Spelling

Find
☑ Misspelled Words
☑ Repeated Words
☑ Uncapitalized Words
☑ Uncapitalized Sentences

FIGURE 2-8   The Spelling page of the Preferences dialog box

Story Editor Display Preferences

NEW TO
**InDesign
CS**

Yes, the built-in word processor from PageMaker is back. However, it is really the word processor from InCopy—that high-end editorial tool that works in conjunction with InDesign. The Story Editor Display page of the Preferences dialog box, shown in Figure 2-9, gives you quite a bit of control over the look of the interface.

For text display, you can choose the font, size, line spacing, background and color. Or you can choose from ink on paper, or three other horrendously ugly reminders of the 1980s: Amber Monochrome, Classic System, or Terminal. (I have to say, if I were forced to use that glaring green on a black background, I would be terminal!)

You can choose whether or not to anti-alias (smooth the type). You are also given four choices of cursors to use: Standard, Barbell, Thick, or Block. Finally, you can choose whether to let the cursor blink. My guess is that using the darker cursor would make you want to eliminate the blinking.

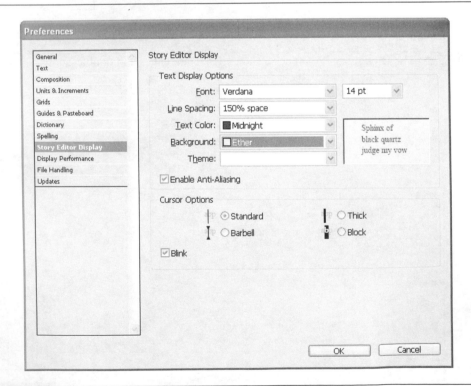

FIGURE 2-9   The Story Editor Display page of the Preferences dialog box

Display Performance Preferences

In the Display Performance page of the Preferences dialog box, shown in Figure 2-10, you can choose whether you want high-resolution images, screen previews, or grayed-out boxes for your documents. None of this affects printing; it is for viewing and working with those graphics on the screen. Your choices are based on the speed of your computer and monitor.

You should set this preference immediately. Otherwise, you will wonder why a graphic looks so horrible after you've imported it. Why Adobe persists in making low-quality display the default after all these years is beyond me. Unless you have a very old computer (and in most cases, computers that old do not run InDesign), you need to be using the High Quality option for your display.

NOTE   *One of the real benefits of InDesign is that it generates its own very high-quality screen previews. Graphics should look better in InDesign than they do elsewhere. Their appearance at least matches, and is often better than, what you see in Photoshop and Illustrator. InDesign's graphics display is far superior to the display in Quark, FreeHand, and Acrobat.*

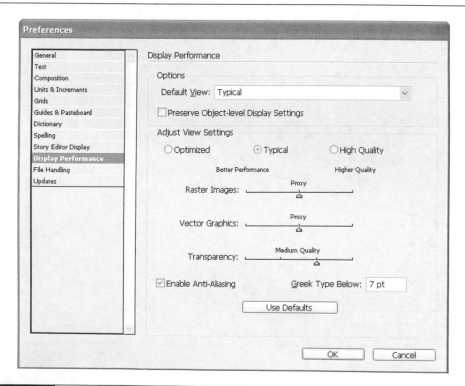

FIGURE 2-10   The Display Performance page of the Preferences dialog box

If you are working on very large files with large numbers of graphics, you may need to go to the Typical display settings to help with redraw speed. Only in rare cases will you need to go to Optimized, which is a flat, gray box that shows only position. This might have been necessary back in 1991 or so, running 4MB RAM (including the video RAM). Memory is no longer a problem for most of us.

The Greek Type Below option relates to the typographic equivalent of choosing Optimized for your display view settings: *text greeking*. With greeking, lines of type are shown as gray rectangles to speed up screen redraw. The default is 7 pt. Because redraw speed is rarely an issue, I set this to 2 pt. I find that even type rendered only 2 pt high shows me enough to know where word breaks, all caps, and other items of interest are located.

File Handling Preferences

The File Handling page of the Preferences dialog box, shown in Figure 2-11, offers options for recovering and saving files. One of InDesign's nicest features is the fact that it almost never loses anything. If the application or your computer crashes, InDesign is usually able open your file again

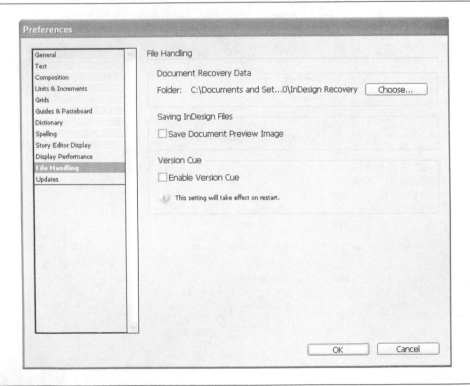

FIGURE 2-11   The File Handling page of the Preferences dialog box

2

automatically, with only a loss of a few seconds or minutes of work. You can choose where to save the file that automatically reopens, but I have always used the default location.

You can also choose to save a preview of your file. In Mac OSX, the preview can be helpful. But it previews only the first page.

Finally, for this set of preferences, you can enable Version Cue. This new ability of the Creative Studio suite enables you to sign out documents, view documents that others are working on, and generally manage large workflows transparently, even when many people on many computers are working on the project. This capability is crucial to publishing newspapers, magazines, books, and the like.

Updates Preferences

The Updates page of the Preferences dialog box, shown in Figure 2-12, lets you check for updates automatically. Why allow Big Brother the opportunity? Adobe is not nearly as sinister as Microsoft in this regard, but I am never happy giving outside agencies regular free access to my computer. Of course, the privacy statement makes me feel much better. If you would like to check for updates automatically, you have a choice of intervals: once a week up to once every three months.

Preferences Wrap-up

So, now you have your preferences set. If you haven't a clue yet, don't worry. Once you are working in InDesign full time, you can fix the ones that irritate you.

Although I've told you how I set my preferences, there really is no right or wrong here. All of these choices are simply your personal preferences (hence the name). But preferences are just the beginning.

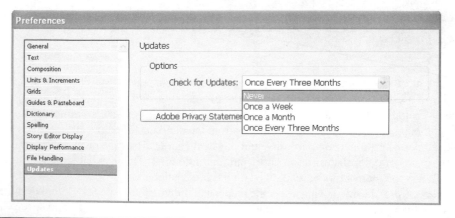

FIGURE 2-12   The Updates page of the Preferences dialog box

Set Your Defaults

One of the most powerful aspects of InDesign is its ability to prestructure the application as well as the specific document, so that much of your formatting occurs effortlessly. Defaults are those things that happen when you click a command, draw a shape, or type in copy without controlling its immediate outcome. Defaults control type, margins, columns, graphics, colors, and everything else in InDesign. There are three major areas that you need to control for efficient production:

- Application defaults, which control how the program reacts
- Document defaults, which control how the specific document reacts
- Interface setup, which controls what is available at a mouse click or keypress

Setting up your interface to fit your working style gives you a huge competitive advantage over those who don't do it. Chapter 4 is devoted to the topic of customizing your interface. Here, I'll explain the importance of using application and document defaults.

Application Defaults

Most of the settings in the entire application are available as defaults. You can determine the page size, margins, and number of columns. Plus, every attribute of type (font, size, leading, set width, color, small cap size, superscript size and location, indents, spacing, alignment, style, OpenType options, and so on) can be predetermined. There are also presets for text wrap, hyphenation, tool performance, paragraph styles, character styles, color swatches, and many other features.

Pick a Design Palette

One of the most important things you must learn about document construction is the principle of prepared production. You must have all the pieces, jigs, and templates readily at hand. One clear analogy is that of a fine-art painter who squeezes appropriate amounts of carefully chosen colors on his palette. He makes choices from the hundreds of colors available based on appropriateness, harmony, compatibility, and physical characteristics. The artist is trying to avoid the chaos of color that turns an entire painting into mud. This is what almost invariably happens when too many colors are allowed on the same palette.

Painters control this by picking a specific media and limiting their palettes. Digital designers take control by designing within the limitations of a specific output technology and specifying their defaults. It is not an optional exercise. If you ignore it, you are forced to deal with the factory defaults for every document you create.

To set an application default, change the setting without any documents open. Your new setting will apply to every document opened from then on. You can tell which settings can be made application defaults by their availability (appearing in black in the menu bar or palettes) when no document is open.

> TIP
>
> *If you do get lost and want to return to the "out-of-the-box" preset factory defaults, the easiest way is to close the application. Then simply relaunch the application while holding down* CTRL-ALT-SHIFT/COMMAND-OPTION-CONTROL-SHIFT. *InDesign will ask if you want to toss the defaults. Say yes, and you are back to where you started when you installed the program.*

Why Set Application Defaults?

The idea is to set your application defaults so that you can begin working in a new document by simply pressing CTRL-N/COMMAND-N, picking one of your document presets (a file you saved with standard page presets), and then pressing ENTER/RETURN. I'll cover document presets in Chapter 3.

When the document opens, everything should be basically set up for your working style. You can just start typing with your favorite font, using your favorite column setup, with a color palette that looks good to you, with style palettes you can apply confidently, and so on.

When Should You Set Application Defaults?

Application defaults tend to change in broad cycles. This is especially true of font choices. There is a strong tendency to use your favorite fonts for most documents. The reason they are your favorites is that you think they are the best solution. As a result, your favorites get boring after a lot of hard use. In addition, as you learn more, your tastes change. As you begin designing, you will change daily, weekly, and then monthly. Gradually that will change to semiannual and annual revisions of your basic style palettes.

> TIP
>
> *The only reasons to change your defaults are fashion, personal style, or boredom. If you produce a thousand documents or more a year (that's about normal for a production designer), changing your default font helps. My solution was to start designing my own fonts, which are available at MyFonts.com.*

Document Defaults

Although application defaults are great, you probably need a different setup for all of your normal documents such as letters, invoices, newsletters, envelopes, and the like. The way to do this is to develop sets of standard document defaults. These are commonly called *templates*, even though few people actually save them in template format.

Setting defaults should become habitual. It should be the first thing you do on every job. When you open a new document, you should use a template, load styles from other documents, or set new document defaults. You can load swatches, paragraph styles, character styles, and so on from any other InDesign document.

In Chapter 8, I will discuss a strategy for setting up paragraph and character styles. These incredibly powerful settings allow you to save styles for paragraphs and local formatting, so you can format type habitually with memorized shortcuts. However, styles are only a portion of the defaults you need to control. Here, we will look at new document defaults and templates.

Set New Document Defaults

Document defaults are the same as application defaults, except that they are changes made with a document open and nothing selected. These defaults can be made when you first open a brand-new, blank document, or they can be changed as needed during the production process. All you need to do is deselect everything and make changes with nothing selected and no insertion point active. This way, you can customize the defaults to the specific project.

After you have set your document defaults, you have the option to save the document as a template. A template is a locked document that normally allows you to open only a copy of the template (keeping the original template unchanged). Most people do not actually save the document in template format. However, templates or documents used as templates are a major part of your workflow (or they should be).

For jobs that repeat only once or twice, it is usually easier to open the file for the most recent job completed and save it under a new name into a new folder. Then place your type insertion point, press CTRL-A/COMMAND-A to select everything, and delete all the old type. Then delete the transitory graphics. This gives you a new, clean document that is set up exactly as the last one was. This procedure is a little slower than using a template. For jobs that repeat often, you should use templates; it's too easy to open the wrong file and get the wrong defaults.

It's usually best to wait for the second or third version of a document to make the defaults. You will not catch all the intricacies of the design for the first few pieces. Usually, by the second or third time through, you have a set that you can use without changes for a long time.

Create Templates

Templates are extremely handy and save a great deal of time. Everything you do on a regular basis should be available as a template. You can literally open a document, place an insertion point, and start typing or importing copy and graphics. Everything will automatically appear as it is supposed to look.

As an example, I regularly use templates for letterhead, books, school handouts, the student newspaper, the department newsletter, lesson plans, invoices, purchase requests, bookstore orders, and other documents.

I use automatic page numbering to number my invoices and purchase orders. For example, my current invoice has Invoice# (auto page number character) on the master page. I started with page number 10000. When I get to 90000 (InDesign's limit), I'll make a new set. However, file size keeps the invoices to sets of ten.

The main reason to use documents saved in template format is for distribution. Templates are the documents normally supplied when producing a corporate-image package. You will need to set up a letterhead template, with a set of paragraph styles and custom-designed margins. You should also create templates for fax cover sheets, second sheets, press releases, and so on.

Newspapers and magazines are other places to use templates, because their defaults remain the same for a long time. Once or twice a decade is considered frequent change.

The best method for producing any template is to open the finished document, delete all of the nonrepeating copy and graphics, and save the file as a template in a location you can remember. If you find pieces that don't work as well as expected, just change the template as necessary.

Navigate in Your Documents

InDesign offers several navigation tools: the Navigator palette, the Pages palette, and controls in the document window. I'll discuss using the Pages palette in detail in Chapter 3. Here, I will just explain why the Pages palette works better than the Navigator palette. Then I'll quickly go over the document window navigation controls.

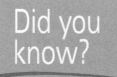

Setting Defaults Saves Time

Setting defaults does take some time, but it does not take nearly as much time as producing a document using local formatting. Just watch yourself as you try to make changes to your basic font decisions in an ad hoc, locally formatted file.

By taking control of your defaults, you can get to the place where your documents are formatted subconsciously. You think headline, and your hand automatically presses the proper shortcut to format that paragraph into the style you have set up for your headlines. You think bold, and your hand automatically double-clicks to select the word, adds the shortcuts to select the other words needed, and types the shortcut to make those words bold from your character styles.

Consider the example of producing a simple 12-page newsletter. The first time you set up this newsletter, you will need to pick fonts, set up page layouts, specify ad sizes, design flags and mastheads, design master pages, and much more. This could take three to ten working days or more—maybe a hundred hours. By the time you are on the fourth or fifth month of the contract, your defaults should be so complete that you can now produce that same document in five or six hours, or less.

Of course, setting defaults saves time only in a mass-production setting, where you are producing a lot of documents. Let's say, maybe a desktop publishing professional might need to set defaults.

The Navigator Palette versus the Pages Palette

I do not recommend using the Navigator palette. As you can see (but not well in grayscale), this palette has a little rectangle (it's red) that tells you what is being viewed in the window of the document.

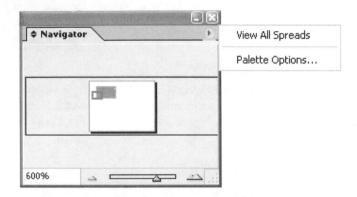

You can also see that you can show all the spreads. But that is not really a big deal. In the following illustration, you can see that the Navigator palette always shows the spreads vertically (Quark style) and can show only 10 spreads in the same area in which the Pages palette can show 36 spreads. Plus, the Pages palette is faster and has many more options.

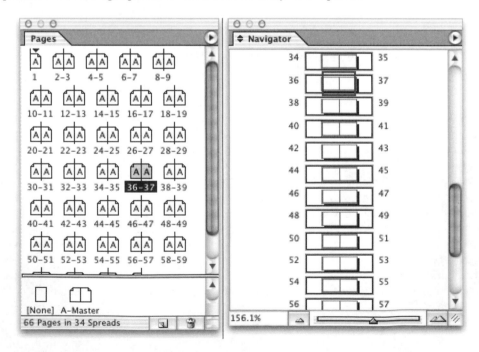

> **NOTE** *I had a student who claimed he always worked with the Navigator palette in Photoshop, and that is what he would use in InDesign. He also said he never used shortcuts and moused everything. I told him that it didn't bother me, as long as he realized that he was giving a massive competitive advantage to other designers who worked so much faster than he does. He said he would think about it. I noticed in a day or so he was sheepishly asking about shortcuts for various actions.*

As you'll see in Chapter 3, the Pages palette offers the best way to move around a document from page to page or page to spread. It allows you to sort pages, apply masters, and control the pages of your document. It is a wonderful tool.

Window Controls

There are some controls for magnification and page navigation available in the lower-left corner of your document window.

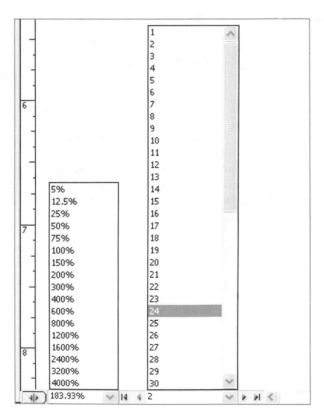

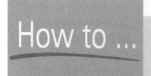 **Navigate a Page or Spread**

Basic navigation procedures are constant in all publishing software (except Quark):

- Use the CTRL-0 (zero)/COMMAND-0 shortcut to fit the image into the window. The only difference in InDesign is the additional CTRL-ALT-0/COMMAND-OPTION-0 command if you need to fit the whole spread in the window.

- Use the CTRL-SPACEBAR/COMMAND-SPACEBAR shortcut to access the Zoom tool.

- Click-drag the mouse to marquee the area you need to work in. The area surrounded by the marquee will enlarge to as large as possible in the center of the window.

- To zoom out a little, add the OPTION/ALT key and click.

- To scroll around, release everything except the ALT/OPTION-SPACEBAR, and you will have the Hand tool to pull the place you need to work into view.

This procedure is by far the fastest way to navigate around a page or spread of pages.

The page navigation controls work well. The single arrows on each side of the pop-up move you to the previous or following page. The double arrows take you to the first page in the document or the last page. The pop-up gives you fast access to any page.

The magnification pop-up is not particularly helpful. It gives you very little control. However, it will center what is selected at larger magnifications. You'll probably need to try several different magnifications before you get what you need. The CTRL-0/COMMAND-0 and CTRL-SPACEBAR/COMMAND-SPACEBAR marquee method is much faster, plus it centers exactly what you need in the window on the first try.

This completes our discussion of setting up preferences and defaults, as well as using some basic navigation techniques. Expect to be modifying your setup regularly for the first few months. You just need to find where the settings are located.

Chapter 3

Open Documents, Old and New

How to...

- ■ Set up new documents
- ■ Open existing documents
- ■ Convert QuarkXPress and PageMaker documents
- ■ Work with the Pages palette
- ■ Use the Pages palette's commands
- ■ Create master pages
- ■ Make multiple-page spreads
- ■ Add sections to your document
- ■ Use the Layout Adjustment feature

InDesign is the premier page layout application. Although you can write in it, and you will certainly create graphics in the application, InDesign is primarily designed to assemble pieces that have been created elsewhere. You will frequently open a new document, and then import graphics and word processing files into that document. Or you will open an existing file, created in InDesign or another application, and continue working in that file.

This chapter covers opening new and existing documents. Then I'll show you how to use the Pages palette, which helps you access and manage the pages in your documents. The final topic is InDesign's Layout Adjustment feature, which you might find useful if you decide to change your page layout.

Set Up New Documents

After all the discussion about parts of the interface, we're ready to actually open a document. InDesign CS gives you many controls for your new documents, before you even open them. The New Document dialog box (which appears when you select File | New | Document or press CTRL-N/COMMAND-N) looks simple enough when you first open it. But all you need to do is click the More Options button to get a hint of what is available. Figure 3-1 shows the expanded New Document dialog box.

Open a Document Preset

The first new addition is right at the top of the New Document dialog box. You can now save as many standard page presets as you like.

You should set up some basic page styles before you even get started working with documents. Choose File | Document Presets | Define to open the dialog box shown in Figure 3-2. Here, you have controls to make new presets, edit existing ones, save presets as a file that can be transported wherever you like, and load saved preset files.

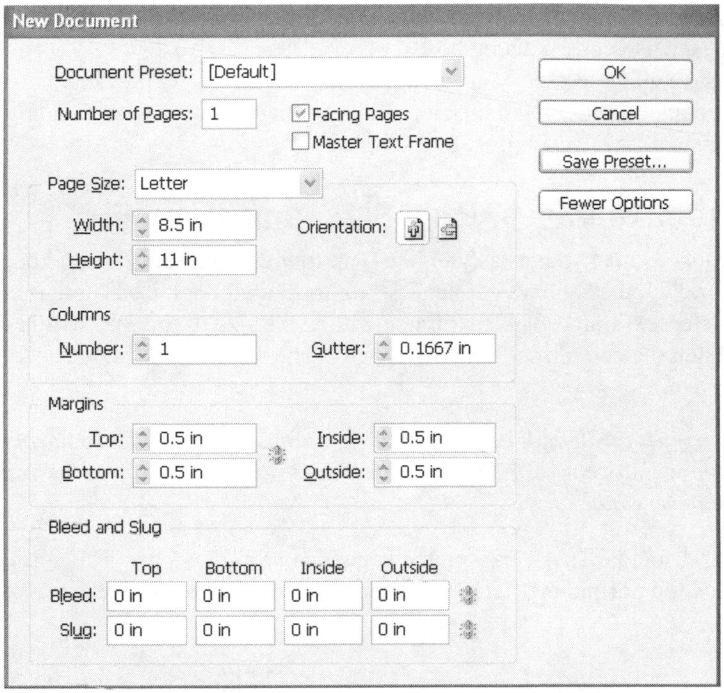

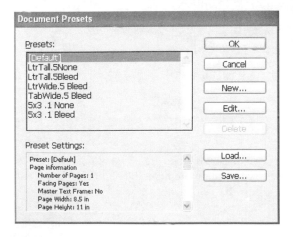

FIGURE 3-1   The New Document dialog box, the More Options version

FIGURE 3-2   The Document Presets dialog box, for managing your presets

As you can see in the example in Figure 3-2, I have added six presets, which are for some of my normal page sizes. If you click New, the New Document Preset dialog box opens. This dialog box looks like the New Document dialog box.

I suggest you save all the presets you can think of as soon as you understand how the settings work. For the first couple months, you'll probably add a dozen or more presets. Building a collection of document presets will save you a great deal of time.

Set the Number of Pages, Page Size, and Columns

You can make almost as many pages as you like—up to 9,999 pages. You can keep them as individual sheets or click the Facing Pages check box for bound booklets. There is also a check box to create a master text frame. This text frame will be the size of the area within the margin guides and will match the column settings you specify. The master text frame is added to the A-Master master page.

 *A-Master is just the default name of the first automatically produced master page. The second one will appear as B-Master in the Pages palette. You can name your master pages whatever you like.*

There are several standard page sizes in the Page Size drop-down list. The normal American sizes are there, plus the normal metric sizes. Often, you can choose one of these to start your saved preset.

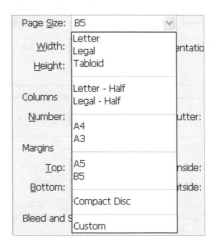

The Width, Height, and Orientation options are obvious. The same is true of the Number and Gutter choices for columns. If you want more than 20 columns, you are out of luck. The gutter width is limited to 20 inches as well.

Specify Margins

With the Margins settings in the New Document dialog box comes yet another new improvement. To the right of the Top and Bottom fields, you can see a little icon that looks like a couple of bugs, but it's supposed to represent a broken chain link. If you click that icon, it becomes three links of a chain. Then when you type a setting in the first field, the rest of the fields automatically get the same measurement.

In any field in any dialog box in InDesign, you can use whatever measurement you like: 1p = 1 pica, p1 = 1 point, 1i = 1 inch, 1mm = 1 millimeter, 1cm = 1 centimeter, or 1c = 1 cicero.

Add a Bleed or Space for a Slug

One of the major InDesign advances for production designers is the ability to add bleeds and slugs. As you can see in Figure 3-1, both of these New Document dialog box options have the link bug icons to the right. Click the bugs, and fill in the first field. The rest of the measurements will be added automatically.

A *bleed* is used when you want the ink to come to the edge of the paper. You need to print oversized, and then trim back to the final size. This ink printed beyond the edge of the trim is called a bleed. (See Chapter 16 for more on bleeds and bleed production issues.)

A *slug* is a standardized setting of type placed outside the trim and bleed areas to contain job-ticket information, a signature line, or whatever else is required by the production department at your company.

A well-designed slug can go a long way toward helping eliminate common production problems and lack of proof signatures. Job-ticket numbers, deadlines, and so forth are good slug additions to consider.

Open Your New Document

When you have all of the New Document dialog box options under control, click OK, and your new document will open. As you can see in Figure 3-3, InDesign's window looks like almost any other, with a couple additions in the lower-left corner. These are the magnification pop-up and page-navigation controls described at the end of Chapter 2. All of the other controls are normal for the operating system. In every other way, the window is standard for your operating system, with your normal scroll bars, title bars, minimize button, maximize button, and so forth.

As soon as your new document is open, save it with an understandable name into a folder that is equally well named, to hold all of the pieces for the project.

The first thing to do in any project is to make a folder with a well-written name. Keep all the pieces for the project in this folder.

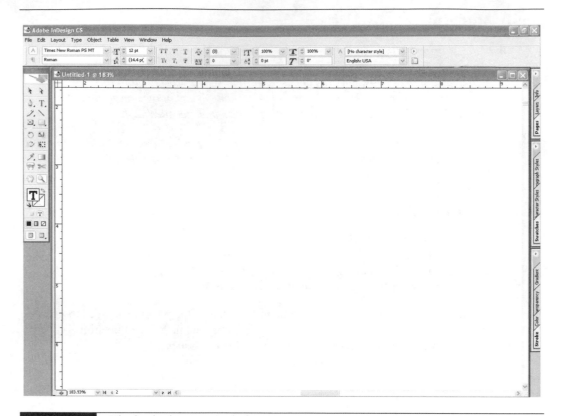

FIGURE 3-3   The basic document window

Open Existing Documents

There are many reasons to open existing documents. You will open a document you use as an informal template. You will also regularly open existing documents for minor changes. When you choose File | Open or press CTRL-O/COMMAND-O, you see the relatively standard Open a File dialog box, as shown in Figure 3-4. Just navigate to the document you want open in your normal fashion. You can open the original or a copy, or just open the document normally (which is the default).

You cannot open any graphic or word processing files from the InDesign Open a File dialog box. Graphics and word processing files must be placed (imported) into an already open file. Placing text is covered in Chapter 5, and placing graphics is covered in Chapter 12.

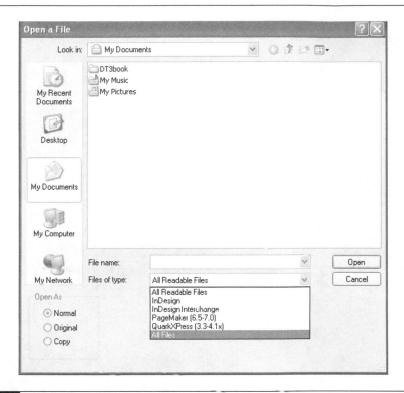

FIGURE 3-4   The Open a File dialog box

As you can see in Figure 3-4, readable files that you can open are InDesign documents, InDesign Interchange files, QuarkXPress 3.3-4.1x documents, and PageMaker 6.5-7.0 files.

Find Missing Fonts and Graphics

Normally, when you open an old file, you will be presented with two dialog boxes. The first will list missing fonts. As you can see in Figure 3-5, the Missing Fonts dialog box has a Find Font button. If you click that, InDesign's standard Find Font dialog box opens.

The Find Font dialog box, shown in Figure 3-6, gives you the opportunity to change the fonts in the dialog box temporarily. You will be able to print normally, and everything will look okay on the screen. However, the Find Font dialog box will not actually fix your paragraph or character styles; you will need to fix those manually.

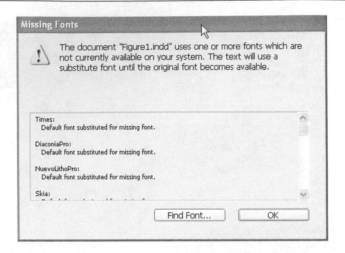

The Missing Fonts dialog box may appear when you open an old file.

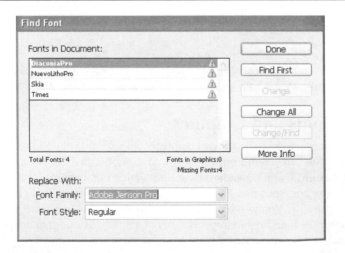

The Find Font dialog box lets you fix fonts temporarily.

The other dialog box that might open is an alert box, which appears if InDesign does not know where your imported graphics are located. In most cases, you can fix the problem simply by clicking the Fix Links Automatically button.

However, InDesign will find the graphics automatically only if you have kept them in the same folder as your InDesign document. If you have not, you will need to show the application where the graphic files are located. In this case, clicking the Fix Links Automatically button opens the Links palette first, and then opens the Relink dialog box, which has a Browse button to click so you can show InDesign where you hid the graphics. In the Links palette, the red stop sign with the question mark appears next to all missing graphics.

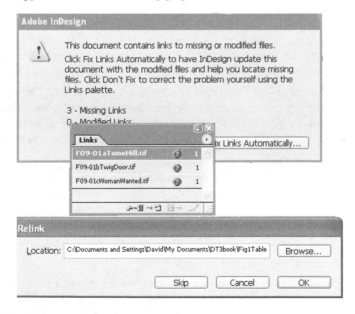

   *If you do not know where the missing graphics are located, you will need to re-create them. The missing graphics will print only as the 72 dpi, RGB preview version, and are worthless for real printing. Chapter 12 explains previews.*

Convert QuarkXPress Documents

As you first start working in InDesign, you may want to keep some of your old files in Quark and work on them in Quark. However, within a couple of months, you will no longer be able to tolerate the missing features in Quark. The good news is that InDesign does a very good job of converting old Quark files to InDesign format.

The bad news is that InDesign will not open Quark 5 or 6 files. You will need to save the file to Quark 5, open it in Quark 5, and save it back to Quark 4. However, you will rarely receive a Quark file that is not already in 4.1 format.

NOTE   *As all the industry commentators have said, InDesign's competition is not Quark 5 or 6 but 4.1. Quark was stunned by the industry's rejection of Quark 5. There is not much of a move to Quark 6 either.*

You will not be able to open multiple-language files from Quark Passport. You will quickly come to realize that InDesign can handle these multiple-language projects out of the box. The standard installation of InDesign has dictionaries in 20 languages. You can, however, save Passport files in single-language format to open them in InDesign.

You will also not be able to open Quark files that require an Xtension (like the beloved Pasteboard XT). However, you will be able to open the vast majority of old Quark files.

Once you have a Quark file open, you will see that InDesign did a credible job of conversion. Of course, there are some quibbles:

- **Nonprinting objects**   If you have suppressed the printing of any object in Quark, InDesign will move this to a separate Non-Printing layer in InDesign. You can move those objects wherever you like and print them.

- **Guides**   These might shift a very small amount during conversion. The conversion is accurate to two decimal places in inches. A three decimal point location might be shifted half the third point—0.003 to 0.0025, for example. I doubt if that will ruin your design. Point dimensions are rounded to the nearest whole point. Again, this is not a critical move.

- **Font styles**   Quark has check boxes to apply styles. This method can easily result in asking for fonts that really do not exist (like Papyrus Bold Italic). InDesign does an excellent job of guessing what Bold and Italic styling means. However, it does not support the Shadow style at all. Outline is formatted with a one-quarter point stroke and a fill of Paper. There is a dialog box to warn you of missing fonts.

- **Master page items**   All master page objects, as well as QuarkXPress guides, are placed on the corresponding InDesign master pages.

- **Text wraps**   Text wraps applied in QuarkXPress require that you select Text Wrap Only Affects Objects Beneath in the Composition page of the Preferences dialog box (accessed from the Edit menu on PCs and the InDesign menu in OSX). That is the way that text wraps work in Quark.

3

- **Color profiles**   Because QuarkXPress uses different color profiles, they are ignored in InDesign.

- **Graphics created with an Xtension**   InDesign does not support Quark Xtensions. If you open a file that has graphics created with an Xtension, those graphics will not appear. You will need to export those graphics from Quark in an acceptable format, such as EPS or PDF.

- **Strokes and custom strokes**   All strokes and lines (including paragraph rules) are converted to the stroke styles they resemble most closely. Custom strokes and dashes are converted to custom strokes and dashes in InDesign and will be available in the Stroke palette.

- **Groups**   Grouped objects stay grouped. However, where nonprinting items are included in a group, they will be ungrouped.

- **Some color conversion issues**   Most colors convert exactly with these exceptions: QuarkXPress 3.3 HSB colors are converted to RGB; 3.3 colors from the color library are converted using their CMYK values; QuarkXPress 4.1 HSB and LAB colors are converted to RGB; 4.1 colors from the color library are converted based on their RGB or CMYK values.

- **Multi-ink colors**   This type of color from QuarkXPress is mapped to a mixed-ink swatch in InDesign, if it uses a spot color. If the multi-ink color does not contain any spot color, it is converted to a process color instead. (See Chapter 13 for information about mixed-ink swatches.)

Other than these issues, the conversions are almost flawless. All styles are converted to InDesign styles. All text and graphics links are preserved and appear in the Links palette. The documents will look the same. You may need to change some of the layer colors just because they irritate you visually. You will probably need to make other minor adjustments, which is not surprising, since you are converting from one paradigm to another.

Convert PageMaker Documents

InDesign does an even better job of converting PageMaker files than it does of converting Quark files. This is to be expected, since InDesign is the replacement for PageMaker.

NOTE   *You can also convert PageMaker 6.5 and 7 documents simply by opening them. For the same reason I keep an old version of Quark to fix problems in old Quark files, I also keep a copy of PageMaker 6.5 to convert older PageMaker files to a usable format.*

Tables created in PageMaker are converted to InDesign tables. Styles are converted to InDesign styles. Text and graphics links are preserved and appear in the Links palette. Color profiles for PageMaker files are converted directly. All master pages and layers are converted to InDesign masters and layers. (If you have any problems converting Adobe PageMaker layers, see the Support area of the Adobe Web site.)

The following are some areas that may require adjustments:

- **Pasteboard items**   Any items on PageMaker's universal pasteboard are placed on the pasteboard of the first spread in InDesign. Like Quark, InDesign has a separate pasteboard for each spread.

- **Embedded graphics**   Graphics added and embedded in the original document using the Paste command are not converted. You will need to find a copy of the original graphic or re-create it.

- **Baselines**   PageMaker has three methods of leading. InDesign's comes closest to the baseline method. Paragraphs formatted in proportional or top-of-caps leading will shift up or down a little.

- **Font styles**   PageMaker has check boxes to apply styles. This can easily result in asking for fonts that really do not exist (like Papyrus Bold Italic). InDesign does an excellent job of guessing what Bold and Italic styling means. However, it does not support the Shadow style at all. Outline is formatted with a one-quarter point stroke and a fill of Paper. There is a dialog box to warn you of missing fonts.

- **OLE**   InDesign does not support Object Linking and Embedding (OLE). If you open a file that contains OLE graphics, those graphics will not appear. You will need to convert the OLE graphic to a usable format.

- **Guides**   PageMaker document guides are placed on the Default layer in InDesign.

- **Color conversions**   PageMaker HLS colors are converted to RGB colors. Colors from the color library are converted based on their CMYK values.

Convert Documents from Earlier Versions of InDesign

There are very few issues with older InDesign documents. Adobe does suggest that you immediately save the converted document with a new name. But that is standard procedure anyway.

NOTE   *To open an older InDesign document, sometimes I need to change the name to make sure it has the .indd extension (the InDesign filename extension). Cross-platform files need this extension to open. In fact, I have yet to open a file from a Mac on a PC without copying the Mac file to the PC first.*

If third-party plug-ins were used in the older InDesign documents, you should always check with the manufacturer to make sure that they are compatible with InDesign CS before you convert the document. Libraries created in InDesign 2.0 cause no problem. Libraries created in InDesign 1.*x* will need to be re-created.

When you convert a document, you may see an alert message asking if you want to use the exception word list in the user dictionary or the one in the document. Personally, I recommend that you use the user dictionary, and then spell-check the document.

Work with the Pages Palette

The Pages palette is the best I have seen in any page layout program. Here, you have access to any page in the document or master page. In most cases, this palette is the fastest method of page navigation. All you need to do is double-click a page or master in the Pages palette to move to that page and center it in the document window. If you double-click the numbers under the spread, that spread will become centered in the document window.

Set Up Your Pages Palette for Better Page Control

A problem is that this marvelous palette opens crippled by default, to make converters from Quark more comfortable. As you can see in Figure 3-7, a lot of space in the palette is wasted. It is showing only 13 of the 56 pages and 7 of the 29 spreads. You can see the settings in the Palette Options dialog box for the palette (displayed by selecting Palette Options from the Pages palette's option menu).

A far better setup for the Pages palette is shown in Figure 3-8. One change is that the pages are on top, and the master pages are on the bottom, but this is not the important modification. What does matter is that the Show Vertically option in the Palette Options dialog box is now unchecked. As you can see in Figure 3-8, the new style can easily show all 56 pages in the same size palette, with room to spare. This makes page control simple, allowing for page shuffling and many other options.

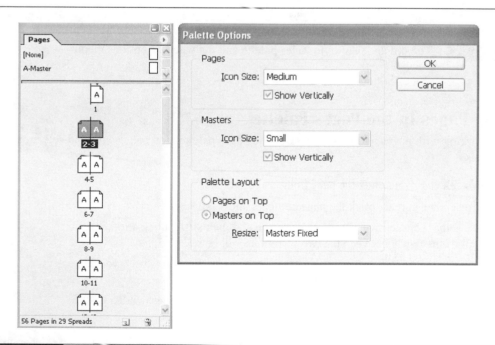

FIGURE 3-7   The default Pages palette setup, wasting space

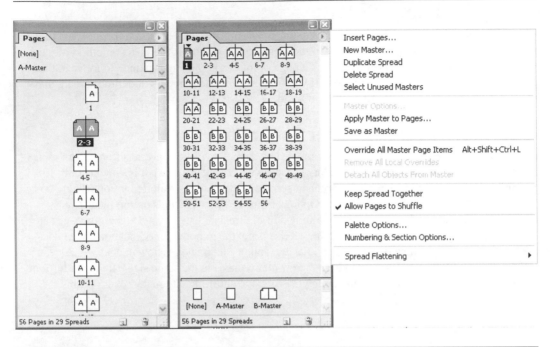

The old and new style Pages palette and the palette's options menu

Select Pages in the Pages Palette

When working with pages and master pages in the Pages palette, you can use normal selection techniques:

■ To select a page, click the page in the Pages palette.

■ To select a spread, click the page numbers under the spread.

■ To select consecutive pages, select a page and then SHIFT-click another page. All of the pages between the two selections will be selected.

■ To select nonconsecutive pages, CTRL/COMMAND-click. This way, you can select pages that are noncontiguous (in any order).

■ You can make a SHIFT-selection, and then add or subtract pages with a CTRL/COMMAND-click.

You can apply these selection techniques in any order to select the pages you need to change.

Use the Pages Palette Commands

The Pages palette's option menu (see Figure 3-7) includes some important commands for adding pages, working with master pages, adding sections, and other common tasks. Let's work our way through these commands.

Insert New Pages

Choose Insert Pages from the Pages palette's option menu to open the Insert Pages dialog box. You can insert almost as many pages as you want, up to a total of 9,999 pages. You can insert them before or after any existing page. You can also apply an existing master page.

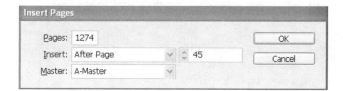

Work with Master Pages

Master pages (along with styles and swatches) are helpful for building a consistent look. Master pages are a major tool for increasing production speed on repetitive documents like newsletters and magazines. Any page layout that is repeated month to month or issue to issue should be made into a master page: table of contents, masthead, full-page ad, newspaper or magazine columns, and so on.

A master page is the place to add automatic page numbering (which is covered in Chapter 6). You can add specific text frames with replaceable type that is already formatted appropriately. You can add standardized locations to insert sidebars with colored backgrounds or whatever your layout requires. You can save a complete set of masters in a template, along with all paragraph and character styles, color libraries, other styles, and presets you might need for your project.

If you need a set of masters with slight variations on one basic design, you can create masters based on other masters. You might have four columnists in your magazine who write regular columns, for example, where the only changes are the picture, name, and colors of the header frames. When you change the parent master, those changes appear in the child also (unless you have modified those objects in the child).

Like document pages, master pages can contain multiple layers. You can use layers to determine how objects on a master overlap objects on a document page. The Layers palette is covered in Chapter 11.

> **TIP** *InDesign's Layout Adjustment feature enables you to control layouts with changes to the master page. If you change column or margin settings on a master, or apply a new master with different column and margin settings, you can force objects on the page to adjust to the new layout automatically. This feature is discussed later in the chapter, in the "Use Automatic Layout Adjustment" section.*

There are a few limitations to using master pages, but they are all logical results of the master page concept. You can thread text frames on a master page only across a single spread. (In Chapter 5, I'll show you how to automatically flow text across multiple spreads on the document pages.) Master pages cannot contain sections, but you can create a unique master page for each section in a document. I'll cover sections in the "Add Sections to Your Document" section later in this chapter.

Make a Master Page

Choose New Master from the Pages palette's option menu to create a new master page. You can make as many master pages as you need (and most documents need only a few). Even magazines rarely use more than 30 pages in a rigidly controlled template.

If you need custom spreads in your document (such as a three- or four-page foldout in a magazine), any master you apply should contain the same number of pages. You can have up to ten pages in a custom-spread master page. I'll show you how to create custom spreads in the next section.

Another easy way to make a master is to simply set up a page the way you want it to look, and then save that page as a master by choosing Save As Master from the Pages palette's option menu.

Apply a Master Page

You apply master pages by dragging the master page icon on top of the page icon in the Pages palette. You can also select a page (or multiple pages) in the Pages palette and apply the master to it by choosing the Apply Master command from the palette's option menu.

Change Master Page Options

You can change master page options by selecting the Master Options command from the Pages palette's option menu. The dialog box that appears allows you to set the prefix, name, what the master is based on, and how many pages are in the master.

Control Your Master Page Items

InDesign has a practical view of master page application. Unlike PageMaker, where master pages are rigidly locked, and unlike Quark, where applied master pages objects are fully editable, InDesign's master page items are normally locked, but any object can be released for editing when necessary.

To view the master items on a document page, navigate to that page or spread, and then choose View | Show Master Items. This is a toggle command, so you can choose it again to remove the master items from the view.

There are times when you need a specific page to be slightly different from a master page. In this situation, re-creating a new master page would be a waste of time. You can customize any master page object or object attribute; other master page objects on the document page will continue to update with the master page. There are several ways to customize master page items on a page.

Override Master Page Objects   You can selectively override one or more attributes of a master page object to customize it without breaking its association with the master page. Attributes that you do not want to override, such as color or size, continue to update with the master. You can override strokes, fills, contents of a frame, and any transformations (such as rotating, scaling, or skewing). If you later want to make the object match the master page, you can remove the override.

Overriding is a simple procedure. On the page or spread you need to modify, press CTRL-SHIFT/COMMAND-SHIFT as you click any master page object to select it. You can now change the object. You can select the overridden object in the same way that you select any other page object, but it retains its association with the master page. Attributes that have not been overridden will still update if you change the master page.

Detach Objects from Their Master   You can also detach a master page object from its master page. When you do this, the object is copied to the document page, and its association with the master page is broken. Detached objects do not update with the master page.

To detach a master page object from its master page, press CTRL-SHIFT/COMMAND-SHIFT to select the object on the page, and then choose Detach Selection from Master in the Pages palette's option menu. This option will be available only when you have overridden objects selected on a page or spread.

Override All Master Page Items   To override all items on a master page, you target a page, spread, or spreads in the Pages palette. Then choose Override All Master Page Items in the Pages palette's option menu. You can now select and modify any or all of the master page items on the selected pages.

Detach All Overridden Master Objects on a Spread   If you want to detach all the master page objects you've overridden, navigate to the spread that contains those objects, not to the master page that contained the original item. Then choose Detach All Objects from Master from the Pages palette's option menu. If the command is not available, there are no overridden objects on that spread.

NOTE   *The Detach All Objects from Master command detaches all overridden master objects on a spread. It does not affect objects that are not overridden. If you want to detach all master objects on a spread, you must override all master page items first.*

Make Custom Spreads

You can easily add multiple-page spreads, which Adobe calls custom spreads in InDesign CS (early versions called them island spreads). This is handy for foldouts and brochures, or any other type of design that uses more than two pages in a spread.

To create a custom spread, choose Keep Spread Together from the Pages palette's option menu and drag pages, as shown in Figure 3-9.

Add Sections to Your Document

You can start new sections anywhere in your documents. You simply select a page in the Pages palette, and then choose Numbering & Section Options from the Pages palette's option menu. The first page of the section will be marked with a little, black, reversed triangle over the page where the section starts.

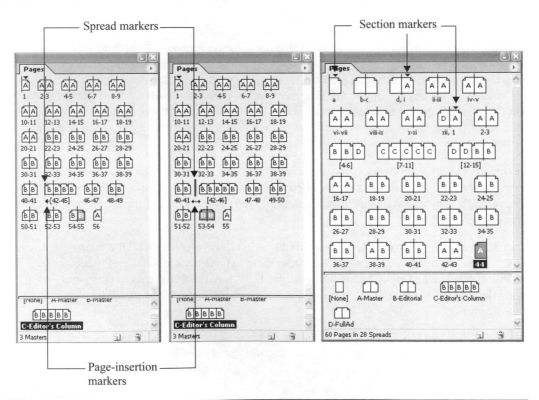

FIGURE 3-9   Dragging pages to form a double foldout that is five pages wide

You can set the section marker (the black triangle) to label section pages automatically. If you are changing the numbering options for any page other than the first page of the document, check Start Section in the New Section dialog box.

If you choose Automatic Page Numbering, the page numbers of this section will follow the numbering of the previous section. When this option is checked, this section's page numbers update automatically when you add pages before the first page of this section.

The other choice for page numbering, Start Page Numbering At, is crucial if you have a document that has frontmatter. Using this option, you can make the first page of this section start at a specific number, regardless of where it is in the document. Just type the number you want to start with, or type 1 to restart the numbering. The remaining pages in the section will be numbered accordingly.

NOTE   *If you choose a non-Arabic page-numbering style for the Style option (such as Roman numerals), you still must type an Arabic numeral in the Start Page Numbering At box.*

Choose a Numbering Style

When you select Style in the New Section dialog box and choose a page-numbering style from the drop-down menu, that numbering style applies only to the pages in this section.

Each section can have its own numbering in its own numbering style. You have five choices:

- 1, 2, 3, 4
- I, II, III, IV
- i, ii, iii, iv
- A, B, C, D
- a, b, c, d

Figure 3-9, shown previously, illustrates what is basically a 54-page booklet, in three sections. You can see one section triangle over page *a*, a second one over page *i*, and a third one over page 1. (The six pages added to make the foldout—4–6, 7–11, and 12–15—make the numbering strange.)

Add Prefixes

You can label each section with a prefix and include the prefix as part of the page number, table of contents entry, cross-reference, index entry, or any other automatic number. To add a prefix, click in the Section Prefix field in the New Section dialog box and type a label for this section. You can use up to eight characters for your prefix.

You need to include spaces or punctuation as necessary, so that the automatic number will appear as *Sec: 4* instead of *Sec4*, for example. If you need blank spaces, use em, en, thin, and/or hair spaces. If you specify Sec: 5- for Section Prefix and place an automatic page number on page 37 of a document, the page number will appear as *Sec: 5-37*. This same prefix and number will also appear in the table of contents or index.

If you want to show the section prefix when you generate a table of contents or index, or print pages that contain automatic page numbers, check the Include Prefix When Numbering Pages box at the bottom of the New Section dialog box. If you leave this option unchecked, the section prefix will display in InDesign, but it will be hidden in the printed document, index, and table of contents.

Add a Section Marker on a Page or Master

A section marker is text that you add to label a section. You enter the text in the Section Marker field of the New Section dialog box. I've typed up to 96 characters in the Section Marker field (and you might be able to include more), so you can make a short paragraph for a section marker.

You can insert the section marker anywhere on any page in the section. To add this marker on a document or master page that you're using in a section, drag the Type tool to create a text frame large enough for the section marker text, or click in an existing frame. Then right-click/CONTROL-click and choose Insert Special Character | Section Marker from the context menu.

Manage Sections

You can end, edit, and remove sections as follows:

- To end the section, start a new section after the section you just created.

- To change settings for an existing section, double-click the black section triangle that appears above the page in the Pages palette. Another method is to select a page with a section marker and choose Numbering & Section Options from the Pages palette's option menu.

- To remove a section, in the Pages palette, select a page with a section marker. Then either double-click that marker or choose Numbering & Section Options in the Pages palette's option menu. Uncheck the Start Section option and click OK.

Rearrange the Page Order

You can shuffle the page order by simply dragging and dropping the icons. But first, you need to choose Allow Pages to Shuffle from the Pages palette's option menu. This is a toggle that prevents page order rearrangement when it isn't selected.

On the left side of Figure 3-9, shown earlier in this chapter, you can see I have dragged page 55 up to add to the left side of the custom spread. The little arrow pointing left from page 42 shows that the dragged page will be added to the spread before 42 and not placed between the spreads. (The bar at the left edge of the spread is hard to see in the figure.) In the center palette, pages 53 and 54 are being dragged between the two spreads. You can see the double-ended arrow and the vertical black bar between the spreads. The palette on the right side of the figure shows the finished arrangement with the sections added and the masters applied.

Use Automatic Layout Adjustment

Changing a layout setting that affects page size, margins, or columns usually requires some adjustments to the page guides and objects on that page. InDesign's Layout Adjustment feature makes these modifications automatically, using a set of rules to move and resize the page guides and objects. The Layout Adjustment feature attempts to approximate the proportions of the old layout in the new layout by following these rules:

- **Margin guides**   It will reposition margin guides but maintain margin widths, if the page size changes. It does this by moving column and ruler guides to maintain proportional distances from page edges, margins, or column guides.

- **Columns**   It will add or remove column guides at the right side of the page, if the new layout specifies a different number of columns.

NOTE   *If you made columns within a text frame by using the Object | Text Frame Options dialog box, the Layout Adjustment feature will affect those columns differently than it does normal page columns. If Layout Adjustment resizes the frame itself and Fixed Column Width is not selected, the columns are resized proportionally. If Fixed Column Width is selected, columns are added or removed as necessary.*

- **Object positioning**   It will move objects already aligned to any margin, column, or ruler guide, or to any two guides perpendicular to each other. The objects will stay with those guides if the guides move during layout adjustment.

- **Resizing**   Objects already aligned to two parallel margin, column, or ruler guides or to guides on three sides will be proportionally resized if those guides move during layout adjustment.

- **Moving**   Objects will be moved to keep them in the same relative position on the page, if the page size changes.

TIP   *The Layout Adjustment feature works better when a layout is tightly structured by snapping objects to a framework of margins, page columns, and ruler guides.*

To turn on this feature, select Layout | Layout Adjustment, and check the Enable Layout Adjustment option in the Layout Adjustment dialog box.

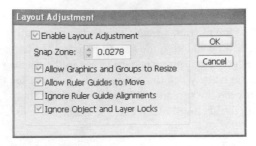

The Layout Adjustment dialog box also lets you modify the adjustment rules. Along with the snap zone size, you can choose whether to allow graphic resizing, group resizing, and moving ruler guides. You can also choose whether to ignore rule guide alignments and locks for objects and layers. Sometimes, you will need to try the change, undo and check or uncheck an option, and then retry the adjustments, to get things to work the way you like. In general, however, this feature works surprisingly well.

The Layout Adjustment feature and Pages palette help you set up the pages in your documents. Now that you are familiar with the procedures for opening documents and preparing them for layout, we can talk about another important step before you actually begin adding type and graphics: customizing the interface. As you'll learn in the next chapter, InDesign offers amazing interface control.

Chapter 4

Customize the Interface

How to...

- Create a tabbed palette group
- Create a docked superpalette
- Stash your palettes
- Use the Control palette
- Save your workspace
- Customize your shortcuts
- Save your shortcut set

As you have seen, InDesign is an application that is very powerful. That is the normal euphemistic expression used by Adobe for a very cluttered interface. You will be using many palettes and dozens, if not hundreds, of keyboard shortcuts to produce your documents efficiently. You must take control of this situation, and you have many options.

In this chapter, I will show you how to set up your interface for efficient production. As you know, the deadline demands in this industry are intense. In many cases, the production speed that results from a well-setup workspace is what gives you the time to be creative and add the decorative niceties you want to provide your client.

Consider Access Times for Frequent Tasks

Before you learn how to set up your workspace, we need to discuss relative access times for the various methods you can use to do your work in InDesign. To give you an idea, here are some approximate times for accessing commands through menus, palettes, and shortcuts:

- **Menu commands: 4–7 seconds**   Whether you are using the menu bar at the top of the screen or one of a palette's option menus or dialog boxes, it will take you several seconds to access a command, or more if you need to continue into a submenu. This is just the time spent to get to the command or dialog box. Actually adjusting the settings offered by the menu command takes even longer.

- **Palette fields: 1–4 seconds**   Using palette fields is a little faster than using menu commands, unless it involves a pop-up menu in a palette. The speed is on the lower edge of the range if you use shortcuts to access the palette and tab through the fields.

- **Keyboard shortcuts: 0.2–0.5 second**   A keyboard shortcut is struck subconsciously in tenths of a second or less. Once you learn your shortcuts, you can hit a shortcut as fast as you can type.

Let's say you pick fonts 60 times a day. Using the Type menu, it took me 15 seconds to pick a font near the bottom of the rather long list of fonts I use. So, if I do this 60 times, it takes

Did you know?

Customizing the Interface Saves Time

Customizing your interface and setting up your shortcuts can save you hours a day. Setting up your personal workspace and your own set of customized shortcuts is essential to keep up with the pressures of deadline-driven digital publishing and stay competitive.

I am not talking about a small savings of time here. My students report a time savings of around 25 to 75 percent of what they were spending when they started learning the program. I am sure you have a clear memory of the last time you spent many seconds (that felt like minutes) looking for a palette, only to find it hidden under another group of palettes, located at the bottom left of the screen, instead of the top right where you normally put it.

The good news is that setting up your workspace is not difficult. It merely takes time and effort. The largest effort will be expended watching yourself work, so you can make changes to the setup to smooth your workflow. Then you'll be amazed at how much time you save in your production work. This frees up time for creativity.

15 minutes per day. Picking the font with the palette field took 9 seconds, for a total of 9 minutes per day. Using a shortcut takes a fraction of a second, for less than 1 minute for a day's total. If your font choice is limited by standard client usage, you can assign shortcuts to each font used.

The basic concept is to set up your interface to streamline all the operations and commands you use the most. The times to access commands and palettes that you rarely use do not cause much penalty. These items can be hidden away in a safe place. So what if it takes you a minute to find and execute a command you use only once a month?

Arrange Your Palettes for Speedy Access

You want to set up your palettes so you can habitually use them without needing to look for them. The default setup of InDesign's palettes, shown in Figure 4-1, is not really useful for anyone.

Here is a quick list of the problems I see with the default setup:

- The toolbox is not in a handy place and it covers the zero points on the rulers.
- The palettes are all stashed on the right side of the screen (as a left-handed designer, this is too far away for me).
- It has several palettes open by default.
- In the default palette groupings stashed on the right are several palettes that I rarely use.
- It is missing several that I use all the time (like the Links palette and the Table palette).
- Three of the most important palettes—Transform, Character, and Paragraph—are not open at all. When I do open them, they pop up dead center on the screen.

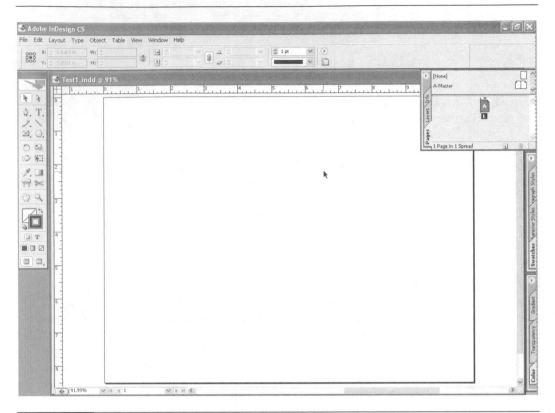

FIGURE 4-1 The factory default workspace setup: a mixed-up mess

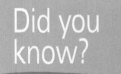

A High Percentage of Creative People Are Left-Handed

Many (some say most) designers are left-handed, as I am. All applications are, by default, set up for right-handed people.

I have found that I can save great amounts of time by setting up my applications so they work better for left-handed operation. Just moving my docked palettes to the left side of the screen saves me about 5 percent in production time. You should look into it. It can really help your work go faster and feel better. Right-handed designers may find similar comfort by doing some rearranging, such as putting the toolbar on the right side of the screen.

InDesign gives you several options for arranging your palettes, including tabbed palette groups, docked palettes, palettes hidden behind tabs, and scattered palettes. You need to pick the one that best fits your working style.

After you move the palettes into an arrangement you like, it's easy to save that arrangement. When you close and relaunch InDesign, your saved arrangement will reappear. You should probably save your arrangement as soon as you have it set up, because if the application or computer crashes, the setup will return to what it was when you launched InDesign the last time. I'll show you how you can save your workspace after going through the palette arrangement options. You can save several workspaces for different types of projects.

Create a Tabbed Palette Group

All Adobe applications come with default tabbed palette groups. The Layers/Channels/Paths group in Photoshop and the Transform/Character/Paragraph group in InDesign, Illustrator, and Photoshop come to mind immediately. A tabbed palette group is the best way to show multiple palettes in the smallest possible space.

The most common mistake is to accept the factory-default groupings as wise and true. Some palettes you use often; others you use rarely, if ever. Often, you want several specific palettes to be available at the same time. You need to look at the palettes available and group them in ways that make sense to you. This will take a little while (at least a month of working every day), and even after that, you may still slightly adjust locations when you see a way to make the palettes you use easier to access. However, with practice, you will be able to set up your palettes in an upgrade or new installation in about two or three minutes.

The creation of tabbed groups is just the beginning of arranging the palettes you use into a useful setup. However, these groupings are central to the concept of setting up your interface. Every type of arrangement uses grouped palettes. They are even used in the scattered palette arrangements opened by shortcut that might be attractive to Quarksters.

Create a Docked Superpalette

Obviously, there are only so many tabs you can add to one group before the tabs begin overlapping and you can no longer read or efficiently find a palette. Another option, common to Adobe applications, is to dock tabbed palette groups above and below each other.

A docked palette is one that is locked into a permanent relationship above or below an existing palette or group. A docked palette does not cover up a palette above or below it in the docked stack. I am not talking about the ability of Adobe palettes to snap into alignment with each other. While this alignment is pretty, it is not docking. Docking allows expansion and contraction of a palette group without any overlaps. You can avoid the situation shown in Figure 4-2.

What I call a *superpalette* is a permanent grouping of many palettes in a docked relationship that gives you instant access to any palette you use regularly. Palettes never overlap, which is an obvious benefit. More than that, it allows you to lock your palette arrangements into a position that remains consistent every time you open a document. Very quickly, you will find yourself

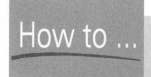 **Arrange a Tabbed Palette Group**

Almost all palettes have tabs. To move a palette from one group to another, just drag it by its tab. Start with two palettes next to each other.

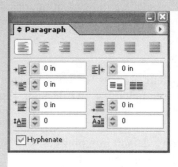 

Then click a palette tab and drag it to the other palette or palette group.

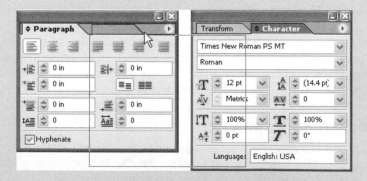

When you release the tab, it is added to the newly changed tabbed group.

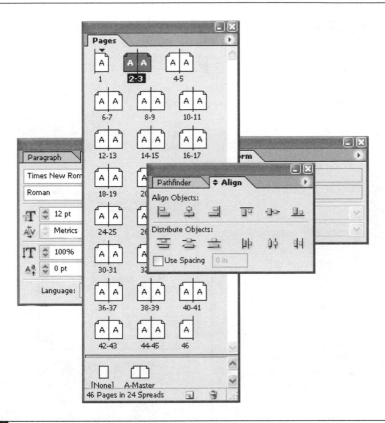

FIGURE 4-2   A bad palette overlap

accessing palettes habitually. You won't even need to look to see where a palette might be, because it is always at the same location. At that point, you think Transform palette, for example, and your hand and cursor often arrive on top of the palette before your eye switches over there (especially on a 20-inch or a 23-inch cinema display).

The only real problem with a superpalette is that the entire palette is open all the time. It is huge, and it takes up valuable room on your screen. You can close and open it by pressing the TAB key (if you're not setting type). A second solution is to put it on the right or left of your screen with the document window next to it. If you place it on the left side of your screen, you will need to do a little manual adjustment each time you open a new document (saved documents will remember the setup, though).

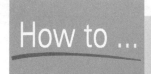 **Dock Your Palettes into a Superpalette**

You can easily solve the problem of overlapping palettes if you learn to dock your palettes into a superpalette. Here's how to create a superpalette:

1. Arrange your palettes so you can easily drag tabs where you want them. This is an important step to make the building of your superpalette easy. It helps if you have them in tabbed groups already.

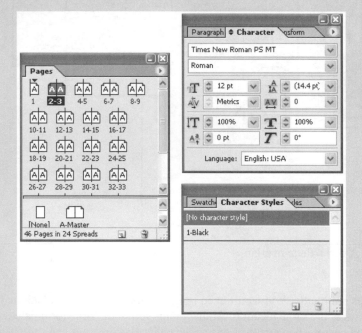

2. To dock a palette under an existing group, drag a tab to the bottom of that group until a dark line appears. This may take some care as you move the cursor around, up and down.

4

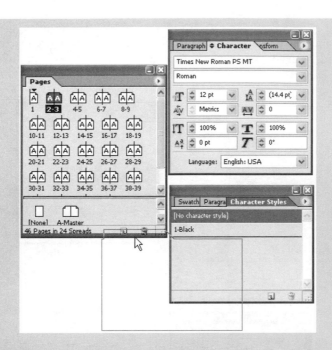

3. When you release the mouse button, the palette will be docked in a new row under the existing group. If you choose a taller palette in a group above, the group below will simply move down to make room. You can add as many tabs as you like to the new row.

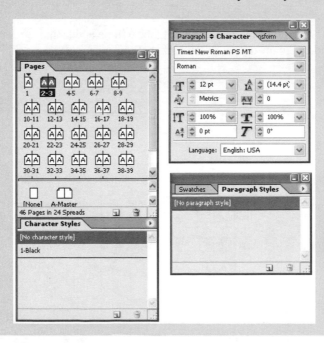

4. To dock a palette above an existing tabbed group, drag the tab above the row of tabs until a dark or tubular line appears. Again, you will need to be careful and watch the interface cues.

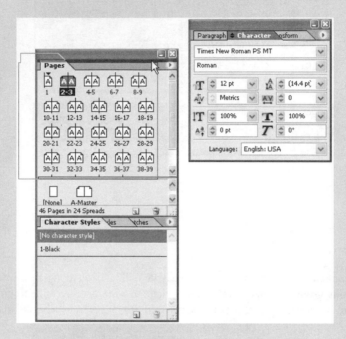

5. When you release the tab, a new row of tabs will be added above the existing group. You can add as many tabs as you like to that row also.

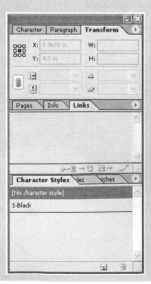

Stash Your Palettes to Open Up Your Workspace

Like GoLive and InCopy, InDesign CS has the ability to stash your palettes to the sides of your monitor. They are hidden there under a little tab that hangs on the side of the monitor. When you click the tab, the full palette expands onto the screen. When you click the tab again, the palette (group) retracts to its hidden position.

This new stashed setup takes a little getting used to, and you'll need to find the setup that works best for you. Personally, I like positioning the stashed palettes on the left side of the screen, because I am left-handed.

 **Stash Palettes**

Here is a simple, step-by-step demonstration of how the new stashing feature works:

1. Drag a palette tab to the left or right side of the screen.

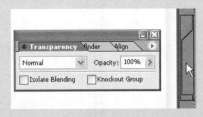

2. When you release the mouse button, it will stash itself there.

3. If you click that tab, it will expand onto the screen.

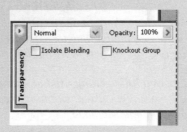

You can drag as many tabs as you can fit into that stashed tab. It does take a little care. If you miss the stashed tab, you can easily make another tab on top of the first one. Make the tab larger or smaller by clicking the dark line inset on the bottom edge of the stashed group and dragging it up or down.

Use the Control Palette

The new feature that really makes stashed palettes work is the Control palette. This is a combination of PageMaker's Control palette and Quark's Measurement palette, plus a lot more. The new Control palette is strongly reminiscent of the Option palette in Photoshop 6 (or newer), but it is much more powerful. Most of the fields of the Character, Paragraph, and Transform palettes are on the Control palette. This is a palette you should leave open all of the time.

You have a choice about where you want the Control palette to appear. The normal design is to dock the Control palette right under the menu bar across the top of the document window.

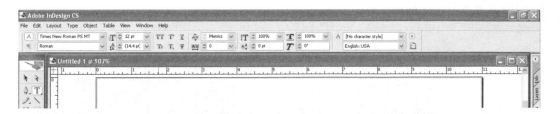

You can also let the palette float, but then it tends to get in the way.

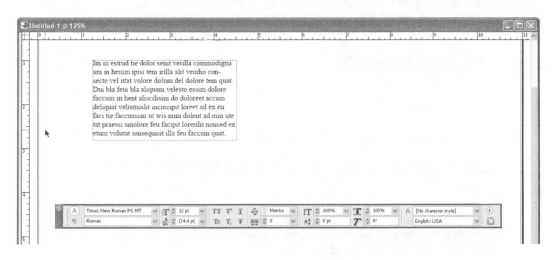

As a third choice, you can dock the Control palette at the bottom of the screen. This can cause problems because it makes for many mousing runs from top to bottom and back to the top.

The default location, docked at the top, is probably the most comfortable for many designers, who already have habitual movements in that direction for the Option palette in Photoshop. Also, we are all accustomed to moving to the top of the screen to access the menu bar.

The shortcut for activating the first field in the Control palette is CTRL-6/COMMAND-6. *This is very helpful for those of you coming from Quark who are accustomed to opening a dialog box with a shortcut and then tabbing through the fields.*

Once you have the cursor active in a field in the Control palette, you can change a setting to larger or smaller by simply pressing the UP ARROW and DOWN ARROW keys.

 *Make sure to remember to hit the* ENTER *key to execute the command you just set in the Control palette and return to having the insertion point active. Otherwise, you will keep typing in the palette field.*

The Control palette is fully contextual. This means that the contents change according to the tool you are using. When you have the Type tool insertion point placed, either the type version or the paragraph version of the Control palette appears (depending on whether you last used the Character palette or the Paragraph palette). The type version contains most of the Character palette fields.

The paragraph version contains most of the fields from the Paragraph palette.

You can switch between the type and paragraph versions by clicking the little button with the *A* on top or the button with the paragraph mark on the bottom.

When you have a shape or frame selected, the Control palette contains most of the fields from the Transform palette.

If you cannot find a field that you know is in the palette, simply click the Palette button on the far right side of the Control palette. This opens the relevant palette in each tabbed palette group, if there is one. As you can see in this example, clicking the button while in the type version brings the Character and Character Styles palettes to the front.

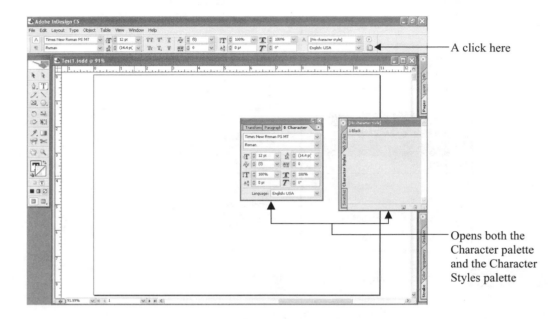

A click here

Opens both the Character palette and the Character Styles palette

The Control palette is much more effective when using stashed palette groups. If you are using a superpalette, clicking the Palette button opens the whole thing with the best palette on each row in focus. With scattered palettes, the relevant palettes open in focus. In both these cases, the palettes are right on top of the document, unless you are very careful with your palette locations. In addition, Adobe's definition of relevant palettes will probably be different from what you expect or desire.

For a Quark Approach, Use Scattered Palettes

One of the major differences between QuarkXPress and InDesign is that Quark uses dialog boxes, whereas InDesign uses palettes. If you are migrating from Quark, you may want to keep the palettes in separated groups that mimic what you get when you open a dialog box in Quark.

You can open each palette with a shortcut. In most cases, the shortcut used is the same as the one used to open the dialog box in Quark. Figure 4-3 shows a sample setup of tabbed palette groups that would work.

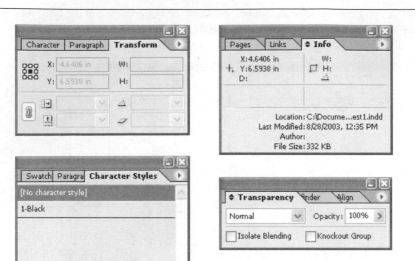

FIGURE 4-3   A scattered palette arrangement that mimics Quark

Learn the shortcuts to bring up each palette that you use often. The shortcuts are toggles; that is, the first time you press the shortcut key, the palette opens, and the second time, it closes. This gives you an all-shortcut-tab-through-the-fields approach that is similar to the normal Quark working style. You will just need to remember to hit the shortcut key a second time to close the palette, instead of pressing the RETURN key.

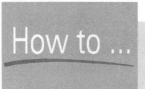 **Move Your Workspace to Another Computer**

You can move your workspace to another computer very easily. The workspaces are saved as XML files in the Workspaces folder, within the Adobe folder, within your Preferences folder. Just copy the file (in my case, it is named David's.xml) onto removable media or attach it to an e-mail. On the other computer, put the XML file in the same place it was stored on its original computer (for example, on a Mac OSX, this would be User/Library/Preferences/ Adobe InDesign/InDesign CS/Workspaces).

Save Your Workspace

After you have your palettes set up the way you want them, you can save that workspace and give it any name you want. To save your workspace, use the Window | Workspace | Save Workspace command. Simply name the workspace, and that name will be added to the list of workspaces at the top of the Window | Workspace menu. As you can see in this example, I am using four different workspaces at this point.

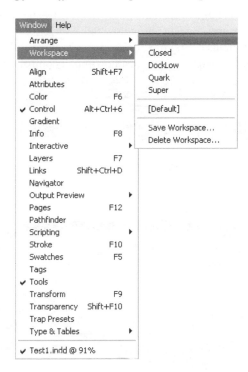

Use Shortcuts to Increase Workflow

Learning shortcuts is one of the tasks that many designers put off. It's easier to simply go looking for the command you need or the palette that holds that command. However, as you saw in the access time comparisons at the beginning of this chapter (in the "Consider Access Times for Frequent Tasks" section), shortcuts are the fastest way to work.

There are hundreds of shortcuts available. No, you are not expected to memorize them all. Shortcuts are learned slowly, as you notice you have a need. Watch yourself as you work. When you see yourself using the same command repeatedly, look on the menu and see what the shortcut is. If there is no shortcut, you can create one. If you don't like the default shortcut, you can change it.

Customize Shortcuts

InDesign's support of shortcuts is one of its real strengths. In InDesign, you can change or add a shortcut to any tool, command, and style. Do not allow this capability to confuse you. When you first look at the Keyboard Shortcuts dialog box (opened by choosing Edit | Keyboard Shortcuts), shown in Figure 4-4, it is not immediately clear just how much control you have.

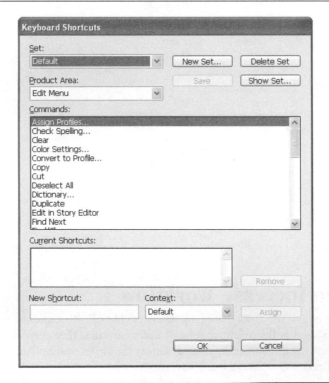

FIGURE 4-4   The powerful Keyboard Shortcuts dialog box

When you click the Product Area arrow to see the drop-down menu, the sheer quantity of choices can be overwhelming. Each area has dozens of commands that you can control. For example, each menu is listed in the Product Area drop-down menu.

There are also Product Area lists for Object Editing, Japanese Typography, Other, Palette Menus, Text and Tables, Tools, Views, and Navigation.

When you first begin working with InDesign, you should choose Edit | Keyboard Shortcuts and make the simple choice between Default and Shortcuts for QuarkXPress 4.0. The Default set is the modified PageMaker set of shortcuts. It is also quite close to FreeHand and Illustrator's set of shortcuts. The other choice is for those of you coming from QuarkXPress.

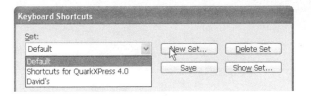

The first shortcuts to customize are those you have memorized that are different in InDesign (or Quark, if you've chosen Shortcuts for QuarkXPress). You will probably be amazed at how many shortcuts you already know. Even if you are new to desktop publishing, shortcuts like COMMAND-S/CTRL-S to save a document, COMMAND-P/CTRL-P to print, and COMMAND-N/CTRL-N to open a new document are probably firmly in your memory banks.

NOTE   *As an example of staying with what you know, when I first started desktop publishing, the shortcut for the Ungroup command was* COMMAND-U/CTRL-U *in all applications. The problem is that Adobe and Macromedia applications changed to* COMMAND-SHIFT-G/CTRL-SHIFT-G. *I've tried to learn the new shortcut, but the old one is too firmly embedded in my memory. So, I routinely customize the Ungroup command's shortcut to the one I memorized.*

When you select a command in the Commands list in the Keyboard Shortcut dialog box, its currently assigned shortcuts appear in the Current Shortcuts box beneath the list.

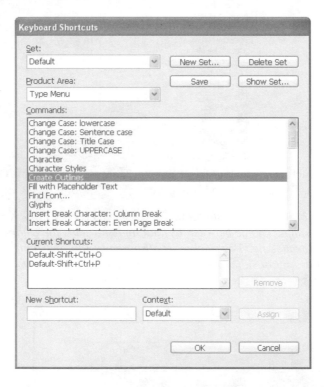

In this example, you can see that the Create Outlines command on the Type menu currently has two shortcuts, listed as Shift+Ctrl+O and Shift+Ctrl+P. The first one is the one I added (the same as FreeHand's Convert to Paths command), and the second is the InDesign default.

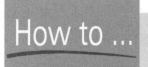

How to ...   Create or Change a Shortcut

Follow these steps to add or change a shortcut:

1. Choose Edit | Keyboard Shortcuts.

2. In the Keyboard Shortcuts dialog box, click the arrow next to Product Area and select the area of the command from the drop-down list.

3. In the Commands list, find and select the command that you want to give a new shortcut (or change the predefined one). The commands are in alphabetical order.

4. Click in the field labeled New Shortcut and type in the shortcut you want to use.

5. Click Assign, and then click the Save button at the top of the dialog box.

6. If you want to delete the old shortcut, you can click to select it, and then click
the Remove button to the right of the Current Shortcuts list. However, this is not
necessary, because you can have several shortcuts active for the same command.

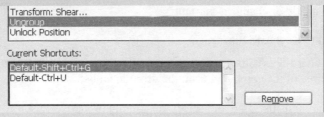

Make Context-Sensitive Shortcuts

One of the really powerful options in the Keyboard Shortcut dialog box is the Context selection
in the Context pop-up at the bottom of the dialog box. This allows you to make shortcuts that work
only in certain contexts: in alerts and dialog boxes, in the text context (setting type), in Story Editor,
in a table, or when coding XML. The Default choice has the shortcut work anywhere a context
does not override it.

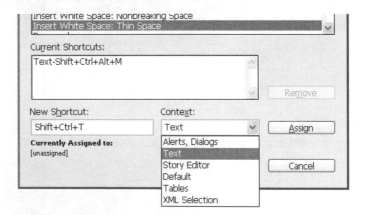

For example, I have a complete set of customized shortcuts that work only when I am in the
text context. I can use some of the same ones that are used normally in other contexts. One of
these is COMMAND-G/CTRL-G to open the Glyphs palette. Other places, this is the Group command
shortcut, but you cannot group anything while you have the Type tool selected, so it works well
in this context.

How to ... **Print Your Set of Shortcuts**

As you are learning and fixing your shortcuts, it is helpful to have a list of them. If you click the Show Set button at the top of the Keyboard Shortcut dialog box, InDesign will save the set as a text file and open it in the default text editor in your system (TextEdit in OSX and Notepad in Windows). Along with the saved file, you might want a printout of these shortcuts. You can keep the printed list in a handy location in your work area.

Save Your Shortcut Set

When you start making changes to the shortcuts, you should save your shortcuts in a set. Just click the New Set button at the top of the Keyboard Shortcuts dialog box and give your set a name (you can call it anything you want). That name will be added to the Set drop-down list.

As with workspaces, you can move your shortcut set to another computer very easily. The sets are saved in your application folder: InDesign CS/Presets/InDesign Shortcut Sets.

This Is Important

When you set up your personal workspace and your customized shortcut set, you are not involved in some exotic procedure done only by power users. This is normal stuff required to save your career under the pressures of our deadline-driven industry. This chapter did not talk about optional steps to take. You really do need to examine your working style and set up InDesign to help you work faster and more efficiently. It's really not difficult; it's just time-consuming.

The key is learning which palettes you use and which ones you never use. You watch yourself work, noticing which commands you use hourly, daily, and weekly or less. As you come to understand how you work, you add shortcuts and palette locations to streamline your production. Your goal is to work fast enough to free up additional paid time to be creative.

Now let's go and set some type.

Part II

Add Typography

Chapter 5

Set Type Professionally

How to…

- Understand basic type terminology
- Add a text frame to contain type
- Flow text in text frames
- Manage text frame links
- Import existing copy to your documents
- Choose and style fonts with the Character palette
- Use the Character palette's option menu
- Control the layout of your paragraphs with the Paragraph palette
- Use the Paragraph palette's option menu

When we talk about setting type in InDesign, we are addressing the core of what we do as graphic designers. Typesetting is the central skill of the professional graphic designer. Most clients don't really care how well you draw and design. They care that you can set type well, producing easy-to-read copy that is attractive to the reader.

For those of you just getting started to page layout, we are now entering a new world. It is a vast world with a new language, new abilities, new responsibilities, and new power. Even for those of you with several years' experience with PageMaker, QuarkXPress, or earlier versions of InDesign, this may be new.

In the ongoing debate over the relative primacy of QuarkXPress or InDesign, this is where the argument ends for professional typographers. InDesign has added typographic capabilities that designers have needed for years. InDesign can now set type better than any of its competition—standing alone at the top, without a serious competitor.

This chapter will introduce some of the tools you use to set type professionally with InDesign. First, we will review some of the basic terminology related to typesetting. Then we will cover how to add type to documents. Finally, you will learn about the basic options for laying out and styling type.

Understand Basic Typesetting Terminology

The world of typesetting has its own language. For those of you with no type background, as well as the many designers who are largely self-taught and are not familiar with the lingo, I will cover the basic terms you need to know to set type. To begin, carefully study Figure 5-1.

It is important that you know all of the measurement lines shown in Figure 5-1—baseline, x-height, descender, ascender, cap height, point size, and optical alignment—and their purpose. For example, the *baseline* is the line on which the type apparently sits. However, you can see that some character points (as in *W*) and curves (as in *O*) go below that line. If they did not, they would look like they were sitting too high. This principle of *optical alignment*, which has always been a part of type design, is also used in optical margin alignment, which we will cover toward the end of the chapter, in the "Align the Margins of Your Paragraphs" section.

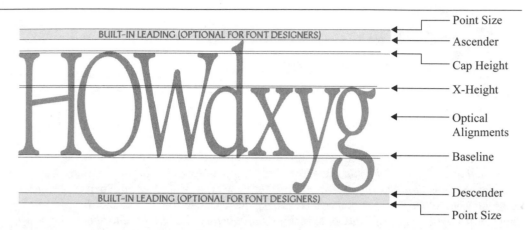

Yes, this type is badly stretched vertically to show the measurement lines more clearly.

FIGURE 5-1   Type terms and measurements

Along with the terms shown in Figure 5-1, there are four more terms you need to understand:

- **The return**   This is a paragraph return, often called a *hard return*. Windows has introduced some confusion about the key used to enter this character by calling it the ENTER key. In fact, it is the end-of-paragraph key, which is labeled ENTER in Windows systems and RETURN in Macintosh systems. This key has a very different function from the ENTER key at the lower-right corner of the numeric keypad. That ENTER key is for entering commands, executing dialog boxes, and so on. Throughout this book, I will call the end-of-paragraph key RETURN or a *hard return*. When I refer to the ENTER key, I mean the key at the lower-right corner of the keyboard.

- **The paragraph**   The RETURN key determines paragraphs. The RETURN key, in type, ends the previous paragraph and starts a new one. A paragraph can be one letter, one word, one line, or many lines.

- **The soft return**   The SHIFT-RETURN key combination produces what is normally called a *soft return*. InDesign calls this a *forced line break* (sounds like something Patton did in World War II, doesn't it?). A soft return breaks a line without starting a new paragraph. It is most commonly used for what is called "break for sense" in heads and subheads. In this case, you break multiple-line subheads into equal-length lines, where each line is a complete phrase. These line breaks are created when a space character is replaced with a soft return.

- **The story**   A *story* is usually a string of paragraphs, but it can be a single paragraph. It is an unlinked text frame. In page layout, a story can be a single headline, an entire chapter, or an entire book (although that rarely happens).

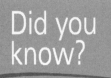

Typography Skill Is a Great Assumption

If the thought of clients expecting you to be a typography expert scares you, don't be concerned. Most of your competitors are in the same boat. They're just too embarrassed to admit it. It is assumed that you understand this stuff, but few people actually do. So, no one ever talks about it.

To be a step ahead, you need to do a little studying. I recommend my most recent book, *Introduction to Digital Publishing* (OnWord Press), produced with InDesign. Another excellent book is *Stop Stealing Sheep & Find Out How Type Works* by Erik Speikerman and E. M. Ginger (Adobe Press). And then there is the modern classic, *The Elements of Typographic Style* by Robert Bringhurst (Hartley & Marks). *Introduction to Digital Publishing* is the best basic introduction. *The Elements of Typographic Style* is the most complete (but a little dry). *Stop Stealing Sheep* is possibly the most entertaining.

Now that you know the basic terms, you're ready to do some typesetting. The first step is to put a text frame on the page.

Add a Text Frame to Contain Type

All type in page layout must be in a text frame. Sometimes that frame is hidden (as in PageMaker). Sometimes it must be created with a special tool before you can start typing (as in QuarkXPress). InDesign's approach is the simplest and easiest to understand once you recognize the visual cues (as in FreeHand).

In InDesign, you can make any shape or frame into a text frame by simply clicking it with the Type tool. You can draw that frame with a frame tool, a shape tool, the Pencil, or the Pen tool. You can also make a frame by marqueeing an area with the Type tool. This means that you do not need to start with a separate tool to add text. You simply use the Type tool to marquee the area you want filled with type (often using the margins as guides), and then start typing.

NOTE   *You can modify shapes to fit your text frame needs using the Direct Selection tool and Pen tools (as explained in Chapter 11). However, if you modify the left side of the frame so it is not a vertical line, some extra work is required when using indents and tabs. We will talk about this in Chapter 7.*

When you click a shape or frame to make it a text frame, the only visual indicator of this change is the little squares set into the upper-left and lower-right sides of the frame. The *in port* on the upper left is used for links from preceding frames. The *out port* at the lower left is used for links to following frames. These links between frames are called *threads*. All the linked frames are called a *story*. If the frame is not linked, that frame contains one story.

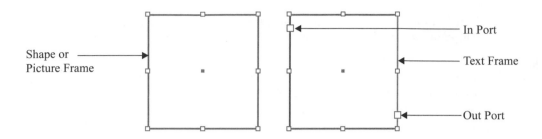

Shape or
Picture Frame

In Port

Text Frame

Out Port

Handle Text Frame Overflow

The out port also indicates if there is overflow type. This is type that cannot fit into the frame at the frame's current size. It is indicated by a little, red plus sign inside the out port.

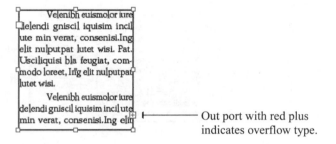

Out port with red plus
indicates overflow type.

TIP   *One small irritation is that this little, red plus will often show up if you add a paragraph return to the last line in the text frame. You can see this return by selecting Type | Show Hidden Characters. (You will also see another character that does not print: an end-of-story character, which looks like an italic number symbol.) You can delete that last paragraph return to eliminate the red plus.*

When you click that red plus in the out port with the Selection tool, the overflowed text is loaded into the cursor, making it easy for you to fix the problem. There are five types of text flow you can produce from that loaded cursor. Each of these is represented by a special icon, and some require keypresses to generate the type of text flow, as follows:

    Loaded cursor.

Loaded cursor when moved over an existing, empty text frame.

Autoflow, which will flow text into all linked text frames (often adding pages as needed). The autoflow icon appears when you hold down the SHIFT key as you click to flow the type.

Semi-autoflow, which fills the frame you click, and then automatically reloads the cursor with the rest of the text. The semi-autoflow icon appears when you hold down the ALT/OPTION key as you click to flow the type into place.

Start-it-here autoflow, which begins the autoflow at the point you click in the frame or column. The start-it-here autoflow icon appears when you hold down the ALT/OPTION-SHIFT keys as you click to flow the type into place.

With your text-loaded cursor, just click the frame you want to fill, and the text flows in. In the sample below, I flowed the rest of the text into the frame on the right. Then I changed my mind and added the frame in the middle, clicked in the out port of the left frame again, and flowed the text into the middle frame. The link with the right frame was maintained automatically. Threads maintain themselves, in general.

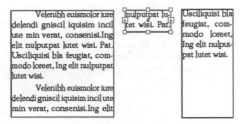

When you have text loaded in the cursor, you can do many things, including turning pages, creating new pages, and zooming in and out. For example, you can click the in port of a frame with the Selection tool, and then marquee the area where you want a frame to precede your existing frame. Any existing text will now begin in the new first frame you just added. If you have type flowing through two frames and click the in port of the final frame, when you make a new frame, the type will flow from the first frame to the new frame to the last frame.

If you start to thread two frames and change your mind, you can cancel the loaded cursor by clicking any tool in the toolbox. You are safe—no text will be lost. The text will just go back to the way it was before you loaded it into the cursor. If you delete a text frame in the middle of the flow, all the text in that text frame will be added to the following frames automatically.

Manage Your Text Frame Links

If you select View | Show Text Threads, and then click any of the linked frames with the Selection tool, you will see the links. This helps you determine how your type is flowing. For example, viewing links can be helpful if you have confused yourself by changing links after you have imported the type.

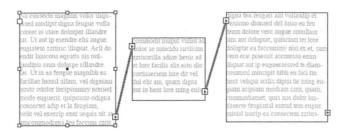

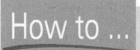

While you are fiddling around with your links, you will also see a couple of new icons added to your loaded Selection tool cursor: Link and Unlink. These icons appear when you are adding frames to existing threads, or when you want to break a link. If you click a port in an existing thread, when you move the loaded cursor over an existing frame that is empty, the link cursor will appear. When you click, that frame will be added to the thread—in front of the in port, if you clicked that, or after the out port, if you clicked that.

To break a thread, first click in either the in port or out port of a linked frame. Then place your cursor over the frame you want to unlink. The unlink icon will appear (although you might not be able to see it clearly because of the type in the frame). When you click, all the text will be loaded in the red plus in the preceding out port.

How to ...

Disconnect a Frame from a Thread while Keeping the Copy

If you need the text you see in a frame to stay in that frame, and you also need that text unlinked from the thread, simply select that frame and cut it to the Clipboard (Edit | Cut or CTRL-X/COMMAND-X). When you paste that stored frame, a copy of the text will remain in the frame, but all links to the original thread will be gone. This also works with multiple frames. If you copied several frames that were linked, those links will remain.

No text will be lost from the original thread. You will need to delete the original copy of the text you removed. It simply flowed into the following frames in the original thread. It's a bit of a pain, but it's what you must do.

This can be pretty tricky and visually confusing. I always save the document before I do any of this stuff. The good news is that all of it can be undone with a simple CTRL-Z/COMMAND-Z.

Import Existing Copy into Your Documents

Typically, you will typeset existing copy, supplied by a client or copywriter. Therefore, importing text is a common task. Adobe calls this function Place, and it is accessed under the File menu. Here, we will go through the steps for importing text, beginning with making sure that the text you want to import is in a file format that InDesign will accept.

Pick a File Format to Import

Normally, you can import text from other InDesign documents, Word, Excel, text editors, and table editors. You can also import text from any application that can export text in Rich Text Format (RTF) or ASCII format. In Windows, file formats that can be placed are listed in the Format pop-up menu in the Place dialog box.

 *You'll need to clean up formatting errors in your imported copy. InDesign's Story Editor is a great tool for this cleanup. Chapter 6 introduces Story Editor, and Chapter 16 provides some tips for fixing imported copy.*

ASCII Files

Virtually every program understands ASCII, but no application speaks it as its native tongue, because ASCII is too clumsy. Nevertheless, ASCII is by far the most universal text format, usually called a text-only file.

The problem with ASCII is simple: It can't do much. The major lack is the inability to add formatting. Most of us have probably tried to use ASCII text in another program. It's never a problem to import it. The problem is the shape it's in when it arrives. Usually, there is a hard return at the end of every line. There is no font assigned, so it comes into your program in whatever your default font is. There are no bold or italic characters, tabs or first-line indents, and so on. ASCII is simply raw copy.

Word Processor Files

Most of us use a word processor regularly. The problem with word processors is that each has its own file format. Worse than that, each version has its own version of the file format. The newer versions can work with the older formats, but the older versions cannot open the newer formats.

In order for a program to import another program's file format, it uses filters. InDesign has relatively few filters. For copy, it can read only recent Word and Excel files (Word 95 or newer), recent PageMaker files (6.5 or newer), and older QuarkXPress files (3.3 or 4.1).

If you need to import text created with a word processor other than Word, those files need to be saved as RTF files, with an .rtf extension. RTF files exported from AppleWorks, WordPerfect, Publisher, and other word processors work fine with the InDesign import process.

 *It has become very hard to find a word processor that just writes, quickly and easily with great editing power. I use Mariner Write or AppleWorks whenever possible. There are other small, fast, powerful word processors out there. I strongly suggest that you get one.*

RTF Files

RTF has become the universal word processing format. All word processors can save in this format, and all professional graphics programs can import it. When you accept a job from a client, you should probably get in the habit of asking that all files be sent to you in RTF. In general, the text-import process is the smoothest when you use RTF to transfer the copy.

Choose Where Imported Text Will Be Inserted

Before you use the Place function to import text, you need to indicate where the imported text will go. You can do this in one of the following ways:

5

- ■ **Place in a new text frame**   To put the text in a new text frame, make sure that no insertion point is present and that no text or frames are selected. The text will appear in a new frame that is small and centered in your monitor.

- ■ **Replace selected text**   To replace existing text within a text frame with the imported text, with the Type tool, select the text you wish to replace. The text you place will replace the selected text.

- ■ **Add to an existing text frame**   To add the text to an existing text frame, click in the existing frame to place an insertion point. The text you place will be added at the insertion point.

- ■ **Replace all of a text frame's contents**   To replace all the contents of an existing text frame with the imported text, with the Selection tool or the Direct Selection tool, select the frame. The placed text will replace the contents of the frame, even if it is a graphic.

TIP   *If you accidentally pick the wrong method, choose Edit | Undo (CTRL-Z/COMMAND-Z). This will reload the text you're placing into the cursor.*

Select to Place a File

When you're ready to import text into a document, choose File | Place or use the CTRL-D/COMMAND-D shortcut. (Quarksters are accustomed to using the E instead of the D.) This will open the Place dialog box, shown in Figure 5-2. In this dialog box, navigate to the file you wish to import and select it.

If you wish to control the formatting of the imported text, check the Show Import Options box (or SHIFT-click the Open button). If you want the placed file to replace the text or frame you've selected, check Replace Selected Item; if not, make sure it is not checked.

If you checked the Show Import Options box, the Import Options dialog box will appear when you click Open. Figure 5-3 shows an example of the import options for RTF files.

FIGURE 5-2   Use the Place dialog box to import text.

The Import Options dialog box has several options:

■ You can include or exclude the table of contents, endnotes, footnotes, and index.

■ You can convert straight quotation marks (called *quotes*) and apostrophes to typographic quotes and apostrophes by checking Use Typographer's Quotes.

■ You can strip all text and/or table formatting, or leave it in.

■ You can convert table formatting to unformatted tables or unformatted tabbed text.

■ You can preserve manual page breaks, convert them to column breaks, or strip them out.

Click Open or select the import options for the type of file you're placing, and then click OK to start the import process.

RTF Import Options

Include

☑ Table of Contents Text   ☑ Footnotes and Endnotes

☑ Index Text

[OK]

[Cancel]

Formatting

☑ Use Typographer's Quotes

☐ Remove Text and Table Formatting

Convert Tables To: Unformatted Tables ▼

Manual Page Breaks: Preserve Page Breaks ▼

FIGURE 5-3   The RTF Import Options dialog box

Flow Imported Text

If you haven't already selected existing text or a frame to receive text, the cursor will become a loaded text icon, ready to flow the text wherever you click or drag. You have the same text flow options as discussed in the "Handle Text Frame Overflow" section earlier in the chapter.

Placing imported text makes a link to the outside copy source. In general, you will want to go to the Links palette and unlink your text. The Links palette is covered in Chapter 12. Alternatively, you can set a preference to avoid the linking: Select Edit (PC) or InDesign (Mac) | Preferences, go to the Text page, and uncheck Create Links When Placing Text and Spreadsheet Files.

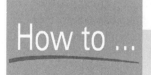

Copy/Paste or Drag-and-Drop Existing Copy

Importing text is not the only way to add existing text to your document. You can copy and paste the text from another open document. In most cases, the formatting in the existing document will be retained by the Clipboard as you copy and paste. A copy/paste operation does not make a link to the outside copy source.

You can also simply drag-and-drop a file with text into your InDesign document. All you need to do is have the folder window open to show the file. Then drag-and-drop that file's icon onto the frame you want to contain the text. Using drag-and-drop to insert copy makes a link to the outside copy source. As with placed text, you will probably want to unlink the text, which you can do by using the Links palette.

Format Text According to Your Sense of Style

There are three methods for formatting text:

- Select it with the Type tool.
- Select a frame containing text with the Selection tool. This will format all the text in that frame.
- Apply a paragraph or character style by placing an insertion point in the paragraph for a paragraph style or by selecting the text for a character style. (This is the best way to format text, and you will learn how to do it in Chapter 8.)

But what do we mean by formatting text? That's the subject of the rest of this chapter and the next four chapters. Here, we will start with font choices, and then cover the paragraph choices.

Choose and Style Fonts

One of the major aspects of your personal style is the fonts you choose and the layouts you use. You need to spend a lot of time and thought developing your style. In fact, this will be an ongoing process throughout your life.

Use the Character Palette

The options for formatting fonts are found in the Character palette, as shown in Figure 5-4. (Many of these choices are also available in the Type menu at the top of your screen, but that is a very slow

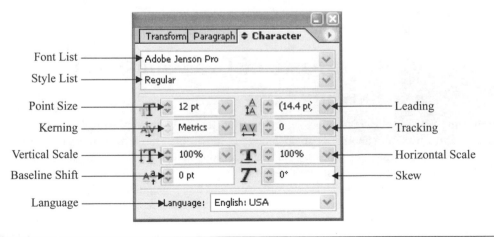

FIGURE 5-4   The Character palette contains the options for formatting fonts.

and clumsy way to access these controls.) Although these are fairly standard, they are important settings. One of the worst things you can do in your designs is to just pick fonts and sizes by using factory defaults. It makes your work look like bureaucratic output. Only bureaucrats use Times or Times New Roman and Helvetica or Arial (or designers trying to reach bureaucrats).

Let's go through all the decisions that need to be made in this palette: from top to bottom, from left to right.

> NOTE
>
> *All of the options on the Character palette are also available on the Control palette. In addition, the Control palette has buttons for All Caps, Small Caps, Superscript, Subscript, Underline, and Strikethrough. If you are using OpenType fonts, these options will be typographically designed characters, not the proportionally reduced nasties made by programs that can use only the 256-character TrueType or PostScript fonts.*

Font

The top drop-down list in the Character palette is where you pick the font you will use. The same choices are available under Type | Font.

> NOTE
>
> *What font should you use? To decide, you need to learn about font choices. Take a look at my book* Introduction to Digital Publishing. *Also, study every piece of printed material you see, looking for fonts you find attractive or ugly.*

One of the major advances in InDesign is how it handles fonts, using a technology called *CoolType*. Let's take a quick tour of some CoolType benefits.

Font Families   InDesign groups fonts into their families. It puts a small, right-pointing triangle next to any font that has more than one style installed on your machine. You used to need to buy an extra utility to do this (and you still do for non-Adobe applications). In Windows, the font family indicators show up in the Type | Font menu. They are in all of the font menus on Mac systems.

Rasterized Fonts   InDesign rasterizes special screen images for the fonts you are using. This makes Adobe Type Manager unnecessary, and InDesign's screen versions look better than TrueType.

Fonts Folder   Because InDesign handles fonts itself, you can put any font—Mac or PC, TrueType, PostScript, Multiple Master, or OpenType—in the Fonts folder within the InDesign folder, and it will read and use it. Yes, cross-platform fonts work in InDesign. While having an individual font folder in an application causes shuddering or worse to a Mac user, it does solve a very real problem. In addition, it is almost certain that the Fonts folder in the Application Support folder will add these capabilities to all Adobe products in the near future.

OpenType Support   A huge advantage of InDesign it that it supports all of the normally used features of OpenType. Because OpenType fonts can have thousands of characters (instead of the paltry 256-character limit of all previous font formats in common use), many extremely necessary functions are now available to normal typesetting. For years, typesetters have been hampered by characters missing from their fonts: true small caps, discretionary ligatures, swashes, old-style

Some Fonts Don't Have Bold or Italic Versions

One of the most common printing problems is styled fonts. These are fonts that have Bold or Italic styles applied to them, when there really isn't a bold or italic version of that font. Many fonts—like Papyrus, Pepita, Friz Quadrata, and thousands more—do not have a bold and/or italic version. You need to be aware of the styles you are using and which fonts you have installed in your computer.

numbers, and the like either have not been available at all or were found only in rare expert sets like Adobe Caslon Expert. Now they are commonly available in OpenType Pro fonts. Plus, these fonts are cross-platform.

To get fonts with these features, you need to purchase fonts that have *Pro* in their name. For example, one of the fonts I designed, Diaconia Old Style, had the normal 256 characters, and I needed to offer a second font, Diaconia Old Style Small Caps, to provide many of the necessities of typography. The new OpenType version, DiaconiaPro, has all the characters of the second font, plus many more.

Style

InDesign has completely solved a big problem related to styling fonts. It will not allow you to choose fonts that do not exist. You must pick your fonts from the style list, right below the font list. It lists only the styles that are installed. As you can see in the example shown here, Adobe Jenson Pro has Light, Light Italic, Regular, Italic, Semibold, Semibold Italic, Bold, and Bold Italic, as well as all the opticals—a total of 32 fonts in this family. If you were allowed to style it Bold, you would have no idea what you would get.

The most common question I hear from students new to InDesign is, "What are these pink boxes in back of my type?" These boxes appear when you ask for styles or fonts that do not exist. In the following example, I applied a character style asking for Bold. However, since Impact does not have a Black version (but it has a Regular version), the result is the pink box. This tells me to fix my style or to reformat the type under the box to Impact Regular.

5

The same font styles are available in the submenus accessed by moving the mouse over the little triangles to the right of fonts that have more than one style in the font list under Type | Fonts. This works fine for applying styles. It is just a lot slower to access.

Point Size

Point size is measured from the top of the ascender to the bottom of the descender (see Figure 5-1, at the beginning of the chapter), with a little extra space normally added by the font designer. You can set type in any size from 0.10 point to 1,296 points (18 inches), in thousandth point increments.

The little up/down arrows at the left of the field let you adjust the size up or down, one point at a time. Clicking the shaded up/down button on the right side of the field gives you a pop-up menu with the basic size choices: 6, 8, 9, 10, 11, 12, 14, 18, 24, 30, 36, 48, 60, and 72. These options are also available under Type | Size. Choosing Type | Size | Other places the focus on the Size field in the Character palette.

Many pros just roughly size type, and then adjust it with keyboard shortcuts. CTRL-SHIFT-./ COMMAND-SHIFT-. *makes the type a point larger.* CTRL-SHIFT-,/COMMAND-SHIFT-, *makes the type a point smaller. Adding the* ALT/OPTION *key does five times as much to each command.*

Leading

In the Character palette shown earlier in Figure 5-4, you can see that there are parentheses around the leading number. This means that autoleading is applied. Autoleading is 120 percent of the point size, by default. (You can change the autoleading value by choosing the Justification option from the Paragraph palette's option menu, as explained in the "Set Your Preferences in the Paragraph Palette's Option Menu" section later in this chapter.)

You can adjust the amount of leading in one-point increments by clicking the little up and down arrows on the left side of the field. Clicking the shaded up/down button on the right side of the field pops up a menu with the basic size choices: 6, 8, 9, 10, 11, 12, 14, 18, 24, 30, 36, 48, 60, and 72. The maximum leading is 5,000 points (or more than 69 inches of line spacing).

You can see the amount of leading applied by selecting some type. The reversed bar behind the selected type is the leading slug. It not only shows you the amount of leading, but also shows where it is located in relation to the type selected.

For Quarksters, finding leading in the Character palette causes a paradigm problem. You are accustomed to paragraph-level leading. You can make this your default by checking Apply Leading to Entire Paragraphs on the Text page of the Preferences dialog box (Edit | Preferences on PCs or InDesign | Preferences on Macs), as mentioned in Chapter 2.

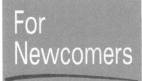

Leading Guidelines

Leading (pronounced like the metal, *lead*) is line spacing. A few of you coming from Word may be a little bewildered that there is no space, space and a half, or double space option. None of these options works for leading. As a general rule, line spacing varies with the point size of the type and how you are setting the type: all caps, small caps, or lowercase. Here are some rough guidelines for type set normally with lowercase letters:

- Type smaller than 7 points is set solid (that is, the leading is the same as the point size).
- Type set from 9 points to 14 points is set +2 (for example, 10/12—10-point type on 12 points of leading, which is normal for body copy—or 14/16).
- Type set from 14 points to 24 points is set +1 (for example, 18/19).
- Type set larger than 24 points is set solid (for example, 26/26).

You also might need to consider negative leading. If you are setting type in all caps or small caps, there are no descenders. Descenders are usually about a third of the point size below the baseline. So, a headline set in small caps at 36 points might be set 36/28 or so. You'll need to make your own judgments about what reads well and looks good.

5

Many pros adjust their leading with keyboard shortcuts. In text, ALT-DOWN ARROW/ OPTION-DOWN ARROW makes the leading a point larger, and ALT-UP ARROW/OPTION-UP ARROW makes the type a point smaller. Adding the CTRL/COMMAND key does five times as much to each command. This seems backward to me, so I reverse the arrows to help me remember them (through Edit | Keyboard Shortcuts, as discussed in Chapter 4).

Kerning

Here, we have yet another InDesign innovation. That new capability is optical kerning. You can see the choice in the pop-up.

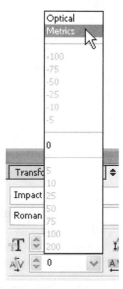

If you use optical kerning, the application measures the area between each letter pair and adjusts the font optically. It is not perfect, but it produces very good results. I have experimented with fonts that have bad kerning, and optical kerning solved the problem.

Let's look at an example. Here, we have two different fonts and three point sizes: BilboPro 44-point for the *A*, BilboPro 40-point for the *we*, and Skia 42-point for the *struck*. The spacing is horrible, compounded by the point size changes.

Awestruck

Here, we simply track the letters together. The *struck* is better, but the *Awe* is terrible.

Awestruck

Next, we change to optical kerning. Notice that the spacing is much better, but the spacing between the *A* and the *w* is still bad, because of the point size change.

Awestruck

Finally, we make the final adjustments by hand-kerning.

Awestruck

Many, if not most, of your subheads and headlines will need to be kerned by hand. You can manually kern by placing the insertion point between the two characters that need to be adjusted and clicking the up or down arrow in the Kerning field of the Character palette. These change the kerning by 10/1000 em. Adding the SHIFT key makes the changes in 25/1000 em increments.

 *It's much easier to use the shortcuts for hand-kerning.* ALT-LEFT ARROW/OPTION-LEFT ARROW *moves the letters together, and* ALT-RIGHT ARROW/OPTION-RIGHT ARROW *moves them apart. If you add the* SHIFT *key, the kerning will be five times as much every time you press the arrow key. You can set the amount of movement for the shortcuts in the Units & Increments page of the Preferences dialog box (opened with Edit | Preferences in Windows or InDesign | Preferences in Macs).*

Tracking

Tracking adjusts the spacing between groups of letters. InDesign offers the same tracking functionality as you find in Quark, with much more control than PageMaker. Normally, tracking is adjusted in a paragraph style, so it affects entire paragraphs. The up and down arrows to the left of this field change the kerning or tracking by 10/1000 em. Adding the SHIFT key makes those changes in 25/1000-em increments.

 Normally, all character-spacing measurements use ems. *An* em *is the width of the point size of the type set. For example, 14-point type has an em that is 14 points wide.*

Vertical Scale and Horizontal Scale

The Vertical Scale and Horizontal Scale fields allow you to make a font taller or shorter and wider or narrower, without changing the point size.

As you might expect, these are the type of options that drive font designers crazy. *"You ruined my font!"* However, the reality is that you can use these well—with care. The major problem is that horizontal strokes of a font are normally thinner than vertical strokes. Scaling the fonts too tall or too narrow causes the horizontal strokes to become the same thickness as the vertical strokes, or even thicker. This is not attractive.

Baseline Shift

The Baseline Shift field allows you to move type up and down relative to the baseline of the font. The baseline is the apparent line that type sits on. Normally, you will use this option last, and as a last resort.

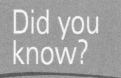

Tracking Can Cause Problems

As you probably know, the main attribute of excellence in typography is smooth type color. This is where InDesign stands far above any of its competition (including the other applications in the Creative Suite). Type color refers to the even gray produced by the body copy portions of the text. It needs to be smooth and even to provide the gray background that makes the headlines and subheads work.

Tracking causes two problems. First, one of the major causes of blotchy type color is changing the tracking. If you make the tracking tighter for a paragraph, that paragraph will look darker—irritatingly darker (not looking like you did it intentionally). Second, font designers put a lot of effort into making the character spacing of a font match the look they want for a font. Changing the tracking messes up the font's design.

Extremely shifted type (up or down) can be difficult to work with, because you can shift it completely out of the leading slug. You must select the type where it was before you shifted it.

Skew

The Skew, or false italic, field allows you to slant type. It should be used rarely.

Please do not skew your type! It not only looks horrible, but it also looks extremely amateurish. Use the italic version of the font instead.

Language

InDesign CS comes with 20 languages out of the box. You can use multiple languages in a paragraph. This means you can spell-check phrases in French or German, for example, while you are writing in any other language.

```
[No Language]
Catalan
Danish
Dutch
English: UK
English: USA
English: USA Legal
English: USA Medical
Finnish
French
French: Canadian
German: Reformed
German: Swiss
German: Traditional
Italian
Norwegian: Bokmal
Norwegian: Nynorsk
Portuguese
Portuguese: Brazilian
Spanish: Castilian
Swedish
```

Unlike with Quark, with InDesign you do not need to buy a special version for languages, unless you want Hebrew, Arabic, Chinese, Japanese, or another language with left-to-right writing. There are also special editions of InDesign with Cyrillic languages (like Russian) and those needing special characters (like Greek).

Find Additional Control in the Character Palette's Option Menu

Like most Adobe palettes, the Character palette has an option menu that pops out when you click the little, circled triangle in the upper-right corner of the palette.

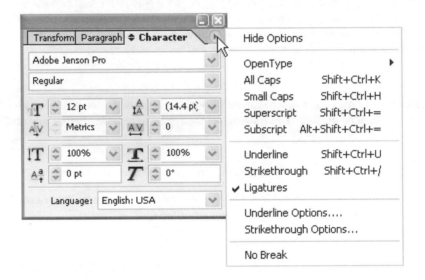

This menu contains critical options:

- ■ **Hide Options** This removes the display of the Character palette's scaling, shifting, skewing, and language options.

- ■ **OpenType** As I said earlier, in the discussion of the font settings, this is a big deal! The future of type is found in these options. The way to read these options is simple. If there are brackets around a set, it is not available in the font chosen. As you can see in the example shown on the next page, Adobe Jenson Pro has discretionary ligatures, fractions, ordinals, small caps, numerators, denominators, superiors, inferiors, and all five versions of numbers.

5

- **All Caps**   This sets everything selected in capital letters. This reduces the font's readability about 40 percent, or looks like you are shouting. All caps are rarely used in professional typography.

- **Small Caps**   This makes the lowercase letters into small capital letters. If you do not have a font with true small caps, this option proportionally reduces the capitals to this height, making them look much thinner and lighter. So, unless you have a font with true small caps, you should not use this option.

- **Superscript and Subscript**   These produce numbers like a^2b^3 (Superscript) or H_2O (Subscript). These are also proportionally reduced in all fonts except Pro fonts. The thin, light, small numbers are the only option you have for fractions when using TrueType and PostScript fonts, with their 256-character limitation.

- **Underline**   Typographers never use the Underline option. Designers sometimes do. Normally, you have a simple choice to make. Should the underlined copy be set as bold or italic? If you decide you must use underlining, try the new Underline Options, a few options down on this menu.

- **Strikethrough**   This is used only for editing or for copy you need to make look like it was edited. The Character palette's option menu also offers a new Strikethrough Options choice.

■ **Ligatures** This is checked by default. This means that any ligatures in the font will be automatically applied to the copy. (A *ligature* is two or more characters combined into one character to make them fit better.) If you are using cheap fonts, you do not want this to happen. In many fonts, the ligatures look like small, dark blotches in the type color. Take a good look at the font you are using to determine if you want to use this option.

NEW TO
InDesign CS

■ **Underline Options and Strikethrough Options** Finally, designers have real choices that might work for underlines. However, it will still not produce excellence in typography for high-quality products. It might work well in ads meant to look cheap—like grocery store, flea markets, or discount store ads. Basically, these options give you all the control available in the Stroke palette to apply to your underlines and strikethroughs.

When you select Underline Options from the Character palette's option menu, you are presented with a dialog box of options, as shown in Figure 5-5.

As you can see, you can set the weight of the line up to 1000 points wide. You can set the type of line using the standard options shown (plus you can make your own options for this pop-up in the Stroke palette). You can set how far the underline is offset (up or down). So, you can make overlines (sic) if you like. Because you can do the same with strikethrough lines, you could set up lines of any type or color above and/or below any type.

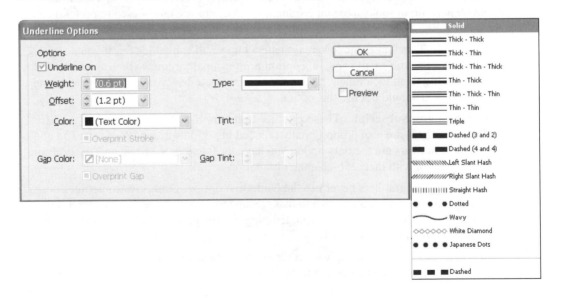

FIGURE 5-5 The Underline Options dialog box and the stroke options that appear in the Type field's drop-down menu

The last option on the Character palette's option menu, No Break, is not documented, but it takes any selected type—hyphen, line, paragraph, column, or page—and refuses to allow InDesign to break it in any way.

Control the Layout of Paragraphs

Although picking your fonts and setting the size and spacing is a critical part of typography, you cannot read those marvelous characters in that exquisite font you chose if the paragraphs are not set up for easy reading. Here, we will look at the InDesign options for formatting paragraphs.

Use the Paragraph Palette

The paragraph settings are found in the Paragraph palette, shown in Figure 5-6. This palette is normally closed because the same options are available on the Control palette.

You will want to memorize the shortcut to open the Paragraph palette. The default shortcut is new: CTRL-ALT-T/COMMAND-OPTION-T. *(I immediately change it to the one I remember from PageMaker,* COMMAND-M, *using Edit | Keyboard Shortcuts, as discussed in Chapter 4.)*

Alignment and Justification

The alignment buttons at the top of the Paragraph palette reveal some of the amazing changes possible in InDesign. Notice that there are seven alignments, instead of the normal four or five. We have left, centered, right, left justified, centered justified, right justified, and full justified. The four variations of justified copy refer to how the sentence fragment at the end of the paragraph is aligned.

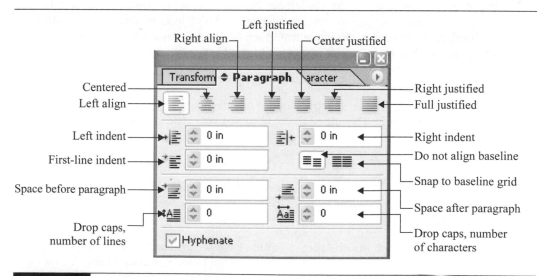

FIGURE 5-6 The Paragraph palette contains the options for formatting paragraphs.

One of the major problems with automated justification in other programs is that it works line by line. Remaining space at the end of a line is distributed into all the word spaces of that line. This sounds good, but in practice, it means that every line of a paragraph has different word spacing—often radically different. These word-space variations are made much worse by narrow columns. This is why newspaper type looks so bad.

InDesign solves this problem by applying paragraph-level justification. This means that the program actually adjusts word spacing on a paragraph level. This gives us far smoother and much better type color. The proverb stating that professional type must be set flush left is no longer true. In InDesign, justified copy is so smooth that you will find yourself using it more and more.

Indents

As you would expect, you can set the left indent, the right indent, and the first-line indent. The left and right indents are measured from the column guides or frame edges. They are measured in whatever measurement system you are using. The little up and down arrows at the left of the fields change the indents as follows:

- If you are using inches, 1/16 inch (0.0625 inch), or 1/4 inch with the SHIFT key
- If you are using points, 1 point, or 10 points with the SHIFT key
- If you are using picas, 1 point, or 1 pica with the SHIFT key
- If you are using millimeters, 1 millimeter, or 10 millimeters with the SHIFT key
- If you are using centimeters, 1 centimeter, or 10 centimeters with the SHIFT key
- If you are using ciceros, 3 points, or 1 cicero with the SHIFT key

The important thing to realize is that the left and right indents are measured from the column or frame edges. You cannot use negative numbers with left and right indents. The first-line indent, on the other hand, is measured from the left indent. It can be a negative number, but no larger than the left indent. This will become important when we talk about hanging indents and lists in Chapter 7.

Baseline Grid

The icons below the Right Indent field control baseline grid alignment. The one on the left does not align the type to a baseline grid. The one on the right causes your type to snap to a baseline grid.

As explained in Chapter 2, you set the size of the baseline grid on the Grids page of the Preferences dialog box (Edit | Preferences on PCs or InDesign | Preferences on Macs). You set it to the size of the leading of your body copy (including any space before or after your body copy paragraphs).

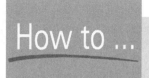

Align Type Across Column Gutters

There are people who believe it really matters that every line of type is aligned across the column gutters. In InDesign, this is relatively easy, provided you take a little care with your paragraph design. The trick is to make sure that all of your headlines and subheads use leading plus paragraph spacing that is a multiple of the grid.

For example, if your body copy is set 10/12 (10-point type on 12 points of leading), your baseline grid should use 12 points as its basic measurement. Now, you need to make all of your paragraph styles for your project's headlines, subheads, kickers, pull quotes, and so on use leading that is a multiple of 12 points. So, a headline could be set at 36/36, with 8 points before the paragraph and 4 points after. Your subheads could be 24/24 or 22/22, with enough space before and after the paragraph to add up to a multiple of 12 for the entire paragraph. You can use any combination where the total leading and paragraph spacing in the paragraph lines up to 12, 24, 36, 48, 60, 72, or 84 points.

To make this easier, you should set your vertical ruler to points (in the Rulers & Increments page of the Preferences dialog box).

Space Before and Space After

The Space Before and Space After fields control the spacing above and below your paragraphs.

As you know by now, paragraph spacing is one of the keys to smooth type color and consistent layouts from page to page. This is one of the reasons typographers never use the double return—it adds too much white space between paragraphs. These fields offer the delicate control you need to make your type readable.

Normally, with body copy paragraphs, you will have a couple of points before or after your paragraph to help your reader see the beginning of a new topic. Anything more than a couple points ruins the type color. If you are having your type snap to a baseline grid, you will usually use no extra spacing at all. It is just too hard to figure out extra spacing, which will vary for almost every paragraph.

However, with headlines and subheads, you need quite a bit of space. The white space added around the heads and subheads is one of the things that makes these paragraphs stand out. Normally, you will want to have more space before the paragraph than after to help the heads attach themselves to the paragraph of body copy that follows. Like the indent settings, the space before and after settings are controlled according to the measurement system you are using.

TIP *Because most designers in the United States work in inches and set type in points, InDesign provides an easy way to always add spacing in points (which is the most common way). Just type the letter p before the number of points you want to add. But be careful, because if you type the p after the number, you will get picas. For example, 2p is 2 picas (or 24 points); p2 is 2 points.*

Drop Caps

The drop caps options at the bottom of the Paragraph palette offer a special way to craft paragraphs, for a specific purpose. InDesign allows you to drop many lines and as many characters as you like. Drop caps are covered in Chapter 7.

Hyphenation

The last item in the Paragraph palette is the Hyphenate button, which turns on or off hyphenation. For example, you probably do not want hyphenation in headlines. We will discuss the hyphenation options in the next section.

Set Your Preferences in the Paragraph Palette's Option Menu

I call the options available on the Paragraph palette's option menu *preferences*, because they are normally long-term decisions you will want to make.

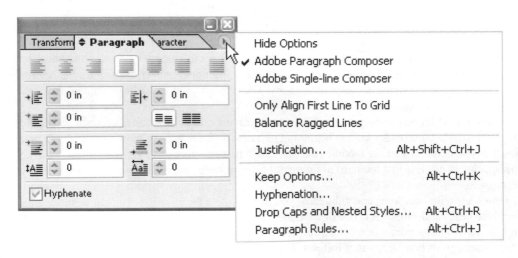

Several of these choices should be set with no document open so they apply as application defaults (covered in Chapter 3). They also can be adjusted in paragraph styles (covered in Chapter 8). The first three items show the long-term nature of these choices. Now, we will see what each of these options does. The only exceptions are the last two options, the Drop Caps & Nested Styles and Paragraph Rules, which are covered in Chapters 7 and 8.

Hide Options

The Hide Options choice hides the Space Before field, the Space After field, and the Drop Cap fields on the Paragraph palette. You do not want to do this. On the relatively rare occasions that you need to open the Paragraph palette (instead of using the Control palette), you want see the entire palette, not a truncated version.

Adobe Paragraph Composer and Adobe Single-Line Composer

The Paragraph Composer is one of InDesign major advances in typography. The Paragraph Composer is checked by default. You should leave it alone! There is never an advantage to switch to single-line justification (unless you're trying to mimic old-fashioned type set in the 1990s).

Only Align First Line to Grid

If you are a user of baseline grids, the Only Align First Line to Grid option will allow you to make the first line of a subsidiary text frame align to the grid. This is commonly used when you have an element, such as a sidebar, with different leading. If you use this option a lot, set a shortcut for it (using Edit | Keyboard Shortcuts, as explained in Chapter 4). Again, this is an option normally set in paragraph styles. There is a drop-down menu for this choice at the bottom of the Indents and Spacing page in the New Style dialog box, accessed from the Paragraph Styles palette (see Chapter 8).

Balance Ragged Lines

Balance Ragged Lines is a new option that tries to adjust lines in very short paragraphs (like subheads or lists) so the line length is as close as possible to the same length in each line. Again, this is an option normally set in paragraph styles. There is a check box for this choice on the Indents and Spacing page in the New Style dialog box, accessed from the Paragraph Styles palette (see Chapter 8).

Justification

The Justification option displays the dialog box shown in Figure 5-7. These are some important settings that have a lot do with how your paragraphs look. Again, justification is normally set in paragraph styles.

The Justification dialog box

NOTE   *The proper settings for word spacing, letter spacing, and glyph scaling for the paragraph are areas of intense debate. What everyone agrees on is that there is no agreement. The needs of different industries vary widely. Plus, they also reflect personal taste. Here, I give you my opinions, which, of course, reflect my personal taste.*

The Justification dialog box settings are as follows:

- **Word Spacing**   This is expressed in a percentage of the word spacing built into the font you choose. All fonts vary, so you cannot just leave this alone. Some fonts are very tight; some are very loose. The defaults of 80%, 100%, and 133% for Minimum, Desired, and Maximum, respectively, mean that in a justified paragraph, the word spacing will never be allowed below 80 percent of the designed space or more than 130 percent of that space. I think these allow too much variance. I set mine at 85%, 97%, and 115% for most fonts I use. I know of newspapers that use 65%, 100%, and 200%. Obviously, you have a decision to make, although the defaults are not too bad.

- **Letter Spacing**   Most professionals agree that you should never allow the letter spacing to vary. So, in this case, the defaults should be left alone: 0% for the Minimum, Desired, and Maximum.

- **Glyph Scaling**   This setting adjusts the horizontal scaling of the characters in the paragraph. Adding this to the Justification settings is unique to InDesign. Setting these options to 97%, 100%, and 103% will help eliminate many widows (or runts) automatically. (*Widows* or *runts* are unacceptably short fragments for the last line of the paragraph.) This amount of scaling is invisible.

UNIQUE TO
**InDesign
CS**

- **Autoleading**   The default is 120%. This figure is a percentage of the point size. The default works for small body copy from 9 points to 14 points. From 14 points to 24 points, 110% works better. For type larger than 24 points, such as headlines, you should use 100% for capitals and lowercase. However, in many cases, it is better to set numerical leading of your choice.

- **Single Word Justification**   Because this is an unacceptable fragment for the last line of the paragraph, you should set this to Align Left. The other choices are Full Justify, Align Centered, and Align Right.

- **Composer**   This should always be set to Adobe Paragraph Composer.

Keep Options

What the heck are Keep Options? This is actually an area of pretty intense debate among typographers. This is supposed to be where you can control your widows and orphans. However, these terms mean different things to different people. My definitions are simple: *orphans* are paragraph fragments left at the top or bottom of a column or page, and *widows* are the short sentence fragments left at the end of paragraphs. A modern digital definition is that both widows and orphans are paragraph fragments, and there is no real name for sentence fragments at the end of a paragraph (except possibly *runts*).

What we all agree on is that the paragraph fragments can be eliminated automatically with Keep Options and that sentence fragments must be eliminated by hand. As a result, the presence of short sentence fragments at the end of paragraphs is a far more telling sign of typographic slovenliness.

When you choose Keep Options from the Paragraph palette's option menu, you see the Keep Options dialog box, shown in Figure 5-8. Here, you can adjust settings to eliminate paragraph fragments. These can be set for any given paragraph. They also can be set as part of a paragraph style for global document control.

The first field, Keep with Next, is for headlines and subheads and keeps them attached to the first lines of the next paragraph. In almost all cases, this option should be set to 2. In other words, if there are fewer than two complete lines of the next paragraph attached after a headline or subhead, the head will automatically be bumped up to the top of the next frame or column.

The Keep Lines Together check box determines whether you will allow a paragraph to be broken into pieces. Obviously, for heads and subheads, you want the paragraphs to remain in one

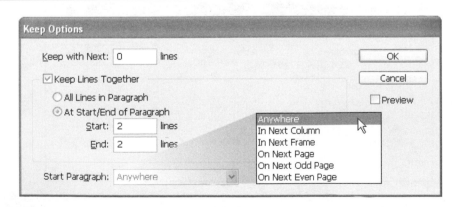

FIGURE 5-8   The Keep Options dialog box

piece. Under this option there are three options. You can choose to keep all the lines together, keep at least the first two lines together, or keep at least the last two lines together. Most typographers would like to set these at three lines. However, modern writing styles, with their short paragraphs, make this impossible.

The final option in the Keep Options dialog box is Start Paragraph. This allows you to set where you want the paragraph to start if it is kicked up to the top of the next column or frame. The choices are Anywhere, In Next Column, In Next Frame, On Next Page, On Next Odd Page, and On Next Even Page.

Hyphenation

Choosing Hyphenation in the Paragraph palette's option menu brings up the Hyphenation Settings dialog box, shown in Figure 5-9. These are relatively easy choices regarding where you allow hyphens and how many hyphens you will allow. I will offer my opinions, but there is not nearly as much debate here as there is with some of the spacing options.

The first choice, Hyphenate, is whether you want to hyphenate or not. In many cases, you do not. Headlines, subheads, and lists are usually not hyphenated. Beyond that, if you decide to hyphenate, there are many choices:

- **Words with at Least** This sets the minimum number of letters in a word to hyphenate. Most people agree that five letters is the minimum; some think as many as seven letters should be the minimum.
- **After First** This sets the first syllable size. Most designers agree that two letters is the minimum.
- **Before Last** This sets the last syllable size. It should be either two or three letters. It depends on whether you think words like *gated* should be hyphenat-ed.

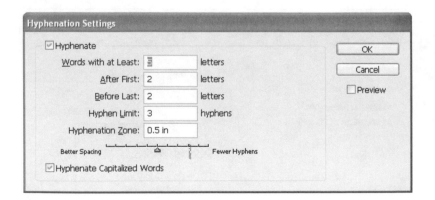

The Hyphenation Settings dialog box

- **Hyphen Limit**   This sets how many hyphens you will allow in a row. There is a little debate here. Some people set this at one; most use two. All agree that three is too many.

- **Hyphenation Zone**   This sets how close a word must be to the end of a line before it is hyphenated. A half inch is the norm.

- **Better Spacing/Fewer Hyphens**   With this slider, you can set, on a sliding scale, whether you want better spacing or fewer hyphens. It is a fine line. In general, leave it at the default setting.

- **Hyphenate Capitalized Words**   Are you going to allow this or not? In general, hyphenating capitalized words is a good idea.

Align the Margins of Your Paragraphs

At the beginning of this chapter, we went over some type terminology, and I mentioned that all type characters are optically aligned to the baseline. You could see how that worked in Figure 5-1. This is necessary to make the characters in the words look like they are accurately aligned vertically. This is normal type.

Another paragraph alignment feature is hanging punctuation. Many other programs have an option to hang punctuation beyond the edge of the right column guide. Quark, FreeHand, and Adobe applications have been able to do this for years. This makes hyphenated words look like they go beyond the edge of the column, for example. However, it has always been a kludge that looked bad, because the entire punctuation character hung and other letters were not affected.

InDesign's capabilities go far beyond hanging punctuation. Many people did not use hanging punctuation because it looked so bad. This is understandable because the periods, commas, hyphens, and so on simply hung outside the column. It looked silly (although it actually helped to smoothen the type color a little for justified paragraphs). But remember, professionals saw justification as in opposition to quality typography in the old paradigm. Optical margin alignment is another story entirely, as you can see in Figure 5-10.

This new capability (as of the original version of InDesign) is more like a preference, but it is actually set through a separate little palette. It is turned on in the Story palette, accessed by choosing Type | Story. There are only two options.

The first option is a check box for Optical Margin Alignment to turn it on or off. This setting affects the entire story. So, if you have a story linked from page to page for 147 pages, it will optically align the entire story. If you check this box with no document open, all new stories will have margin alignment turned on.

The other option is a point size field. Adobe recommends that you set the point size to the same as your body copy size. Smaller point sizes make the adjustments more visible, and larger point sizes make them less visible. If you set this at 60 points, while using 12-point body copy, your body copy will actually be indented a little.

| Yes, these examples are poorly set. The columns are too narrow and the optical margin alignments are exaggerated to make the point. However, if you look in the ellipses, you will see where the left side of the right column is optically aligned also. | As Raqhel looked out over Lake Farnuel, her loneliness increased a little. This surprised her. Usually the Lake, at least, gave her a sense of peace. Today, nothing was working. Damn Cyrill! Czuqqin' pervert! This morning in the hall outside her bed- | As Raqhel looked out over Lake Farnuel, her loneliness increased a little. This surprised her. Usually the Lake, at least, gave her a sense of peace. Today, nothing was working. Damn Cyrill! Czuqqin' pervert! This morning in the hall outside her bed- |

FIGURE 5-10   Optical margin alignment applies to the left and right margins.

> **TIP**
>
> *Adobe suggests setting the optical margin alignment at the point size of your body copy. The lower the point size chosen, the more the alignments will overhang the column edges. I recommend that you use about 2 points larger than the point size of the body copy. Because this setting affects the entire story, sizes too small will cause extreme overhangs for the heads and subheads.*
>
> *This is a very important setting. Many people do not like optical margin alignment at first. However, it makes the edges of your columns look much smoother. Think of it as anti-aliasing for columns.*

Take This Seriously

Obviously, many of these choices discussed in this chapter make up your personal design style. They are very important. Many designers think that these choices are less important than color, layout, graphics, and so on. That is far from the truth. In reality, they are much more important. Your job as a designer is to clearly and easily convey your clients' messages to their customers. That message is in the type.

Remember that there are no right or wrong settings. These choices are all about personal taste and style, coupled with the needs of your clients. These are much more important choices than your drawing skill.

Chapter 6

Edit Type in Your Document

How to ...

- Select text quickly and accurately
- Add glyphs
- Manage fonts
- Use special typographic characters
- Find and replace with Story Editor
- Spell-check with Story Editor
- Edit your type with the Type context menu
- Practice setting type
- Use tagged text
- Use Version Cue and InCopy for large workflows

The goal of this chapter is to show you how to edit type—fast! InDesign has every option you could want to edit your type. It probably has a few dozen options you didn't even know existed.

Let's get one thing out of the way immediately. InDesign does not have drag-and-drop text editing. However, that is the only ability it lacks. Earlier versions of InDesign had a problem with editing speed. This problem is now eliminated with the new built-in word processor, Story Editor.

Before you can edit any type, you need to select it, which is the first topic in this chapter. Then you can use the many options on the InDesign Type menu to edit and format your text. If you want word processing capabilities, including spell checking and a full-featured Find/Change option, you will be pleased with the new Story Editor. After we've gone over all of the methods for editing type, we will step through a simple example to demonstrate what you've read about. Finally, we'll talk about using tagged text, which is particularly useful for handling large workflows.

Select Text Quickly and Accurately

Yes, you can select type by clicking to place the insertion point and dragging with the mouse, but you do not want to do this. There are two major reasons not to use this technique:

- Click-drag selections are very slow. They also take a lot of coordination. If you miss the starting slot you want, all you can do is stop and start over again.
- Click-drag selections are inconsistent. They are one of the major reasons you find fonts in your document that you know you quit using days ago. With hand selection, it is very easy to leave characters behind in a forgotten font. Figure 6-1 illustrates the problem. The boxes in back of the type show what was actually selected.

 *Many designers do not realize that a single character often requires the entire font at the printer. And that single character may be an invisible one, such as a return, a soft return, a tab, or a space.*

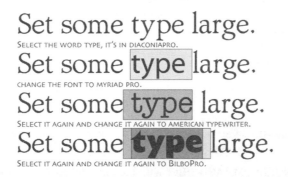

FIGURE 6-1   This sentence requires four fonts to print because of formatted invisible characters: *Set some* in DiaconiaPro, the space before *type* in American Typewriter, *type* in BilboPro, and the space after *type* in Myriad Pro.

Select Text with Multiple Clicks

There is a way to select text accurately and consistently with the mouse: by multiple clicking. You have two choices: Quark style or Adobe style. In the Text page of the Preferences dialog box (Edit | Preferences on PCs or InDesign | Preferences on Macs), there is a Triple-click to Select Line check box. Uncheck it for Adobe behavior. Check it for Quark behavior. Here is the difference:

- **Unselected Triple-click to Select Line (Adobe style)**   You click to place the insertion point, double-click to select a word, triple-click to select a paragraph, and quadruple-click to select an entire story.

- **Selected Triple-click to Select Line (Quark style)**   You click to place the insertion point, double-click to select a word, triple-click to select a line, quadruple-click to select a paragraph, or quintuple-click to select the entire story.

Speed and consistency are the result of either choice (although many of us feel that quadruple-clicking to select a paragraph is too much clicking). You will select a paragraph dozens of times a day. You will rarely want to select a line. You will want to select an entire story even less often (and CTRL-A/COMMAND-A selects the entire story faster than using the mouse).

The consistency of multiple clicking is a major feature of using this technique. A double-click always selects the word—nothing more or less. Clicking to select a line (if you choose that option) always includes the soft return at the end. Triple-clicking to select a paragraph always selects the return at the end of the paragraph also. This way, you are not leaving returns that are formatted with a former font. You always select the same amount. So, no matter how many times you change your mind, there are no leftovers.

Add to Your Selection with Shortcuts

The basic selection shortcuts used in InDesign come from Aldus, PageMaker, and early versions of Word. In other words, they have been around for a long time. They are surprisingly important.

 *One of the nicest things added to InDesign CS is the ability to simply double-click in a text frame to convert to the Type tool automatically. However, this works only when you're coming from one of the selection tools. This emphasizes the need for a good, fast shortcut (with a CTRL or COMMAND key modifier) to force yourself back into the selection tool of your choice.*

Shortcuts really save time when you are adding to your selection. Here are some of the handiest selection shortcuts:

- Holding down the SHIFT key and using the LEFT ARROW or RIGHT ARROW key adds or subtracts a letter at a time to the selection.

- Pressing CTRL-SHIFT/COMMAND-SHIFT with the LEFT ARROW or RIGHT ARROW key adds or subtracts a word at a time.

- With the UP ARROW or DOWN ARROW key, SHIFT adds a line at a time up or down.

- Pressing CTRL-SHIFT/COMMAND-SHIFT with the UP ARROW or DOWN ARROW key adds or subtracts a paragraph at a time.

These shortcuts are by far the fastest methods of selecting parts of text, such as the first few words in a paragraph to make them bold (other than using the new run-in styles now available, which are covered in Chapter 8). If these shortcuts are not enough, there are dozens of additional shortcuts available. To set shortcuts for text, select Edit | Keyboard Shortcuts and choose Text & Tables in the Product Area drop-down list (see Chapter 4 for details on creating custom shortcuts).

Use Type Menu Options to Edit and Format Your Text

Once you have your text selected, you can format it as you wish with the Character and Paragraph palette options, as described in Chapter 5. You can also move pieces around by using the Cut, Copy, and Paste functions available on the Edit menu.

CAUTION *Before you start formatting type, be aware of the dangers of* local formatting. *This is formatting applied to selected text, without using a paragraph or character style. This chapter and the previous one describe the formatting options in a local context, just to explain how to edit type. You'll be applying most of your formatting through styles. You'll learn how to use styles and avoid local formatting in Chapter 8.*

There are many additional editing and formatting options on the Type menu, which we will go through now. As usual, we will simply go down the menu from top to bottom, but skip some that we have already covered or will discuss in a later chapter.

In Chapter 5, we covered the top four Type menu options: Font, Size, Character, and Paragraph, as well as the Story option. We'll talk about the Tabs option in the next chapter. The Paragraph Styles and Character Styles options are the topic of Chapter 8. Create Outlines makes type into a graphic that looks like type, so we'll cover that in Chapter 11. The Type on a Path option, which is a graphic treatment of type, also will be covered in Chapter 11. Here, we'll begin with the sixth choice, Glyphs, another major InDesign advance.

Add Glyphs of Your Choice

UNIQUE TO
**InDesign
CS**

For many of you, glyph *is a new term. A glyph differs from a character in that there can be many glyphs for a given character. For example,* a, A, ᵃ, *and* ₐ *are four different glyphs of the lowercase* a *character: normal, small cap, superscript, and subscript. There can be many other variants. Figure 6-2 shows examples of glyphs, as well as several unusual ligatures and contextual alternatives. Notice how the lowercase* k *in the Caflisch Script Pro font has five contextual alternatives.*

All of the glyphs shown in Figure 6-2 were added with the Glyph palette, which you can display by choosing Type | Glyph. This palette, shown in Figure 6-3, displays all the glyphs available to a font. The Show drop-down list at the top of the palette allows you to see the alternate glyphs for the selected font, the entire font, or all the OpenType classes that are built into the font. At the bottom of the palette, you will find a Font drop-down list, followed by a Style drop-down list, and then a set of Magnify/Demagnify buttons.

There can be well over a thousand glyphs for OpenType fonts. The new Adobe Creative Suite applications have access to these glyphs. No other programs do at this time, except for a few obscure, nonprofessional Windows XP applications. The good news is that InDesign adds many of these glyphs automatically with its OpenType feature options.

You can manage your glyph sets by using the commands on the Glyph palette's option menu (see Figure 6-3). For example, the Edit Glyph Set command displays the dialog box shown in Figure 6-4. Here, you can see (and change) the font and style of glyphs, and delete glyphs from a set, if desired.

Manage Your Fonts

One of the nicest features of InDesign is its ability to check all the fonts in a document, find out which ones are being used, replace bad or missing fonts, and determine where they are stored on the hard drive. This feature is called Find Font. The Find Font dialog box, shown in

A lower case a: *a á ă â ä à ā å ã* ᵃ • a A ᵃ • a A ᵃ

A lower case k in Caflisch: *k k k k k make work*

Lower case ct st sp: *ct st sp* • • ct st sþ

Lower case sy: *sy sý sÿ sy sý sÿ sy sÿ sÿ sy sý sÿ* • •

A Th combination: *Th Th* • Th Th Th Ţh • Th Th

Some Caflisch ligatures: *bjext ey fr iss of öff offi oft ot ott oy rr ss tt xt among many others...*

FIGURE 6-2   These alternative glyphs (separated by bullets) are from Caflisch Script Pro, DiaconiaPro, and Adobe Jenson Pro.

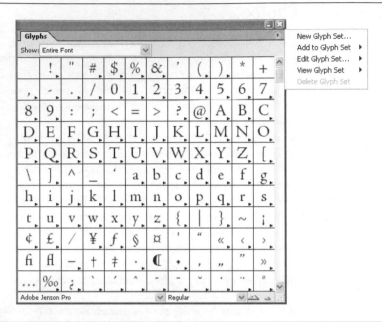

FIGURE 6-3   The Glyph palette and its option menu

Figure 6-5, opens automatically whenever you open or print a document that has missing fonts. Or, you can open this dialog box by selecting Type | Find Font.

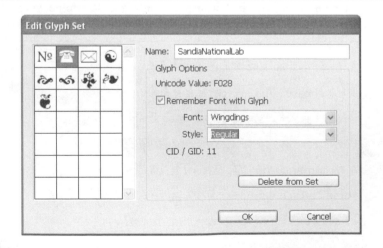

FIGURE 6-4   The Edit Glyph Set dialog box

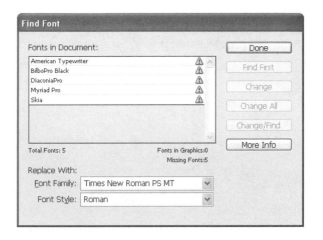

FIGURE 6-5   The Find Font dialog box helps you find and replace bad or missing fonts.

The Find Font dialog box in Figure 6-5 shows the fonts in a document I used to demonstrate glyphs. When I opened that document (created on a Mac) on a PC that didn't have those fonts, InDesign let me know about the problem immediately.

To fix a missing font, just select the font in the Fonts in Document list, choose a font and style from the Font Family and Font Style choices below the list, and then click the Change All button. Clicking the More Info button expands the dialog box to show the selected font's entire name, type, and location on the hard drive.

Change the Case of Your Fonts

Here's strange terminology: the Change Case option on the Type menu. The case of a font refers to old letterpress usage, where the majuscules, or capital letters, were in uppercase, the minuscules were in lowercase, and the small caps and special characters were in a separate case.

In InDesign, there are four case settings you can use: UPPERCASE, lowercase, Title Case, and Sentence case. Title case capitalizes all the words in the selection. Sentence case capitalizes the first word after every period in the selection.

NOTE   *There are no predefined shortcuts for the case conversions. To create shortcuts for them, choose Edit | Keyboard Shortcuts and select Type Menu from the Product Area drop-down list.*

Use Special Typographic Characters

The next three commands on the Type menu—Insert Special Character, Insert White Space, and Insert Break Character—give you easy access to most of the special characters you need to make your typesetting look professional.

Automatic Page Numbering

Selecting Type | Insert Special Character (or right-clicking/CONTROL-clicking when the Type tool is active and selecting Insert Special Character from the context menu) brings up a long list of special character choices.

Selecting the Auto Page Number option from this menu (or from the context menu while the Type tool is active) adds a page number character. Wherever this special character appears, it will show the page number it is on. The most common use for automatic page numbering is on master pages. All you need to do is add a text frame on a master page to show the page number. You can format this number any way you like, and you can add any copy to that frame.

You can also easily produce what are called *jump lines* for stories that continue to other pages. A jump line might read "*Fires in the West* is continued on page 42," for example. Use the Next Page Number or Previous Page Number options of the Special Characters menu to automatically update the number of the page containing a story's next or previous threaded text frame. These numbers will be automatically updated when you move or reflow the story's threaded text frames. Usually, these jump-line page numbers should be in a text frame separate from the story to which they refer. Then the jump-line page number remains in position, even if the story's text reflows.

How to ... Add an Automatic Jump-Line Page Number

To add a jump-line page number, follow these steps:

1. With the Type tool, create a new text frame that overlaps an existing text frame that contains the story to which you need to refer.

2. In the new text frame, type something like "this marvelously educational article is continued on page."

3. Choose Type | Insert Special Character | Next (or Previous) Page Number, depending on your need.

If the story and the jump-line text frame do not overlap, you can group them. If you need to move the frame and its associated jump-line frame, multiple-select or group them before you move them.

TIP *If an unwanted character appears at the beginning of the page number (your auto-number might read* ...continued on C75 *instead of* ...continued on 75*), you have included a section prefix in the Numbering & Section Options dialog box. Simply edit the prefix there by double-clicking the section marker in the Pages palette (see Chapter 3 for details on document sections).*

Special Hyphens

One tool you will need as you go about achieving excellence in typesetting is the *discretionary hyphen*. If you are coming from the PC world, this may be a new concept for you. Discretionary hyphens are not common in PC applications. The basic concept is simple. A discretionary hyphen is a special character that gives the software permission to hyphenate at that point if necessary. If it is not necessary to break the word, the discretionary hyphen is invisible.

Discretionary hyphens are most commonly used when justification hits a snag with a long word that is not in the dictionary. This happens most often with long proper names or technical jargon. When you see that justification or flush-left line breaks are far too ragged, all you need to do is type in discretionary hyphens between the syllables (choose Type | Special Characters | Discretionary Hyphen, use the context menu while the Type tool is active, or use the shortcut). Then InDesign will make the ending word fragment as long as possible before hyphenating it.

Another special hyphen is not used quite as much, but it is equally important. This one is more common in the PC world. It is the nonbreaking hyphen, which is used in compound words to prevent them from hyphenating. The Nonbreaking Hyphen option is listed below the Discretionary Hyphen option on the Special Characters menu.

 *The shortcuts for special hyphens are easy. They are in the text context, meaning that they work only when you have an active insertion point. The discretionary hyphen is* CTRL-SHIFT-HYPHEN/COMMAND-SHIFT-HYPHEN. *The nonbreaking hyphen is* CTRL-ALT-HYPHEN/COMMAND-OPTION-HYPHEN. *(I wouldn't be surprised if both of these need to be used in setting the typographic monsters of these keystrokes.)*

White Spaces: Em, En, and Beyond

Most of you know about ems and ens. Some of you know about thin spaces. InDesign goes way beyond that.

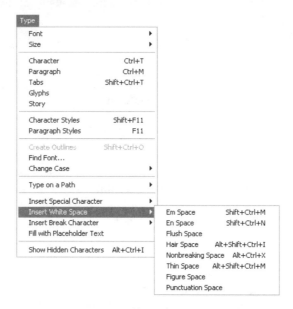

A thin space has no standard width. In various applications, it has been a third, a fourth, or a fifth of an em. InDesign's thin space is an eighth of an em. In addition, InDesign has a hair space that is a twenty-fourth of an em for fine adjustments.

 *I use four text context shortcuts for white spaces:* CTRL/COMMAND-SHIFT-M, -N, -T, *and -I. The first two are the built-in shortcuts, and the last two are custom ones. You will need to use white spaces a lot if you modify the left edges of your text frames (discussed in Chapter 7), so shortcuts for them are very handy.*

Column, Frame, and Page Breaks

The options on the Type | Insert Break Character menu help you manage your document flow. You can move the rest of the text in a frame or column to the next column, the next frame, the next odd page, the next even page, or the next page.

Make a Dummy Document for a Proposal

Most designers need to make a proposal before they have any real copy to use. The Type | Fill with Placeholder Text command is the solution to this problem. PageMaker has a Latin document. Quark has Jabberwocky (which is marvelous). InDesign has Latin, or you can save any document in text-only format, call it placeholder.txt, and save it into the InDesign CS folder.

Placeholder text is very easy to use. Press T to select the Type tool, and then right-click/ CONTROL-click and select the Fill with Placeholder Text command. If you click a frame, it will be filled with the placeholder text. If you have placed an insertion point, the placeholder text will start there and fill the frame or frames. It will fill all the frames linked to the place from which you start.

Show the Invisible Characters

For some reason (lawyers probably), InDesign regularly changes traditional wording. Although the Type menu option says Show Hidden Characters, these characters are not hidden—they are invisible.

Most of the time, as you are setting type, you want to be able to see the invisible characters: space, tab, paragraph return, soft return, em space, en space, thin space, hair space, and so on. Often, the only way you will have to quickly locate typesetting problems is to see the invisible characters. The practice of going to the next line in a numbered list by hitting the TAB key until the next line happens is just one example of why it's a good idea to display invisible characters.

You can easily turn on the display of invisible characters by pressing CTRL-ALT-I/COMMAND-OPTION-I. *I suggest you make this your default.*

Edit Your Story in InDesign's Word Processor

InDesign's built-in word processor, Story Editor, is very fast. It shows all the paragraph styles. It is a good place to edit multiple pages of copy. Spell checking is snappy. Find/Change is a quick operation. The more you use Story Editor, the more you'll like it. Its only shortcoming is the lack of drag-and-drop capabilities.

One of the primary reasons to use Story Editor is for its Find/Change feature. You will use Find/Change a great deal to clean up supplied copy.

Clean Up Your Document with Find/Change

One of the most common requirements when you import supplied copy is to clean it up. This is a fact of life to most of us in desktop publishing. Most of the copy you receive (unless you work for a large in-house design department producing books, newspapers, or magazines) will be littered with typographic errors.

NOTE *In Chapter 16, I'll suggest an efficient way to fix common errors in imported copy, using Story Editor's Find/Change feature and styles.*

The Find/Change feature in Story Editor is an incredibly powerful tool for cleaning up copy. You can find and change text in a selection, one or more stories, a document, or multiple open documents. You can find and change anything typographic: invisible characters, special characters, styles, formatting, or whatever you need to fix. The Find/Change dialog box, shown in Figure 6-6, looks deceptively simple.

Where can you look? Your choices in the Search drop-down list depend on what you have done before you selected Edit | Find/Change (or pressed CTRL-F/COMMAND-F). If you have an insertion point in a story, you will see four options: All Documents, Document, Story, and To End of Story. If you have several stories selected, the choices will be All Documents, Document, and Stories. In other words, you can search the entire story you are working on (even if it is several hundred pages long), all the stories selected, the entire document, or all open documents.

The next question is, what can you change? Let's start simply. You can change any word or words to any other word or words. You do need to be careful how you define your search, though. Imagine what would happen if you searched to find *in* and replace it with *is*. The results would be *inspect* to *isspect*, *interest* to *isterest*, and so on—you get the idea. The two check boxes at the bottom of the Find/Change dialog box can help prevent some problems.

- **Whole Word** The example in the previous paragraph has a simple solution. If you had checked the Whole Word check box, you would find and change only *in*. The Change operation would not do anything to *thing*, *sing*, *sin*, *tin*, or any word that merely contains *in*. It changes only whole words.

- **Case Sensitive** This option also helps to limit the changes. If this is checked, and you do a search for *InDesign*, it will not find *indesign*, *Indesign*, or *INDESIGN*.

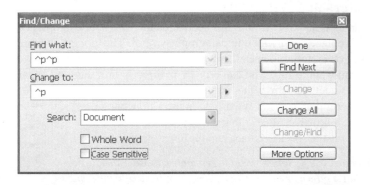

FIGURE 6-6   The simple Find/Change dialog box offers powerful capabilities.

 **Find and Change Text**

Here is the simple procedure for finding and changing text:

1. To search in a story, use the Type tool to click in a text frame. To search only within a selection, select the text you want to search. To search in one or more stories, use the Selection tool to select one or more frames.

2. Open the Find/Change dialog box (choose Edit | Find/Change, press CTRL-F/ COMMAND-F, or use the context menu). Then choose the range of your search by selecting from the Search drop-down menu.

3. Place an insertion point in the Find What field and type or paste the text you want to find.

4. Press TAB to move to the Change To field and to select everything in the field to replace it. Then type or paste the new or changed text.

5. Searching and changing are done with the buttons on the right side of the dialog box. Click Find Next to begin the search. Once you see the first word or words found, click Find Next, Change, Change All, or Change/Find. After clicking Change All, an alert will appear, telling you how many changes were made. Change/Find changes what has been found, and then finds the next instance.

6. Click the Done button (or close the window by pressing CTRL-W/COMMAND-W) when you are finished making changes.

This sounds very simple, and it is. However, keep in mind that you can search for anything.

Special Characters and Wildcards

Figure 6-6 shows an example of searching for special characters—for example, two paragraph symbols, ^p ^p—to replace them with one paragraph symbol. This operation would find all paragraphs with an extra return between them and get rid of that extra return. If you know the special characters you want to find, you can type them directly into the Find What box. But you may find it easier to select them from the list that Story Editor provides.

If you look to the right of the Find What field in the Find/Change dialog box, you'll see a little rectangle with triangle pointing to the right. When you click that, a list of special characters pops up, as shown here.

Yes, this means you no longer need to remember those esoteric codes to find a return or tab character. They are basically the same as PageMaker's set of special characters. So, if you have those memorized, you won't need the pop-up menu. But look at the list! Almost every special character you ever need to search for is here.

At the bottom of the special characters pop-up menu, you will see three very special characters: Any Character, Any Digit, and Any Letter. These are wildcard characters that let you search for words when you cannot remember exactly how to spell them. Just use the wildcard character type you need for the characters you do not remember. (You may need to do this a few times until you get the right number of wildcards.) You can also use wildcards to find things like product codes. For example, *XG???* would find all the product codes starting with *XG* followed by three numbers.

Formatting Searches

One of the more powerful capabilities of the Find/Change feature is not apparent until you click the More Options button in the dialog box. This expands the bottom of the dialog box to give you two more fields. When you click the Format button to the right of the fields, you begin to see how powerful this dialog box really is. This dialog box covers every typographic capability of the entire application.

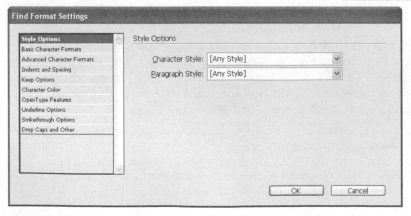

For example, you can select Style Options to find and change any character or paragraph style to any other. (Chapter 8 covers styles.) The Basic Character Formats and Advanced Character Formats options let you find and change any option in the Character palette, such as font, point size, leading, kerning, tracking, baseline shift, and so on. The Indents and Spacing option and Drop Caps and Other option give you find-and-change control over all the options in the Paragraph palette: indents, paragraph spacing, drop caps, autoleading, and more. You can even find and change the color (both fill and stroke) of any piece of type by selecting Character Color. The rest of the format options let you control all the items in the option menus of the Character and Paragraph palettes. So, for example, you can search for all the red, 14-point Garamond Bold and change it to blue, 18-point Caslon Regular and add a half-point purple stroke.

Check Your Spelling

One of the major complaints with earlier versions of InDesign was the slowness of the spell checker. It is much faster in InDesign CS. It is blazingly fast in Story Editor.

SHORTCUT   *Probably the first to change in the spell checker is the keyboard shortcut. InDesign uses* CTRL-I/COMMAND-I. *I doubt if any of you have that one memorized. You might want to change it to one you're familiar with, such as Microsoft Word's (*COMMAND-OPTION-L *or* F7*) or Mac OSX's (*COMMAND-SHIFT-;*).*

InDesign's spell checker looks a little different from the one in other applications, as shown in Figure 6-7, but it performs all the functions you are used to, except grammar checking. If you want to check the grammar or use a thesaurus, you need a third-party plug-in or utility. Alternatively, you can check your grammar in Microsoft Word or whatever word processor you use.

For your Search scope, you have the same choices as in the Find/Change dialog box: End of Story, Story, Stories, Document, and All Documents. Once you click the Start button, InDesign will check the spelling from that point on, wrapping around at the end to come back to where it started, unless you have chosen End of Story. It will flag any word it does not recognize, usually changing the name of the top field to Not in Dictionary, but sometimes it will say Duplicate Word or Improper Capitalization. If the spell checker can make any guesses, it will put possible alternatives in the Suggested Corrections field.

NOTE   *When you first start the spell checker, make sure it is set for the language you are using. Remember that the language control is at the bottom of the Character palette. Also, you can change dictionaries on the fly to check selections set in a different language.*

If you want the spell checker to ignore a word because it is spelled the way you want it to be spelled, click Ignore. If you want it to ignore all instances in the entire document, click the Ignore All button.

InDesign's spell checker is very good. However, like all spell checkers, it needs to be trained. Rare is the field or industry that doesn't have dozens of words that are technical jargon. Adding words to your spell checker is part of the learning process for any new software (or version of that software) and for most new clients. For example, I always add *platesetter, imagesetter, prepress, RIP,* and other typesetting terminology. When the spell checker finds a word that you want to add to its dictionary, simply click the Add button. The dialog box shown in Figure 6-8 will appear.

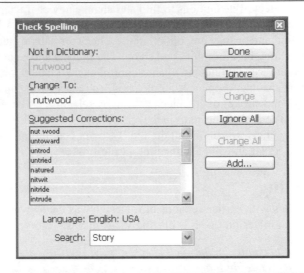

FIGURE 6-7   InDesign's spell checker finds words that are not in its dictionary and offers suggested corrections.

The first choice you must make is where you are going to save the changes. You can save the changes into either the external dictionary installed in the application or the word list inside any open InDesign document. Both or either can include a list of words you have added or removed

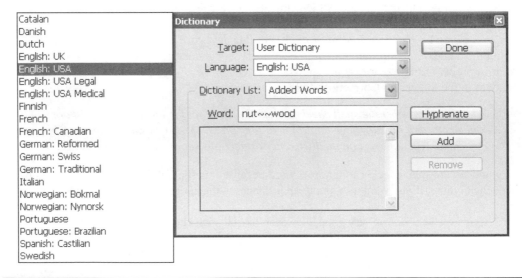

FIGURE 6-8   The Dictionary dialog box with the languages in the standard installation of InDesign

from the dictionary for spelling and hyphenation. (Yes, this is also where you add the hyphenation points.) In addition, InDesign can save a separate set of added and removed words for each installed language.

If you want to remove a word from your dictionary, select a word first, or just choose Edit | Dictionary. If necessary, type the word in the Word field in the Dictionary dialog box. In the Target drop-down list, choose the dictionary from which you want to remove the word. In the Dictionary List drop-down list, choose Removed Words. Then click the Add button, and the word will be added to the Removed Words list for that dictionary. Yes, I know, you think you should click the Remove button—I do too, but it is never active.

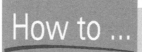

Add Words to Your Hyphenation and Spelling List

To add words to your dictionary, follow these steps:

1. When the Check Spelling dialog box displays a word that you need to add to a dictionary, click Add. Or you can select a word and choose Edit | Dictionary. InDesign will display that word in the Word field. Click Add if it is correct. Or you can type the word you want to add in the Word field and click Add.

2. When the Dictionary dialog box opens, choose the dictionary where you want to store the word from the Target choices: the user dictionary or in any open InDesign document.

3. Make sure that the language showing in the Language field is the one you want to use. If not, choose the correct one.

4. In the Dictionary List drop-down list, choose Added Words or Removed Words, depending on whether you want to add the word or remove it from the user dictionary or your document list.

5. Check your hyphenation by clicking the Hyphenate button to see InDesign's best guess. Tildes (~) will indicate possible hyphenation points. If you actually need a real tilde in a word, type a backslash before the tilde (\~).

6. Click Add, and the word is added to the currently selected Dictionary List choice.

7. If you are finished adding words, click the Done button. If you are still spell checking, move the Dictionary dialog box to an out-of-the-way location. Then go back to the spell checker and click Ignore to resume spell checking.

If you don't like InDesign's hyphenation locations, you can indicate your preferred hyphenation of the word. Type one tilde to indicate the best possible hyphenation point, or the only acceptable hyphenation point; type two tildes to indicate the second choice or choices; and type three tildes to indicate a poor but acceptable hyphenation point. If the word should not be hyphenated, type a tilde before the first letter.

Edit Your Type with the Type Context Menu

Most of the commands we have talked about so far are available in the Type context menu. When you are working in type, you can easily access this menu by right-clicking (or CONTROL-clicking if you don't have a multiple-button mouse for your Mac yet). You'll see this menu:

Along with the commands we have covered, there is also the Paste command, a Text Frame Options command (discussed in Chapter 7), and commands for adding tags or hyperlinks. Using the context menu is usually quite a bit quicker than searching through a regular menu. (But keyboard shortcuts are still the fastest way to go.)

Practice Setting Type

Now that you've read about typesetting, let's try a simple exercise. Here, you will go through the steps to pick a font, leading, and alignment. Then you will add some simple color.

Feel free to modify the exercise as much as you like to make it more interesting. If you have problems with this or any other exercises in this book, e-mail me at graphics@swcp.com.

1. Open InDesign and choose File | New. When the New Document dialog box opens, set the page size at 2 inches wide by 5.5 inches tall. Use 0.25-inch margins and a single column.

2. Choose the Type tool. Click in the upper-left corner of the margins and drag to the lower-right corner to make a text box the same size as the margins. This will leave the insertion point flashing in the upper-left corner of the new text frame.

3. To begin formatting the type for the first paragraph, choose centered alignment in either the Paragraph palette or the Control palette.

4. Pick a font you like and set it at 24 points with 22 points of leading (24/22), using the Character palette or the Control palette.

5. Type the following words. The double arrows, >>, represent a soft return (created by pressing SHIFT-RETURN/ENTER), which will give you a line break but not start a new paragraph. (To see the invisible characters, select Type | Show Hidden Characters).

   Do you >> know >> what >> you are >> doing?

6. Press the RETURN key after the question mark to start a new paragraph.

7. Make this new paragraph justified. Set the font you choose at 12/14.

8. Type the following:

   Actually, I imagine that, at this point, the answer to the question is, "No!" However, you are actually doing digital publishing and setting type. That is a step in the right direction. That this is very easy and extremely boring for some of you cannot be helped. Go on to a harder exercise, type it on a spiral path, or something.

9. Press the RETURN key to end the paragraph.

6

10. Change the font to something you like that is very bold and set it at 48/48 type. Set the horizontal scaling to 10%.

11. Type the following:

    YOU'RE DONE!

12. Select those two words and the exclamation point. Then adjust the horizontal and vertical scaling (in the Control palette or Character palette) and make the type wide enough to fill the entire width on one line. I made my type 47% wide and bumped it up to 62 points to make it fit without breaking into two lines. You may want to start small and gradually make the type larger, or it will overset and disappear into the little, red plus.

13. Place the insertion point in the middle paragraph of the three paragraphs. In the Paragraph palette or Control palette, change the space before paragraph to 0.0625 inch (one-sixteenth inch).

14. Select the entire last paragraph (*YOU'RE DONE!*) and click a color in the Swatches palette to color the type (make a new color if you're in the mood).

15. If you export this document as a PDF (choose File | Export, select PDF as the format, click OK, and then click Export), the final result should look something like what you see in Figure 6-9.

Do you know what you are doing?

Actually, I imagine that, at this point, the answer to the question is, "No!" However, you are actually doing digital publishing and setting type. That is a step in the right direction. That this is very easy and extremely boring for some of you cannot be helped. Go on to a harder exercise, set it on a spiral, or something.

FIGURE 6-9   The results of formatting and exporting text

Use Tagged Text

Some editorial departments work in stripped-down word processing applications that format their text by adding tags—sort of a typesetting version of HTML. InDesign has strong support for tagged text (if you can find a designer who can stand to code). There is a Tags palette to control the tags. You can map the tags to your styles, or map your styles to your tags.

> **TIP** *Many of the older companies use XPress Tags (Quark's version of the process). InDesign cannot read those tags. However, Late Night Software (www.latenightsw.com) has a plug-in called Tag-On that you can purchase to solve this problem.*

You can also use tagged text without knowing how to write it. You can import (or export) a text file capable of taking advantage of InDesign's formatting capabilities by using the tagged-text format. Tagged text files are text files containing information describing the formatting you want InDesign to apply. Properly tagged text can describe almost anything that can appear in an InDesign story, including all paragraph-level attributes, character-level attributes, and special characters. If you want to learn how to write or edit tags, open the Tagged Text.PDF file on the InDesign CD (find the file in the Tagged Text folder, under the Adobe Technical Info folder).

Export to Tagged Text Format

The easiest way to use tagged text is to simply export all your copy in that format, by choosing File | Export and picking the Tagged Text export option. The tagged text format seems to do a better job of keeping everything formatted than Rich Text Format (RTF), which is the second-best choice. When you reimport your copy, everything is there. The major advantage is that a tagged document can be edited in a simple word processor like BBEdit or Notepad.

> **CAUTION** *Do not think you can safely edit tagged text in Word. The fancy word processors seem to think that tagged text is HTML, but it is not. You get some scrambled stuff.*

Import a Tagged-Text File

If you receive a tagged document from someone, simply place it (by choosing File | Place, as explained in Chapter 5). When you import a tagged text file and select Show Import Options in the Place dialog box, the following options are available:

- **Use Typographer's Quotes**   This option ensures that imported text includes curly left and right quotation marks and apostrophes, instead of straight inch and foot marks and apostrophes.
- **Remove Text Formatting**   This option removes formatting—such as typeface, type color, and type style—from the imported text. In other words, you can strip all formatting.

> **TIP** *If you place a tagged text file and find that the formatting is all wrong, it's easy to fix. Simply press CTRL-Z/COMMAND-Z to undo it. Then choose File | Place, select Show Import Options, and choose Remove Text Formatting to import the file without the formatting.*

■ **Resolve Text Style Conflicts Using**   This allows you to choose which character or paragraph style to apply when there is a conflict between the style in the tagged text file and the style in your InDesign document. Select Publication Definition to use the style definition already existing in the InDesign document. Select Tagged File Definition to use the style as defined in the tagged text. This will cause InDesign to create another style name in the style palette, with the word *copy* added after the style name.

■ **Show List of Problem Tags Before Place**   This option will display a list of unrecognized tags. If a list appears, you can choose to cancel or continue the import. If you continue, the file may not look as expected.

Use Version Cue and InCopy for Large Workflows

InDesign offers a lot to large-staff production departments. First of all, there is all the interaction within Adobe's Creative Suite. Within this suite is a program called Version Cue that allows you to keep track of multiple versions of your files. From within the creative applications of the Creative Suite (InDesign, Illustrator, Photoshop, and GoLive), you can visually scan thumbnails of your design files and search for attributes (called metadata)—including resolution, file size, author, keywords, and comments—to locate the version on which you are supposed to be working. Version Cue is designed to allow you to work as part of a networked team, managing shared files and keeping track of who is working on which areas of the project.

Another option has been available for a while. Since InDesign 1.5, Adobe has also sold companion software for editorial staff called InCopy. The new Story Editor is from that code base. With InCopy, editors can check out the copy to work on while the layout artist continues to adjust the layout. The designer cannot make changes to the copy unless the editorial staff allows it.

Now you have been introduced to many of the commands and features that InDesign offers for setting type. However, there is still a lot more information to cover (three more chapters' worth, in fact). Typesetting is complex!

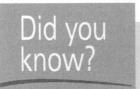

XML and Scripting Are a High-End Solution

A good XML script can solve many of your problems. For seriously dull and repetitive projects, like a phone book, XML scripts are essential. If you do not want to write your own XML, you can have someone else do it for you. You can use your Web search engine of choice to find hundreds of resources.

The fact is that we will all be using XML in the future. Consider that we can write PostScript code, with no problem, simply by using Quark, InDesign, FreeHand, Illustrator, or Photoshop. Remember, Illustrator was simply a WYSIWYG interface to write PostScript code to produce graphics. The same thing will happen with XML—eventually.

Chapter 7

Design Your Paragraphs

How to ...

- Wisely choose page size and column widths
- Add a drop cap to help the reader
- Use tabs creatively
- Use leaders for forms
- Design facing tabs
- Handle indents and tabs in modified text frames
- Set up professional-looking indents
- Make hanging indents
- Use paragraph rules for emphasis and direction
- Control how paragraphs look in text frames with Text Frames Options

In this chapter, you will learn how to craft your paragraphs, both to grab attention and to make them more readable. Excellence in typography is as much about paragraph design as it is about beautiful fonts carefully kerned.

InDesign gives you incredible control over the design of your paragraphs. With just a little planning, you can make powerful communication tools. This chapter discusses some of the decisions concerning paragraphs you must make as you use InDesign. By the end of the chapter, you will know how to make your designs attractive and, most important, easy to read.

Wisely Choose Page Size and Column Widths

Your first choices as you begin to put type on pages are page size and column width. You need to make several educated decisions to choose page size, columns, and gutters.

 Your first decisions outside InDesign are picking your printer and paper stock. There are huge differences in printers' capabilities. For more information about digital printing production, see Chapter 18.

First, we need to revisit the New Document dialog box. It contains most of what you need to set up your pages. You might think these settings are obvious, but they are not.

Consider the New Document dialog box settings shown in Figure 7-1. You can see that this specifies letter-size, eight facing pages, wide orientation, one column, half-inch margins, and one-eighth inch bleed. (This is an unusable page design; we're just using it for demonstration purposes here.) Just by seeing this layout, you know several things. First, two 11-inch-wide pages facing each other with a bleed means this must be printed on a press that is at least 25 inches wide (no presses are 22.5 inches wide, which is what is required). This means a sheet-fed commercial printer, in most cases.

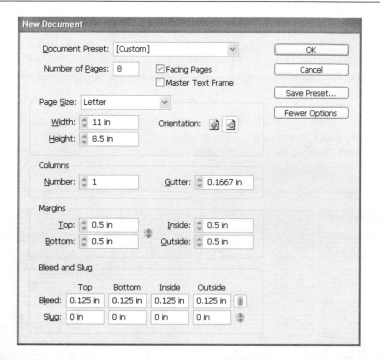

FIGURE 7-1   The New Document dialog box contains settings that affect your design.

But how does this affect the design? Now we get to the heart of the matter. In this example, one column is 10 inches wide. To understand the problem, you must know the basic readability issues of column width.

You should design your columns so they have from 10 to 14 words in an average line. A rough guideline for producing this many words in a line is 40 percent of the point size in inches. In other words, 10-point type should have 4-inch columns.

So, if you have a 10-inch-wide column, the body copy of this document must be around 25-point type to be readable (40 percent of 25 is 10 inches). That is not likely for an eight-page booklet. Normal body copy is 10/12 (10-point type with 12-point leading). In other words, you will need close to a 4-inch column. So, rather than the single 10-inch column, any of the following would be a better choice:

■   Keep 0.5-inch margins and use two 4.8-inch columns with 0.4-inch gutters and a decorative rule between the paragraphs. (The rule is not necessary, but a 0.4-inch gutter is very wide.) A 0.5-inch margin gets the inside copy pretty close to the fold, but this is only an 8-page booklet. If it were a 200-page perfect-bound book, a 0.5-inch interior margin would not be enough.

■ Make the margins 0.875 inch (seven-eighths inch) and use two 4-inch columns with a normal 0.25-inch gutter.

■ Change the outside or inside margin to 1.25 inches, so you can use two 4-inch columns and a 0.25-inch gutter. This would give you a little sidebar on the outside for small pictures and graphics. Or it would add some sophistication to your booklet with a larger interior page gutter.

My choice would be the last one, with the larger interior page gutter. I would also give the page a little breathing room by making the top margin 0.75 inch and the bottom margin 1 inch. The results would look like this for pages 2 and 3:

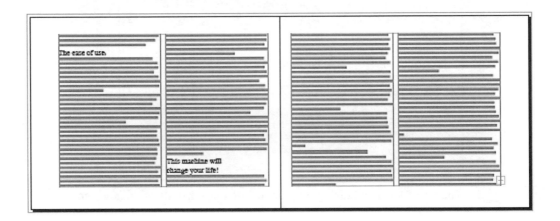

Those are some of the simple issues involved with paragraph crafting. Now we need to go through some more of the options offered by InDesign.

 *As you design paragraphs, remember the guideline for readability: 10 to 14 words in an average line, or 40 percent of the point size in inches.*

Add a Drop Cap to Help the Reader

Adding a drop cap is fairly simple. In the Paragraph palette, there are two fields to adjust.

The field on the left, with the *A* and up/down arrows, is where you set how many lines you want the letter, letters, or graphic to drop. You can drop as many as 25 lines. The field on the right determines how many letters or graphics you want to drop. You can drop as many letters or graphics as you like. Figure 7-2 shows an example of a graphic (as a single character or inline graphic) that has been dropped 25 lines.

As Raqhel looked out over Lake Farnuel, her loneliness increased a little. This surprised her. Usually the Lake, at least, gave her a sense of peace. Today, nothing was working. Damn Cyril! Czuqqin'pervert!

This morning in the hall outside her bedroom, he had actually gotten serious. Being fondled by one's brother was not a pleasant way to greet the morning. She hoped he still ached. Her knee still hurt a little. The problem was she didn't know what to do next. Her father would laugh it off - "boys are like that you know". Her mother would deny it really happened. She was too embarrassed to tell anyone else. The future problem was Cyril's foul temper. Who knew what he would do now?

She turned from the window. She was sitting on one of the window seat/study alcoves built into the wall of the castle. Her particular vantage point this morning was invisible from the floor of the library - as usual. She was nearly forty span above the library floor in front of one of the windows on the south side of the palace next to the history archives. The Harvest sun was low enough, now, to flood the main floor of the library with light.

The palace wall, up this high, was only about seven span thick. The windows that had been cut into the wall made perfect little three-sided rooms, with the window on the outside and a narrow walkway on the library side. They were set up for right-handed people with a dark green padded seat on the left side of the window and a built-in desk on the right with a small bookshelf and pen holders.

As far as Raqhel could tell from the original plans, these alcoves were an after thought. Originally the walkway was simply to access the windows in case one of them broke or leaked. She had never been able

---

FIGURE 7-2   An inline graphic placed as the first character and dropped 25 lines, through almost three paragraphs

NOTE   *To drop a graphic, place a graphic into an insertion point. After that, the graphic is treated as a type character. Graphics treated as type characters are discussed in Chapter 11.*

Once they find out how easy it is to drop a letter, word, or graphic, people new to desktop publishing want to do it all the time. The problem is that readers have a very specific understanding of what a drop cap means: It signals *the story starts here*. It does not start here, here, and here. It can start in only one place. Basically, a drop cap should appear just once a page as a maximum. It should be used only for the beginning of the most important story on that page. It can also be used at the beginning of each chapter, for example.

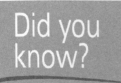

Raised Caps Capture Attention, Too

A variation of a drop cap is to make the first letter of the paragraph large. That is called a *raised cap* or an *initial cap*.

As an example, the most extreme drop/raised cap I ever saw was stunning, as well as tasteful and elegant. It was used in a large 30-by-40-inch poster, single column, with huge indents. All the paragraphs were set in an extremely elegant serif font, centered, maybe 24/40, with a first-line indent to the middle of the page (about an 8-inch first-line indent). The first paragraph had a raised cap in a very narrow, yet bold, sans serif font that was about 3 inches tall, colored with a subtle gradient of grays.

Designers spend a lot of time designing their drop caps. As in any design, if there is not enough contrast, you will merely irritate the reader. Often, the letter used for the drop cap is in a radically contrasting font. Sometimes, the designer wants a text wrap around a huge drop cap that sticks outside the margin. Then the capital letter must be set separately and placed as a graphic with a text wrap, and it will no longer flow with the text.

Use Tabs Creatively

Typesetters' tabs are very different from typewriter tabs. First, like alignment, they also come in four kinds: left, right, centered, and decimal. InDesign has upped the ante by making its decimal tab a special character tab. It can align on any character you choose. As you set tabs, notice that a vertical line appears in the text block to help you line up the tabs.

InDesign's tabs align text as follows:

- **Left tab**   Moves the insertion point to the tab location. The type starts at this point and proceeds normally as it is typed.

- **Right tab**   Moves the insertion point to the tab location. The type grows to the left from that location as it is typed.

- **Centered tab**   Moves the cursor to the tab location, and the type grows in both directions, remaining centered on the tab location.

- **Special character tab**   Moves the cursor to the tab location. Everything before the chosen character extends left, and everything after the special character extends right. This style tab is usually used with periods to easily make accountant-style tabular records, where parentheses and asterisks often stick out to the right of the numbers.

Here's a little example using an *x* for the left tab and a period for the right one. I grayed out the *x* and period on the first line, so you can see them.

Boards:x Price per board:.8' each, Pine

2x2	$.6785
2x4	$1.09
2x10	$4.783
10x16	$76.475

All alignments, indents, and tabs are in relation to the column. For tabs to work as you expect, the paragraph alignment almost always must be flush left. The best way to set up tabs is with paragraph styles, which are covered in Chapter 8.

Add a Leader

7

A *leader* is a set of repeating characters leading into a tab. All of the space between the last character before the tab and the first character after the tab is filled as fully as possible with the character specified for the leader.

Repeat Any Character

You normally associate leaders with layouts like restaurant menus, where a row of dots connects a name with a price. However, there are many types of leaders. Any character can be used to repeat. In fact, InDesign allows any combination of up to eight characters to repeat. Figure 7-3 shows some examples.

Green Chilé Chicken Alfredo............................$9.95 ◄———Period leader

Spearmint Fudge Sundae _____ $2.95 ◄———Below-line rule leader

Need a picket fence any one?|||||||||||||||||||||||||||||||||||||||||| ◄———Vertical-bar leader

°.\|/.°°.\|/.°°.\|/.°°.\|/.°°.\|/.°°.\|/.°°.\|/.°°.\|/.°°.\|/.°°.\|/.° ◄———Leader made with 7 characters

FIGURE 7-3   Examples of leader styles

Here is the Tabs palette with the settings for the leader examples. The vertical gray line indicates the tab location.

InDesign gives you a lot of control over your leader sizes. Simply select the tab character and format it. If you want the leader thinner and lighter, pick a lighter font at a smaller point size. The special sequence of seven characters shown in Figure 7-3 was resized to 13.2 points to make it fit the line properly.

Use Leaders for Forms

One of the best uses for leaders is to create forms. Almost anywhere that you need a group of blank lines to be filled in, you can set it up with leaders.

Figure 7-4 shows an example of using the below-line rule character as a leader to make a form. For the last line, I typed in *State*, two below-line rules, *Zip*, and five below-line rules at the right-tab insertion point, and they grew from the right. I needed to do some kerning in front of *State* and *Zip* to align them. However, a problem with typing the pieces after the flush-right aligning tab is that *State* would not align with anything else in the form.

TIP   *To help people fill out the forms, make sure you have the equivalent of a typewriter double return (24 points of leading, total) to give them enough room to write. Try to fill out the form yourself to see if it works. Make sure the leaders are long enough.*

It is difficult to design forms that people will actually use. Internal alignments help a lot. Figure 7-5 shows a way to set up tabs to keep the internal alignments and help the form hold together.

Name _____

Address _____

_____ ◄—Flush right tab here

City_____ State___ Zip_____

FIGURE 7-4   Below-line rule leaders are handy for creating forms.

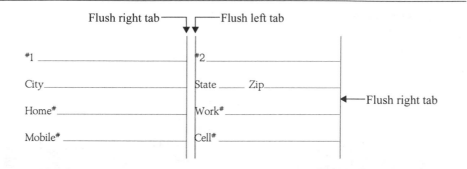

FIGURE 7-5   A form setup that uses tabs to help with the internal alignments. The vertical lines show where the tabs are in the text.

The form setup in Figure 7-5 includes double lines and a blank space between the columns. The right tab at 2 inches has a line leader; the left tab at 2.125 inches has no leader (to give a controlled amount of space before the second word); and the right tab at 4 inches has a line leader. I've drawn vertical, gray lines to show you where the tabs are in the text. This is a style commonly used for invoice headings. It comes in handy for filling in information such as city and state locations, home and work phone numbers, billing and shipping addresses, and so on. Sometimes, you need a third style with three lines or another special alignment.

Once you understand the principle, you can easily create forms without needing to resort to tables or drawing programs. You can have many leaders on the same line. With paragraph styles (described in Chapter 8), it's easy to have different setups for different purposes. Sometimes, it seems like it would be simpler to merely add lines with the Line tool, but those lines do not flow with the copy. In the long run, it takes much more time to draw them.

Design Facing Tabs

There are times when you want two text blocks to face each other, with the left block flush right and the right block flush left. This is an arrangement I call *facing tabs*. Here, you need two tabs: a flush-right tab for the left side and a flush-left tab for the right side. You type a tab, then the left copy, then another tab, and then the right copy.

Figure 7-6 shows a couple of examples of facing tabs. The top example uses bullets for the leader in the second tab. The more common use for this type of arrangement is for numbered or lettered lists, where you need to deal with numbers or letters that vary in width, as shown in the second example in the figure.

TIP   *Uses for indents and tabs are limited only by your creativity. Simply keep this idea in the back of your mind:* The solution to this might be a tab. *File it next to this thought:* There is no excuse for hitting the SPACEBAR more than once.

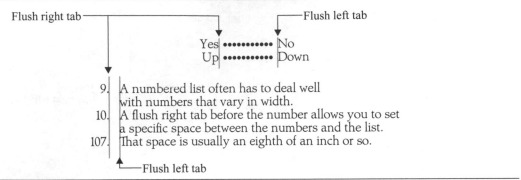

Facing tab arrangements are used for blocks that face each other.

Handle Indents and Tabs in Modified Text Frames

As you learned in Chapter 5, you can modify text frames with the Direct Selection tool and Pen tool. However, if you change the left side of the frame so that it is no longer a vertical line, and you want to use indents or tabs, you will need to do some extra work.

For example, you will need to make adjustments for alignment if you make the left side of your text frame curved. Tabs are measured from the bounding box, not the edge of the frame itself.

Figure 7-7 shows an example of how I used a curved text frame. If you look closely at the hidden characters, you will see that I needed to abandon tabs on these pages entirely. The hanging indents are made with different combinations of em, en, thin, and hair spaces. It was a little tedious, but the result was worth it.

Get a Quick Flush-Right Tab

Sometimes, you need a quick flush-right tab, and you don't want to take the time to set up one in the Tabs palette. With a special character, you can add a right-aligned tab at the right indent. This makes it easier to set tabbed text that exactly spans an entire column.

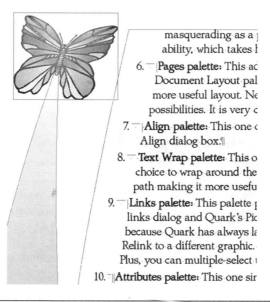

masquerading as a ¡
ability, which takes I

6. ⌐ Pages palette: This ac
Document Layout pal
more useful layout. Ne
possibilities. It is very c

7. ⌐ Align palette: This one c
Align dialog box.¶

8. ⌐ Text Wrap palette: This o
choice to wrap around the
path making it more usefu

9. ⌐ Links palette: This palette ¡
links dialog and Quark's Pic
because Quark has always la
Relink to a different graphic.
Plus, you can multiple-select ¡

10. ⌐ Attributes palette: This one sir

FIGURE 7-7   A curved left frame edge requires special space characters (em, en, thin, and hair spaces) to give the appearance of indents and tabs.

Right-indent tabs are different from regular tabs. A right-indent tab aligns all subsequent text to the right edge of the text frame. If the same paragraph includes any tabs after the right-indent tab, those tabs and their text are pushed to the next line.

 **Insert a Quick Right-Indent Tab**

To set a right-indent tab, follow these steps:

1. Use the Type tool to click an insertion point where you want the flush-right copy to begin.

2. Choose Type | Insert Special Character | Right Indent Tab, or right-click and select that option from the Type context menu.

You can also insert a right-indent tab character by pressing SHIFT-TAB with the insertion point active.

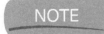 *A right-indent tab is very different from a right paragraph indent. A right paragraph indent value moves the* entire *right edge of the paragraph away from the right edge of the text frame or column. The right-indent tab special character aligns the rest of the paragraph with the right indent, whatever you set it to be.*

A right-indent tab is a special character available through the Type menu (or Type context menu), not the Tabs palette. Therefore, a right-indent tab cannot be part of a paragraph style.

Set Up Professional-Looking Indents

With indents, again, we run into one of the major differences between nonprofessional word processing and typesetting. It is not that indents cannot be made with most word processors. In truth, word processors have most of the controls that InDesign has available. The problem is that indents are much clumsier to set up in a word processor than in InDesign.

Visually, InDesign has its indent settings on the Tabs palette. On the left side of the ruler, you see two right triangles. The lower one is the left indent. If you move it, the upper one moves along with it. The upper triangle is the first-line indent. It can move independently of the lower-left indent. The left and right indents work much as you expect (as long as you remember that they are measured from the edges of the text frame, frame insets, or column sides).

 You can also simply type the indents you need in the Paragraph palette or Control palette.

Understand First-line Indents: Positive and Negative

A concept that some people have trouble understanding is how a first-line indent is measured. A first-line indent is not measured from the column or frame edge; it is measured from the left indent.

The first-line indent can be either positive or negative. The norm is a positive number that indents the first line farther to the right. But a negative number indents the first line less than the rest of the paragraph. A positive first-line indent is set off to the right from the left indent. A negative first-line indent is set off to the left of the left indent. It's important to remember that these indents use the *left indent* as their starting point.

Here is an example of a negative first-line indent:

Negative first line – As you can see, this looks a bit strange because you are used to seeing all the lines in a paragraph line up to the same margin or having the first line indented to the right a little. The left indent grabs your attention. But, because the first line just runs into the paragraph the impact is weakened. It looks unprofessional.

And the following shows what I did to create the example. I set the left indent to 0.75 inch and the first-line indent to −0.75 inch (or three-quarters inch to the left).

Make Hanging Indents

A *hanging indent* is another specially crafted paragraph style to help the reader know what is important in your copy. The first line can be as large negatively as the left indent is large positively. In other words, a left indent of 1 inch and a first-line indent of −1 inch would start the first line exactly on the margin, but every other line in that paragraph would be indented 1 inch.

However, a negative first-line indent, by itself, is not a hanging indent. A hanging indent sets a tab for the first line that matches the left indent to produce formats such as bulleted or numbered lists. Here is an example of a hanging indent (the dingbat is a capital *E* from Webdings):

> Hanging indent with a tab at left margin: This time everything is neat and tidy. This is why hanging indents work so well. First of all, they are much neater and tidier. We normally like to see things lined up on the left side. The large left indent attracts our attention. Secondly, a hanging indent greatly emphasizes the bullet, graphic, or dingbat so that the eye is further drawn to the paragraphs involved. They do attract attention.

The tab added to make this hanging indent is directly on top of the left indent at 0.75 inch.

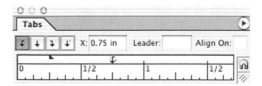

Because the left tab is exactly on top of the left margin, matching the left indent of the rest of the paragraph, everything before the tab hangs off to the left of the left margin. This way, the hanging characters serve to grab the reader's attention and direct it to the paragraph. The left indent provides the white space to the left of the paragraph that makes this work.

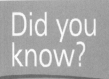

Bulleted Lists Attract Attention

Bulleted lists are one of the better devices used to attract readers. Surveys have conclusively shown that bulleted or numbered lists are third or fourth in attractiveness, right after captions, heads, and possibly pull quotes.

Why do bulleted lists get attention? Partly, it is the layout and the rhythm of the hanging characters. Partly, it is because we are all in a hurry and a list gives us hope of a synopsis, so we can determine if we need to read the material.

Use a Special Indent Character

You can use the Indent to Here special character to indent lines in a paragraph without regard to a paragraph's left-indent value. This special character is different from a normal left indent in several ways. The Indent to Here character is part of the text flow, as if it were a visible character. If text reflows, the indent moves with it. It affects all lines after the line where you've added the special Indent to Here character. This enables you to indent just some of the lines in a paragraph.

NOTE   *If you place more than one Indent to Here character on a line, InDesign uses the one farthest to the right.*

Insert an Indent to Here Character

To add an Indent to Here character, follow these steps:

1. Use the Type tool to click an insertion point where you would like to indent.

2. Choose Type | Insert Special Character | Indent to Here from the Type menu or the Type context menu.

The Indent to Here character looks like the dagger character (a cross) when you turn on hidden characters.

Use Paragraph Rules for Emphasis and Direction

One of the unique capabilities of page layout software is the ability to add paragraph rules above and below any paragraph. These rules may appear simple, but they are actually very powerful.

To create a paragraph rule, select the Paragraph Rules option on the Paragraph palette's option menu. You will see the Paragraph Rules dialog box, shown in Figure 7-8.

Here are some facts about the paragraph rules you can set up using InDesign's options:

- They can be very large. A rule can be up to 1,000 points wide (a little less than 14 inches).

- They each can offset up or down as far as you like. Actually, the limit is plus or minus 18 inches.

- They can be as wide as you want. The actual limit is plus or minus 120 inches. You can set them to the width of the column or the width of the text, but the left and right indents can be measured plus or minus from either the right or the left.

- They can be any color, including gradients. You will need to add the gradient to the Swatches palette to use it, though. The gaps of the dotted or dashed stroke styles can be any other color you like.

- They can be any type of line. You can use any kind of dotted, dashed, or striped stroke style your fertile imagination can develop in the Stroke palette's option menu.

- They are layered. The above rule is at the bottom, the below rule is on top of that, and the type is on top of both of them. So, it is easy to make light type reversed on a dark box.

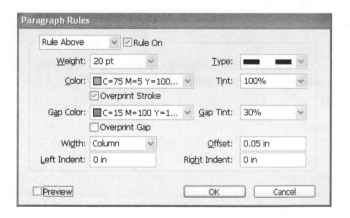

FIGURE 7-8   The Paragraph Rules dialog box contains some powerful options.

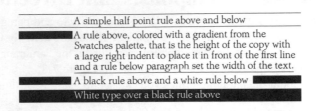

FIGURE 7-9   You can create various types of paragraph rules.

Using paragraph rules, you can automatically make square bullets of any color or lines that shoot the entire way across the page (even if the type column is only a couple inches wide). You might add rules to set off graphics like product shots, or simply to add extra emphasis and spacing to certain types of special paragraphs like pull quotes. Figure 7-9 shows some examples of various kinds of paragraph rules.

It does take a while to set up rules as you want them to look. This is why they are usually part of a paragraph style. You will learn how to set up paragraph styles in the next chapter.

Control How Paragraphs Fit in Text Frames

Another powerful feature of InDesign is the ability to control almost every aspect of how your paragraphs fit within a text frame. If you choose Options | Text Frame Options, you see the dialog box shown in Figure 7-10.

The Text Frame Options dialog box lets you set many options and preview how they will affect your text:

- **Columns**   Set the number of columns and the gutter between the columns, how wide you want the columns to be, and if you want them to be a fixed width.

- **Inset Spacing**   Set text insets from the frame edge on all four sides.

- **First Baseline**   Set where you want the first baseline in the frame to start. You can offset by ascent, leading, cap height, x-height, or fixed. (You may need to experiment with these settings to get the look you want.)

- **Vertical Justification**   Control the vertical justification of all the copy in the frame. There are four alignments: top, bottom, middle, and justified. Justified vertical alignment is used to add space between all of the lines of text to make the top and bottom of the column line up with the frame edge's top and bottom. If you change the maximum space between paragraphs, the paragraph spacing will justify as far as possible first, and then line spacing will be added as needed.

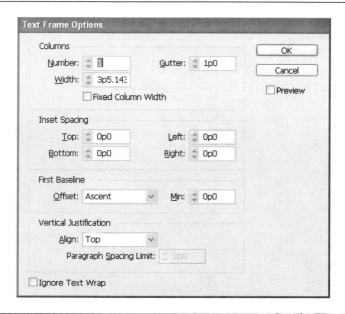

7

The Text Frame Options dialog box lets you take control of how your
paragraphs fit in text frames.

NOTE

*Many designers think that excellence in typesetting means that the tops and bottoms
of all columns align across the pages, vertically justified or snapped to a baseline grid.
Personally, I think the vertically justified spacing is worse than the irregular column
bottoms and that horizontal-line alignment looks too rigid and boring.*

- ■ **Ignore Text Wrap**   Lets the selected frame ignore any text wraps that are pushing it
  around.

I usually use the Text Frame Options dialog box for insets and vertical justification (which is
the most important control in this dialog box). This is the only place these controls are available.

Now that you have been introduced to all of the typographic controls, you're ready to learn how
to set up paragraph and character styles. They are the most important aspect of production speed
and formatting control of your documents.

Chapter 8

Format Your Document Using Styles

How to...

■ Define paragraph styles

■ Use paragraph styles

■ Set up your character styles

■ Use character styles

■ Make a table of contents or an automatic list

■ Practice your formatting skills

■ Set up your default styles

This chapter is the core of the book, because it talks about the core of page layout: paragraph styles and character styles. InDesign's Paragraph Styles and Character Styles palettes allow you to have page layouts that are both consistent and flexible. The major advantage of using paragraph styles is global control over the entire document. If you decide that you just don't like Baskerville font for this project and want to use Caslon, simply change the relevant style, and the entire document changes automatically.

Style palettes are a collection of specialized typographic defaults that can be accessed at the click of a mouse or stroke of a key. You can set up styles for headlines, subheads, body copy, hanging indents, bylines, captions, tabular matter, or whatever you desire or imagine. (Just keep your style list as simple as possible.)

It is possible to have a set of styles that apply to virtually all situations. All it takes is a little thought and some planning.

Define Paragraph Styles for Global Document Control

You can create and apply styles using the Paragraph Styles palette. All of the styles you create are listed in the Paragraph Styles palette in alphabetical order. Figure 8-1 shows an example of a Paragraph Styles palette with a set of styles.

Because they are paragraph styles, they are applied to the paragraph as a whole. This means that all you need to do is place an insertion point anywhere in the paragraph and click the style in the Paragraph Styles palette to apply it (or press the shortcut you have chosen).

Because it provides the ability to reformat documents globally, the Paragraph Styles palette is indispensable. You should always use it, unless you are setting only one or two lines of type (in which case, you are probably in FreeHand, Illustrator, or Photoshop anyway). In addition, styles ensure consistency.

What Styles Do You Need?

The two main type elements on pages are body copy and heads. So, you will need a set of styles for the various parts of your body copy and a set of styles for your different level headings.

FIGURE 8-1   The Paragraph Styles palette lists the paragraph styles you've defined.

Body Copy Styles

Typically, you use a serif face for the body copy styles and a sans serif font for the head styles. *Body copy* refers to everything that is formatted in the basic serif font family used by the bulk of the readable words of your manuscript or word processing file.

There are several styles of body copy elements, which are used in almost every document, that need to be on every Paragraph Styles palette:

- **Body copy**   The style for your basic readable materials. Normally, you use a serif font, 10/12, with a first-line indent. Invitations use a script face 18/24. Posters use around 20/22 for their body copy. It all depends on reading distance.

- **Hanging body**   This style is used within the body copy to deal with lists of concepts, ideas, and so forth. Hanging body styles include bulleted lists (like this list of body copy styles), numbered lists, definition lists, and so forth.

NOTE   *As noted in Chapter 7, bullets and numbered lists are one of the most important factors in readability and used for recapturing the readers' attention. Readers use these lists as a synopsis. Normally, they are created as hanging indents, with the left indent equal to the first-line indent of the body copy.*

- **Quotes**   There often needs to be a special style to handle long quotations of materials, using different indents and often a different alignment. However, it is usually in the same font and size as regular body copy. Commonly, the left indent and the right indent are the same size as the first-line indent of the body copy.

- **Captions**   Captions are probably the most important part of your copy. They, too, are usually based on the style of your body copy because of its readability. They are usually a little larger than the body copy, maybe 12/13, without a first-line indent.

- **Bylines**   Using a standard style, based on your body copy, for bylines is an excellent method of maintaining consistency. However, modern usage often uses bylines that are a small subhead, coupled with a bio at the end of the article in a modification of the subhead styles. These styles vary.

- **Forms paragraphs**   These are paragraphs, again built on the body copy style, that contain the tabular setups necessary for filling in information needed by the client. Setting up forms is discussed in Chapter 7.

- **Body heads**   These are small subheadings that are really boldface body paragraphs with several explanatory body copy paragraphs between. They are the same as the body copy, but bold. They are usually the third or fourth level of subhead.

You will be using a couple of these styles in every project. The rest are determined by the type of job at hand.

Headline Styles

Headlines are used to grab readers' attention as they page through your final printed materials. As such, they are normally brief, focused topic statements about the material that follows. In most cases, heads are eight words or less (like a billboard).

 I am aware (and I agree) with David Ogilvey's position that headlines can actually be quite long. This is particularly true in the context of ads that are presented as tightly focused posters in a magazine spread.

Headline styles are more concerned with legibility rather than readability. Sans serif fonts are easier to grasp quickly, but they are very poor for reading in large doses. As with body copy styles, there are several headline styles that are used in almost all documents:

- **Headline**   This is the style used as the opening attention-grabber for a story, article, chapter, poster, ad, or flyer. Heads are usually very bold. Sizes vary by reading distance. For example, newsletters may use 30/30 left or centered. Posters need 100-point to 300-point type (it must be readable easily from many yards away).

- **Subhead 1**   This style has the same basic purpose as the headline, but it is used to indicate the beginning of more important sections within the story, article, chapter, poster, ad, or flyer. The size should be 60 to 80 percent of the head's size, maybe 16/17 for a newsletter or brochure.

- **Subhead 2**   These lesser headers are used as lead-ins for important points in ads, posters, and flyers. They are also used as lead headlines for subsections of the sections delineated by the first-level subheads. The size should be 40 to 60 percent of the head size, maybe 14/15 for a newsletter or brochure.

- **Subhead 3**   This level of headlines is usually used only in books, longer articles, and stories. Often, body heads serve this purpose. These are almost always flush left, a couple points larger than the body copy, maybe 12/13 for pieces held in your hand to read.

- **Kicker**   This style is for a small introductory statement leading into a relatively important headline or subhead. Kickers are mainly used in newspapers, but they can be effective in indicating the most important article on a page of several articles. These are small, often underlined, often in all caps or small caps, maybe 9 to 11 points in the same font as the head or subhead.

- **Pull quote or callout**   This style may be necessary for newsletters, magazines, and books. Pull quotes or callouts need to be very dramatic, usually italic or a different font, often with rules before and after, outsized quotes, or color. Pull quotes are used as graphics to reattract wandering readers.

Of course, this does not cover it all. You will probably need a different set of headline and body styles for your sidebars (these may even be in a complete set of styles using a third font family). You may have special column headers, chapter heads, questions, or footnotes. Most documents need a couple of special styles, as you will see in the writing sample shown in the "Make a Conscious Effort to Use Paragraph Styles" section later in this chapter. The key is to leave room in your standard Paragraph Styles palette for these special styles.

8

TIP   *Simplify and streamline your styles. There is no need for dozens of styles. You will never remember them all. Except for books, newsletters, and the like, you should rarely use more than 8 to 10 styles. More than that, and you'll lose consistency—that great typographic virtue.*

Create New Paragraph Styles

To create a new style, choose New Style from the Paragraph palette's option menu. This opens the New Paragraph Style dialog box, shown in Figure 8-2.

Another way to create a new style is to click the tiny document icon at the bottom of the Paragraph Styles palette. This adds a new style to the palette, based on the specifications of the paragraph where your insertion point is located. It will be called Paragraph Style 1 (for the first one), and you can double-click the style to open the Paragraph Style Options dialog box (which is the same as the New Paragraph Style dialog box).

TIP   *You may want to pick a keyboard shortcut for opening the New Paragraph Style dialog box. Choose Edit | Keyboard Shortcuts and choose Palette Menus in the Product Area drop-down list. You will find this dialog box listed under Other, alphabetically.*

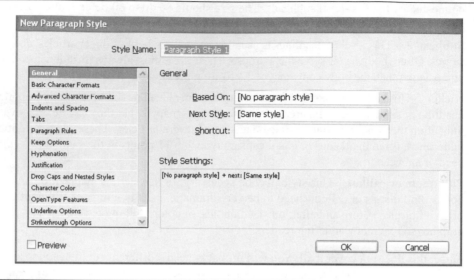

FIGURE 8-2   Create a style using the New Paragraph Style dialog box.

We'll begin with the important settings on the General page of the New Paragraph Style dialog box.

Name Your Styles

Your first choice is what to name your style. The simple trick I have learned is to number my styles, such as 1-Body Copy, 2-Hanging Body, and so on.

If you look at the lists of body copy styles and headline styles in the previous section, you will see that there are four styles that are used in every project: body copy, hanging body, headline, and subhead 1. In addition, there are five more styles built on the body copy style and four more built on the headline style, plus a few others. Numbering the styles not only puts them in a standard order in the Paragraph Styles palette, but it also can show you what the shortcut is for that style.

Remember that consistency is the most important consideration. You need to have the same styles with the same names for all of your documents. This way, you can easily remember them and apply them without conscious thought.

Base Styles on Other Styles

The Based On option in the New Paragraph Style dialog box lets you base your new style on any other style. This means that when you change the first style, all the styles based on that style change also. The only attributes that do not change are the specific changes in the derivative styles.

In well-designed documents, all the headlines and subheads are tied together; all the body copy, hanging indents, bulleted lists, bylines, captions, and so on are tied together; and all the sidebar heads, sidebar body copy, and special paragraphs are tied together. This means that the look of the entire document can often be controlled by simple changes to two or three styles.

If all the heads are based on the headline style, and all the copy is based on the body copy style, an entire document can be reflowed by simply changing those two styles. This saves a lot of time on one- and two-page documents. You can imagine how much time it saves in 100-page booklets.

Specify the Next Style

To increase the efficiency of applying styles, using the Next Style option, you can set up any style to change to another style when you press the RETURN key. For example, you can have every head, subhead, and specialized style automatically return to the body text when the RETURN key is struck. This happens, on average, three times a page. It takes three seconds to pick up the mouse and click the Paragraph Styles palette. So, if you were writing a 200-page document, you could save approximately 600 seconds, or 10 minutes, with this simple default.

Set the Style Shortcut

The Shortcut field is where you make your shortcut for your styles. This is where the real power is, as far as production speed is concerned. InDesign has some limits here. You can use only the numbers on the numeric keypad for your shortcuts, along with any combination of three modifiers. Windows systems use CTRL, ALT, and SHIFT as the modifier keys, in any combination. Mac systems use the COMMAND, OPTION, and SHIFT keys. (No, InDesign will not allow you to use the CONTROL key on a Mac for these shortcuts.) That gives you 60 possible shortcuts. I never use more than 30 styles: 20 paragraph styles and 10 character styles.

The important thing to remember when setting up your styles is consistency throughout all your documents. For example, I use COMMAND-6 for my headline style, COMMAND-3 for the hanging indent style, COMMAND-7 for a second-level subhead, and so on.

If I am doing a poster, my main head is COMMAND-6, and my body copy (limited though it is) will be COMMAND-2. After I key in the copy, it is a matter of a few seconds or a couple of minutes to reflow and set up the entire poster, changing 2-Body and its subsets to 24 points, for example. This greatly speeds up my work, because I think headline, and my fingers press COMMAND-6, without conscious thought.

8

For example, here are the styles and shortcuts in my default Paragraph Styles palette:

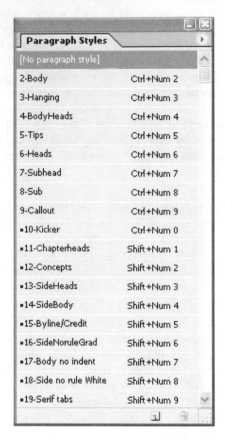

Notice that I added bullets in front of the style names for styles after number 9. (The character will vary with the operating system you are using.) If I didn't do that, styles 10 through 19 would appear before 2-Body.

For all of my documents, paragraph styles 2, 3, 6, 7, 8, ~13, and ~14 remain the same. The sidebar styles actually serve as a sans serif body copy set. Styles 3 through 5, ~11, and ~12 are all based on 2-Body. Styles 7, 8, ~10, and ~13 are all based on 6-Heads. All the sidebar copy is based on ~14. I can change the fonts for the entire document by simply changing 2-Body, 6-Heads, and ~14-SideBody—talk about global document control!

It is important that you find a palette setup that works for you. When you use a standard palette, looking for the miscellaneous styles is simple, because they are always in the same place. Also, if you always use the same basic palette, you will find that the shortcuts are quickly added to your publishing design repertoire. You will be able to format with styles habitually.

Format Your Style

The other pages in the New Paragraph Style dialog box are where you can format your style:

- The Basic Character Formats and Advanced Character Formats pages cover everything in the Character palette.

- The Indents and Spacing page has most of the options from the Paragraph palette. The rest are on other pages of the New Paragraph Style dialog box.

- The Tabs page offers the complete Tabs palette.

- The Paragraph Rules, Keep Options, Hyphenation, Justification, OpenType Features, Underline Options, and Strikethrough Options pages add all of the capabilities from the option menus of the Paragraph and Character palettes.

- The Drop Caps and Nested Styles page offers some enhanced drop caps options and the brand-new nested styles. You can now automatically apply any character style to your drop cap. This allows you to automatically change the font, color, or anything else available in a character style. Nested styles allow you to automatically format character styles within your paragraph styles. Nested styles are covered in the next section.

- The Character Color page lets you make characters any color possible, both their fill and stroke, as long as it is in the Swatches palette. The necessity of the Swatches palette is not a limitation. It is a safety device that I will discuss in Chapter 13.

Use Nested Styles

Using the new nested styles feature, you can automate your formatting even more by adding character style definitions into your paragraph style definitions. Figure 8-3 shows the Drop Caps and Nested Styles page of the New Paragraph Style dialog box. As it says in the box under Nested Styles, you click the New Nested Style button to create a nested style.

Then you can pick any character style and apply it to words in the paragraph style by specifying the number of words (through or up to) and picking a place to end the style. You have 15 choices for how to end a nested style:

- **Sentences**   InDesign looks for periods, question marks, and exclamation marks that indicate the end of a sentence. If a quotation mark follows the punctuation, it is included as part of the sentence.

- **Words**   InDesign looks for any space or white space character that indicates the end of a word.

- **Characters**   InDesign counts the characters. Any character other than zero-width markers is included. *Zero-width markers* are characters like anchors, index markers, XML tags, and so on. Ligatures are counted as a single character.

- **Letters**   InDesign counts all characters except punctuation, white space, digits, and symbols.

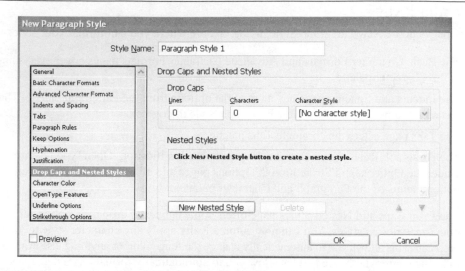

FIGURE 8-3   The Drop Caps and Nested Styles page

- **Digits**   InDesign counts the Arabic numerals 0 through 9.

- **End Nested Style Character**   InDesign extends the nested style up to or through the End Nested Style special character you insert. To insert this character, choose Type | Insert Special Character | End Nested Style. If you are showing hidden characters, it looks like a backslash.

- **Tab Character, Forced Line Break (soft return), Indent to Here Character, Em Space, En Space, or Non-breaking Space**   InDesign extends the nested style up to or through the character chosen.

- **Inline Graphic Marker**   InDesign extends the nested style up to or through an inline graphic marker. When you place a graphic into text, this marker appears in the word processor.

- **Auto Page Number or Section Marker**   InDesign extends the nested style up to or through the automatic page number or section name marker. This includes automatic jump numbers.

You can add as many nested styles as you want to your paragraph style. The only limit is your imagination. For example, you could have a paragraph style—say, 10-point, Caslon Regular, black—with nested styles for 12-point Myriad Bold Semi-extended, red, up to the colon; then 11-point Caslon Italic, maroon, through the em dash (the End Nested Style Character used as the delimiter); then 10-point Myriad Semi-extended Regular, black, until the tab.

How to ... Add a Nested Style to a Paragraph Style

To use a nested style to add a character style to your paragraph style, follow these steps:

1. Click the New Nested Style button. A nested style is added to the Nested Styles list box.

2. Click [No character style]. You can pick any character style for the nested style.

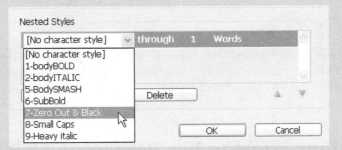

3. Click Through, and a pop-up appears giving you the choice of Through or Up To.

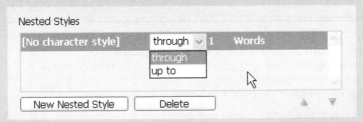

4. Click the number next to Through. It becomes a field into which you can type any number up to 999.

8

5. Click the field next to the number. A pop-up with 15 choices for ending the nested style appears.

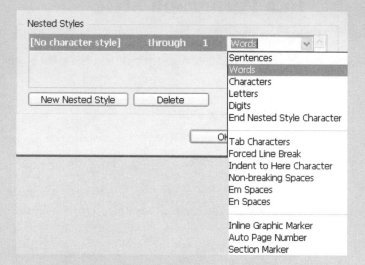

You can add more nested styles by clicking the New Nested Style button, or delete a nested style by selecting it and clicking the Delete button. The up and down arrows to the right allow you to shuffle the order of the nested styles.

Make a Conscious Effort to Use Paragraph Styles

Observe yourself as you work and add styles as you use them. Consciously try to set them up in a way that is logical and easy for you to remember. Do the best you can to keep the same styles in all of your documents, and you will find your formatting speed doubles or triples.

Using styles, you can genuinely make writing (or importing) and formatting text a semiautomatic procedure. The writing sample shown in Figure 8-4 demonstrates how this works.

To create the meeting notes shown in Figure 8-4, first I set up four styles:

- A Meeting style, with a Next Style of Topic
- A Topic style, with a Next Style of Speaker
- A Speaker style, with a Next Style of Location
- A Location style, with a Next Style of Meeting

After I set this up, I merely needed to select the style for the first meeting (1-Meeting), and everything else was formatted automatically. I just kept typing, and the returns caused the change to the new style. Using the paragraph style shortcut for the Meeting style made the work go even more quickly.

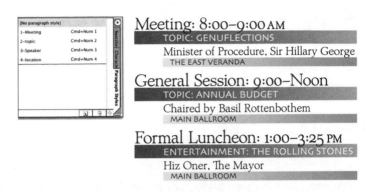

Meeting: 8:00–9:00 AM
TOPIC: GENUFLECTIONS
Minister of Procedure, Sir Hillary George
THE EAST VERANDA

General Session: 9:00–Noon
TOPIC: ANNUAL BUDGET
Chaired by Basil Rottenbothem
MAIN BALLROOM

Formal Luncheon: 1:00–3:25 PM
ENTERTAINMENT: THE ROLLING STONES
Hiz Oner, The Mayor
MAIN BALLROOM

FIGURE 8-4   The styles in this Paragraph Styles palette were used to produce the text on the right, automatically.

8

I set up all of the formatting you see in the meeting notes in Figure 8-4—the white type in the first paragraph rule; the size, length, and color of the rules; the indents; the spaces before and after paragraphs; the font changes; the size changes; and all the rest—in the four paragraph styles. This gives you an idea of how much variety you can build into a style.

As you can see, having a set of styles can save you a great deal of time. Using a well-set-up Paragraph Styles palette, you will be able to write and format as fast as you can type.

Another problem solved elegantly by the use of styles is the common one of needing to have a certain amount of pages. For example, you might end up with a little more than 16 pages of copy in a saddle-stitched booklet, but not nearly 20 pages. The number of pages must be divisible by four in saddle stitching, so you are forced to cut to 16 pages or stretch to 20. With a Paragraph Styles palette adjustment, you can simply cut the leading of the body copy style by a half point and save several inches (every 72 lines saves half an inch if you cut the leading a half point).

NOTE
If you no longer need a style, you can easily remove it from the style palette. Just select the style and click the little trashcan icon at the bottom of the palette. You can also drag-and-drop a style onto the trashcan to get rid of it.

Copy Your Styles from an Existing Document

Another powerful use of the Paragraph Styles palette is to copy styles from an existing document into a new one. The only requirement is that the styles in the existing document have the same names as the styles you want to bring in. Only the names need to be the same; everything else about the styles can be different.

You can simply import copy from a word processor that has styles with the same names as the style palettes you are using. Then copy the styles from the template, and the chapter reflows in the new format.

 **Make a Standard Set of Styles**

Copying styles is the easiest method of adding a standard set of default styles. Once you determine your normal use, close all open documents, and then go to either the Paragraph Styles palette or the Character Styles palette and choose Load All Styles from its option menu. They will become your standard styles in all new documents.

To copy styles, just open the Paragraph Styles palette's option menu and choose the Load All Styles command. In fact, you don't even need to import the styles. If you have your style palettes set up with styles of the same names, the existing styles automatically change to match those in the palettes. A quick check for widows, orphans, and similar problems, applying character styles where needed, and the copy is formatted!

Work with Imported Styles

If you have a client who knows enough to use styles while writing the copy you will be using, you are in good shape. When you place the supplied file, all the styles will be added to your style palettes. They will have a little icon of a floppy disk (as a reminder of days long past where people actually still used floppies).

All you need to do is double-click the style to open the Paragraph Style Options dialog box. After you set up the style as you want, add a shortcut, and close the dialog box, the floppy will be gone. And you will know that you have made the style your own.

Get Rid of Local Formatting

One of the biggest temptations to new designers is to attempt to fix small problems or create specialized paragraphs by applying formatting options directly from the Character palette or Paragraph palette. This is called *local formatting*, because it affects only the paragraphs, or the copy in the paragraphs, selected at the time. The problem is that locally formatted type is not reformatted when you make changes to your styles (through the Paragraph Styles and Character Styles palettes).

You will often see a little plus sign (+) after a style's name in the Paragraph Styles palette. You can see one after the 7-Subhead 1 style in Figure 8-1, shown earlier in the chapter. This means that there is local formatting somewhere in that paragraph. To remove the local formatting, select the style and ALT/COMMAND-click the style. If there is also a character style involved, the plus sign may not go away. Then you add the SHIFT key (ALT/COMMAND-SHIFT-click) to eliminate local formatting plus any character styles.

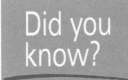

Local Formatting Is Only for Cleanup

There is a time and place for local formatting. It's appropriate for eliminating widows and orphans and for adjusting vertical justification. The rule is this: *Use local formatting only for final cleanup.*

All local formatting should be done last, if possible. Its appropriate function is massaging the copy into its final configuration. Even then, it should be done very sparingly. Extensive local adjustments can make simple reflow a nightmare that costs you an amazing amount of extra time and aggravation. Our world is stressed enough without self-inflicted pressures.

Set Up Your Character Styles to Eliminate Local Formatting

In addition to its paragraph-styling power, InDesign offers a very powerful Character Styles palette, shown in Figure 8-5. This palette enables you to format selected text. It gives you global control over what used to be local formatting run-in heads (InDesign calls these nested styles), italicized periodical names, bolded proper names, body copy emphasis, and so on. It is meant as an addition to the Paragraph Styles palette. (Notice that these are the same styles offered for nested styles in the New Paragraph Styles dialog box.)

FIGURE 8-5   The Character Styles palette

Create New Character Styles

To create a new style, choose New Style from the Character Styles palette's option menu (you can set up a shortcut if you like). This opens the New Character Style dialog box, shown in Figure 8-6.

As you can see, the General page of this dialog box looks similar to the one for creating a new paragraph style. Give your character style a descriptive name. As I recommend for paragraph styles, numbering character styles has the advantage of arranging them and helping you to remember the shortcut key.

You can base your character style on another style. The other pages offer all of the options available from the Character palette and its option menu. You have control over which character attributes will be changed. Just change what is needed. Any attribute left blank will not be touched. So, you can make a character style that makes the selected copy bold and maroon, and leaves all of its other attributes the same as the rest of the paragraph, for example.

 *Be careful to remember what you are using. If you apply a Bold character style to a font that has only the Heavy style, you'll receive the dreaded pink box as a prize (showing that you have missing fonts, as explained in Chapter 2). Appropriate style names are crucial.*

You will also want to add shortcut keys for your character styles. In Figure 8-5, notice that I use the ALT/OPTION key as the modifier with all of my character styles. This gives me ten character

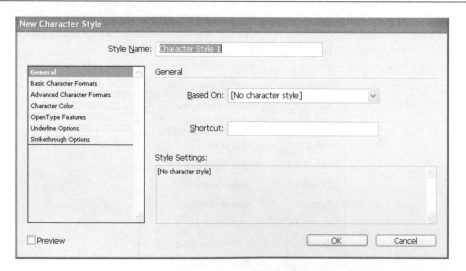

FIGURE 8-6   The New Character Style dialog box

styles, which is far more than I have ever needed. If I forget the shortcut key, I just open the relevant palette, and I can quickly see what the shortcut is by glancing at the number before the style name.

Use Character Styles

The Character Styles palette gives you global control of local formatting. If you change the character style, everything formatted with that style is changed also.

I have created six character styles for various purposes, mainly when I need to temporarily go to a different font, type color, or point size for some purpose. By doing all of my local formatting with the Character Styles palette, I retain global control over the formatting.

Make a Table of Contents or an Automatic List

One of the nice uses of styles is for making Tables of Contents (TOCs). The basic procedure is to pick the styles you want to use to make your TOC or list. Then InDesign gathers those styles, applies the styles you want to use for your list, and loads your cursor so you can place the newly gathered list wherever you want. The procedure takes a little time, but it is a lot quicker than hand gathering—or worse yet, handwriting.

Set Up TOC Styles

To set up your TOC styles, choose Layout | Table of Contents and click the More Options button. You will see the expanded dialog box shown in Figure 8-7.

It will help you a lot if you create the styles you are going to need for the TOC in advance. For example, I have created a TOC 7-TOCSub1 paragraph style. It uses smaller point sizes, tabs, leaders, and lighter fonts than my other styles. I also created a character style named 6-TOC#s for the TOC numbers, and I used 1bodyBOLD for my leaders.

There's a lot here. Let's work our way through:

- **TOC Style**   In the drop-down list, you can pick one of the TOC styles you have saved (saving your TOC style is described a bit later in this section).
- **Title**   You can pick the title for your TOC or list (or not).
- **Style**   You can pick a style from the styles available on the Paragraph Styles palette.
- **Styles in Table of Contents**   Here, you have two list boxes: Include Paragraph Styles and Other Styles. You double-click a style on the right to add it to the list on the left. If you like going slow, you can click a style, and then click the Add button. Actually, it is sometimes faster to SHIFT-select or CTRL/COMMAND-select styles, and then click the Add button to add them all at once.

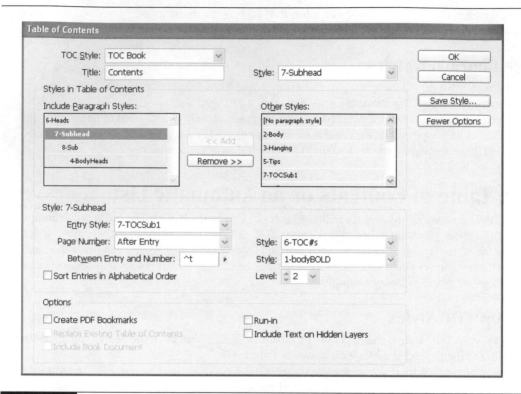

FIGURE 8-7 The Table of Contents dialog box

Once you have your styles added, you click them one at a time and set up what you want to happen when that style is collected.

- **Entry Style** This is the style that will be used for that paragraph in the collected list.
- **Page Number and Style** This specifies where the page number (if any) appears and its style. Your choices in the Page Number drop-down list are After Entry, Before Entry, or None.
- **Between Entry and Number and Style** You have 13 choices for the character to place between the TOC entry and the page number. (^t appears in the field when you choose the tab character.) Then you can pick a style, such as one that has a leader to go with a tab setting.

Bullet Character
Tab Character
Right Indent Tab
Forced Line Break
End Nested Style

Em Dash
Em Space
En Dash
En Space
Flush Space
Hair Space
Nonbreaking Space
Thin Space

Nonbreaking Hyphen

Once you have you the Table of Contents dialog box set up the way you like, you should save it so you can use the style elsewhere. (Again, it really helps if you have a standard set of styles you use.) To save the setup, click the Save Style button and give it a name (such as TOC), and then click the OK button.

InDesign will gather those paragraphs, apply the styles you have chosen, and load the cursor. Figure 8-8 shows an example.

If you make a mistake, simply open the Table of Contents dialog box again, make your changes, and check the Replace Existing Table of Contents option at the bottom of the dialog box. InDesign will make a new TOC and replace the one you already have in the document.

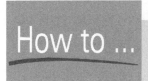

Make a List of Authors, Illustrations, Products, or Other Items

You can also use the Table of Contents dialog box (Layout | Table of Contents) to create lists. As with TOCs, you just specify the styles you want to collect into a list. So, if you have a separate style for bylines, captions, creators, products, or whatever, you can gather those items into a list.

Beyond that, you can place a text frame over each illustration with the artist's information, for example. You can then either put that text frame into a hidden layer or make it nonprinting by using the Attributes palette (covered in Chapter 14). The Table of Contents dialog box has a Sort Entries in Alphabetical Order check box and an Include Text on Hidden Layers check box. So, it is easy to make a list of illustrations and another list of artists that is alphabetized and that shows on which page the illustration can be found, for example.

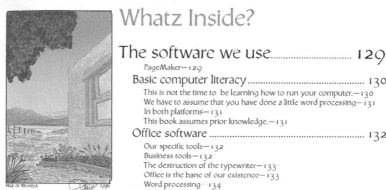

Whatz Inside?

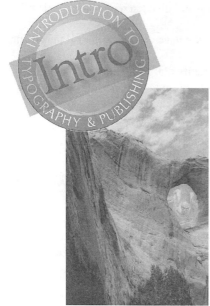

FIGURE 8-8   A sample TOC generated by InDesign after you specify the TOC styles

NOTE   *In Chapter 17, you will learn how to gather multiple documents into a book. You can make a TOC for that entire book.*

Import TOC Styles from Existing Documents

One of the real advantages of using a consistent set of styles becomes apparent when you want to import TOC styles from an existing document. Just choose Layout | Table of Contents Styles and click the Load button. Navigate to the document that has the styles you want to import, and click Open.

The only problem is if you are asking for styles that do not exist in the new document. If there are any, you will need to spend some time fixing your styles.

Practice Your Formatting Skills

To practice what you've learned so far, you can work through the example in this section. Here are a few things to be aware of before you begin:

- To set the shortcuts for the styles in Windows, you *must* have Num Lock on. Otherwise it won't work.

- For the character style, you may need to use CTRL-ALT for your shortcut, depending on which version of Windows you are using.

TIP   *If you do not want to type in the copy, go to http://kumo.swcp.com/graphics/pneumatika and click the DTP200 InDesign CS class.*

You should read the instructions before you start this exercise.

> Formatting a document
> Copy the type out of here — starting with the "Formatting a document" headline above. From here on down, simply follow the instructions as you make this document.
> Open new document:
> Set page size at 6" × 10", tall, margins at .5", single column
> Set up paragraph styles:
> Here, you need to set up your Paragraph Styles palette. Start by selecting all the styles and deleting them (by using the palette's option menu). Then make a new style and call it 2-body. We've talked about the reasons for numbering the styles. Each style is just a listing of specs. You will make five styles in all.
> 2-Body Georgia, 10/auto, left justified, 1st line indent .4", tracking 0, Metrics kerning, based on No Style, next style same, 2 points before paragraph (type p2 in the field), black, shortcut Command/Control-Num 2

8

3-Hanging Select 2-Body in the palette and choose new style (making it based on 2-Body), flush left, small caps, leading 11, horizontal scale 90%, left indent .4", 1st line -.25", tab left 1", 7 points before paragraph, shortcut Command/Ctrl-Num 3

5-Headline Select no style and make new style, Trebuchet Bold, 24/24, flush left, Metrics kerning, no indents, based on no style, next style 2-Body, 4 points before paragraph, 1 point after, Color: 30% gray, shortcut Command/Ctrl-Num 5

6-Subhead Based on 5-Headline, 16/17, all caps, left indent .4", rule below paragraph, 5 point, 50% gray, offset 2 points, width of column, color: black, shortcut Command/Ctrl-Num 6

7-Sub2 Based on 6-Subhead, 12/12, no rules; Command/Ctrl-Num 7

Set up character styles:

Now, you need to set up a character style to make the style names bold. So, open the Character Styles palette and choose New Style in the option menu. Make the name of the style 1-Bold:

1-Bold: Style, Bold — leave all the other fields blank. All we are changing is the weight of the font. If the fields are blank, nothing is changed when you apply the style. Shortcut: Alt/Option-Num 1

Format the type:

Place your insertion point by click-dragging a text frame to fit the margins. Paste in the copied text. Select All and press Ctrl/Command-Num2 to format everything in body copy. Then place your insertion point in the first paragraph and hold down the Ctrl/Command key. Then type the following string of characters — slowly and methodically, while continuing to hold down the Ctrl/Command key.

5-down arrow-2-down arrow-6-down arrow-2-
down arrow-6-down arrow-2-down arrow-3-down arrow-
3-down arrow-3-down arrow-3-down arrow-3-down arrow-6-down arrow-2-down arrow-3-down arrow-6-down arrow-2-down arrow-7-down arrow-2-down arrow-6

Select the style names and format them with the character style.

Now everything is formatted nicely — and should fit perfectly.

Figure 8-9 shows the finished product resulting from your formatting sample.

Formatting a document

Copy the type out of here — starting with the "Formatting a Document" Headline above. From here on down, simply follow the instructions as you make this document.

OPEN NEW DOCUMENT

Set page size at 6" × 10", tall, margins at .5", single column

SET UP PARAGRAPH STYLES:

Here you need to set up your Paragraph Styles palette. Start by selecting all the styles and deleting them (by using the Option menu off the palette). Then make a new style and call it 2-body. We've talked about the reasons for numbering the styles. Each style is just a listing of specs. You will make five styles in all.

2-Body Georgia, 10/auto, left justified, 1st line indent .4", tracking 0, Metrics kerning, based on No Style, next style same, 2 points before paragraph (type p2 in the field), black, shortcut Command/Control-Num 2

3-Hanging Select 2-body in palette and choose new style (making it based on 2-body), flush left, small caps, leading 11, horizontal scale 90%, left indent .4", 1st line -.25", tab left 1", 7 points before paragraph, shortcut Command/Ctrl-Num 3

5-Headline Select no style and make new style, Trebuchet Bold, 24/24, flush left , Metrics kerning, no indents, based on no style, next style 2-Body, 4 points before paragraph, 1 point after, Color: 50% gray, shortcut Command/Ctrl-Num 5

6-Subhead Based on 5-Headline, 16/17, all caps, left indent .4", rule below paragraph, 5 point, 30% gray, offset 2 points, width of column, color: black, shortcut Command/Ctrl-Num 6

7-Sub2 Based on 6-Subhead, 12/12, no rules; Command/Ctrl-Num 7

SET UP CHARACTER STYLES:

Now you need to set up a character style to make the style names bold. So, open the Character styles palette and choose New Style in the Options menu. Make the name of the style 1-Bold:

1-Bold: Style, Bold — leave all the other fields blank. All we are changing is the weight of the font. If the fileds are blank, nothing is changed when you apply the style.. Shortcut: Alt/Option-Num 1

FORMAT THE TYPE

Place your insertion point by click-dragging a text frame to fit the margins. Paste in the copied text. Select All and press Ctrl/Command-Num2 to format everything in body copy. Then place your insertion point in the first paragraph and hold done the Ctrl/Command key. Then type the following string of characters — slowly and methodically while continuing to hold down the Ctrl/Command key.

5-down arrow--2-down arrow-6-down arrow-2-down arrow-6-down arrow-2-down arrow-3-down arrow-3-down arrow-3-down arrow-3-down arrow-6-down arrow-2-down arrow-3-down arrow-6-down arrow-2-down arrow-7-down arrow-2-down arrow-6

Select the Style names and format them with the character style.

NOW EVERYTHING IS FORMATTED NICELY — AND SHOULD FIT PERFECTLY.

8

FIGURE 8-9 An example created using InDesign's formatting capabilities

Set Up Your Default Styles

Now that you know how to use the Paragraph Styles and Character Styles palettes, you need to set up your default styles. The largest problem with using the style palettes is simply the time it takes to set them up. Some designers have a mental block with this sort of thing. Somehow, they have the idea that formatting copy is done by underlings, as if it were some sort of production busywork that has little to do with "true design" (whatever that is).

If you leave this part of design to your assistants, all of your projects will look like they were done by amateurs (and it will be true). Also, your assistants will get all the good experience, and you will end up working for them!

The style palettes are what set the tone and layout of your design. In reality, you should set up the style palettes for your assistants to use, so you can control how the project looks.

Other designers set up a new set of styles for every project. Because they have no palette continuity from project to project, it takes them an inordinately long time to set things up, so they give up in frustration. But if you follow my recommendations, you will not need to set up new styles every time you start a project. You will see the consistency of all projects. They will all use a similar set of body text and headline styles. The point sizes, fonts, and so on will change, but the styles are always there.

Chapter 9

Add a Table

How to…

- Understand table terminology
- Add a table to a text frame
- Set up tables
- Modify tables with table options
- Control the size and content of cells
- Add text to cells
- Fine-tune your table design
- Build a simple table
- Find solutions with tables

Page design often includes text that lines up in columns and rows. Traditionally, this type of layout has been created with tabs. However, this is a perfect use for a table. If you need a box around your paragraph, this is also an excellent reason for a table.

Tables were always the poor orphan children of desktop publishing. Word processors could make tables, but not set type. Page layout could set type, but not do tables. This is no longer true. InDesign's tables are extremely powerful. In this chapter, you will get some ideas about how to use tables.

Understand Table Terminology

Before we begin to explore how to use tables, you need to understand some specialized terminology. Figure 9-1 shows an example of a table produced in InDesign, with its various parts labeled.

A table is made up of *cells*. These cells are arranged in rows and columns. Each cell can have a fill and a stroke. The stroke can be different on all four sides of a cell. The outside edges of a table are called the *border*. If two or more cells are made into one cell, they are *merged*.

Each table can optionally have a header and a footer added to every frame filled by that table. Header and footer rows can be added through many pages. For the example in Figure 9-1, the title Cities & Towns of New Mexico and column headings (Photo, Location, Name, and Description) form a two-row header that goes on top of every page. The footer row at the bottom of the table in Figure 9-1 includes the page number and copyright information.

Add a Table to Your Text Frame

As far as InDesign is concerned, tables are part of type. They must be created within a text frame, and they are designed with the Type tool. A table is a grid of smaller text frames attached together and embedded within a larger text frame. This may sound complex, but InDesign makes it easy to insert a table in a text frame.

Beginning a table is simple. With an insertion point active, choose Table | Insert Table or use the shortcut CTRL-ALT-SHIFT-T/COMMAND-OPTION-SHIFT-T. This brings up the Insert Table dialog box.

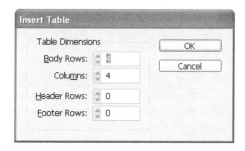

In the Insert Table dialog box, you pick the number of rows, columns, header rows, and footer rows. Header and footer rows can automatically appear on every frame in which the table appears. This is one of the unique aspects of InDesign's tables: They can flow from frame to frame and page to page.

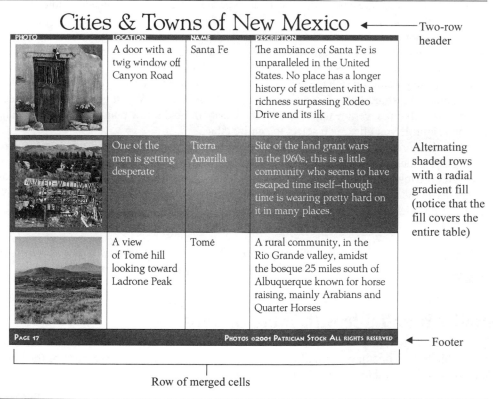

Row of merged cells

FIGURE 9-1   An InDesign table, with standard and optional parts

Do not agonize over your choices in the Insert Table dialog box, because you can always change them. You just need to decide whether you want a header and/or footer, and make a rough guess of the number of rows and columns.

 *In the Keyboard Shortcuts dialog box (Edit | Keyboard Shortcuts), Table is a context area. There are many shortcuts that are available only while you are working in a table. In addition, there is a specific context menu that is only available when you have more than one cell selected.*

Set Up Your Table before You Add Type

It will greatly streamline your production if you set up your table before you add your copy. The first step is usually to select cells to roughly format them.

Select Cells and Resize Rows or Columns

All the manipulation of the table is done with the Type tool. Once you click inside a table, it becomes the Table tool.

To select more than one cell, simply place your insertion point and drag to select whatever you desire. The only parts you cannot select in this manner are the headers and footers, which must be selected separately or as part of selecting the entire table.

You need to carefully watch the cursor. If you move it over the border of your table (top or left), it will change to a short, bold arrow, pointing at a row or column. When you click, you select that entire row or column. Over the upper-left corner, the short, bold arrow points at a 45-degree angle, down and right. If you click, you select the entire table.

When the cursor moves over any other cell boundary, it changes to a double-ended arrow, showing you which way you can drag the boundary to resize the row or column. When the cursor moves over the lower-right corner of the table, the double-ended arrow is diagonal, indicating that you can resize the table. When you are resizing from the borders, hold down the SHIFT key to keep the cells proportional. Otherwise, you will simply change the size of the column to the left or the row above.

 When resizing cell boundaries, you resize the entire row or column. The only way to make an individual cell wider is to merge it with an adjacent cell or cells.

Modify Your Table with Table Options

The Table Options dialog box is critical to setting up your tables. You should normally select your entire table before opening this dialog box (by clicking in the upper-left corner of the border). You can access the Table Options dialog box in five ways:

- Choose Table | Table Options.
- Choose Table Options from the Table palette's option menu.
- Select Table Options from the Control palette's option menu when more than one cell is selected.

■ With more than one cell in the table selected, open the context menu and click Table Options.

■ Press the shortcut, which is CTRL-ALT-SHIFT-B/COMMAND-OPTION-SHIFT-B by default.

The Table Options dialog box has five tabbed pages. We will discuss the options page by page. Each page has a Preview option, so you can see your changes interactively.

Set Table Setup Options

Figure 9-2 shows the Table Setup page of the Table Options dialog box. This page has four main sections:

■ **Table Dimensions**   This section contains the same choices as the Insert Table dialog box. If you guessed wrong there, you can change it here at any time.

■ **Table Border**   The table border is the line that goes around the entire outside edge of the table. You can make it any weight, type, color, and tint. (The color needs to be listed in the Swatches palette for either the line or the gap.) If you choose a fancy line type, you can also choose the gap color and tint. The Preserve Local Formatting check box lets you control all the cell edges that have not been changed locally. For example, in Figure 9-1, the top header row has a stroke of none that was chosen by selecting just that row. The rest of the table has a quarter-point black stroke.

9

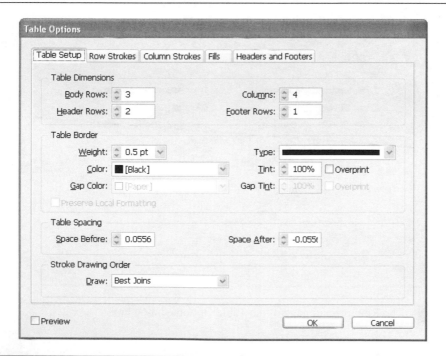

FIGURE 9-2   The Table Setup page of the Table Options dialog box

- **Table Spacing** The fields in this section are similar to those with the same name in the Paragraph palette, for setting the space before and after a paragraph. Here, you can set the spacing before and after your table in the text frame (or frames) that holds it.
- **Stroke Drawing Order** This section has a Draw drop-down list, which offers four choices: Best Joins, Rows Strokes in Front, Columns Strokes in Front, and InDesign 2.0 Compatibility. Best Joins has InDesign make the best guess about which stroke order and type will look best. It's the default and works well.

Choose Row Stroke and Column Stroke Options

As you can see in Figure 9-3, the Row Strokes page lets you set options for the strokes of the rows. You can choose the width, type, and color of the lines between the cells. The Column Strokes page has the same options for columns.

The first choice is whether you want an alternating pattern. The choices are None, Every Other Row, Every Second Row, Every Third Row, and Custom. For example, if you choose Every Third

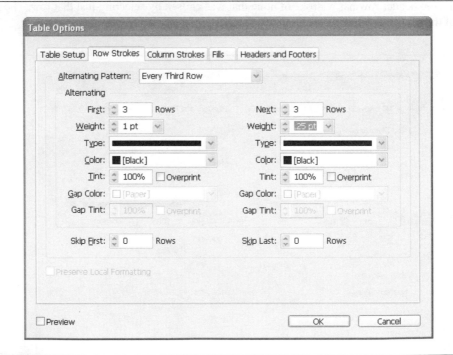

FIGURE 9-3   The Row Strokes page of the Table Options dialog box

Row, the table rows are three of one pattern and then three of the other pattern. For columns, you have the same alternating pattern choices.

If you choose to use an alternating pattern, you set up the two patterns in the Alternating section. Choose the number of rows (or columns) to appear in each pattern and set the stroke attributes. Strokes can be any width (up to 800 points), any stroke type including custom strokes you've saved, any color in the Swatches palette, and any color gap (if the style you choose has gaps). Finally, you can tell InDesign to skip first or last rows (or columns), up to 10,000 rows and 100 columns each. (Chapter 10 describes how to set stroke attributes and create custom strokes.)

NOTE   *The 10,000 row and 100 column limits seem like overkill to me, but desktop publishing has a history of going to the limits as soon as they are available. I remember people on the Photoshop team complaining about a 1,000-layer limit.*

The Preserve Local Formatting option lets you retain individual stroke adjustments you have made outside the controls in the Table Options dialog box.

Choosing Table Fills

The Fills page of the Table Options dialog box has the same basic options as the Row Strokes and Column Strokes pages. However, here we run into the first serious limitation: You cannot have alternating rows and columns in the same table— so plaids are out.

Set Up Table Headers and Footers

In the Headers and Footers page, you can not only set up how many rows you want for the header and footer, but you can also specify whether you want them to appear with every column, every frame, or every page. As you can see in Figure 9-4, the header and footer have separate controls.

You can set and reset the controls on any of the Table Options dialog box pages as you continue to work on your table. You can also pick options for just selected cells, as explained in the next section.

Control the Size and Content of Your Cells

You can do the local formatting of your table by using the Cell Options dialog box. To open this dialog box, use one of the following methods:

- Select Table | Cell Options.
- Choose Cell Options from the Table palette's option menu.
- Choose Cell Options from the Control palette's option menu when one or more cells are selected.
- With one or more cells in the table selected, open the context menu and click Cell Options.

This dialog box has four pages: Text, Strokes and Fills, Rows and Columns, and Diagonal Lines.

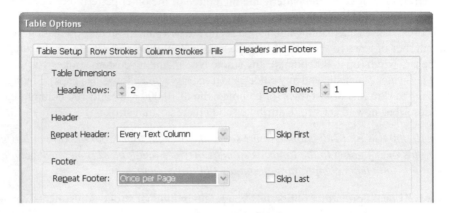

FIGURE 9-4 The Headers and Footers page of the Table Options dialog box

Format Cell Text

Figure 9-5 shows the Text page of the Cell Options dialog box. This gives you most of the control of the Text Frame Options dialog box for the selected cells:

- **Cell Insets** You can set the text inset within the cell, on each of the four sides.
- **Vertical Justification** Your choices for this justification are Top, Center, Bottom, and Justify. The Paragraph Spacing Limit setting limits the amount of paragraph spacing before line spacing occurs. InDesign will space the paragraphs first, until the limit is reached.
- **First Baseline** The choices for offsetting the baseline are Ascent, Cap Height, Leading, X-Height, and Fixed. You can also set the minimum amount of the offset.
- **Clipping** The Clip Contents to Cell option is for when a placed graphic or large type extends outside the cell boundaries. You can then clip the cell's contents—in effect, making the cell borders a mask.
- **Text Rotation** I am a little surprised that InDesign allows only 90-degree increments for cell text rotation: 0°, 90°, 180°, and 270°. It does not allow skewed cells either (unless you skew the entire table).

Set Cell Stroke and Fill

In the Strokes and Fill page, shown in Figure 9-6, you have the normal controls over stroke and fill, with one large exception. At the top of the Cell Stroke section is a cell proxy. This allows you to specify which strokes you want to affect. You can turn on or off any side of the border, the horizontal

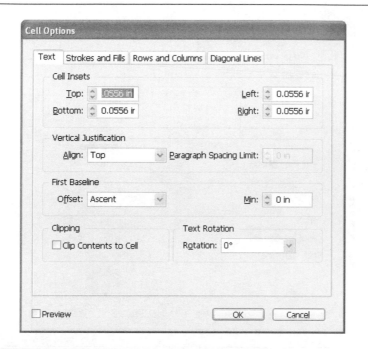

FIGURE 9-5   The Text page of the Cell Options dialog box

interior strokes, and the vertical interior strokes. You can specify a different stroke for each of the six choices, if you like. This affects only the selected cells.

Specify Individual Row and Column Settings

On the Rows and Columns page, you can specify the height of the rows exactly or within minimum and maximum ranges. You can also make all of the columns a certain width. If the columns are different widths, leave this field blank.

This page also offers a Keep Options choice. You can tell a row where to start: Anywhere, Next Column, Next Frame, Next Page, Next Even Page, or Next Odd Page. A check box lets you tell a row to keep with the next row.

Place Diagonal Lines over a Cell

The Diagonal Lines page, shown in Figure 9-7, gives you three options for placing diagonal lines over a cell. Those lines can have any stroke you want. More than that, you can create them in front of or in back of the content of the cell. The ends of the diagonal strokes are clipped by the edges of the cells.

FIGURE 9-6   The Strokes and Fills page of the Cell Options dialog box

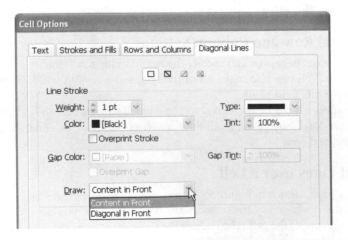

FIGURE 9-7   The Diagonal Lines page of the Cell Options dialog box

Why would you want to place diagonal lines over a cell? Perhaps in a table for a catalog where you wanted to cross out sold-out items (and you do not have time to properly redo the table). Maybe if you were laying out a game board or a Web site and had blank boxes until the copy came. You might never need to use this option, or you might discover that it's just what you need for some purpose.

Add Text to Your Cells

Now that you have your table designed to hold the copy, it is time to enter it. As mentioned, each cell is like a separate text frame, with one major difference: You cannot link one cell to another in a thread of cells. If there is too much copy for a cell, a little, red dot will appear in the lower-right corner of the cell. You can make the copy a smaller size or edit it to fit. You can format the text in a cell with your styles, in the same way that you format any other text.

When you're working within a table, a TAB will move the next copy to the next cell, and a RETURN will move the next copy to the beginning of the next row.

The TAB *key moves you to the next cell. If you need a tab in a cell, press* OPTION-TAB *on a Mac. Because* ALT-TAB *switches applications on a PC (and it's hard-wired), you'll need to make your own shortcut on a PC. Or you can choose Insert Special Character from the Type menu or Type context menu.*

Along with typing in the text, you can add text to your table in the following ways:

- **Copy and paste your cells into your table**   You can add tab-delimited copy to your table, and it will automatically fill the cells in order. So, you can either copy and paste cells from one table to another, or you can copy tab-delimited text and paste it into your table. If you use this method, make sure that you have at least as many or more cells as there are in the area into which you paste.

- **Import tables directly from Excel or Word files**   InDesign will retain as much of the formatting as it can, and you can fix the table after the import. You can also select an area of cells in Excel or Word and copy/paste it into a similar area of cells in InDesign. If you import a table or cells, a link is made to the original file. You will want to break that link or embed the table, so you do not accidentally lose the formatting changes you made in InDesign.

- **Convert text to a table**   If you have copy properly separated by tabs and returns, all you need to do is choose Table | Convert Text to Table. InDesign will make a new cell in the row for every tab and a new row for every return.

You can also select a table in InDesign and choose Table | Convert Table to Text. For example, you might want to do this to make tab-delimited copy to bring into your spreadsheet application.

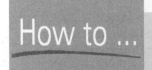 **Make Floating Heads with a Two-Cell Table**

One of the frustrating things in page layout is figuring out how to set type where the headlines float in the margin to the left of the copy. Tables give you a simple solution. Here's how to set up floating heads:

1. Make sure that you have a large left indent on all your copy on the page. This will leave space for the floating heads.

2. Insert a one-row, two-cell table in front of the paragraph where you need the floating head.

3. Adjust the cell sizes to fit.

	repair and other emergencies. She removed a small hatchet.
	" Becareful of this. It's as sharp as the knife. It won't work for trees, butyou'll be surprised how many times you'll use it. I've used it to cut uppheasant after roasting, for example." Finally she pulled out a sealed whorlhide packet. After laying it open, shesaid,
	" A dull edge slipsand can cause horrible jagged cuts. A sharp edge only cuts when you arecareless (like you were a minute ago). Even then the cut is so thin andsmooth that it heals up almost instantly with that salve. Even bad cutsheal better after bandaging because the sides of the cut fit so much betterand there is much less tissue damage.
	" So, I want to make sure all your blades are sharp. In the process you willget your

4. Copy and paste the paragraph into the right cell.

5. Add the headline to the left cell.

6. Adjust the margins and cell boundaries until the copy fits as you intended.

	repair and other emergencies. She removed a small hatchet.
	" Becareful of this. It's as sharp as the knife. It won't work for trees, butyou'll be surprised how many times you'll use it. I've used it to cut uppheasant after roasting, for example." Finally she pulled out a sealed whorlhide packet. After laying it open, shesaid,
Learning to sharpen	" There is one final thing I need to teach you this morning. This packet contains several of the best sharpening stones available. The onething you must understand is that a dull tool is much more dangerous than asharp one." Seeing Raqhel's quizzical look, she explained further,
	" A dull edge slipsand can cause horrible jagged cuts. A sharp edge only cuts when you arecareless (like you were a minute ago). Even then the cut is so thin andsmooth that it heals up almost instantly with that salve. Even bad cutsheal better after bandaging because the sides of the cut fit so much better~~and there is much less tissue~~

7. Select all the cell boundaries and turn them off. This will make the table invisible.

8. Copy and paste the table into position for the remainder of the floating heads, and change the copy inside the table.

Fine-Tune Your Table Design

The Table menu (and Table context menu) offer commands that can be useful for designing your tables:

- **Merge or Unmerge Cells**   With these commands, you can merge any selection of cells into a single cell. (If you refer back to Figure 9-1, you will see that I did this with the top header row and the footer row.) You can also unmerge a merged cell. All of the copy in the merged cell is placed in the upper-left unmerged cell group.

- **Split Cells, Horizontally or Vertically**   You can take any selected cell and split it in half horizontally or vertically. For example, you can merge three cells, and then split the new cell into two equal halves. These split cells can make a new row or column.

- **Add or Delete**   You can add or delete as many rows or columns as you like.

- **Convert**   You can convert any type of row (header, body, or footer) to any other type of row.

- **Distribute Rows or Columns Evenly**   This makes all of the selected rows or columns the same size.

- **Select**   There are commands to select a row, a column, or a table. You can also select all the header rows, all the body rows, or all the footer rows.

- **Go to Row**   This command opens a dialog box that lets you pick a row by number in the header, body, or footer rows.

- **Edit Header or Edit Footer**   You can easily make changes to the table header or footer.

All of the commands, options, and dialog boxes we have mentioned are also available in the Table palette or its option menu. You will be using these options a great deal as you work with your tables in InDesign.

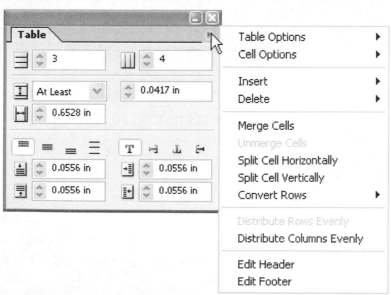

9

There are actually more controls in the table version of the Control palette than there are in the Table palette. The Control palette adds basic text formatting options and simple stroke options. In addition, almost every option has a default shortcut, or you can assign the shortcut of your choice.

Build a Simple Table

For some practice in table production, we'll work through a relatively simple table (although tables, by their very nature, are not simple). We'll make a supplies list (adapted from a graduation party a couple of years back; I'll leave it to you to imagine the party).

Set Up the Table

To set up the table, follow these steps:

1. Open a new document. Make it 4.5 by 8.5 inches wide, with 0.5-inch margins.

2. Drag a text box the size of the margins with the Type tool.

3. Choose Table | Insert Table. In the Insert Table dialog box, set the table to have 7 rows, 6 columns, and 1 header row.

4. Select the top row (click in the first cell and drag to the right until the top row is selected). Then right-click/CONTROL-click and choose Merge Cells in the context menu.

5. You need to merge the cells in the footer row also. Select all these cells and choose Merge Cells in the context menu.

Add the Copy to the Table

After you've set up the table, type the following copy into the cells, tabbing from cell to cell. The double bars (||) indicate a tab. You will need to drag the cell boundaries around to make it look like the table shown in Figure 9-8. When the Type tool is moved over a cell boundary, it turns into a double-ended arrow. At that point, you can click-drag the cell boundaries as necessary.

Party Supplies

NUMBER || PRODUCT# || QUANTITY || DESCRIPTION || ITEM PRICE || TOTAL PRICE

1 || XGC512 || 6 || Tubular electric vibrator, 110V, stainless steel, 2"x36", knurled rubber tip, rosewood handle || $75.37 || $452.22

2 || KTY387 || 45 || Stir rod, glass, 27" || $1.23 || $55.35

3 || VG524 || 3 || Galvanized steel vat, specially vulcanized acid-resistant rubber lining,

2'Hx2'Wx4'L, tempered glass rolled lip, thermostatic heater element || $1476.97 || $4430.91

4 || PUU27 || 144 || Hydrofluoric acid, 1 gallon, brown glass bottle || $11.23 || $1617.12

5 || AFK21 || 1 || 64-pack, aniline dyes, 6 oz. bottles with glass eyedroppers || $286.87 || $286.87

Total: || $6842.47

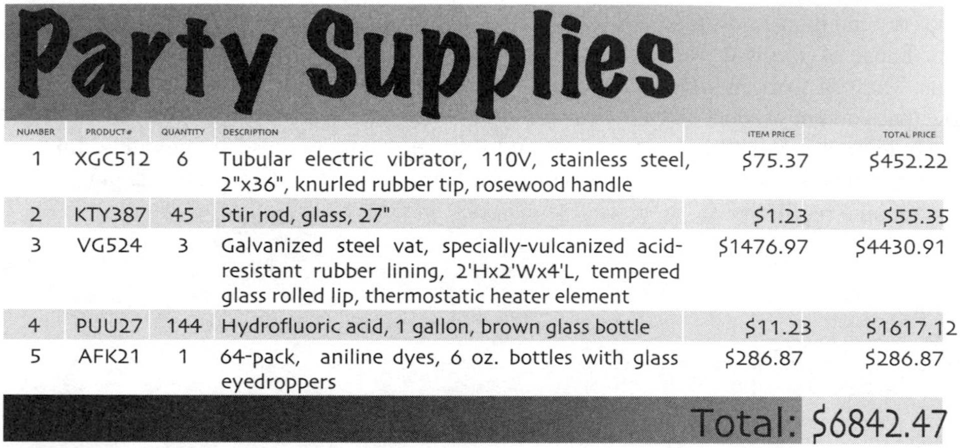

NUMBER	PRODUCT#	QUANTITY	DESCRIPTION	ITEM PRICE	TOTAL PRICE
1	XGC512	6	Tubular electric vibrator, 110V, stainless steel, 2"x36", knurled rubber tip, rosewood handle	$75.37	$452.22
2	KTY387	45	Stir rod, glass, 27"	$1.23	$55.35
3	VG524	3	Galvanized steel vat, specially-vulcanized acid-resistant rubber lining, 2'Hx2'Wx4'L, tempered glass rolled lip, thermostatic heater element	$1476.97	$4430.91
4	PUU27	144	Hydrofluoric acid, 1 gallon, brown glass bottle	$11.23	$1617.12
5	AFK21	1	64-pack, aniline dyes, 6 oz. bottles with glass eyedroppers	$286.87	$286.87

Total: $6842.47

FIGURE 9-8   A completed party supply table

Format the Table

The column name headers are 4-point, all-caps type (you can make them really small, and people can still figure them out). In most cases, you can select cells and change their fills with a simple right-click/CONTROL-click. I selected all of the cells in the bottom six rows. Then in the context menu, I chose Table Options | Alternating Fills. This same command is available in the option menu of the Table palette.

Choose any fonts you like. I used Party LET and Skia for the fonts. You might find it easier to open the Character palette to format the type.

A version of the completed table is shown in Figure 9-8. You do not need to match the table exactly. The idea is to experiment. Just have fun! Use your own copy if you like. (If you use my copy, you might be tempted to figure out just what kind of party it was—you really don't want to know.)

Find Solutions with Tables

There is very little you cannot do with InDesign's tables. As you saw at the beginning of the chapter, in Figure 9-1, you can add graphics to table cells. Just place or paste a graphic into an insertion point. We will cover this process in detail in Chapter 11.

You can insert another cell into a cell of an existing table. If you need a word, line, or paragraph with a box around it, insert a single-cell table. For complex column setups, a table is often the simplest solution. Those of you with Web design experience are already accustomed to outrageous table gyrations. They all work in InDesign.

Now that you know about all of InDesign's typesetting capabilities, you're ready to move on to InDesign's impressive graphic creation tools and abilities. Many of these are unique to InDesign. Some, like gradient strokes, are so unique and helpful that you will find yourself creating graphics in InDesign on a regular basis.

Part III

Add Graphics

Chapter 10

Produce Graphics in or for Your Document

How to...

- ◾ Understand how PostScript works
- ◾ Use the tools that work with paths
- ◾ Create frames and shapes
- ◾ Draw freeform lines with the Pencil tool
- ◾ Draw with the Pen tool
- ◾ Choose stroke weights
- ◾ Use caps and joins
- ◾ Align a stroke to a path
- ◾ Create custom strokes

Adding graphics to a page layout has traditionally meant inserting items produced elsewhere. In digital page layout, you typically add pieces from programs like Illustrator, Freehand, and Photoshop. However, InDesign has changed that considerably. It is possible that you will be producing many of your graphics in InDesign.

If you already have some experience with FreeHand or Illustrator, many of the topics we will cover in this chapter will be familiar. Almost two-thirds of InDesign's toolbox tools are Illustrator's drawing tools. InDesign can do much of what Illustrator can do, and sometimes do it better (probably because InDesign's interface is easier to control). The main point to understand is that InDesign is a PostScript program, as are all professional publishing programs for print. So, I'll begin this chapter with an explanation of how PostScript drawing works. Then I'll cover the basics of using InDesign's drawing tools.

Understand How PostScript Works

As in FreeHand and Illustrator, drawing in InDesign is a specific type of vector drawing called *PostScript illustration*. No matter what type of drawing you want to create, PostScript illustration must be approached as a combination of objects belonging to two simple categories: lines and shapes. A shape is just a line that returns to its starting point. So, everything is line.

Drawing in PostScript is a uniquely digital solution of mathematics. It takes all of the pieces and describes them through the use of mathematical equations. These equations are used to generate outlines (curved and straight) that are called Bézier curves (named after the Frenchman who defined the equations). Because all these shapes are mathematical, they are much smaller than bitmaps.

NOTE   *This type of image is often called a* vector image *or* object-oriented drawing. *PostScript is a variant of this, and it is the absolute standard in publishing.*

For Newcomers

Drawing in PostScript

When discussing drawing in PostScript, it is helpful to consider the fine-art technique of collage. This is where you glue separate pieces on top of each other to produce the final image. It is not like a montage, where you assemble photos into a larger photo (most often seen in composite-layer images from Photoshop). In a collage, you can use any type of object and arrange it any way you wish, piling pieces on top of pieces.

Imagine that you are about to create a collage with an inexhaustible supply of lines and shapes. Each line and shape can be stretched, bent, and otherwise reshaped however you choose. Virtually any color can be applied (even blends of color, from one to another by using hundreds of shapes piled on top of each other). You can then paste these manipulated lines and shapes on your collage in the locations and order that you decide are best for your image.

Because it exists only in digital code, this collage is infinitely flexible. You can select any line or shape and move it to a new position, slip it between two other objects, or discard it altogether. Any element can be exactly duplicated, manipulated in a new way, or left as is. It is as if each shape were on a separate sheet of perfectly transparent, infinitely thin Mylar, and you can shuffle these sheets at will.

This scenario is actually a reasonably accurate description of the PostScript drawing process. You have a totally fluid, incredibly malleable drawing medium. It has taken "inkwork," or line art, to new heights, adding color, type, patterns, shading, and much more. It is a wonderful set of tools.

10

What's the Difference between PostScript and Bitmap Images?

To understand the difference between PostScript and bitmap (InDesign and Photoshop), let's consider the simple drawing shown in Figure 10-1. This is a light-gray page, outlined in a thin, black line, with a black circle in the middle. It is 10 inches wide and 8 inches tall, with a 4-inch circle centered in the image.

The Bitmap Version

First, let's assume that we have drawn the image shown in Figure 10-1 in Photoshop, at normal printing resolution (300 dots per inch, or dpi). If this Photoshop drawing is 10 inches wide by 8 inches tall, at 300 dpi, it contains millions of pixels: $(10 \times 300) (8 \times 300) = 7,200,000$ pixels. Because it is in grayscale mode (8-bit color, or 1 byte per pixel), it would be 7.2MB of data. If it were in RGB mode (24-bit color), it would be 21.6MB. If it were in CMYK mode (32-bit color), it would be 28.8MB.

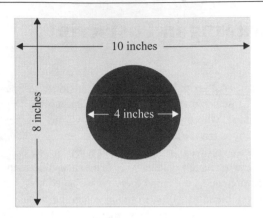

FIGURE 10-1   A simple ball in a rectangle: 7.2MB bitmap or 62KB vector

> **NOTE**   *These image file size figures are accurate only conceptually. Photoshop adds some other data, such as creation date, file type, and so on. Also, it's true that compression schemes ease this problem somewhat.*

The size is the same for any image in a 10-by-8-inch area, regardless of what type of image it is. Bitmaps do not care what the pixels are. Every pixel must be described individually. This is why the background is opaque white when you place a TIFF file from Photoshop. How can you get rid of that opaque background? Only PostScript can clip the image or hold the transparency. (But now the inventor of PostScript, Adobe, has brought transparency to all its applications.)

The PostScript Version

With PostScript, we are dealing with a programming language, specifically a page description language. The good news is that to draw with PostScript, you don't need to know anything about PostScript programming. However, you must understand conceptually what is going on. Basically, what PostScript does is describe shapes by their starting and ending points, locating them on a grid with a 0,0 point in the upper-left corner that is included in the page-size description.

To produce the image shown in Figure 10-1, we have something like this (assuming the start and end locations are measured from the upper-left corner): Draw rectangle: start 0,0; end 3000,2400; fill 10% black; stroke 0.5 pt 100% black; draw circle, start 900,600; end 2100,1800; fill 100% black. This is my version, not PostScript code, of the basic PostScript instructions. The important thing to understand is the simplicity of this approach. Assuming that each character in this description is 1 byte of data, my language used about 100 bytes to completely describe this simple drawing. That is 100 *bytes*—not 100 kilobytes (100,000 bytes) or 100 megabytes (100 million bytes of data). So, on a floppy disk, where the minimum recording segment is 256 bytes, this would show up as a 1KB file in your window. It is so small that Finder or Program Manager would not even list its size correctly.

Now, the saved document would need to have a path location, a document creator descriptor, a creation time and date, a modified time and date, and so forth. The additional information brings the document up to the 400KB mark. Adding type, arrows, and gradient strokes on the arrows would result in a bigger file size, but it's still remarkably small when compared to the 7.2MB necessary in Photoshop for a bitmap file of the same grayscale image.

In my "interpreted" version of the PostScript instructions, did you notice there was no description of resolution? That is because, for a PostScript workflow, the printer defines the resolution. In other words, PostScript files are completely independent of resolution. If you send an image to a 600 dpi laser printer, it prints at 600 dpi. If you send it to a 2,400 dpi imagesetter or platesetter, it prints at 2400 dpi. For a bitmap image, you need to make a separate file for each resolution, unless you put it into a PostScript page layout application like InDesign. Then InDesign can package it in a way that lets the PostScript printer set the resolution.

Work with PostScript's Stack of Shapes

All shapes and lines in InDesign are described in this PostScript, resolution-independent manner, even bitmaps brought into your documents. All of these shapes are simply described and piled on top of each other, the last one on top of the first ones. Because each of these shapes is independently described as a specific object, it's very easy to reshape or rearrange shapes by rewriting the description.

As far as PostScript is concerned, every shape is on its own layer; a stack of sheets of infinitely thin Mylar is a good analogy. You can move those shapes forward and backward at will. As shown in Figure 10-2, it is easy to reorder the layering and shuffle shapes up and down in the stack. There are no layers in this illustration, but the lizard is grouped.

NOTE   *If you decide to gather a large bunch of those shapes and keep them together, separate from the other shapes in the document, you can assign groups of shapes to a uniquely named layer in the Layers palette (as explained in Chapter 11). However, this is rarely a good idea.*

10

FIGURE 10-2   PostScript shapes are easy to rearrange and reorder.

Learn PostScript Terminology

As explained in the previous section, almost any drawing can be expressed as an interacting collection of lines and shapes. PostScript has specific terms for these lines and shapes, as well as how they interact.

Bounding Boxes

A *bounding box* is what PostScript uses to contain a shape. A bounding box is made up of the horizontal and vertical lines that touch the far left, far right, top, and bottom extremes of a shape. Points placed at those locations are called *extrema*. Shape locations use the upper-left corner to start the bounding box and the lower-right corner to end the bounding box.

In InDesign, the bounding box shows up when you select an object with the Selection tool. Even bitmaps brought into one of your documents are placed into a bounding box.

Paths, Points, and Segments

A line connects points. If you remember your geometry, a straight line is the shortest distance between two points. Any line starts at one point and ends at another. Lines can be very short (millionths of an inch) or stretch for great lengths. They can be straight, curved, or any combination of straight and curved sections. In PostScript, lines are called *paths* and are defined by *points*.

Segments are drawn between points to connect them. A segment can be straight or curved. Segments can connect two points in the shortest distance or indirectly in a curve, bending along the way. PostScript segments are linked together so that neighboring segments share a common point.

In this way, you can think of a line (or path) as a connect-the-dot puzzle. Each point is a dot. You draw one segment from dot A to dot B, a second segment from dot B to dot C, a third segment from dot C to dot D, and so on. The completed image is a *path*. A path may consist of only one segment, a thousand, or more. Figure 10-3 illustrates a path with five points, four segments, two handles, a start point, and an end point.

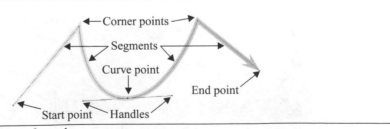

Anatomy of a path

Curve Points and Corner Points

Obviously, the form of each straight and curved segment in a path determines an image's overall appearance. The appearance of a path is equally affected by the manner in which one segment meets another segment at a point. Segments can meet at a point in two ways:

- Two segments can curve on either side of a point, meeting on the common tangent to the curves passing through the point. This kind of point is called a *curve point*.

- Two segments (straight or curved) can meet to form a corner. If two curves meet at a corner, each of those curves will have a different tangent. The point where they meet is called a *corner point*.

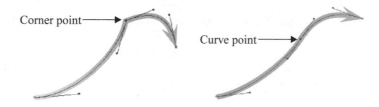

A tangent *is the line passing through a point on a curve that touches the curve only at that point, without cutting through the curve. Think of a coffee can sitting on a table. If you slide a ruler over on the table until it touches the can, the edge of the ruler shows the tangent to that point on the curve of the can.*

10

In Figure 10-3, there is one curve point and four corner points. That figure shows a straight segment between points 1 and 2, and another between points 4 and 5. There is a curved segment between points 2 and 3, and another between points 3 and 4.

In PostScript, assembling segments is much like drawing curving lines using French curves in drafting plans. If you match the tangents, you get a smooth curve. If the tangents do not match, there is a bump or corner in the resulting curve.

PostScript curve points have a single tangent for both curved segments meeting at that point. As a result, the curve flows smoothly through the point without a bump. Corner points have separate tangents for each curve, or one of the segments is a straight line that is at a different angle than the tangent of the other curved segment. The result is a point—sometimes sharp, sometimes subtle.

Ingoing and Outgoing Segments

All paths—the segments going from one point to another—have direction. In PostScript, this is important information. (In PostScript jargon, this is called *winding*.) The direction is determined by the order in which you place the points. (But, as you will learn in Chapter 11, you can change the direction with menu commands.)

What you need to know now is simple: All points (except the first and last) have an *incoming segment* and an *outgoing segment*, which are determined by the direction of the segment.

Point Handles

As you can see in Figure 10-3, only one of the points (the curve point) has visible handles. However, the other four points have handles also.

All points have two handles:

- An *incoming handle* describing the tangent of the segment attached to the previous point
- An *outgoing handle* that will determine the curve of the next segment generated when you click to produce the following point

Point handles are a central part of PostScript illustration. In PostScript, two points and two handles describe every segment.

Handles are the tools you use to manipulate the curves of segments. They have two basic attributes: a handle indicates the tangent of the curve of the segment it is attached to, and the length of the handle determines the amount of curve of the segment. Every segment has a handle at each end. When you click on a point, four handles appear (if they have any length at all): the outgoing and incoming handles for each segment attached to the point.

When the Handle Is Missing   If you cannot see the handle, it has a length of zero (and is hidden by the point). You always have the option of dragging the handles out.

Often, you cannot see one or more of the handles. For example, if you simply click to produce corner points, you get straight lines connecting the dots. A corner point with straight segments coming into and out from the point will appear to have no handles. In fact, both handles have zero length in this case. In other words, when the handles have zero length, the segment is as short as possible. Remember that the shortest distance between two points is a straight line. The tangent of these zero-length handles is the straight line between the two points.

When the Handles Are Visible   When the handles have length, that length is added to the segment. As a result, the segment must bend, and the tangent shown by the angle of the handles determines the shape of those bends. Here is a two-segment path with corner points, with the handle of the middle point drawn out:

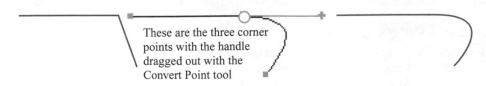

These are the three corner points with the handle dragged out with the Convert Point tool

As you can see, the length of the handle is added to the segment. This is not a one-to-one relationship, but conceptually this is what happens.

PostScript Paths Do Not Vary in Width

One of the main advantages of using a technical pen (the old-fashioned kind that uses ink) is that all its lines have a common thickness. A half-point pen produces a half-point line and nothing else. This is also a disadvantage, and the major reason why technical pen drawings tend to look too perfect and somewhat sterile. PostScript has the same problem: Its lines do not vary in width, producing drawings that look unreal and too clean (well, like computer drawings).

In nature, almost all lines vary in thickness. Only man-made lines are a constant width. Consider, for example, the difference between a vine strung between branches and a phone line hung on poles. The only ways to use a constant line to depict organic forms are crosshatching, stippling, or filled shapes. PostScript uses the latter approach. If you need a line that varies in width, you must draw a long, skinny shape that varies in width. Freehand and Illustrator automate this with a brush tool, a brush stroke, or a graphic tablet. InDesign does not produce these options.

Here is a simple brush stroke from Illustrator, showing the complex paths necessary to create it:

You may want to draw a brush stroke in Illustrator, and then copy and paste it into InDesign to use for various effects.

10

When the handles are showing, you can make any point into either a corner point or a curve point. You will see how this works when we talk about the Pen tool, later in this chapter.

All of this sounds very complex. However, once you start practicing with the point-creation tools, it becomes second nature. Soon, you will find it hard to draw well without the aid of those controlling points and handles. Of course, this assumes that you will practice!

Shapes, Fill, and Stroke

Like a geometric line, a PostScript path is a purely one-dimensional shape. It has length but no width or height. More appropriately stated, you can make a path any width in PostScript (including a width of none). A path is merely a description of a line, no matter what form it takes.

When a path goes back to the originating point and connects the last point with the first point, it becomes a closed path, which artists call a shape. The area enclosed by the closed path is the shape.

In PostScript, the attributes of the area are called the *fill*. The attributes of the path are called the *stroke*. All shapes have stroke and fill. Open paths can also have both stroke and fill. For an open path, the only difference is that PostScript creates an unstroked, straight segment that contains the fill between the beginning and ending points.

Open path

Closed path

Just like the stroke of a line, the fill of a shape may be black, white, none, or colored. Either the stroke or the fill can even combine many colors fading into one another in linear or radial gradients. To rephrase, the stroke is the color and size of the path, and the fill is the color of the area enclosed by the path. The limits of stroke and fill are very broad. They can be any color supported by InDesign: spot, RGB, CMYK, or LAB. Stroke width can be from 0 to 800 points, in increments of thousandths of a point. Colors can blend from any color to any color.

 *Every shape must be described by one continuous path around the outside of the shape. You cannot fill or control a shape made by groups of short lines.*

Use the Tools that Work with Paths

As I have already mentioned, InDesign has most of the path-producing tools from Illustrator, except for the Brush tool and some of the fancier shape tools.

Select and Edit Paths

The Selection and Direct Selection tools are identical to Illustrator's in appearance. The Direct Selection tool does path editing. The Selection tool selects the bounding box of the shape or path, which we call a frame in InDesign.

Selection tool

Direct Selection tool

The Selection tool lets you move and manipulate the path as a whole. The Direct Selection tool gives you access to the points and handles and lets you move them, but it does not allow you to create or change point types.

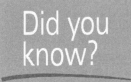

You Need a Shortcut to Force Yourself into the Proper Selection Tool

As I mentioned earlier in the book, I have made customized shortcuts for both the Selection and Direct Selection tools, using a CTRL/COMMAND key combination. This is very important.

Using my shortcut, no matter what I'm doing, I can force myself into whatever selection tool I need at the moment. As many of you know, you can always temporarily access the last selection tool you used by holding down the CTRL key in Windows or the COMMAND key in Mac. This works in almost all applications. However, there will be many occasions when you actually must be in the selection tool of your choice, not temporarily accessing it. I will mention this requirement when it applies.

You can pick any Selection tool and Direct Selection tool shortcuts that work for you (see Chapter 4 for details on setting up custom keyboard shortcuts), but you really do need to have them.

TIP *As explained in Chapter 5, you can make any frame into a text frame by simply clicking in the frame with the Type tool. This is true of any path you draw (assuming that the fill is large enough in area). If you select it with the Selection tool, and then click it with the Type tool, you can add type within the shape.*

10

The Scissors tool simply cuts a path. Just select the tool and click on the path to break it at that point.

Create Frames and Shapes

The six frame and shape tools are a little confusing, because Adobe has put them in two separate pop-ups in the toolbox. But it doesn't really make any difference which one you are using. The frame tools have diagonal lines in an X from corner to corner; the shape tools do not.

Rectangle tools

Ellipse tools

Polygon tools

The frame tools have no stroke or fill, but they are easy to move because you can click anywhere on them. The shape tools have a stroke (of whatever you have made your default stroke) and a fill of none. So, to move them, you must click on the frame edge or the little blue spot that marks the center. Other than that, the frame and shape tools function in the same way.

These tools draw their shapes in a standard way, from handle to handle. You can constrain the shape (for example, to a circle or square) by holding down the SHIFT key. If you hold down the ALT/OPTION key, the tools draw from the center out.

Although you can make stars with the Polygon tool, this function is severely limited. In the Polygon Settings dialog box, which appears when you double-click the tool, you must guess the shape of the points of the star. And you don't have a preview to help you see how the star will turn out.

Add Straight Lines

What can I say? The Line tool draws lines. Hold down the SHIFT key, and it draws horizontal, vertical, and 45-degree lines. However, an important feature of InDesign is that it allows you to assign a gradient to a line.

You can also add arrowheads automatically at the end of each line. One of the nice new features in InDesign is that the arrowheads match the line length. In earlier versions, the arrowhead or tail was added to the end of the line, beyond the ending point. This made drawing little callout arrows an exercise in frustration. Now the end of the arrow is at the starting or ending point of the line point. You can pick the arrowheads and tails you like in the Stroke palette, as explained in the "Add Arrowheads, Tails, Balls, Bars, and Circles" section later in this chapter.

Draw Freeform Lines with the Pencil Tool

Along with the regular Pencil tool, which draws freehand, you get the Smoother and Eraser tools. You can select the Smoother tool while drawing by holding down the ALT/OPTION key. The Smoother tool progressively smoothes out the line (without any real control, although it often does a nice job). It does this by changing corner points to curve points, as well as adding points. The Eraser tool erases the path from where you click to where you drag.

All three Pencil tools work on any path you draw, with any tool. They even work on type converted to paths (described in Chapter 11). The main thing to remember about using the Pencil tool is that you do not have any choice about point placement. Lines drawn with the Pencil tool will always look hand-drawn, unless you spend a lot of time cleaning them up. Usually, once you get used to drawing in PostScript, you will want the control offered by the Pen tool.

Draw with the Main Tool: The Pen

The Pen tool gives you the control you need, both to edit and to create paths.

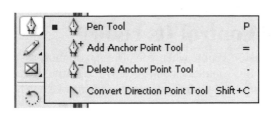

The basic operation of the Pen tool is the same as all Pen tools in PostScript applications. You click to produce a corner point. You click-drag to make a curve point, holding down the mouse button until the handles are dragged out to the length you need. InDesign adds some nice touches, though. If you click a second time on the corner point you just created, the Pen tool automatically changes to the Convert Point tool, which allows you to drag out a handle in the direction you want the outgoing segment to go.

TIP   *The SHIFT-C shortcut for the Convert Point tool works reasonably well for right-handed people (though it is a long reach that usually takes your eye off the screen), but it is a disaster for lefties. I suggest you change the shortcut for the Convert Point tool to zero (0). This way, all four shortcuts are right next to each other, and it is very handy to use them for the tools.*

Watch the Pen tool while you're working with a path to find out what is happening. If you see a little plus next to the tool, a click will add a point. If you see a little minus, a click will subtract one. If you see the little open V-shape pointing to 11 o'clock, you will change the point type from smooth to corner or vice versa. The Add Point and Subtract Point tools are automatic. You access the Change Point tool by holding down the ALT/OPTION key.

The following are the basic points to remember when you're using the Pen tool:

- Holding down the CTRL/COMMAND key changes you back to the last selection tool you used.
- Holding down the ALT/OPTION key switches you to the Convert Point tool.
- To drag out handles on a corner point, click the corner point and drag with the Convert Point tool. Then move the tool over the handles that result. At this point, the Convert Point tool allows you to drag the handles individually.

The Pen tool is a central PostScript drawing tool. If you're not used to using this tool, it does take some practice, because it is a very different paradigm to drawing on paper or canvas.

NOTE   *An assignment I give my students when introducing the Pen tool is to produce 48 drawings in two weeks, using only the Pen tool. You might want to try an approach like this. Quality does not matter at this point. The only thing that matters is quantity. You need to become accustomed to the tool.*

10

Set the Stroke and Control Its Look

Once you have a path, to make it visible when you print it, you must assign a stroke and/or a fill. The color of the stroke (and fill) should be controlled by the Swatches palette, which I'll cover in Chapter 13. Here, we are concerned with the options on the Stroke palette, shown in Figure 10-4.

Choose a Stroke Weight

The first option you see in the Stroke palette is for the weight of the stroke. InDesign's limit for stroke width is 800 points (or a little over 11 inches wide). The full range of widths is from 0 to 800 points, in thousandth of a point increments.

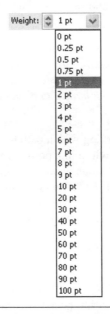

FIGURE 10-4   The Stroke palette

Did you know?

Some Strokes Are Too Thin to Print

Be very careful of strokes that might be too thin to print. Depending on the technology you will be using to produce your artwork, there are some limits to how thin you can make your strokes. Here's a short list:

- **Web** You want to be sure that your stroke is fairly wide, if you want your color to be consistent all the way around the shape. Two-point strokes are usually necessary, and they may need to be a little wider. The anti-aliasing of the screen blurs the edges, but it also makes 1-point strokes that do not fit the grid exactly twice as wide and a tint of the chosen color.

- **Screen printing** It depends on what you are printing. If you are printing on a smooth T-shirt or something similar, you can probably print a 1-point stroke, if it's solid. However, on a coarser weave like a hat, screen printers often use a 50-line screen, which requires at least a 1.5-point stroke width.

- **Quickprinters** Because of the limitations of black-plate platemakers, any stroke thinner than 0.6-point will probably fade in and out. Half-point strokes are pushing it a little, and may or may not be satisfactory, depending on equipment and press operator experience. If the printer is using plastic-plate platesetters (CTP, or computer-to-plate), 0.5-point strokes should not be a problem.

- **Commercial printers** With uncoated stock, you will have little problem down to 0.3-point. With coated stock, 0.25-point strokes are easy. For #1 premium, coated papers, you can go as thin as 0.15-point strokes.

If there is any doubt, ask your printer before you send in the artwork. The printer will know the applicable limits.

Use Your Caps and Joins

The six little icons at the top right of the Stroke palette are not familiar to many designers. However, they are a normal part of PostScript paths. Many times, controlling the Cap and Join options will be the only way to create the effect you need. The Cap and Join options may seem esoteric, but they actually provide a solution to the problem of how to end a line.

Caps are line endings. There are three cap types, represented by the icons at the top right of the Stroke palette: the left icon is Butt, the middle icon is Round, and the right icon is Projecting. Joins are corner-point renderings in the middle of a stroke of caps. There are also three types of joins: the left icon is Miter, the middle icon is Round, and the right icon is Bevel. You can use any combination of these caps and joins. This gives you nine combinations.

Butt cap and miter joins

Round cap and round joins

Projecting cap and bevel joins

Choose Caps

The caps are easy to understand:

- ■ Butt caps cut off directly at the end point at a 90-degree angle to the handle of that point.
- ■ Round caps end the stroke with a half circle centered on the point with a radius of half the stroke.
- ■ Projecting caps extend the 90-degree cutoff a distance of one-half the stroke width beyond the end point.

Choose Joins

Joins are a little more complicated because they include what is called a *miter.* As far as PostScript is concerned, a miter is the corner defined by two intersecting lines of the same width, where the extra line length on both sides is trimmed off even with the outer edges of the corner. This rather complicated definition can be seen easily in the following example. The white line is the path. The black shape is the miter that results from a stroke as wide as the two light-gray intersecting boxes.

Miter

The Miter Limit field, below the Weight field in the Stroke palette, limits how long the point can be by cutting off the miter extension at a predetermined length beyond the corner point. This solves the supposed problem of miters extending several inches beyond the point. The little x indicates how many times the stroke width is multiplied; the limit is 500x.

NOTE

In practical experience, miters extending beyond points are not a real problem, other than sometimes the tips of the points can be cut off when you do not want that to happen. It really matters only when you are using wide stroke widths and very narrow angles. At this point, the miter limit is a pain. I have often used 80x or higher to get the entire point to show. Eventually, I made my default miter length 200x.

There are three types of joins at a corner point:

- Miter joins trim the corners, as just explained.
- Round joins connect the outer edges of the corner with a circular arc whose radius is half the stroke width.
- Bevel joins work just like miter limits, except that they cut off the miter at the corner point.

Regarding the bevel join, Adobe says that this "squared" corner "abuts" the point. However, that happens only at very acute angles. On wider angles, the cut-off corner extends beyond the point by an unspecified amount. By the way, the angle of the bevel cut is perpendicular to the bisector of the angle produced by the handles of that corner point (this may be meaningful if you remember your geometry).

Align Your Stroke to the Path

InDesign has added another major new capability to the mix. Historically, strokes have always been centered on the path (except for an aborted attempt in PageMaker 5 or 6). Now, the Stroke palette offers three stroke alignment choices: Center, Inside, and Outside. Here is how they affect the stroke placement. In this example, the black line is the path with the stroke in gray, aligned using the three choices. The paths are identical in size.

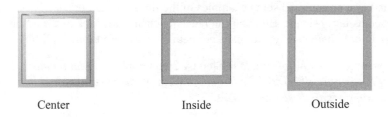

Center   Inside   Outside

These stroke alignment options may not seem impressive, but you will be surprised how many times they solve a problem you have while making an illustration or a layout. (Photoshop seemingly has had these options for years, but *those apply to pixels, not paths.)*

Change the Type of Stroke or Add Dashes

One of the complaints of Quarksters has been that InDesign could not make fancy strokes. InDesign 2 added a few limited options, but there was no control of the gap color. Needless to say, this has all changed. First, there are now 18 standard stroke types: double lines, triple lines, wavy lines, dashes, dots, diamonds, and so on. But this is just the beginning.

10

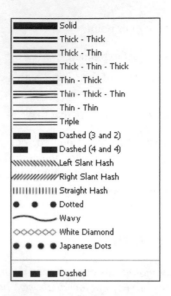

If you drag your mouse to the bottom of the Type pop-up in the Stroke palette, you will see the Dashed choice. By selecting that, you radically change the bottom of the palette. Those of you who are familiar with Illustrator will recognize the dot and dash options. These six fields allow you to make three dashes and three gaps of any length you desire (up to 800 points). Figure 10-5 shows the dashed line options and some examples of the lines you can create.

Again this seems fairly simple. But, you can radically change the look of the dashes with caps and joins. You can only have one type of caps per path—so you are limited a little.

NOTE   *A few years ago, I saw an article in* Step by Step Graphics *about a man in Georgia who had built an entire illustration style out of layers of dashed and dotted lines. There's a lot you can do with these line choices.*

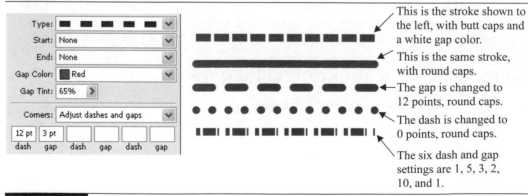

FIGURE 10-5   The settings for dashes and some sample lines

The Corners pop-up, at the bottom of the dashed line settings, lets you adjust how InDesign fits the dashed line into the corners of shapes. This can help a lot when you're trying to put a fancy frame around a rectangle, for example. The choices are None, Adjust Dashes, Adjust Gaps, and Adjust Dashes and Gaps.

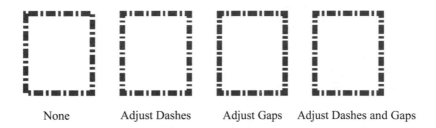

None   Adjust Dashes   Adjust Gaps   Adjust Dashes and Gaps

As you can see here, you definitely want to adjust the corners. I tried dozens of different dash setups. In this example, None doesn't work. The other three choices are almost identical. I suggest using the default Adjust Dashes and Gaps setting.

Create Custom Strokes

One of the major new advances in InDesign is the ability to make fancy custom stroke styles and save them for reuse. In fact, you should make the styles you use often part of your defaults.

Custom Styles is the only command in the Stroke palette's option menu. The Stroke Styles dialog box, shown in Figure 10-6, lists seven default styles. These cannot be deleted or edited (which is a real shame).

When you click the New button, you get the New Stroke Style dialog box. Like most options of this type, you can waste a lot of time making styles you need. There will be a lot of trial and error. You also need to be aware that any stroke style you make will work only for certain widths of strokes.

The main problem with custom stroke styles is the ease with which you can make your stuff look overdone and amateurish. You need to watch out for the "Look, Ma! See what I did!" phenomenon. Using software as an expensive video game is far too common.

The first choice to make is Type: Dash, Dotted, or Stripe. The options change slightly for each type of stroke. In general, you can define the stroke's pattern, cap, and corner attributes.

Create Custom Dashed Lines

Let's look first at the custom dash options. Figure 10-7 shows the New Stroke Style dialog box when the Dash type is selected, along with some sample dashed strokes.

10

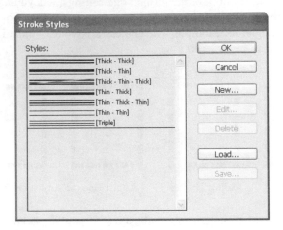

The Stroke Styles dialog box shows the default styles.

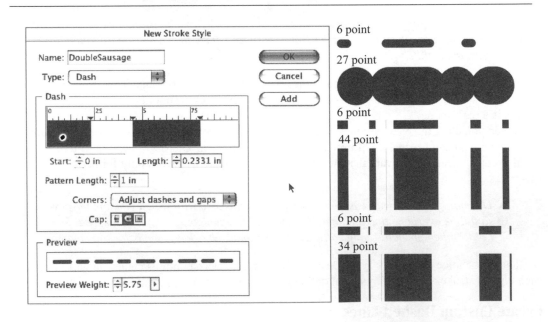

The New Stroke Style dialog box for dashed strokes and some samples

The first thing you see in the Dash area is a ruler of the same style as the Tabs palette's ruler. There will be a dash of the default length, starting at zero. You cannot get rid of that dash. However, you can click the little, black triangle pointing down and make it a length of zero. After that, you simply click or click-drag in the ruler to make up to five dashes. If you use round caps, you get dots or sausage shapes of whatever length you need.

You should be aware that the use of either round or projecting caps makes the custom stroke style very sensitive to point-size restrictions. Remember that the round and projecting caps go half the stroke width beyond the point. So, if you have a gap of 12 points with either of these caps, the dashes will touch at 12 points (6 points at each side of the gap). You can see this in the 27-point sample stroke in Figure 10-7, where the round-ended shapes are beginning to overlap. If this line had projecting caps, the solid line would start as soon as they touch.

All the dashes will have a starting point, a length, and a pattern length. The length can be from 0 to 9,999 points long, although the pattern length must be a minimum of 0.25 point.

If you do not like any dash you add (beyond the original one), just click the dash itself (the black rectangle) and drag it off the ruler to make it disappear. Simply drag the little, black triangles in the ruler sideways to change the length of that dash. Click the dash itself and drag it sideways to change the starting point.

At the bottom of the New Stroke Style dialog box is a limited preview, which gives you an idea of what you are producing, up to 20 points wide. The up and down arrow buttons let you change the Preview Weight setting in increments, and the button to the right of that field gives you a slider for adjusting the setting.

Create Custom Dotted and Striped Strokes

When you choose the Dotted type in the New Stroke Style dialog box, the options are similar to the ones for dashed lines. The stroke length is always zero with round caps. You can add up to five dots, spaced as needed. If you make a mistake, you can correct it by dragging dots off the ruler. Because of the round caps, the stroke width is limited to half the smallest gap before the dots begin to touch. Once the width is the same as the gap, that portion of the dot pattern becomes solid.

The Striped type of custom stroke has the same options vertically as dashes do horizontally. The only difference is that the stripe width is expressed as a percentage of the total stroke width.

 You can click to make a stripe of zero width, just as you can with dots or dashes. However, zero-width striped strokes probably will not print, even though they show up on the screen.

Save Your Custom Strokes

After you have created your custom stroke, just click Add in the New Stroke Style dialog box. Your new stroke style is added to all the Stroke Style pop-ups throughout InDesign. When you have all the strokes you need, click OK.

If you want to be able to load your custom styles in other documents, somewhat like paragraph and character styles, you will need to first save them individually, one at a time, separately from any

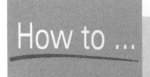 **Add Custom Strokes as Document Defaults**

You can save your custom strokes from the Custom Styles dialog box and load them in any new document. Here's how:

1. In the Stroke palette, select the Custom Styles command in its option menu.

2. Create the styles you want.

3. Select the styles in the Stroke Styles dialog box and click Save.

4. Save the file in a location of your choice. It will have an .inst extension.

5. In the Stroke Styles dialog box, click the Load button.

6. Navigate to the style or styles you have saved and click OK.

The styles you loaded will be added to your document. The custom styles show up at the bottom of the Type pop-up in the Stroke palette. If you want custom stroke styles in all new documents, just make the new stroke styles and add them to the Stroke palette with no document open.

document. To save the custom stroke style you made, select the style in the Styles list in the Stroke Styles dialog box (see Figure 10-6) and click the Save button. You can save the custom stroke file wherever you like, but I recommend that you make a new folder in Presets in your application folder to hold your custom strokes. You need to use the .inst extension for the style, in case you go to a foreign operating system.

After you've saved your custom stroke, you can load it anywhere else. Just open the Stroke Styles dialog box from a document, click Load, and find the style you saved. You will need to load each custom style you want to use, one at a time.

Add Arrowheads, Tails, Balls, Bars, and Circles

Below the Type pop-up in the Stroke palette there are two pop-ups labeled Start and End. These offer 11 choices for items you can add to the start or end of a stroke. These are marvelous for callouts and illustrated drawings.

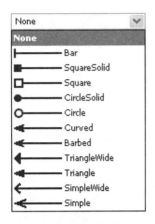

For those of you who have used FreeHand, with its customizable ends, let me ask you a question: Did you ever successfully make an arrowhead that was better than those supplied?

The good news is that you are not forced to deal with those monstrous attachments found in Illustrator—the ones that are not even part of the stroke. The really good news is that these attached graphics are no longer added to the end of the stroke, beyond the end point. Now, the end point of the path it also the tip of the arrow. This makes adding callout arrows effortless. No longer do you need to guess at the line length to get the tip of the arrow where you want it. No longer does the tip move when you change the point size of the stroke. (Unless, of course, you make the point size so large that the arrowhead is longer than the original line.) My only quibble is that the open circle and the open square do not have a white fill. But then, you can never have everything.

Color the Stroke Gap

Beneath the Start and End pop-ups in the Stroke palette is the Gap Color pop-up. The gap will be the same width as the point size you have chosen, even in dotted lines. The gap color can be anything you have added to your Swatches palette (covered in Chapter 13). Also, you can pick a tint of the gap color. Basically, you can make any stroke into any two colors you like.

On Graphics Production

After a while, InDesign's graphics implementation seems very elegant and obvious. However, I'm still firmly convinced that, for almost all graphic creation work, Illustrator users will go back to Illustrator and FreeHand users will go back to FreeHand. Even for Illustrator users, there are just too many things missing in InDesign (envelopes, blends, brushes, filters, and the like). However, I've found that I rarely make typographic graphics in either FreeHand or Illustrator, because they

10

are just not powerful enough with type. Personally, I use InDesign for graphic production more than I use Illustrator.

The stroke capabilities of InDesign are unique. Many of these options are simply not available to FreeHand or Illustrator (even Illustrator CS). As you've seen, InDesign amply equips you to make any type or width stroke you might need, with very few restrictions. The good news is that these features are available to paragraph rules, underlines, strikethroughs, and so on. Once we get to the chapters about applying color (Chapters 13 and 14), you'll discover that you can make any of these strokes any color or any gradient, as well. InDesign is truly an amazing page layout program.

Chapter 11

Edit Graphics in Your Document

How to...

- ■ Edit shapes and frames
- ■ Add graphics to text
- ■ Convert your type to graphics
- ■ Use type and shapes as a mask for graphics
- ■ Add type to a path
- ■ Use the full transparency of Adobe
- ■ Add a drop shadow
- ■ Feather your objects
- ■ Align objects
- ■ Arrange the pieces in your layout
- ■ Group objects in layers
- ■ Transform your objects
- ■ Combine your paths
- ■ Wrap your text
- ■ Use step and repeat

Now that we have covered the basics, we can talk about the many ways you can manipulate graphics. These techniques range from simply editing the points in your shapes to transforming objects and combining paths. We will also explore some graphic treatments of type, including converting type to graphics and adding type to a path.

Much of design in PostScript involves the assembly of multiple shapes into a finished whole. Actually, this is true of type also. Every character is made of one to five paths. In this chapter, I will show you how to access those paths to make typographic changes far beyond what you can accomplish with your fonts.

Edit Shapes and Frames

As explained in Chapter 10, several toolbox tools are useful for editing graphics. The Selection tool edits the shape as a whole. The Direct Selection tool selects the path and allows you to edit the points on the path by moving them or manipulating the handles. The Smoother tool changes corner points to curve points. The Eraser tool erases segments. Figure 11-1 shows some examples of a shape edited with these tools.

However, if you want to add, subtract, or convert points with any kind of control, you must use the Pen tool.

| FIGURE 11-1 | From left to right, a 17-pointed star, with some points moved around by the Direct Selection tool, with a side smoothed, and with two segments erased |

Edit with the Pen Tool

It is essential to learn how to use the Pen tool and to become comfortable with it. Remember that you access the Convert Point tool by holding down the ALT/OPTION key. If you do that over a curve point, the handles will be retracted to zero length. If you ALT/OPTION-click-drag a corner point, you will drag out symmetrical handles for a curve point. If you ALT/OPTION-click-drag on a handle of a curve point, you will be able to move each handle independently, thereby making it a corner point. Figure 11-2 shows some examples of paths edited with the Pen tool.

As I emphasized in Chapter 10, you need to practice drawing with the Pen tool. It does not matter what you draw. You just need to draw several dozen drawings.

Add a Corner Effect

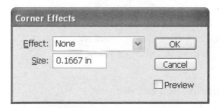

Here, we start to see a real difference between InDesign and the two dedicated drawing programs (FreeHand and Illustrator). InDesign has a dialog box that lets you put effects at corner points of a shape. To open the Corner Effects dialog box, select a path and choose Object | Corner Effects.

Your choices in the Effect drop-down list are None, Fancy, Bevel, Inset, Inverse Rounded, and Rounded. These effects are shown in Figure 11-3. As you can see in the example of the nine-pointed star, these effects can gct complex.

These effects work well, and you can apply them quickly. If you use them a lot, make a shortcut for the dialog box.

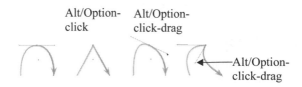

| FIGURE 11-2 | From left to right, a three-point path, with the top point converted to a corner, with the top point dragged out to a new curve, and with the handles moved individually |

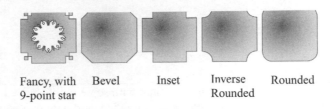

Fancy, with   Bevel   Inset   Inverse   Rounded
9-point star   Rounded

FIGURE 11-3   The five basic corner effects plus a nine-pointed star with fancy corners

You can modify the shapes that have corner effects as much as you like, but the effects themselves are not editable. In other words, you can modify the shape, but the Direct Selection tool does not give you access to the points that make up the corners.

Add Graphics to Text

InDesign allows you to either paste or place a graphic that is already created into an insertion point. This creates what InDesign calls an *inline frame*. In Quark-speak, the term is *anchored*. I call them *inline graphics*.

There are some major advantages to inserting an inline graphic:

- Because it is part of the text, it flows with the text. If the paragraph containing the inline graphic moves to the next page, so does the graphic. If you change the font or point size, the inline graphic moves with the type.

- Because InDesign considers an inline graphic as a type character, you can use it as a drop cap.

- If you put an inline graphic in a paragraph by itself, type will not overlap it. You can control it with the space before paragraph and space after paragraph settings. You can align it with the left, right, and centered alignments.

- Because you can place an unlimited number of graphics into text, you can make patterns, borders, and many other designs that would be time-consuming to do in any other way.

Add an Inline Graphic

There are three main ways to insert an inline graphic on a page:

- **Pasting a frame**   Select the frame you want to use as an inline frame and cut (CTRL-X/COMMAND-X) or copy (CTRL-C/COMMAND-C) it to the Clipboard. With the Type tool, click in an empty text frame or place an insertion point where you want the inline graphic to appear, and then paste (CTRL-V/COMMAND-V).

- **Placing a graphic file**   With the Type tool, click in an empty text frame or place an insertion point where you want the inline graphic to appear. Choose File | Place (CTRL-D/COMMAND-D). Then locate and select the graphic document you want to import and click Open. InDesign will place the graphic as an inline graphic at the insertion point.

> **NOTE**   *If autoleading is turned on, the inline graphic will increase the leading of the line into which it is placed. To remove this extra space, either resize the inline graphic or specify a fixed leading value for the paragraph.*

- **Create an inline frame by creating outlines**   You can use the Type | Create Outline command to convert your selected type to a graphic that looks like type. Using the Type tool, select the characters that you want to convert to outline shapes. When you do this for a portion of the text in a frame, the converted type becomes an embedded inline graphic in the text frame. We'll cover converting type to text after the next section.

Adjust the Position of an Inline Graphic

As you can imagine, once a graphic is placed inline, its movements are highly restricted. Basically, you can move it that same way you would move any character.

- You can select it with the Type tool and move it up or down by adjusting the baseline shift (on the Character palette).
- You can place an insertion point before or after the graphic and kern the graphic left or right.
- In addition (and unique to inline graphics), you can select the graphic with either selection tool to move it up or down. If you move it with the Direct Selection tool, the inline frame will crop it. If you move it with the Selection tool, you will be limited to moving the bottom of the frame up to the baseline or the top of the frame down to the baseline. To go farther than that, you will need to use a baseline shift setting.

> **TIP**   *The easiest way to adjust spacing around an inline graphic is to use the Selection tool to adjust the size of the frame, and then the Direct Selection tool to move the graphic around inside the frame.*

11

Convert Your Type to Graphics

As mentioned in the previous section, one way to create an inline graphic is to use the Type | Create Outlines command to convert type to a graphic. Although InDesign calls the command Create Outlines, what it really does is convert type to the paths that are already there. All type formats that you normally use are built from paths. PostScript Type 1 fonts use PostScript paths, and TrueType and OpenType fonts use paths also.

A major change happens when you use the Create Outlines command. You can get access to the paths that make up the type characters you just converted, but you no longer have type that can be edited as type. This graphic looks exactly like type, but it cannot be edited, spell-checked, reformatted, or anything else you would do to type. It is no longer type.

So, why would you want to do this? There are many reasons, but the two most common ones are to use type shapes as a mask for a placed graphic and to customize type character shapes for graphic purposes.

NOTE   *To be honest, you will usually want to convert type to graphics in Illustrator or FreeHand (using FreeHand's appropriately named Convert to Paths command). FreeHand does it better and faster, but FreeHand does not have access to OpenType's additional characters. However, InDesign can do a credible job (as good as Illustrator, in most cases).*

Use Type (or Shapes) As a Mask for Placed Graphics

Using type as a mask for graphics is commonly done. It is rarely done wisely. The problem is that using type as a mask often makes both the type and the graphic unreadable. However, with care, masked graphics can have a powerful impact.

Figure 11-4 shows an example of a masked image. I needed to radically modify the character outlines to eliminate white space around and within the characters. As you can see, the image is irritatingly cut up. This is often the result of masking. This entire process takes great care.

Of course, you do not need to use type as a mask for a bitmap. Any shape functions as a mask. If you resize the containing frame with the Selection tool, you can crop any portion of the image. With the Direct Selection tool, you can click the image and move it around inside the masking frame. And you can modify the frame with the Direct Selection tool and the Pen tool.

Edit the Character Shapes

After you select the type you want to convert and choose Type | Create Outlines, you have outlines of the characters that you can modify to your heart's content with the Direct Selection, Pen, and Pencil tools. Anything that InDesign can do to a graphic, you can now do to this converted type. Figure 11-5 shows a simple example, but you can do anything you can imagine.

FIGURE 11-4   A distant landscape masked by some type

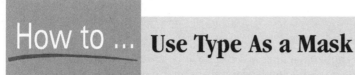
Use Type As a Mask

The procedure for using type as a mask is relatively simple:

1. Create the type as close to final size as possible (optional) and select it.

2. Choose Type | Create Outlines. This converts the type to paths.

3. With the Direct Selection tool and the Pen tool, modify the character shapes until you have removed as much white space as possible.

4. Choose File | Place to place the graphic you want to mask.

5. Move the graphic to the location where you will mask it to check that it is sized correctly. Bitmaps need to be resized in Photoshop. If it is a bitmap, select it in the Links palette and click the Edit Original button (or open Photoshop and open the graphic in Photoshop for editing). If it is a vector graphic, resize it in InDesign.

6. Cut the image to the Clipboard. Select the converted type and choose Edit | Paste Into.

7. With the Direct Selection tool, move the image around inside the mask as necessary. The Direct Selection tool cursor will turn into the grabber hand when it will move the image.

11

Just remember that after you convert the text, the type is a graphic. It can no longer be edited as type.

FIGURE 11-5   A word converted to a path, and then modified to a simple logo

Add Type to a Path

People are used to seeing type across horizontal lines in rectangular boxes like columns, so type on a path looks like a graphic. First, you should understand that this is not an operation to be undertaken lightly. You must be very careful, *if* you really want readers to be able to read your copy on a path. Keep that proviso in mind as you read through this section.

Putting type on a path is simple to do. Just click a path with the Type on a Path tool, accessed by pressing SHIFT-T (the tool icon is a *T* slanted on a path), and type in the copy.

When you type on a path, the direction of the path matters. Type on a path reads from the start of a path to the end of a path. If the path is from left to right, the type reads normally. If the path is from right to left, the type reads backwards and upside down.

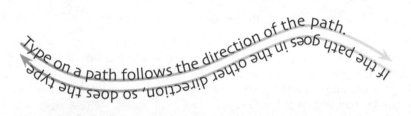

There are some new iconic indicators that appear with type on a path, as shown in Figure 11-6. The vertical lines at the beginning and end of the path are called the start and end brackets. Attached to these brackets are the in and out ports of a normal text frame. These are used to link the text on this path to other frames. This means that you can have normal text flow from a text frame through a squirrelly path to another text frame, if you wish.

> **TIP** *The new Story Editor can be helpful for working with type on a path. When your type is unreadable on a path (like a spiral, for example), simply open the story in Story Editor to edit it.*

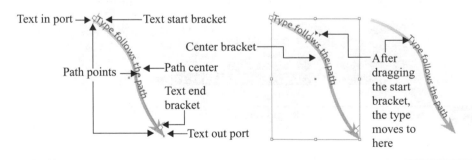

FIGURE 11-6   The parts of the interface for type on a path

Edit Text on a Path

As usual, to edit type on a path, you need to select it first. You can add an insertion point with either Type tool by clicking between any two characters in the type on a path. You can also double-click the path with either selection tool to place an insertion point. Then double-clicking selects the word, and triple-clicking selects the entire path of type.

After you select the type, you can just edit normally. You can apply most of the character and paragraph options to type on a path, including styles. The alignment setting in the Paragraph palette controls the alignment of type on a path, and all the shortcuts work normally. However, some of the specialized options like paragraph rules and the paragraph spacing options have no effect on type on a path.

Of course, you can simply select the type and delete it, as you would remove regular type. In this case, the path remains threaded (if you had linked it). Plus, it keeps all the attributes of type on a path.

Change the Position of Type on a Path

Using the start or end bracket, you can move the type on the path. Use either selection tool to select the path with type on it. Then move the selection cursor over either the start or end bracket of the type on a path. The cursor changes to a filled convert-point cursor, with a vertical bar that has a little arrow pointing to the right (see Figure 11-6). Then click-drag the bracket with the Selection tool to drag the type along the path. Do not position it over the bracket's in port or out port. If the little red plus sign appears, indicating overflowed type, you can simply make the path longer, and then reposition the type.

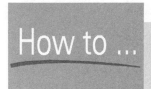 *If you have paragraph indents, they are measured from the start and end brackets.*

11

How to ... **Remove Type from a Path and Type-on-a-Path Attributes**

There is a special method of deleting text on a path that also eliminates the special type-on-a-path attributes. Simply select one or more paths with type attached. Choose Type | Type on a Path | Delete Type from Path (it's not available in a context menu).

If the path with text is threaded, type will move to the next threaded text frame or path with type on it. If the path isn't threaded, text on it is deleted. The path remains, but loses any type-on-a-path attributes—all brackets, in and out ports, and threading properties are removed.

Note that if the path's fill and stroke are set to None, the path will be invisible after you delete the type. The easiest way to make the path visible is to press the D key immediately after you delete the type with the Delete Type from Path command. This will apply the default fill and stroke to the selected path.

Using the center bracket of type on a path, you can manipulate its position a couple other ways. The center bracket is almost invisible on a normal high-resolution monitor. It looks like a simple upside-down *T* (see Figure 11-6), but the lines that draw it are very thin, and they are the color of the layer. It is positioned halfway between the start and end brackets. If you move a selection cursor over a selected path with type on it, the little center bracket icon will appear next to the cursor when you are over the center bracket.

By dragging the center bracket, you can do the following:

- **Slide type along a path**   Use either selection tool to select the type on a path. Slide the cursor over the path type's center bracket until the center bracket icon appears next to the pointer. Drag the center bracket along the path. The text won't move if both the brackets are at the ends of the path. To create some space for dragging text, you will need to drag the start or end bracket away from at least one of the ends of the path. (You might need to lengthen the path.)

- **Flip type on a path by dragging**   With either selection tool, select the type on a path (path or frame) and slide the cursor over the type's center bracket until the little center bracket icon appears next to the cursor. Then drag the center bracket across the path to flip the type upside down and in the other direction.

Use Type on a Path Options

There are several esoteric options that control how the type characters align to the path. These are in the Type on a Path Options dialog box, accessed by inserting an insertion point or selecting the type and choosing Type on a Path | Options from the Type menu or the Type context menu. (As usual, if you use this dialog box a lot, you should make a shortcut for it.)

This little dialog box has a great deal of power. It has all of Illustrator's options, but it adds the ability to align the type to the edges or center of the stroke width. Let's go through the various options, top to bottom. Remember that you can check the Preview box to see what your choices look like before you click OK.

Apply an Effect to Type on a Path

You can apply five different effects to type on a path. The Rainbow effect is the default. The other four may work for specialized designs, but they are rarely used.

You can choose one of the following from the Effect menu in the Type on a Path Options dialog box:

- **Rainbow**   This effect keeps the center of each character's baseline parallel to the path's tangent or the center of the character perpendicular to the path. This is the default setting because it looks relatively normal.

- **Skew**   This effect keeps the characters' vertical strokes vertical, regardless of the path shape, while letting characters' horizontal strokes follow the path. The resulting horizontal distortion causes the type to look like it is standing vertically and is useful for text that goes around a cylinder, such as on a can label.

- **3D Ribbon**   This effect keeps characters' horizontal edges perfectly horizontal, regardless of the path shape, while keeping each character's vertical edge perpendicular to the path. This effect makes the text very hard to read.

- **Stair Step**   This keeps the left edge of each character's baseline on the path, without rotating any characters. This one is also very hard to read.

- **Gravity**   This keeps the center of each character's baseline on the path, while keeping each vertical edge in line with the path's center point. This looks a little like perspective, but the characters tend to distort a bit too much. It's not easy to read.

Figure 11-7 illustrates each of these type-on-a-path effects.

Control the Alignment of Type on a Path

The Type on a Path Options dialog box offers several alignment options. The Align option specifies how to align all characters to the path. Your choices are Ascender, Descender, Center, or Baseline. Baseline is the default setting. These font dimensions are part of the font and specified by the font designer.

11

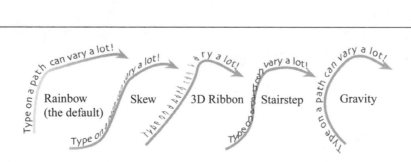

FIGURE 11-7   The five effects for type on a path

In InDesign, you can align the path to the edges of the stroke. In Figure 11-7, for example, I lined up the type by descender to the top of the stroke. You can produce effects like this easily by choosing one of the following in the To Path drop-down list:

- ■ To align the path to the top edge of the stroke, choose Top.
- ■ To align the path to the bottom edge of the stroke, choose Bottom.
- ■ To align the path to the center of the stroke, choose Center. This is the default setting.

For more control over vertical alignment, use the Baseline Shift field in the Character palette (or in a paragraph style). For example, type a negative value in the Baseline Shift field to lower the type.

Flip the Type on a Path

Rather than dragging the center bracket across the path, as described in the previous section, you can select the Flip check box in the Type on a Path Options dialog box. But it's usually easier to simply drag the center bracket.

Control Character Spacing around Turns and Angles

The Spacing option in the Type of a Path Options dialog box provides a way to apply tracking to portions of the type on a path as they go around sharp corners or curves. This Spacing value affects only the way characters fan out around a curve or sharp angle. It has no effect on characters positioned on straight segments. In most cases, normal kerning and tracking controls are faster, easier, and better.

Most People Won't Read Text Added to a Path

Type on a path is one of those things that designers squeal for. However, you need to be very careful when using the feature. It is so far outside the norm that most readers will not read the copy on a path. They will skip to the next copy they can read.

You really need to make sure you have a genuine reason to go so far outside the normal reading patterns of the reader. If you are marketing snowboards, go for it!

Use the Full Transparency of Adobe

Vector transparency has been a major leap in desktop publishing production. In general, full transparency is both easy and simple in InDesign.

As we go through the transparency options, however, be aware that transparency can introduce some complications. Transparency on top of transparency—like a word with a drop shadow on top of a transparent box with a drop shadow—will cause some difficulties. Occasionally, you will run into severe problems. It is possible to have so much transparency that no one can print what you designed. You may need to rethink your design choices. We will cover how to deal with these and other types of production hurdles in Chapter 17.

> **NOTE** *One of the major routines that Adobe has been able to implement fully across the applications is transparency. However, Adobe's transparency is a major scam. Transparency is not part of the basic PostScript language. Ole Kvern, who speaks that language, says Adobe does it with clipping paths, rasterization, and mirrors. (Well, he doesn't mention the mirrors.) But no matter how it's actually accomplished, transparency works very smoothly in practice.*

The Transparency palette itself is deceptively simple. It shows just four items: a Blending Modes drop-down list, an Opacity control, an Isolate Blending check box, and a Knockout Group check box. However, each can have a dramatic effect.

Play with Blending Modes

The blending mode affects how the color on top (to which the mode is applied) changes the colors of the objects below. The drop-down list in the Transparency palette offers 16 modes.

Normal

Multiply
Screen
Overlay
Soft Light
Hard Light

Color Dodge
Color Burn

Darken
Lighten
Difference
Exclusion

Hue
Saturation
Color
Luminosity

11

These are basically lifted directly out of Photoshop, as far as the results are concerned. Here's a list describing each option:

- **Normal**   What do you think? Everything remains normal, and the object does not interact with the objects below it. If you make an object transparent in Normal mode, it just gets transparent.

- **Multiply**   This basically adds the color of the selected object to the colors of the object (or objects) under that object. In other words, it makes the object darker. This is the way shadows work, for example. The colors being shadowed are added to the color of the shadow itself. (Mathematically, they are evidently multiplied.)

- **Screen**   This mode is the opposite of Multiply. You can use this to lighten overlapping areas. The effect is of multiple layers of light. More light makes the colors lighter.

- **Overlay**   This mode lightens the light areas and darkens the dark areas, with no effect on the 50 percent tints. It sharply increases color contrast and can get out of hand easily.

- **Soft Light and Hard Light**   These modes apply effects to the highlights and shadows. Hard Light really exaggerates the highlights, often causing a "plastic" look. These modes have little use in InDesign.

- **Color Dodge and Color Burn**   These two modes increase contrast by intensifying the hues or increasing the saturation (same thing). Color Dodge lightens as it brightens. Color Burn mainly deepens and intensifies the shadows.

- **Darken and Lighten**   These modes work by comparing the pixels on top with those underneath. Lighten only makes changes when it finds a color on top that is lighter than the ones under it. Darken works by changing only colors that are darker on top.

- **Difference**   Here's one of those mathematical wonders. It compares the upper image and the image below it using black as a neutral. If there is no difference in color between the two, those colors are changed to black. It usually results in more saturated color, often psychedelic. Using it, you can produce some ugly stuff.

- **Exclusion**   This is a more subdued version of Difference that creates much less saturated colors (that is, they are grayed out).

- **Hue, Saturation, and Luminosity**   For those of you with fine-art training, these are hue, saturation, and value. In each case, the mode takes that particular information from the object on top and applies it to the objects beneath. Hue changes the colors only. Saturation changes the intensity only. Luminosity changes the value (or grayscale information) only.

- **Color**   This mode applies both the hue and saturation—everything except the value (the luminosity, or light and dark information).

NOTE   *The Difference, Exclusion, Hue, Saturation, Color, and Luminosity modes do not work with spot colors.*

Wonderful! Look at all the options! My response is pretty much, "Ho, hum…." These blending modes are used a lot in Photoshop. For vector objects, they are far less useful. Mainly, you can waste a lot of time fiddling with effects. When you have spare time, play with the modes to find methods that work for your style. Don't try to do it on a client's time, though. You can easily spend hours with nothing to show for it. Most of the time, Normal or Multiply do what you want.

Adjust the Opacity

The Transparency palette's Opacity field is where you can type in a percentage for opacity. Or, you can click the right-pointing triangle to use the slider. This is a crucial ability for transparency.

Most of the time, you want it lighter than you see on the screen. Remember that all printers have some dot gain. The cheaper the printing technology, the greater the dot gain, in most cases. So, in most cases, make it as light as you can tolerate. However, if you make the object too transparent, it may disappear completely.

Isolate the Blending or Knock Out the Group

When you apply blending modes to objects in a group, the effects of the blending modes also affect any objects beneath the group. You can control this with the Isolate Blending and Knockout Group check boxes on the Transparency palette (these appear when you choose Show Options from the palette's option menu).

When you use the Isolate Blending option, only members of the selected group are affected; objects beneath the group are unaffected by the blending modes. Isolate Blending works only for groups containing objects that have a blending mode other than Normal applied to them. It affects only groups or selected frames.

11

> **TIP** *To isolate a PDF containing blending modes, select Transparent Background in the Place PDF dialog box when placing the file. Use the Selection tool to select the file, and then click the Isolate Blending check box.*

With the Knockout Group option, you can make all of the objects within a selected group function opaquely with each other, while still interacting transparently with objects below the selected group.

Here is an example of using both of these options:

Isolate Blending   Knockout Group

Be prepared for frustration and testing when isolating blending or knocking out groups. It took me more than an hour to make the illustration shown here, requiring several adjustments that did not flatten properly when I made the PDF graphic. When you're working with these, do not assume your results will print properly. Make a proof.

Add a Drop Shadow

The major use for transparency is drop shadows. People are fascinated by these, and they are an excellent way to attract attention to an area. They are easy to create, and you can edit a drop shadow at any time, with no penalty. One of the nice things about transparency is that it is not rasterized until it is output and flattened. On the screen, it is flawless. However, the rasterization and flattening can result in some production problems with the use of shadows, which we will talk about in Chapter 17.

To create a drop shadow, choose Object | Drop Shadow to open the Drop Shadow dialog box, shown in Figure 11-8. As you can see, there are many controls.

The Drop Shadow check box turns on the drop shadow. Then you can set the options in the dialog box:

- **Mode**   You can choose any of the blending modes listed in the previous section. Multiply is the normal mode, because this is the way shadows work.
- **Opacity**   This is the normal Opacity slider. The default is 75%. I think that is too dark. I would suggest a starting point of around 50%.
- **X Offset**   This is the horizontal offset of the shadow. The default is 7 points.
- **Y Offset**   This is the vertical offset of the shadow. The default is 7 points.
- **Blur**   This is the distance from the edge of the shadow where you want the blurring to occur. The default is 5 points.
- **Color**   You can use any color in the Swatches palette. Normal shadows are gray or blue-gray.

If you check the Preview box, the preview updates as soon as you tab out of a field. When you click OK, InDesign creates a transparent raster object for the shadow. (That's what the Help section says—don't get mad at me.) As far as I can tell, it is the interaction of these transparent raster objects of strokes, fills, and so on that causes the imaging problems.

Figure 11-9 shows some examples of shadows applied to type. I used the defaults, except for the changes noted in the figure.

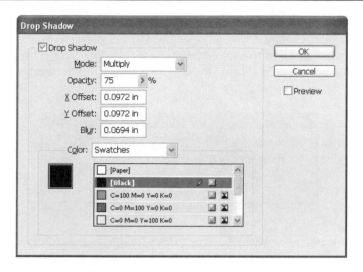

FIGURE 11-8   The Drop Shadow dialog box

11

FIGURE 11-9   Examples of shadows applied to type

Feather Your Objects

There are times when it is handy to have an object fade to transparent along the edges of that object. The Feather command softens the edges of an object in this manner over the distance you specify. All you need to do is choose Object | Feather and check the Feather check box in the dialog box that appears.

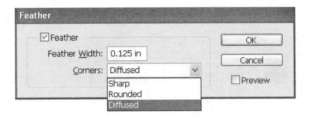

First, set the distance over which the object fades from opaque to transparent by entering a number in the Feather Width field. Then choose a corner option from the three possibilities:

- **Sharp** The gradient follows the outer edge of the shape exactly, including sharp corners. This option is appropriate for any object with sharp corners, such as stars and rectangles.

- **Rounded** The corners are rounded by the feather radius amount set in the Feather Width field; according to Adobe, the shape is first inset, then outset, to form the two contours. It was designed to produce a pleasing effect on rectangles.

- **Diffused** The Adobe Illustrator method is used to make the edges of the object fade from opaque to transparent.

Figure 11-10 illustrates the effects of the three corner options for feathering. Obviously, this will take a little experimentation and you could waste a lot of time, if you're not careful. Select Preview to display the results on-screen while you are experimenting, and then click OK when you're finished.

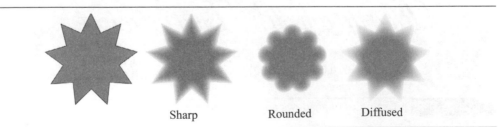

FIGURE 11-10 The three feather options on a 9-pointed star, with a Field Width setting of 0.125 inch

Align Any Objects Any Way

The section heading here may be a little optimistic, but InDesign's Align palette is very powerful. You can use the Align palette to align or distribute objects you select either horizontally and vertically. You can use object edges or anchor points as the reference point for these alignments. In addition, you can distribute the space between objects evenly, both horizontally and vertically. You can see all these options in the Align palette after you've chosen Show Options in the palette's option menu, as shown in Figure 11-11.

NOTE   *The Align palette will not affect objects that you've locked. Also, it won't change the alignment of text paragraphs within their frames.*

To align objects, multiple-select them (by using the Selection tool while holding down the SHIFT key), and then click the Align palette button for the type of alignment you want. You can use the Align palette in the following ways:

- **Simple alignment**   You can align selected objects by the edges of their bounding boxes to the left, center, right, top, middle, and bottom. This works as you would expect. Just remember that the alignment applies to the bounding box. This can be a problem if you have an inset on your text frames.

- **Distribute**   You can distribute objects, by inserting an equal amount of space between the corresponding edges of the bounding boxes of all selected objects. For example, if you click the Vertical Distribute Left button, InDesign makes sure that there is an equal amount of space between the left edges of the bounding boxes of each selected object.

11

FIGURE 11-11   The Align palette with its options showing

■ **Distribute by value**   You can set a measurement for distribution. This inserts a spacing value between the center points or corresponding edges of bounding boxes of the selected objects. This method changes the width of the original selections and can cause severe overlapping. When distributing by value, a negative value moves objects left horizontally or up vertically.

■ **Distribute by spacing**   You can also insert an equal amount of space between the facing edges of the selected bounding boxes: horizontally or vertically. For example, if you put 0.125 inch as the spacing value and click the Horizontal Distribute Space button, InDesign will put one-eighth inch of space between all selected objects. A positive value adds space between objects, and a negative value removes space.

It does take some practice and math to distribute objects the way you would like. But the alignments work very well.

 There are no assigned shortcuts for the Align Objects and Distribute Objects areas. If you use the Align palette a lot, you will want to assign shortcuts for these functions.

Arrange the Pieces in Your Layout

In Chapter 10, I described the PostScript layout as analogous to sheets of infinitely thin Mylar. Here, we will look at the incredible power you have to arrange all those transparent sheets that hold the different objects you create for your layout. We'll start with the simplest.

Change the Stacking Order

Every frame or drawn object has its own order in the stack, arranged by creation time. The newest object is on the top of the stack. Many times, you will need to bring your objects forward or backward in the stacking order. There are four commands on the Object menu to help you do this:

■ Bring Forward (CTRL-]/COMMAND-])

■ Bring to Front (CTRL-SHIFT-]/COMMAND-SHIFT-])

■ Send Backward (CTRL-[/COMMAND-[)

■ Send to Back (CTRL-SHIFT-[/COMMAND-SHIFT-[)

These commands allow you to bring selected objects toward the top or the bottom of the stack of objects in your document.

I recommend better shortcuts: CTRL-F/COMMAND-F *for Bring to Front and* CTRL-B/COMMAND-B *for Send to Back. They are easier to remember, but they do mean you will need to rearrange other shortcuts: the Find command (I use* COMMAND-OPTION-F*) and the Text Frame Options command (I use* COMMAND-OPTION-T*).*

Group Objects in Layers

Above and beyond rearranging the stacking order, you can use the Layers palette to group objects into their own layer. This way, you can lock upper layers to give you access to layers under many other objects, which would be hard to select in any other way. You can also have separate layers for each language in which you are setting the document. Figure 11-12 shows the Layers palette and its option menu.

This is Illustrator's palette from version 9 or 10, with a few additions, and it has all of its benefits and limitations. You can lock layers, name layers, and assign them a custom color for all their bounding boxes.

When you select an object or objects, a small square appears at the far right of the layer. You drag this little box to move things to another layer. It is safer than FreeHand's click-on-layer technique to move objects, but it is much slower.

You can control the layers by clicking on them and dragging them up or down to put them above or below other layers. As with all the palettes, you can multiple-select, double-click to see the options, and so on.

TIP   *The color of the Default layer bothers me, so I change it. If you have the same reaction, you can change a color of a layer by simply double-clicking the layer in the Layers palette and choosing a new color.*

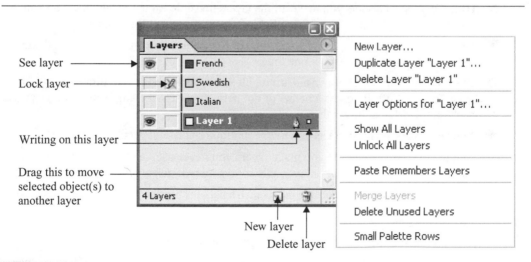

11

FIGURE 11-12   The Layers palette and option menu

Use Layers Palette Options

The Layers palette's option menu contains the following commands:

- **New Layer**   This makes a new layer and opens the New Layer dialog box, which allows you to choose your layer options immediately. More important, it gives you the immediate chance to name your layer. It is much faster to click the New Layer icon at the bottom of the palette to make a new layer if you do not wish to control the options of that layer.

- **Duplicate Layer**   This duplicates a selected layer and opens the Duplicate Layer dialog box, which allows you to choose your layer options immediately and name your layer. It is faster to simply drag the name of the layer on top of the New Layer icon.

- **Delete Layer**   This deletes a selected layer. It is faster to select the layer and click the trashcan icon at the bottom of the palette. Or you can drag the layer by its name to the trashcan icon at the bottom of the palette.

- **Layer Options**   You can name or rename the layer, show it or hide it, show guides or hide them, or you can suppress a text wrap if the layer is hidden. It is much quicker to get to these options by simply double-clicking the layer name.

TIP   *If you uncheck Suppress Text Wrap in the Layer Options dialog box, you can have a text wrap on an object in a hidden layer that affects the visible layers.*

- **Hide Others**   This lets you make all the layers invisible except for the layer on which you are working. This is faster than clicking the eye icon on all the other layers.

- **Unlock All Layers**   This might be helpful if you are using many layers—more than you can see in the Layers palette at one time.

- **Paste Remembers Layers**   This is a toggle command—select it to turn it on, select it again to turn it off. It affects whether or not items copied to the Clipboard will be pasted back on the original layers they were copied from.

- **Merge Layers**   This one lets you merge multiple selected layers.

- **Delete Unused Layers**   If you make layers you never use, or if you cut or move all the items on a layer to another layer, this command will delete all empty layers.

- **Small Palette Rows**   Makes the rows much smaller. They then look like Quark's version, only smaller.

Deal with the Lack of Guides and Nonprinting Layers

If you're used to using a program like FreeHand, you probably noticed that the InDesign Layers palette does not offer a guides layer or simple nonprinting background layer. There is no printing check box or dimming field. If you do not want objects to print, you must use the Non-Printing option in the Attributes palette. If you need to dim your objects on a palette to make irregular guides, you must pick tinted strokes and fills.

Layers Are a Last Resort

Layers are not helpful unless you need them. Too many layers can make it very hard to keep track of what is happening in your document. A new layer should be a last resort. In most cases, a single layer is all that you need. InDesign is a vector program, so everything remains completely editable at all times. I leave the Layers palette closed.

You can have individual guides for each layer, and you can lock those guides. Normally, all you can create are horizontal and vertical guides. Without a guides layer, circles, angled lines, or paths can be saved only to a locked layer that does not print and is dimmed. You can color the shapes as necessary before you lock the layer and move it into position. Normal guides are controlled under the Layout and View menus.

Transform Your Objects

PostScript gives you the ability to transform objects in many ways, providing far more flexibility than most page layout programs. You can scale, rotate, and shear objects. Drawing programs also have reflection or flipping transformations, and InDesign has a couple of options for those, too. The transformations are available through the Transform palette, Transform menu, and toolbox tools.

Use the Transform Palette

The Transform palette deals with very different transformations of objects, even text as an object. Figure 11-13 shows the palette and an example of a rectangle that has been rotated and sheared.

At the bottom of the Transform palette are the Rotate, Shear, Horizontal Scale, and Vertical Scale fields. You can click any of the icons to the left of the fields and use the up and down arrows to change the numbers (based on your Units and Cursor Key settings in the Preferences dialog box, as explained in Chapter 2). For the transformation shown in Figure 11-13, I used the center of the rectangle as the transformation center and clicked the Rotate icon (second from the bottom right). I clicked the up and down arrows until I liked the rotations. Then I clicked the Shear icon (bottom right), and used the arrows to adjust the shear. You can read the angles and percentages in the palette's fields.

Notice the link icon to the left of the Horizontal Scaling and Vertical Scaling fields. This is where you click to constrain the shape to proportional resizing. You can also make proportional changes by pressing CTRL-RETURN/COMMAND-RETURN to apply the transformation, or by holding down the CTRL/COMMAND key before you choose a percentage in one of the scaling pop-up menus.

11

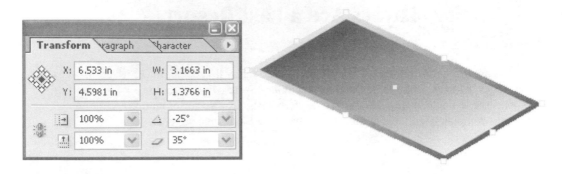

The Transform palette with a rotated and sheared rectangle

Measure Your Transformations

On the upper-left side of the Transform palette, you see a proxy icon (the same as the one used in PageMaker), which shows from which handle your transformations were measured. This proxy allows you to apply transformations from any handle or the center of the object.

In this example, the proxy shows that the measurements are from the center of the object. The center point is 5.5165 inches to the right, measured from the zero point on the horizontal ruler. It is 2.7569 inches below the zero point on the vertical ruler. The width of the object (in the W field) is 1.5956 inches. The height of the object (shown in the H field) is 0.7361 inches. The height and width are centered on the X/Y measurements. So, this is a small rectangle a little more than 1.5 inches wide and a little less than 0.75 inch tall.

You can base your measurements on any of the nine handles by simply clicking the handle in the proxy. This is one of the most useful aspects of this palette. You can accurately locate any object on a page, measured from any point, the center, or the transformation center (if you have moved that by hand). How many times have you wished that you could measure the size and location of an object from the right side or the lower-right corner? Now you can.

Use the Transform Palette Options

The Transform palette's option menu has several important commands.

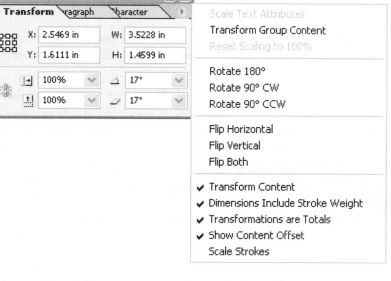

These options work as follows:

■ **Scale Text Attributes**   This command is available only when you have turned off the Adjust Text Attributes When Scaling preference. This preference affects only text frames scaled after the option is turned on, and it does not affect existing text frames. If you need to fix an existing, individually scaled frame, use the Selection tool to select the text frame and choose the Scale Text Attributes option. (It does not affect groups of frames.) Text attributes like size, leading, kerning, and so on are adjusted based on the scaling percentage, and the scaling fields in the Transform palette revert to 100% scale.

NOTE   *The Adjust Text Attributes When Scaling preference is turned on by default. When you triple the scale of 12-point type, for example, the values in the Character or Control palette appear as 36-point type, while the scaling values remain at 100% in the Transform palette. If you turn off this preference, when you triple the scale, the Transform palette indicates 300% scaling, but the text appears in the Control or Character palette as 12pt(36). See Chapter 2 for more information about the effects of this preference.*

■ **Transform Group Content**   Normally, when you transform grouped objects, the settings apply to the entire group, as well as to the individual objects in the group. If you rotate a group 27 degrees, the rotate value in the Transform palette is 27 degrees, whether you select the group or direct select an object in the group. The Transform Group Content command resets the rotation of the group to 0 degrees, while maintaining the actual transformation attributes of the group. In other words, this command makes a new bounding box that is not transformed, while the contents of the group remain transformed inside that new bounding box.

11

■ **Reset Scaling to 100%**   If you want to restart your percentage calculations, choose this option to reset the numbers to 100%.

■ **Rotate 180°, 90° CW, or 90° CCW**   These Rotate options allow you to make quick 180 degrees, 90 degrees clockwise, and 90 degrees counter-clockwise rotations. The old norm (before digital production), was to use only these angles.

■ **Flip Horizontal, Vertical, or Both**   You can use these commands to flip objects.

■ **Transform Content**   This command affects only transformations made with the Transform palette. You can choose whether or not you will transform the content of a frame when you transform that frame.

■ **Dimensions Include Stroke Weight**   If this is checked, the size of your object will be measured by the outside edges of the stroke. If it is unchecked, the path will determine the object size.

■ **Transformations Are Totals**   This affects nested objects (graphics pasted into other graphics). When this command is checked, if a parent (containing) graphic of a nested graphic is rotated 15 degrees, the subselected nested graphic will show a rotation of 15 degrees. If this is unchecked, the nested graphic will still show 0 degrees, because it has not rotated in relation to the parent graphic.

■ **Show Content Offset**   This makes the measurements in the Transform palette show the relative position of the nested graphic as measured from the upper-left corner of the parent graphic.

■ **Scale Strokes**   Here, you can choose whether the stroke width scales with the frame, path, or shape.

Transform with Menu Commands

On the Object | Transform menu, you will find four commands: Move, Scale, Rotate, and Shear. The same commands appear in the context menu when you right-click/CONTROL-click a selected object and choose Transform. Selecting one of these commands opens a dialog box for that transformation. For all of them, you need to choose the point of origin in the Transform or Control palette proxy. All of the dialog boxes include a Copy button that lets you make a copy as you transform, as well as a check box to transform the content of the frame. They also have a Preview option.

The dialog boxes displayed by the menu commands work as follows:

■ **Move**   This dialog box gives you fields to move horizontally, vertically, by distance, and by angle.

■ **Scale**   This dialog box gives you fields to scale uniformly by a percentage or nonuniformly by horizontal and vertical percentages.

■ **Rotate**   This dialog box gives you a field to choose the angle of rotation by degree. Negative numbers are clockwise, and positive numbers are counter-clockwise.

■ **Shear**   This dialog box gives you a field to choose the angle of shear by degree. Negative numbers slant to the left, and positive numbers slant to the right. You also pick your axis of shear: horizontal keeps the horizontal lines horizontal; vertical keeps the vertical lines vertical. You can shear on any other axis at the angle of your choice in degrees.

These transformations are very powerful, clean, and easy to use.

Use the Transform Tools

The transform tools in the InDesign toolbox have been civilized for page layout. They do not have the extreme power found in Illustrator and FreeHand. However, because of the limitations, these tools are much easier to use in InDesign. In the drawing programs, all of the tools, except the Rotation tool, also rotate and flip (reflect) while they transform. You really need to keep track of what you are doing. InDesign's tools do not flip, but they are still powerful enough to get out of control easily.

You need to practice using the transform tools. These tools can quickly transform a shape beyond recognition, until you get used to them.

Understand the Center of Origin

There is a concept that you need to understand to work with the transform tools: the transformations move around what Adobe calls the *center of origin*. I usually call it the *transformation center*. Figure 11-14 illustrates how the transformation center works.

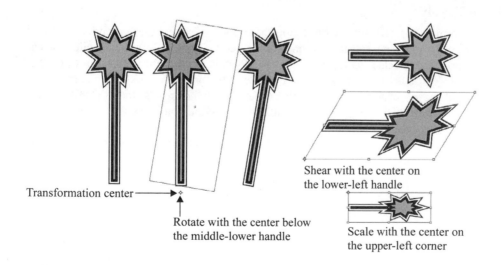

Transformation center ⟶

Rotate with the center below
the middle-lower handle

Shear with the center on
the lower-left handle

Scale with the center on
the upper-left corner

FIGURE 11-14   Some transformations with various centers of origin

11

The transformation center is a little icon that can, and usually should, be moved with the transform tool before you transform the shape. It is a little circle with horizontal and vertical lines sticking out of it, as you can see in Figure 11-14. The transformations move around this center. For example, if you want to move a reflection around the edge of a wheel, you need to move the transformation center to the center of that wheel. The transformation center works in the same way as the nine handles in the proxy in the Transform palette or Control palette, except that you can move it wherever you like.

Rotate, Scale, and Shear

To rotate, select the shape with the Rotation tool. (This tool works like Illustrator's Rotate tool.) When you move the cursor over the transformation center, it changes to a black pointer that allows you to drag the center to wherever you desire. Move the transformation center, and then click-drag the Rotation tool until you get the angle you want. For precise rotation, use the Transform palette, where the center of origin shows in the X/Y fields.

You will get a lot more control of your transformation by clicking farther away from the center of origin.

The Scale and Shear tools work as expected, once you take the transformation center into account. If you hold down the SHIFT key and shear upward, this will constrain your skew to vertical. The preview while transforming is exceptional, but you need to wait until the cursor changes into a solid, black triangle to see it. If you quickly click-drag, all you will see is an outline of the bounding box.

Transform Freely

The Free Transform tool is basically the Illustrator/Photoshop tool. Using the appropriate shortcuts, you can interactively apply any transformation to any object. If the tool is over a handle, you can scale. If it is outside the selected shape, you can rotate. If you hold down the CTRL-ALT/COMMAND-OPTION keys before you drag a side handle on the side of the bounding box (not a corner), the bounding box will shear around the transformation center. If you then release the ALT/OPTION key, the opposite side handle will lock into its original position while you move the selected edge around. There is no perspective option.

To reflect, simply drag a handle across to the other side. You can SHIFT-drag to constrain the tool. It's a wonderful tool!

Add a Transformed Cast Shadow

Let's work through a short exercise to practice using the transform tools.

1. Start with any single word. The only requirement is that there be no descenders in the characters. Even rounded bowls at the bottom of letters like *O* and *G* will cause overlapping problems. Using a very bold font at a large point size will make it easier to see what is happening. I used *WANTED!* set in a font called WANTED and colored black.

2. Choose Type | Create Outlines to convert the type to a path.

3. Select the converted type with the Selection tool and cut it (CTRL-X/COMMAND-X). Delete the original text frame and paste the converted type back into the document.

4. With the Shear tool, using the lower-left handle as the center of origin, shear the type straight up by holding down the SHIFT key.

5. Copy the pasted type and choose Edit | Paste in Place to put a second copy of the type directly on top of the original type.

6. Color that second copy a light gray.

7. With the Selection tool, click the upper-center handle and drag it down until the type is upside down and about twice as tall as the original type. It really does not matter how far up (or down) you stretch the word. All it will change is the apparent angle of the light source.

8. With the Free Transform tool (and the same center of origin), hold down the CTRL-ALT/ COMMAND-OPTION keys and drag the bottom-center point sideways. Release the ALT/ OPTION key as soon as it starts shearing, and the top will remain aligned with the original baseline.

The result is a word standing vertical, with a cast shadow down and to the right. Figure 11-15 shows a summary of the process. I usually add a gradient to the shadow to make it look better.

Now, it can be argued that this type of illustration can be done much more impressively in a 3D rendering program—with multiple light sources, extruded type, and many other embellishments. This is certainly true. But how much more impact will that give the word you have chosen? Are those bits of decorative embellishments going to help your client's target audience decide to buy the product or service? And could you do those fancy 3D renderings in two or three minutes? That is about how long it takes to do this in InDesign.

11

1. Drag the top-center handle of the copy straight down.

2. With the Free Transform tool, hold down Ctrl-Alt/ Command-Option, click the bottom-center handle, and shear it sideways (releasing the Alt/Option key as soon as it starts shearing).

FIGURE 11-15   The word *WANTED!* standing tall with a cast shadow

Combine Your Paths

You may need to keep groups of paths in a permanent relationship for various reasons. There are basically three ways to combine paths with InDesign: grouping, making a composite path, and (for now, let's call it) merging, using the five Pathfinder operations. They all have different rules and produce different effects, as illustrated in Figure 11-16. You need to understand which operations do which things and why you would want to use them. They all start with a multiple selection of paths or objects.

NOTE   *Another way to combine paths is blending, but InDesign cannot do this. Blending requires FreeHand or Illustrator.*

Group for Temporary Handling

Grouping is the establishment of a permanent relationship between multiple objects, without changing any of those objects in any way. For example, if you group a man's hat with his head, whenever you move his head, his hat moves also. To group objects, SHIFT-select them and press CTRL-G/COMMAND-G (or choose Object | Group).

A practical use for grouping is to gather various paths into a temporary unit to enable transformation as a single piece. Any transformation of the group transforms every piece of the group, while maintaining the original relationships. All of the fills remain the same. None of the paths are altered in any way. Usually, you will want to be careful to have the Scale Strokes command in the Transform palette's option menu turned off, to maintain control of your strokes.

Make Composite Paths

Combining paths by making them a composite path actually changes the paths. FreeHand calls this *joining*, which is a good name for it, because the paths are joined into one path. However, it is a very special type of joining. It fundamentally changes the appearance of the paths by giving them a single, overall fill.

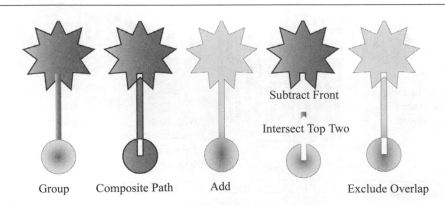

Group   Composite Path   Add   Subtract Front / Intersect Top Two   Exclude Overlap

FIGURE 11-16   Three paths combined using InDesign's seven methods

You Should Ungroup ASAP

Grouping is probably the most overused capability of digital publishing software. Many designers think that grouping is the best way to protect layouts from accidental changes. However, there are some problems with this approach. One is that you may need to fix problems with one or more of the objects in the group, which requires that you access it separately from the group. Also, grouping adds memory requirements when printing. So, in general, you should always remember to ungroup after you no longer need the group (for example, after you've performed the transformation on the group).

The paths to be joined this way must meet these requirements:

■ All paths to be joined must be ungrouped. When type is converted to paths, the entire text block becomes a group. When ungrouped, each line remains a group.

■ All paths must be closed paths.

To combine paths that satisfy these two rules, select all the paths and choose Object | Composite Path | Make.

When paths are made into a composite path, some very special effects appear. First, the new composite path has a single stroke and fill, using the attributes of the path farthest back in the layering of the paths.

The second, and probably most important, attribute of composite paths is that they have even/odd fill. This is where the single fill appears and disappears as it passes through the various sections of the composite path. The most useful part of this even/odd fill is that the unfilled portions are not white; they are transparent, empty, open areas within the composite path.

NOTE *Transparent areas are essential for almost every graphic design. How would we deal with letters like O, R, a, d, and so on, if the counters were not transparent? Every time we placed type over a colored background, we would need to manually select the paths of the counters and color them the color of the background. And what would happen when you placed type over a photo or a gradient fill? It would be impossible to match portions taken from the middle of a gradient. Type is filled with composite paths to solve this problem.*

In Chapter 10, I described how all paths have direction: clockwise or counterclockwise. This attribute is called *winding*. It is used to determine even/odd fill, how type reads when attached to a path, and to which end the arrowhead attaches. All composite paths in InDesign are based on winding. If the paths wind in the same direction, there is no even/odd fill. If the paths wind in opposite directions, even/odd fill occurs.

How to ... Fix a Composite Path

If your composite paths misbehave and do not produce an even/odd fill, you can correct them by following these steps:

1. Choose Object | Composite Path | Release.
2. Select a path at a time and choose Object | Reverse Direction.
3. Remake the composite path.
4. Do this until it works.

Yes, it is a pain. If you want trouble-free composite paths, you need to use FreeHand.

Combine Paths Mathematically with Pathfinder Commands

The path-combining capabilities available from the Pathfinder palette or Object | Pathfinder submenu enable you to combine paths in ways that will greatly enhance your drawing production speed. The Pathfinder palette is simple to use. Just select the shapes and click the button. There are five choices:

- **Add** All the paths became one path that is a combination of all of the shapes. The attributes of the top shape are applied to the newly combined shape. This operation is the fastest way to build a cross, a dunce hat, a crescent moon, a silhouette, and many other shapes.

- **Subtract** This subtracts the paths on top from the path in back, using the attributes of the path in back.

- **Intersect** This usually works only with two paths selected and creates a path with the intersecting areas of those two paths. It uses the attributes of the path on top.

- **Exclude Overlap** This gives you a composite path, but it uses the attributes of the top path instead of the bottom path.

- **Minus Back** This subtracts the underlying paths from the top path, using the attributes of the top path.

You can see examples of using these choices in Figure 11-16, shown earlier in the chapter. Although you probably will not use these commands a lot, they can be very helpful. It was surprising how often the lack of them (in earlier versions of InDesign) made it necessary for me to make the journey to Illustrator or FreeHand. They are a nice addition.

Wrap Your Text

Sometimes, when you add a graphic to a layout, you would like to have the text wrap around the graphic. This uses less space and more closely ties the graphic to the story. In InDesign, text wraps are easy to apply and virtually faultless. You apply text wrap with the Text Wrap palette, shown in Figure 11-17.

The five buttons across the top of this palette are used to apply the text wrap. Your choices are, from left to right, None, Wrap Around Bounding Box, Wrap Around Object Shape, Jump Object, and Jump to Next Column. Clicking one of these simply adds a path with rules that say the type overlapping the text wrap path must stay outside or inside the path. *Path* is the operative word. The wrap is simply a path that can be modified normally with the Pen and selection tools.

If you choose the Wrap Around Bounding Box option, the four fields below the buttons allow you to adjust the measurements for how far the type must stay away from the text wrap. You will not see the text wrap if the offset is zero and you have a stroke on your shape. When you see the text wrap, it looks like a thin path with a quarter-point stroke, in the color of your layer. There is an Invert check box that lets you wrap text inside a wrapping path.

If you place a bitmap, several more options appear in the Type pop-up under Contour Options (see Figure 11-17). If it has a clipping path, you can use that clipping path as the object shape you wish to wrap around. You can ask InDesign to detect edges. You can use an alpha channel. You can use a Photoshop path. The options that are not available will be grayed out.

 *The Detect Edges option produces text wraps that have so many points they become very hard to edit.*

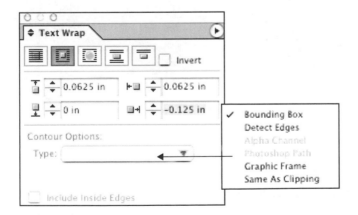

FIGURE 11-17   The Text Wrap palette, with the Contour option Type choices

Here are some tips for text wraps:

- If you want the text to appear in holes in the image (like the image of a doughnut), select the Include Inside Edges option in the Text Wrap palette.

- If you want a block of type to ignore the text wrap, select that option in the Text Frame Options dialog box (choose Object | Text Frame Options).

- If you want the text wrap on a layer to turn off when you turn off that layer, choose that option for that layer (double-click the layer in the Layers palette to open the dialog box that has this option).

- If you want only text that is under the object to wrap, choose Preferences | Composition and turn on that option.

Use Step and Repeat

One often-forgotten feature of page layout programs is step and repeat. This makes it extremely easy to build patterns, set business cards ten-up on a page, and produce many other designs—limited only by your imagination. You simply select something or many things and copy them to the Clipboard. Then choose Edit | Step and Repeat. You will get a little dialog box where you can set how many copies, how far you want to copies to move horizontally, and how far you want them to move vertically.

Here's a quick exercise for you to practice the technique:

1. Draw a 0.5-inch square with a 4-point stroke.

2. Add a drop shadow.

3. Move the square to an appropriate place on the page.

4. Copy the square to the Clipboard.

5. Use Edit | Step and Repeat to paste four copies horizontally. Set 0.6 inch for the horizontal movement and 0 for the vertical movement.

6. Select the row of five squares and copy them to the Clipboard.

7. Use Step and Repeat again to add two rows vertically. This time, set 0.6 inch for the vertical movement and 0 for the horizontal movement.

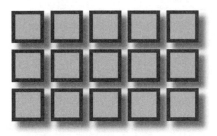

So far, we've looked at InDesign's tools for creating and editing graphics. Although InDesign's graphics capabilities are quite impressive, in reality, most of your graphics will be created in other applications. The next chapter describes how to get those graphics into InDesign.

11

Chapter 12

Import and Export Graphics

How to...

- Decide whether to import or paste
- Pick appropriate graphic formats
- Import graphics
- Understand graphic screen previews
- Deal with cross-platform issues
- Handle clipping paths
- Manage links
- Export text and graphics from InDesign

One of the major confusions about the entire process of desktop publishing and digital printing is the need to import graphics, export graphics, and maintain links. These procedures are essential to building usable digital documents. InDesign handles graphics files very well, but it does take a little knowledge and attention.

This chapter will explain the differences among graphics file formats and which ones are best for particular uses. It will also cover the important topic of managing links. But first we need to address another common question: import or paste?

Decide Whether to Import or Paste

In response to the basic question of whether you should import (place) graphics or paste them into your InDesign documents, the answer is usually that you should place them. Cut, copy, and paste are easy to use, but you must know when pasting is appropriate and when it is not. In most cases, it is not, because of what happens to the copied graphic.

Beware of File Conversions during Pasting

When you cut or copy a graphic (or text) to the Clipboard, in many cases, you change the format. Within the application, almost all applications have a special format that works well. In other words, the cut/copy/paste routine works well if you are copying from InDesign to InDesign, or from Photoshop to Photoshop.

However, all applications convert their copied pieces to something. Most convert text to Rich Text Format (RTF). Adobe products convert graphics to PDFs. Mac OSX also tends to convert things to PDFs (because it is the code used to render graphics on the screen). However, OSX does not make PDFs strictly to Adobe standards, so there are some problems with them. Other applications convert graphics to PICTs, WMFs, BMPs, or even stranger formats.

What Can You Copy and Paste?

As you would expect, you should be able to copy and paste editable paths from Illustrator to InDesign. What may be surprising is that FreeHand paths can be copied and pasted also. You can also copy and paste Photoshop files into InDesign, but all you copy is the low-resolution screen capture. Text copies well in most cases.

Except for text and properly set up Illustrator and FreeHand paths, cut/copy/paste should not be used, except within the application. Within InDesign, it is usually the preferred method.

If you plan to copy and paste graphics from Illustrator or FreeHand, set your preferences in those programs as follows:

- To set up FreeHand, choose Preferences | Export | Clipboard Formats and check Adobe Illustrator and RTF.

- To set up Illustrator, choose Edit | Preferences | File Handling and Clipboard. Change the Clipboard defaults from PDF to AICB (no transparency support), with Preserve Paths checked.

In most cases, you will want to import your graphic files. So, which type of file should you use?

For Newcomers   What Are Foreign File Formats?

Start by imagining that InDesign speaks English, FreeHand speaks German, Illustrator speaks French, Quark speaks Bulgarian, Photoshop speaks Russian, Painter speaks Chinese, Word speaks Italian, WordPerfect speaks Spanish, CorelDraw speaks Ubangi, and so on. The next complication to add to this scenario is that very few of them speak more than their native language.

What this means, on a practical level, is that Quark cannot open a FreeHand file. FreeHand cannot open a PageMaker file. (InDesign can now read Illustrator and Photoshop files for import, but it cannot open them.)

To deal with all of these different languages, software companies have developed translators. In former days, applications had huge numbers of translators. PageMaker, for example, had well over 50. These translators are called filters. These are not like Photoshop filters, which apply complicated mathematical formulas to the selected pixels. These filters can read the foreign format and translate it into a format that can be read by your software.

Pick Appropriate Graphic Formats

There is no graphic format universally accepted by all programs (as RTF is a text format accepted by all professional programs). However, there are three formats that are close: EPS, TIFF, and PDF. In the professional programs used for printing, EPS and TIFF are always accepted. There are also several other common formats that you may encounter.

As a designer, you must know the appropriate formats for a given project. For example, JPEGs are not usable for printing. If you get these from clients, you will usually need to tell them that the quality is simply not good enough for professional results. GIFs are even worse.

Design with Compression in Mind

You need to know about how the different compression schemes work, because you must design your graphics so that they compress well and are not visually damaged by the compression process itself.

Lossy and Lossless Compression

The built-in compression schemes used by the various formats can vary widely. Basically, there are two types of compression: lossy and lossless.

The purpose of compression is to save on file size; compression makes files smaller. But what happens when you decompress?

If you have lossless compression, nothing happens. The decompressed file looks exactly the same as the original file. A typical lossless compression takes an entire area of the same color and says, "Fill this area with this color." This saves a lot of space when compared to, "Make pixel one gray, make pixel two gray, make pixel three gray, make pixel four gray, …"

However, if you have lossy compression, you lose data with every compression. In other words, if you compress and decompress, compress and decompress, and compress and decompress, you end up with obvious compression artifacts. Details disappear, and things appear in your images that were not there when you started.

So, why would you ever want to use lossy compression? Sometimes, it is the only solution to your specific problem. Lossy compression must be approached with care and handled correctly, but given that, lossy compression can make your files five percent of their original size.

LZW Compression

LZW is a lossless compression scheme. It is built into GIFs. It is also an option when used with TIFFs. It is a type of run-length encoding. PSD files (Photoshop's native format) use a similar compression scheme called RLE.

LZW reads all of the pixels, from left to right, top to bottom, row by row, looking for patterns. When it finds a group of pixels, it replaces it with a marker. If it sees another group like that, it simply puts in the marker (which is only 2 bytes or so). Pixels are located and named in *row,column* format (the first pixel in the first row is 1,1, followed by 1,2, and so on). An uncompressed image must define every pixel by location and color. The color is indicated by a number representing the PostScript level from 0 to 255 (0 is black, and 255 is white).

For example, an image that is 2 inches square at 300 dpi, with a white background and a 1-inch black box in the center of the 2-inch document, has 600 rows and 600 columns. Uncompressed, this would be written as 1,1 255; 1,2 255; 1,3 255; 1,4 255; and on and on for the 600 pixels in the first row, the 600 pixels in the second row, and so on. With LZW, the document would be described something like this: The first row is all 255 and becomes a marker; the next 149 rows use that marker; the next row is 150 pixels of 255, followed by 300 pixels of 0, followed by 150 pixels of 255, and this becomes a marker; the next 299 rows use that marker; and the final 150 rows all use the first marker. The LZW description is completely accurate, yet describes the entire document in a couple hundred bytes (0.2KB). Uncompressed, the file needs from 8 to 12 bytes per pixel (minimum). Because there are 360,000 pixels, that is well over 2MB to describe the file.

However, what happens when the image isn't as simple as a black box? Suppose the graphic has multicolored vertical stripes or a photo, in which every single pixel is different. In those cases, LZW will not be able to make the file smaller. In fact, it will make the file size larger.

LZW is superior compression with relatively large areas of flat color, or with horizontal instead of vertical patterns. In other words, GIFs and TIFFs compress best with PostScript illustrations that do not use any gradient fills or patterns. If you do use gradients, you will want to use vertical ones, where the color changes in horizontal bands. For graphics like these, the GIF format can make file sizes very small.

CAUTION

You need to be careful about LZW compression. It can add to file size for continuous-tone images. It should be used only for images with relatively large areas of flat color. When in doubt, do not compress. Also, DOS LZW and Mac LZW are not entirely compatible. If you need the compression on the other platform, it is usually best to save the file uncompressed, and then open the file and compress it on the platform where you will do your page layout.

JPEG Compression

JPEG is a lossy type of compression. JPEG compresses by taking areas of pixels—3 by 3, 5 by 5, and so forth. This sample is then averaged, and either the average color is applied to each pixel in the sample or a simple gradient is used to fill the sample. It would seem that a 5-by-5 sample that is averaged would give you 25-to-1 compression ratios, and that is nearly true. However, the averaging process breaks the image into little squares, and you lose detail.

Because the Web is so crude, even these highly compressed images look great on the monitor. JPEG artifacts are too small to be seen on the screen, even with the most extreme compression options offered by the format. The problem with using JPEG for printed images is that the little averaged squares are visible in top-end process printing. As a result, the huge compressions available cannot be used. The sampling artifacts tend to look like tiny plaid patterns around all the edges in the image.

ZIP Compression

ZIP is a PC-only compression scheme. Macs can now expand it. It has only recently become an option for graphics compression. It can cause problems with some printers and raster image processors (RIPs).

12

Understand the Common Graphics Formats

To choose the appropriate format, you need to recognize the common graphic file formats. Each format is the best choice for certain applications. The general rule is to use EPS, TIFF, or PDF for printed designs. For Web publishing, use GIF, JPEG, or PDF.

EPS Format

EPS is short for Encapsulated PostScript. ESPF is the full acronym for Encapsulated PostScript Files. EPS was invented by Altsys (the original creator of FreeHand and Fontographer). It is still the only universally usable format for printable vector (PostScript) graphics.

Simplistically, an EPS file is a PostScript file written in a universal language that any professional publishing program can read. The PostScript code is encapsulated in code markers. PostScript was designed to save vector information, but it can also include bitmap graphics.

NOTE   *Vector EPS files are being replaced with PDF files. PDFs are almost the same as EPSs, but they include compression, font and graphic embedding, and so on. In the not too distant future, EPSs will probably be only a memory, unless you are in a workflow that uses software from last century.*

With bitmaps, many avoid EPS because of its size; it has no compression scheme. EPS bitmaps (from Photoshop) or EPS graphics with embedded bitmaps have the same resizing and file size problems as all bitmaps. However, EPS files print beautifully and can carry designer-specified angles, dot shapes, and other critical information like clipping paths. In fact, if you need a clipping path or a duotone, EPS is the recommended format to use.

TIFF Format

Aldus (creator of PageMaker) developed the TIFF format quite a while ago. TIFF stands for Tagged Image File Format. This is a file language for bitmaps: 1-bit, 8-bit, 24-bit, and 32-bit. In addition, all nonprofessional applications understand TIFF. It is used by many platforms, including DOS, Windows, UNIX, and Mac. As a result, it is the most common professional graphic format and the best for cross-platform usage. If you want to make a Word template, you will need to use TIFFs. TIFFs also support the LZW (lossless) compression scheme. This means that they can be reduced in size with no data loss. The only place where TIFFs are a problem is on the Web, because of their size.

Because the TIFF format has been around so long and is used so much in the PC world, there are many TIFF dialects. This is primarily because TIFF is so flexible. For example, in Photoshop, TIFFs can have up to twenty-four 8-bit channels and layers. Other programs cannot use this data at all.

TIFFs now can also contain clipping paths. InDesign supports this (and provides controls accessed by choosing Object | Clipping Path). If you want the clipping path as your frame, be sure to open the Import Options box before you import, and then check the Use Clipping Path As Your Frame option. InDesign can edit that clipping path frame, if necessary. I'll cover clipping paths later in the chapter, in the "Handle Clipping Paths" section.

PDF

Another format that is becoming universal is PDF. This is the new format of choice for print publishing. It's a streamlined, cleaned-up PostScript, in essence. In many workflows, PDF is the final output that is sent to be printed. It's still a bit too large for most uses on the Web.

All professional design programs currently support PDFs. However, programs like FreeHand still export older versions of PDF and produce problematic PDFs.

InDesign works transparently with PDFs, importing and exporting them with no special steps. It offers a wide variety of compression options: downsampling, JPEG, ZIP, and others. Use the compression requested by your printer. If your printer does not specify compression for PDFs, do not compress them.

You do need to set up your PDF correctly for where it will be used. There is a huge difference between a PDF generated for prepress use and one generated for use on the Web. Web versions are so compressed and downsampled that they are horrendously ugly when printed. You must keep track of the font-embedding options also. The default for screen-optimized PDFs is to have no fonts embedded, for example. Setting up PDFs is covered in detail in Chapter 18.

PICT and WMF

PICT is short for picture. This was Apple's internal format created by QuickDraw in Mac OS8 and earlier. WMF is short for Windows Mctafile. It was used in older Windows operating systems. Copy-and-pasted graphics were converted to PICTs on the Mac and WMF on the PC.

Both of these formats are old and crude. Usually they are 72 or 96 dpi RGB and compressed to nonrecognition. In general, it is usually best to open either format in Photoshop and save the file in another format. The problem is that when they are saved in another format, they are still not usable for print, in most cases.

GIF

The GIF format is an example of a common specific-use format that is not professional printing quality. GIF was developed by CompuServe and is the primary format for Web graphics. It supports only 256 colors (8-bit) maximum and LZW compression. The small file size makes it popular for transfer over modems. It can also be saved in 3-bit, 4-bit, 5-bit, 6-bit, and 7-bit color for increased size reductions. Simply changing from 256 colors to 64 colors can often save 10 to 25 percent of the file size.

GIF remains the best file format for the Web in most cases, even though a lot of software companies complain about the licensing fees for LZW. Photoshop, ImageReady, and Macromedia Fireworks now can produce lossy GIFs, which are marvelous. Lossy GIFs work by changing colors that are very similar to the same color, so they will compress better. In most cases, you cannot see the difference.

RIFF

Fractal Design developed the Raster Image File Format (RIFF) for use in the Painter, Sketcher, and ColorStudio programs. It supports multiple layers and 32-bit color, and has options for compression.

12

Almost no other program supports RIFF, but it works very well in Painter. If you receive an RIFF file, open it in Photoshop and save it in another format.

BMP

Microsoft Paint and other Windows programs use the BMP format. It is a 24-bit format, using RLE compression. It is used almost exclusively by PCs and is supported by none of the professional design software, except Photoshop. Usually BMPs are 96 dpi and RGB, so they are not suitable for professional printing.

Photoshop PSD

PSD files are produced by Photoshop. PSD has become the format of choice for InDesign, because InDesign can use the transparency in PSDs. No other programs can do this. It uses layers, transparency, included vectors, and much more. The worst problem with PSDs is that they are usually extremely complex and therefore very large. You often need to make a merged or flattened version for use in InDesign.

JPEG

As explained earlier, JPEG is really not a file format; it's a lossy compression scheme. Compressions of up to 20-to-1 are possible. The problem is that JPEG creates many artifacts from its compression scheme, and the artifacts get worse every time you save it.

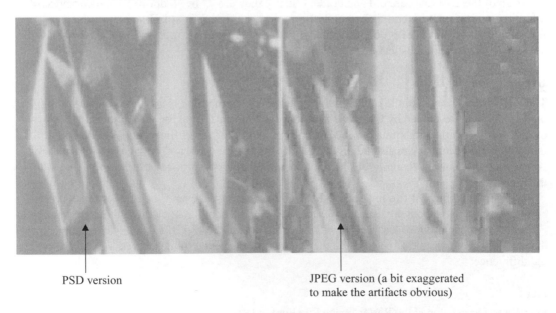

PSD version   JPEG version (a bit exaggerated
                               to make the artifacts obvious)

JPEG has almost no use for print publishing. If you receive a JPEG for print, immediately open it and resave it as a PSD. Most JPEGs are automatically converted to 72 dpi, so you will usually need to resize them without resampling in Photoshop.

PNG

PNG is the touted new format for the Web, with 24-bit color and tight compression. PNG files are 72 dpi. PNG is the native format of Macromedia Fireworks, for example. However, PNGs are not completely supported by all browsers currently in common use.

Specialized Formats

Programs outside the Big Seven (PageMaker, QuarkXPress, InDesign, FreeHand, Illustrator, Photoshop, and Acrobat) often generate dialects of the standard formats that may not import properly. You will have many problems with files from PowerPoint, Word, Canvas, CorelDraw, and other programs. These programs have simply not been blended into the mainstream of PostScript publishing, so far.

Word documents are not too bad. It is common to need to copy graphics used in Word and paste them into Photoshop. Even though these graphics are 96 dpi and RGB, many clients are very attached to them. However, graphics made by the other Office programs (especially Excel and PowerPoint) are useless. They are all 72 or 96 dpi and RGB. Usually, all you can do with them is use them as a background template for hand-tracing.

If the graphic was not made in one of the Big Seven, you should open and resave it simply as preventative maintenance. This will rewrite the code to PostScript compatibility. For example, you should save a CorelDraw file (with an .ai extension) into Illustrator format. Then open the file in Illustrator and save it as an EPS from there. Off-brand TIFFs often need to be opened in Photoshop and simply resaved to make them usable. This is normally necessary with Painter TIFFs, for example.

NOTE
Utilities such as DeBabelizer and MacLink Pro translate files. However, in almost all cases, it is better to save files in a usable format when they are created. In other words, start with a professional PostScript-compatible program whenever possible.

Plan Ahead to Use Proper Formats

You should determine your graphic and text format needs before you start drawing, and certainly before you begin document assembly. By figuring out what you need and how to get there most efficiently, you can avoid many problems.

For virtually every part of your document, there is a best format to use. Sometimes, this is just common sense. Sometimes, it is controlled by the desires of your service bureau or printing firm. The main thing you need to keep in mind is that your choice is important.

For vector graphics, only EPS and PDF work consistently. For non-PostScript applications like Word, PDF may be the only option. Often, the only solution is to rasterize the vector graphics in Photoshop at an appropriate resolution and save them as RGB TIFFs. Then they can be added into Word.

For bitmap graphics, TIFF is almost always the best option. Some workflows prefer EPS, DCS, or PSD for bitmaps. Transparent PSDs are marvelous, but check that fonts are included or rasterized. Also, you should make a flattened copy to control file size. The only exceptions are things like duotones, tritones, and so forth, which need to have correctly specified screen angles. For those, and for graphics that need to have a special screen frequency that is different from the basic document,

12

EPS is the only option. Chapter 17 covers the considerations and procedures for preparing graphics for production.

 *InDesign now offers the capability of working in the final format you will be using. Do it very carefully! For many reasons, having editable graphics (with no original standard for that graphic) is a very dangerous practice. Get in the habit of always having an original in the native format of the creating software, and then exporting a copy in the specific format you need.*

Know the Import Process

You will be importing and exporting constantly. No one program can do it all. You will be scanning halftones and separations in Photoshop; making illustrations in Painter, FreeHand, and Illustrator, and other programs; and placing everything into InDesign for assembly. Every graphic you create or use will have an original document and an exported version for import into page layout. Often, there will be several intermediary files in various formats. For example, a regular routine in common use is this:

- Scan a printed logo into Photoshop. Clean it up and save it as a TIFF.
- Open the file and trace the graphic in Macromedia FreeHand or Adobe Streamline.
- Open the file to generate the final illustration in FreeHand and/or Illustrator.
- Export the file as an EPS or PDF.
- Import the file in InDesign for final positioning.

You may use Adobe Dimension or some other 3D illustration tool. The point is that for many illustrations, you will need to create five files.

However, when you have a finished graphic, moving it into InDesign is a simple two-step process. First, you need to export a copy of your document from the originating application. That program needs to export or save the file in a usable format. For vector graphics, acceptable formats are EPS, AI, and PDF. For bitmaps, you can use TIFF, PSD, EPS, DCS, and PDF.

 *Be careful of PDFs output from Photoshop 7 or earlier. They often have printing problems. If you need to fix the file, open it in Photoshop and resave it as an EPS, TIFF, or PSD. If you have included vector art or a clipping path, EPS is the best choice.*

Second, you open a new or old document in the receiving program and import the exported graphic. InDesign calls this step *placing*.

Place an Imported Graphic

The procedure for placing an imported graphic is the same as for placing imported copy, described in Chapter 5. Choose File | Place (or press CTRL-D/COMMAND-D) to open the Place dialog box. Locate the graphic to place. It should be in the folder you are using for the project. If it is not, move a copy to that folder before you place. Check the Show Import Options box (or SHIFT-click the Open button) if you want to control how the graphic is imported (for example, if you want to use a clipping path as a frame). Click Open or select the import options for the type of file you're placing, and then click OK to start the import process.

<table>
<tr><td>CAUTION</td><td>*Do not try to open a graphic instead of placing it. EPS graphics cannot normally be opened. Even if you are allowed to open the EPS, you will not be allowed to edit the graphic. Even if you can edit it, opening a graphic does not import it into your page layout document for publishing.*</td></tr>
</table>

Drag-and-Drop Graphics

On the Mac, there is strong support for drag-and-drop graphics. Windows systems may have a little trouble, so you'll need to experiment.

You simply select the graphic in the other application's window and drag-and-drop it into InDesign's window. Your monitor needs to be large enough to open the two windows side by side. Using two monitors makes this easier.

If you're using this method, be careful that the links are made and that you actually have a copy of the graphic or text in the folder with your document. Embed the text, and link the graphics.

In general, I suggest the normal, traditional procedure of exporting/importing because it avoids many problems. However, with care, InDesign handles drag-and-drop very well.

Handle Cross-Platform Imports

What if you need to import a graphic file created on a Mac on a Windows system, or vice versa? It is relatively easy to open and convert PC graphics to Mac graphics. The opposite is not usually true.

Windows still requires a three-character filename extension to indicate the file type. Mac OSX also requires the extension to be typed into the name. Make sure you do not hide extensions in either operating system. To open a PC file on a Mac, you can usually simply change the name to add the Windows filename extension. This works most of the time, if you have any idea what the originating software was. The main problem is still fonts. Cross-platform graphics usually need to have all the type converted to paths.

<table>
<tr><td>TIP</td><td>*When working cross-platform, it is still wise to use the old 8.3 naming convention. This means that names should not use anything but letters, numbers, hyphens, periods, and underscores. Internet service provider's UNIX servers often require 8.3 names for files attached to an e-mail message.*</td></tr>
</table>

To open or use a Mac graphic on a Windows machine, it must be saved in a PC version of the format, the extension must be there, and the name must not have any spaces or special characters. (This can cause problems when trying to make cross-platform CDs, for example.) Normally, a PC can read any Mac file produced by the same software with the same version, as long as it has the proper extension. However, some Windows machines may require specially purchased software to read Mac files.

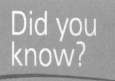

What You Can and Cannot Do with Imported Graphics

Imported graphics should not be edited in page layout. Vector graphics (EPS and PDF) can be resized, flipped, skewed, rotated, scaled, or transformed as a whole.

Bitmap graphics should be placed at 100 percent scale and kept at that scale. You should avoid resizing bitmap graphics. Unless you are very careful, resized bitmaps do not fit the pixel grid any more. As a result, resized bitmaps are usually blurred. Many people do it all the time. However, they are also usually the persons who complain about the quality of computer halftones.

One-bit TIFFs can be recolored. However, the best practice for all graphics is to transform them only by returning to the creating application, making the changes, and then reexporting and reimporting. InDesign's Links palette makes this procedure relatively painless.

Understand Screen Previews of Graphics

One of the major difficulties with graphics, in general, is their sheer size. Text-only files run in dozens of kilobytes. Graphic files are much larger. Full-color bitmaps are commonly dozens of megabytes or more. One of the results is that exported graphics are normally at least two-part files.

NOTE *DCS EPS has five separate files (or more) that are linked to each other. DCS stands for Desktop Color Separations, which is an ancient Quark format. It comes from the days when no application, except Photoshop, could accurately separate CMYK images.*

If the full-resolution graphic were rendered on the monitor, screen redrawing would take virtually forever. In addition, the monitor cannot display all the information because of its extremely low resolution (72 or 96 dpi).

To solve this problem, all graphic formats have a screen preview. This is a low-resolution image that interprets the high-resolution image as well as it can at monitor resolutions. When you import a graphic from another program, only the preview can be seen. The inexperienced are constantly frustrated because the screen image does not look like what they expect to see. After all, it was gorgeous in the originating program. InDesign draws its own previews from the file information, and they are excellent, but they are still low resolution.

NOTE *A generic EPS usually does not have a preview at all. As a result, EPSs brought to another platform often show only a box with an X through it. However, in most cases, InDesign will now construct a better preview using the PostScript information in the file, so this problem is usually avoided.*

Keep the Original Image File

The high-resolution image is not used until the document is output to a printer, imagesetter, or press. This means that the high-resolution image must be available for the document to print. Many assume that because the image has been imported, it is in the document, and the original can be deleted. This is certainly not the case. The low-resolution preview is the only thing in the document. The high-resolution image is only linked to the file.

When the document prints, the printer or imagesetter searches for the original, high-resolution file. It is very important to make sure that the imported file (or a copy of it) is contained in the same folder as the final document. Printers and imagesetters are instructed to look in the same folder as the final document. If they do not find the high-resolution original there, the output is messed up— one way or another. The printer might use the low-resolution screen version or simply not print the graphic at all.

Handle Clipping Paths

Clipping paths are a common addition to a bitmap graphic. A clipping path is a PostScript path saved in the Paths palette in Photoshop and included with the TIFF or EPS file exported from Photoshop. The purpose is to eliminate the background from an image when it prints. The most common example of this is when you select an image in Photoshop and make the background disappear.

InDesign can automatically recognize clipping paths, alpha channels, or user-modified paths. However, you may need to handle clipping paths in InDesign, particularly if a Photoshop file has clipping paths and alpha channels. Then you can choose which one you want to use. InDesign provides controls for clipping paths in the Clipping Paths dialog box, accessed by selecting Object | Clipping Paths. Choose the path you want to use from the Type drop-down list, as shown in Figure 12-1.

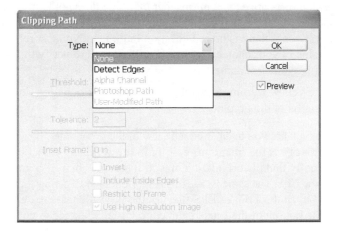

12

| FIGURE 12-1 | The Clipping Path dialog box lets you choose which type of clipping path to use. |

As you can see in Figure 12-1, the Clipping Path dialog box also offers a Detect Edges option. You might use this option when you have an image without a clipping path or an alpha channel, and you want InDesign to detect the edges. In general, this is not a good idea because InDesign's internally produced clipping paths are exceedingly complicated and usually useless. It's better to produce the clipping path or alpha channel in Photoshop and update the link.

Usually, to avoid any problems with clipping paths, the best solution is to make the background transparent in Photoshop, save it as a merged PSD, and import that file. InDesign will read the transparency (using Photoshop's transparency mask). However, you may not have this option, especially when you are using graphics supplied by others.

Manage Links

Once you have imported your graphics, you need to make sure that all of your links to those files are up to date. You do not want any of the graphics in your document to show up in the Links palette with a yellow, triangular warning sign or a red, octagonal question sign. Figure 12-2 shows the Links palette with these signs.

To avoid missing link problems, keep your linked filed in the same folder as your document. Then relinking is automatic.

Fix Links

If either of the dreaded icons appears in your Links palette, you need to click the appropriate button at the bottom of the Links palette:

■ If the red question mark appears, it means that InDesign does not know where that graphic went. Click the Relink button, and then click the Browse button. Locate the file in the dialog box that opens. Even if there is no red question mark icon, you can relink and change to a different graphic of your choice. (InDesign will ask you to verify that you want to link to a graphic with a different name.)

■ To get rid of the yellow warning sign, click the Update Link button. InDesign will import the changed version of the graphic.

The Go to Link button takes you to an enlarged view of the graphic in place in your document. The Edit Original button opens the image for editing in the application that created it. In many cases, this does not actually find the originating object. It assumes that EPS graphics are editable, for instance, and opens the EPS. The same is true of TIFF or duotone EPS files that have an original PSD file. InDesign will open the TIFF or EPS file, not the PSD file that created it.

The four icons at the bottom of the Links palette are visually vague, so you may need to use the palette's option menu, where these functions are listed as the first four commands, until you have memorized the buttons.

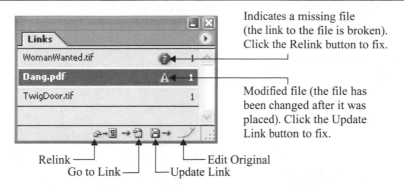

Indicates a missing file
(the link to the file is broken).
Click the Relink button to fix.

Modified file (the file has
been changed after it was
placed). Click the Update
Link button to fix.

Relink
Go to Link
Update Link
Edit Original

FIGURE 12-2   The Links palette showing three placed graphics, indicating some problems

TIP

Tool tips show the name of the button on the palette. If you set Tool Tips for Fast on the General page of the Preferences dialog box (opened by choosing Edit | Preferences in Windows or InDesign | Preferences on Macs), you will not need to wait too long to see the name.

One of the reasons Adobe put these commands in the option menu is to let you assign keyboard shortcuts to them. If you use them a lot, you should do that.

To see information about a linked file, double-click its entry in the Links palette. Figure 12-3 shows an example of the Link Information dialog box that appears for a modified file (a file marked

12

Link Information

Name: Dang.pdf	Done
Date Modified: Tuesday, August 26, 2003, 7:05 AM	Prev
Size: 400 K	Next
Page: 1	
Link Needed: Yes	
Color Space: NA	
Profile: NA	
File Type: Adobe Portable Document Format (PDF)	
Content Status: ⚠ File Modified	
Workgroup Status:	
Location: C:\Documents and Settings\David\My Documents\InDTest\Dang.pc	Relink...

FIGURE 12-3   Link information about a modified file

with the yellow warning sign). Notice that this dialog box also has a Relink button, so you can fix a link from there.

Use Link Options

The Links palette's option menu includes the same commands as the buttons at the bottom of the palette and several other commands you may find useful.

The other option menu commands work as follows:

- ■ **Embed File** Not only does this increase the file size of the InDesign file dramatically, but it also means that you can no longer access the graphic for editing purposes. You cannot export the embedded graphic back out of the document. You almost never want to do this. However, you almost always want to embed text files.

- ■ **Link File Info** This shows you the metadata (descriptive information) associated with the file.

- ■ **Link Information** This shows you the filename, type, color space, path, and more. It is the same information dialog box you get when you double-click a link (see Figure 12-3).

- ■ **Sort by Name, Page, or Status** The default sorting order is by status, and that is the best choice. This will put the missing and modified files at the top of the list, where you can see them easily. However, if you have a huge number of placed files, you may want to see an alphabetized list, produced by choosing Sort by Name.

- ■ **Small Palette Rows** This option gives you the Quark look, which shows more files per inch.

How to ...   Add Metadata to a File

The Link File Info option on the Links palette option menu displays the metadata associated with the file. You can add this metadata to your files.

According to InDesign's help page:

"Metadata (file info) is descriptive information that can be searched and processed by a computer. Adobe's eXtensible Metadata Platform (XMP) lets you embed metadata into a file to provide information about the contents of a document. Applications that support XMP can read, edit, and share this information across databases, file formats, and platforms."

You can add this metadata to a file, so that it will appear when you (or someone else) choose to view file information. Select File | File Info to open the File Information for *File* dialog box.

The pages available for this dialog box depend on the system you are using:

- The Description page lets you enter the title, author, description, keywords, and copyright information.
- The Origin page gives you a place to enter when and where the graphic originated, the headline, instructions, transmission data, urgency, and other information.
- The Advanced page shows you the information that will be displayed for various metadata formats, such as PDF, TIFF, XMP, and so on.
- The Workgroup category will be available only if you have Version Cue enabled.

Additionally, Macs will also have the following pages:

- The Camera Data 1 page is the place to enter data about your traditional camera: make, model, lens, ISO speed, F-stop, and so on.
- The Camera Data 2 page is the place to enter data about your digital camera: pixel dimensions, resolution, compression, color space, and so on.
- The AP Categories page lets you pick the appropriate Associated Press (AP) category for the document.

Export Text and Graphics from InDesign

To export graphics or text, choose File | Export (or press CTRL-E/COMMAND-E) and choose the format you want to use in the Export dialog box.

- InDesign can export the text from its documents as Adobe InDesign Tagged Text, Rich Text Format, or Text Only. Tagged Text and RTF save the formatting, including paragraph styles, character styles, and tables.
- InDesign exports generic EPS files. These can be used for graphics sent to companies that are still using Quark, for example.
- InDesign exports excellent PDFs with all the control of Adobe Distiller. InDesign CS has added the ability of exporting PDFs using the PDF/X-1a standard, which will ensure that your PDFs are printable. It can also export PDFs using PDF/X-3 for printers and service bureaus using RIPs with color management. Chapter 18 covers these options in detail.
- The InDesign Interchange format exports files in a format that can be read by InDesign CS. It contains everything in the file and is said to be a safety backup.

NOTE *Originally, the Interchange format was going to be used by a plug-in in InDesign 2 to provide backward compatibility. The InDesign 2 plug-in may be available in the future.*

- You can export JPEGs of the InDesign file for use on the Web.

- SVG and SVG Compressed are the Adobe version of Flash's SWF format.

- Package for Web enables you to export a package that can be read by GoLive 7 (which is also part of the Creative Studio). In GoLive, you open the package and drag-and-drop the pieces into your Web pages. Paragraph and character styles are converted to Cascading Style Sheets (CSS) automatically. This feature is discussed in Chapter 15.

In general, you will find that InDesign works with import and export issues flawlessly. However, as emphasized in this chapter, you do need to be aware of the formats that work and those that do not. Also, keep in mind that link management is one of the most important aspects of digital production. It is a bit tedious, but it needs to become a normal, fully integrated part of your production workflow.

12

Part IV

Add Color

Chapter 13

Add Color to Your Pages

How to...

- Know your color spaces
- Be prepared for the costs of color
- Use reproducible color
- Use the color libraries installed with InDesign
- Pick the proper color-application palette
- Use the Gradient tool
- Set up your Swatches palette
- Apply color from the Swatches palette
- Add a gradient swatch
- Mix your colors and build a mixed-ink group
- Manage your colors
- Practice your graphics and color skills

Now we come to the most complex issue outside of typography: color. Black-and-white design is complicated enough. Color increases the complication to an entirely new dimension. For this reason, it will be wise for you to work in black and white as much as possible to develop your skills. More than that, you will find that even your color pieces should be proofed in grayscale to see the structure of the design more clearly. Color usually lessens your contrast and confuses your eye. There is no stronger contrast than black and white.

Having said that, I must acknowledge reality. One of the primary results of the digital revolution is a vast increase in color usage. It has become increasingly easy to work in color, proof in color, and print or publish in color. The problem with this is that many desktop publishers know little about commercial printing or Web publishing necessities. As a result, many projects are ruined because of bad color.

In this chapter, I will show you the color capabilities of InDesign and suggest some relatively simple ways to avoid problems with color. We'll begin with a brief review of color spaces and color systems.

Know Your Color Spaces

To design with color, you need to understand that the colors used in digital publishing come from several color sources and theories, none of which are completely reproducible in the other output. In other words, reality is not reproducible. Monitor color cannot be reproduced by printing inks without substantial color shifts. Printing color cannot be viewed on the screen (unless you spend a lot of money for the software and hardware to calibrate your monitor, printer, scanner, and so on).

Color space is the term used to describe the colors available in a given color theory using primary colors. A *color system* is a standard set of colors—a classic example being the 64 standard colors found in the Crayola system. There is a color space for TV, a color space for printing, a color space for fine art, and so forth. In addition, InDesign supports several standardized color systems.

The problem is that the different colors existing in the various color spaces may not be available in other spaces or systems of color. To work with digital publishing, it is necessary to be familiar with several different color spaces and color systems. But before we talk about the specifics for digital color work, let's start with an old standard.

Understand the Problem with Primaries

You learned about the first color space in elementary school. You were told that any color could be made with the three primary colors: red, blue, and yellow. As you found out (if you played with color at all), this is not so. I still remember the frustration of trying to generate a vibrant purple by mixing red and blue. Unfortunately, color does not lend itself to neat, tidy analysis. The only way you can produce the illusion of reality in the red, blue, yellow (RBY) color space is by carefully adding the hundreds of pigments together.

The problem with the RBY color space is simply that there are no true RBY primary pigments. The theory works well when trying to predict what colors will result when mixing cobalt yellow and ultramarine blue, for example. However, the practical use of the color space has nothing to do with mixing primaries. It simply becomes a way to describe how the various fine-art pigments are going to interact. More important, RBY has almost nothing to do with printing color. It has nothing to do with monitor color. It is the world of fine art. It is really not reproducible.

Use the Color of Light

A rose in your garden looks different in the yellow of sunrise, the much bluer glare of noon, or the diffuse light of a hazy sky. Artificial light sources are even more problematic. Incandescent lighting is very yellow. Called tungsten lighting, it is named after the material used to make the filaments in the light bulbs. Fluorescent lighting is normally very blue or green, although it is possible to find warm fluorescents that are tinted pink. The pink tint mixes with the blue light to make something that is less harsh. It's weird color, though, and simply doesn't look natural. The greenish tint of fluorescent lights is what makes people look lifeless in its light.

Printers deal with these problems by using a concept called *color temperature*, measured by the Kelvin (K) scale, named after the inventor, Lord Kelvin. This concept uses a temperature scale that begins at absolute zero (that place where all molecular activity ceases). This is 273°C below zero. If we place a theoretical black-body radiator into a furnace and begin heating it, we can watch it go through color changes as it gets hotter. As the heat increases, the color changes, passing from red, orange, yellow, through white to blue white. Incandescent light bulbs have a very yellow color at about 3,500°K. The color of the light at noon at sea level is around 4,800°K to 5,600°K, depending on how clear it is—still yellowish. The color at noon in Santa Fe, New Mexico, is closer to 6,500°K—a little past pure white into a slight bluish tint.

13

But all you really need to know is that printers need lights with a predictable color. The standard used by printers for viewing printed color pieces is special fluorescent lighting at 5,000°K. This is an average white light. It is very close to the white light from the sun, which is around 5,400°K. A light source of 7,500°K is recommended for checking press output for color uniformity. The bluish tint to the light aids the human eye in detecting minute color differences and color misregistration.

Any printing company that is serious about quality color reproduction will have a 5,000°K color booth, with the walls of the booth painted a specific neutral gray. Often, all of the lighting in the press room will be 5,000°K. This is not because the color looks better under this lighting. It is because a standard is needed when jobs are printed in multiple facilities in different areas of the country. Designers also need a standard for color comparison. Color will always look the same in a 5,000°K light booth, no matter where it is. If you produce a lot of critical full-color printing, you need a color booth.

Wise designers do the best they can to design their work so it shows best under the light source their readers will be using. Needless to say, this is a guessing game at best. It would be a good idea to take your printed pieces into an incandescent environment to make sure it is still readable. The yellowish light of our normal light bulbs greatly reduces the contrast of creams, beiges, tans, and so on.

Learn to Communicate Colors Accurately

Like all areas of design and publishing, color has its specific terminology. Again, the goal is communication with our peers. There is no room here for nondefinable frivolities such as blush, mauve, lime, peach, and so on. These names are simply fashion and mean different things to different people. What we are looking for is a language that can be understood by anyone who is not color-blind.

Fine artists are taught to break color down into three parts: hue, saturation, and value. Printers tend to substitute the word *brightness* for *value*. These are defined as follows:

- *Hue* is the name of the color: blue, red, yellow-green, and so forth. There are only six hues (plus white and black): red, orange, yellow, green, blue, and violet (or purple).

- *Saturation* is the intensity of a color, or how far it varies from neutral gray. For example, grass green in the spring is more saturated than forest green in late summer. *Saturation* should be used instead of terms like *dull* or *brilliant*, because these terms could include value variations.

- *Brightness* (or *value*) refers to the lightness or darkness of a color. The same hue of green may be a dark green or a light green. This is different from the saturation changes that would be referred to as dull green or intense green.

Any color can be described in terms of hue, saturation, and brightness or value (HSB or HSV). Neon red, for example, could be described as an extremely saturated, fairly bright red. Barn red could be referred to as an unsaturated, very dark red. The color hue could be the same for both of these colors.

Use the Artists' Color Wheel

The wavelengths of visible light are measured in billionths of a meter and cover the range from 400 to 750 millimicrons. The color change here is linear, starting from invisible ultraviolet through violet, blue, green, yellow, orange, red, and invisibly ending with infrared. This is the spectrum we see in a rainbow.

The fascinating thing about a color wheel is that though the spectrum is linear, the color relationships are circular. In other words, red does not end things. Instead, it blends through violet-red, and red-violet, to violet, and then continues.

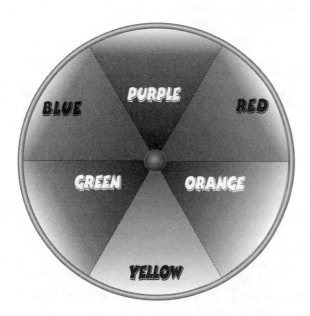

In addition to being continuous, some color relationships work in a circular fashion, and there are specialized terms to describe these relationships. I have already mentioned one of these relationship terms: primary colors. The three primary colors here (of pigment) are yellow, blue, and red. With these three, you can theoretically make any color. All three together make black. You can mix any two primaries and produce the color between them on the wheel. These are called secondary colors. This is true, even though red is at one end and blue at the other end of the spectrum. If you mix them, you get violet or purple (even though highly saturated purples cannot be mixed).

Know That Mixed Complementary Colors Deaden Color

A complementary color pair is a primary color and the secondary color on the opposite side of the color wheel: red/green; blue/orange; and yellow/violet. These three color pairs have the same relationship with each other. Two complementary colors of equal saturation and value will produce a vibrating edge between them, for harsh, garish, exciting, compelling, maximum color contrast. This is true even when the colors are low in both saturation and value, such as maroon and hunter green. Just make sure that you are using complementary hues.

The most useful aspect of complementary color is seen when you mix a primary with its complementary secondary. The result is neutral gray. The same neutral gray is produced no matter what the complementary pair is. Purple and yellow produce the same gray as red and green.

The major factor to remember is that complementary color affects brightness. If your red seems toned down and weak, it is probably because it is contaminated with green. Orange or brown contaminates and deadens blue. Yellow deadens purple. In many cases, control of the complementary portion of the color determines the intensity.

Be Prepared for the Costs of Color

When printing color, economics play a huge role. Every separate pigment requires a separate plate and an additional printing cylinder. In practical terms, every additional plate costs about the same as the first color to produce (disregarding paper costs). Two-color is almost twice as expensive, three-color is three times as expensive, and so on.

So, a fine-art painting that used 30 different colors of paint would cost 30 times as much to print (plus the cost of the paper). Even if this could be done (and it cannot, under normal circumstances), the economics would prevent it. The only place we find such treatment is in classical Japanese woodcut prints, for which dozens of plates were used.

The solution involves using a different color space—cyan, magenta, and yellow (CMY) instead of RBY. With the addition of black (because the cyan is weak), printers can print a full-spectrum color space that gives a convincing illusion of reality using only four colors. CMY use cheap pigments that cost only about 60 percent more than black (which is by far the cheapest pigment). Black is simply soot.

As we go on to what color spaces are available to InDesign, you must remember that color printing is expensive. Color may be free on the Web. It is certainly not free in print. Primarily because of equipment requirements and the experience needed, full-color printing is often ten to a hundred times more expensive than black-and-white printing. You can see this with simple laser prints. Black-and-white prints cost about five cents. CMYK (the *K* stands for black) laser prints usually cost a dollar each. What is called spot color saves a lot of money, but it also requires that you give up on the illusion of reality.

Use Reproducible Color

Now we're ready to talk about the color spaces you will be using on a regular basis. I call them *reproducible color*. This means that it is possible to make many copies of an image that are very close to the same color. The world of graphic design uses five color spaces and systems: black and white (grayscale), spot color, RGB, CMYK, and LAB color.

Maintain Contrast with Grayscale

The most common color space is grayscale. More than 50 percent of all printing is grayscale. This means all that is used is black ink or toner. Most of this work is reproduced by black-and-white laser printers (like the Xerox DocuTech). These printers use 600 dpi black dots to build the images, producing around 120 letter-sized copies per minute.

In this area, the professionalism of your typography is the key to your success. This equipment poorly reproduces photos. You need to work at maintaining contrast and helping the reader through the printed piece.

On the other hand, grayscale on a printing press can have amazing impact. You have the largest contrast available when working with black ink or toner on bright-white paper. The quality of the project is determined by your skill, not equipment limitations.

NOTE *Remember that there are sizable portions of your readers who are color-blind—more than 10 percent of your male readership. Your pieces must work even if reduced to grayscale. Color should be added only when required by your client or circumstances.*

Use Tints of Color

One of the most common questions from those new to the industry concerns tints: If this is a one-color job in slate-blue, can I use a 50 percent blue or a gradient of that blue? The answer is yes. All you need to know is how a tint is produced.

A *tint* for our industry is a percentage screen of a color. We have no way to add white other than letting the paper show though. We call this *linescreen* (named after the old hand-scribed glass plates used to make the screens). All colors and grays, other than areas of solid spot color, are printed with tiny dots. A tint is a solid color broken up into dots that are described as a percentage of area covered. For example, a 50 percent screen of square dots looks like a checkerboard. Half the area is one color square, and half is the other color. For printers dealing with negatives, half the area is solid, and half is clear. A 10 percent tint would have tiny dots of solid color that cover 10 percent of the area.

Develop Skill with Spot Color

Spot color is the use of custom-mixed colors, each on its own plate. In the context of color spaces, spot colors are specific RBY colors. They can be custom-mixed or bought by the can. They can fit into a color system or not. The main thing is that they are printed separately, on a separate printing plate.

Spot color, however, is mixed pigment. It is not blended by overprinting tints, as with CMYK or process color, but with a paint knife on a mixing table. Brilliant red, warm red, Van Dyke brown, and colors like these have no specified relationship to CMYK. In fact, many of these colors cannot be produced with process color. These colors are referred to as standard colors. This is sort of funny, because they are not standards for anyone. They are really colors manufactured by a specific ink company. They are only standards for that particular company. One company's warm red might be very different from another's warm red.

13

Standard colors became a real problem. In the mid-1960s, a company named Pantone gave our industry the first standard color system that was accepted industry-wide in the United States. It is called the Pantone Matching System, or PMS. Although there are some other systems around the world, PMS is the only universal, spot-color system standard that you normally need to be familiar with, if you are working in the United States.

PMS color is not a full-spectrum system. Even though it covers many colors outside the RGB or CMYK color spaces, it is not based on primary colors. All PMS colors must be described by RBY or HSV, and 35 percent of PMS colors cannot be reproduced with the tint overprints of CMYK. Many of them cannot be reproduced with RGB.

PMS (spot) is a completely separate color system. At present, PMS uses 15 standard colors that are mixed into more than 1,000 standard mixes. The mixes can be seen in swatch books, which have a swatch of the printed color next to a formula used to mix that color. This formula tells the printer which of the standard colors to use and what percentages to mix to create the specified standard mix.

In addition, Pantone has metallic and neon swatch books that add another couple hundred standard Pantone spot colors. These are very interesting, and often very beautiful, custom colors. You will pay a little extra with special press washup fees. It's very difficult to get the metallic particles off the rollers. And there is no digital press equivalent.

With a swatch and a PMS number, anyone can match any PMS color in any facility that puts offset lithographic ink on paper. PMS inks are also available for some other printing methods. However, you must be careful, because unless your printing method can use Pantone inks, PMS colors cannot be matched. Pantone sends employees to work in the various ink-manufacturing plants to ensure color accuracy. All Pantone-approved color has the word Pantone in the name on the label.

Remember to figure ink-mixing charges when using spot color. Printing companies usually charge from $10 to over $75 to mix the spot color for your use. No one stocks all the PMS colors. They are normally custom-mixed for every job. However, if you can use one of the colors the printer already has mixed, you can avoid the mixing charges.

NEW TO
InDesign
CS

One of the real problems with spot colors over the years has been the inability to mix these colors. Designers always wanted to make gradients from one spot color to another spot color. Until recently, this was impossible. Now it is simply unwise, unless you have an educated client. As you will see in the "Mix Your Colors" section later in this chapter, InDesign offers this new capability through the Swatches palette.

Deal with the Limitations of Your Monitor: RGB

The color space of your monitor is called RGB, for the three primaries used: red, green, and blue. These are the primaries used by light and light sources. They are called *additive color*. They are additive because adding all three primary colors gives white light. This is the reverse of RBY, spot color, or CMYK. To make yellow, you add green to red, for example.

Everything you see on your computer screen is RGB. RGB is a full-spectrum color space like RBY or HSV. However, RGB is the first color space we have discussed that is severely limited. Many colors that are seen in reality are not available in RGB color. In fact, only a small percentage of the colors seen in the real world can be duplicated by RGB. The human eye sees trillions of colors. Digital RGB is 16.7 million colors.

This is normally not a problem. When in the color space, it seems as though every color is available. This is because it is a full-spectrum space; there is a good representative sampling of all six hues, most of the values, and quite a few of the saturations available in reality. However, if you bring a TV with a video of your garden into your garden, you'll see a vast difference, and not just brightness and saturation differences. Many of the hues will be different on your screen.

In fact, if you visit your local electronics or computer superstore, you'll quickly see that every TV or monitor reproduces the colors differently. Some TVs will show that shirt as blue, some as purple, some as teal. We have run into the bane of our industry: accurate color reproduction. Accurate reproduction of color is a virtual impossibility, even on a theoretical level.

Know the Limitations of Process Ink: CMYK

In the past, the problems of printing full-spectrum color were severe. Most of the problems originally involved the number of colors needed. Japanese woodcuts often used 30 to 60 colors, and even they were not remotely realistic. After a full-spectrum color space for printing inks was developed (just before 1900, from research funded by Mr. Montgomery Ward), the main problem became *registration*. This is the ability to place two or more colors in exact alignment with each other, image after image after image. Process printing tolerances for registration are a half dot, or about 0.03 inch. Any more than that, and the colors shift.

What we call full-color printing uses four inks: cyan, magenta, yellow, and black. Printing tints of the four process colors on top of each other produces the full-spectrum color space of process color. A typical color might be described as 100c 50m 0y 10k. These numbers refer to the tints of the color used. The *k* is used for black to avoid confusion with blue, which is *c*, because it is really cyan. In this case, there is solid cyan, overprinted with 50 percent magenta, no yellow, and 10 percent black. This produces a rich shade of royal blue.

This is the major full-spectrum color space you need to know for printing. For most of us, CMYK is understandable color because it works under the same basic rules we learned for RBY.

13

RBY and CMYK are both *subtractive* color spaces. These primaries absorb light. When added together, they absorb all light, leaving black. Printing uses the complementary opposites of light. Here is how the RGB and CMY primary colors are related:

It was discovered that camera shots of color originals using red, green, and blue filters created negatives that could be printed in the subtractive primaries to reproduce the original colors. These subtractive primaries are cyan, magenta, and yellow (CMY). This process is called *color separation*. The following shows you how CMY colors are related to RGB when starting with white light and white paper:

- ■ Magenta is the printed color seen when all green light is eliminated.
- ■ Cyan is the printed color seen when all red light is eliminated.
- ■ Yellow is the printed color seen when all blue light is eliminated.
- ■ Black is the printed color seen when all red, green, and blue light is eliminated.

Process color uses the separation concept to print full-spectrum images. Separations are produced when you convert RGB color to CMYK. There are some real problems, however. Like RGB, CMYK covers the entire spectrum, but it misses many colors. CMY covers even less than RGB. This is further confused by the fact that RGB cannot reproduce some CMY colors, and CMY cannot reproduce many RGB colors.

Again (due to the fact that this is a full-spectrum color space), if you restrict yourself to the color space, it seems real. Printed color photos look real. However, we are in worse shape now. CMY cannot reproduce RGB. Neither of them can come close to the real world.

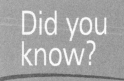

Did you know?

Why CMYK Needs Four Colors

Why do we need black with three-color primaries—CMY? The problem is the pigments used. CMY inks are really not very close to theoretical CMY. Some of this is due to economics. The CMY pigments available are not economically feasible, not quite the right color, not strong enough, poisonous, or some combination. The compromises we presently use are reasonable and economically viable. They are all a little more expensive than black, but in the acceptable range.

However, they are inaccurate. The three primaries added together do not make black, they make an ugly, muddy brown. This is primarily because the cyan used is weak. In addition, all three pigments have impurities. As a result, a fourth color is used: black.

Keep in mind that RGB is not CMY, and neither is RBY. For our purposes, we are discussing three separate color spaces. This is true on a practical level, even though reality contains all RBY, and RBY contains all RGB and all CMY color. This explains why fine-art reproduction is such a frustrating exercise, why it is so difficult to print the newest fashion colors, and why a photo of the Grand Canyon can never capture the reality.

Make the Conversion from RGB to CMYK

As you create your designs, you will be drawing in RGB (on the monitor) and printing in CMYK. Some software and/or hardware will make the conversion before the cyan, magenta, yellow, and black inks hit the paper. As mentioned, RGB is weak in yellows, and CMY is weak in blues and reds. The dilemma is that many of the colors on the screen cannot be printed. As a result, you will need to be using printed swatch books to judge final printed color.

13

A set of swatch books is really not optional. It is true that you can spend a lot of money and get a monitor that is reasonably accurate. However, a monitor will always be a glowing light source, and ink on paper is a very different thing.

Your results will become more predictable with experience. In fact, with enough experience, you will begin to think in CMYK and know what a color like 75c 15m 100y will look like before it is printed.

CAUTION   *If you are new to process-color printing, the first printed pieces you design are going to be horrible shocks. The color will be muted, dull, and, in many cases, a different hue.*

The background color space to all these machinations is *LAB*. This is a color space that covers the entire visible spectrum of the human eye. It is one of those theoretical things that mere humans have trouble understanding. It has two color channels and a grayscale, or value, channel. When you make a conversion from RGB to CMYK, the computer actually converts from RGB to LAB to CMYK. It is the standard on which color management is based.

Meet the Color Libraries Installed with InDesign

InDesign installs color libraries for several standardized color-matching systems for spot color, RGB, and CMYK. You can install additional color libraries and load swatches from them in InDesign. Here are brief descriptions of each of the libraries that come with InDesign CS:

- **DIC Color**   This is a Japanese system that provides 1280 CMYK mixes to be used as spot colors from DIC Process Color. Colors may be matched against the *DIC Color Guide*, published by Dainippon Ink & Chemicals, Inc. The advantage is that all of these colors can be duplicated in CMYK.

- **Focoltone**   This is a printed process-color system with 763 CMYK colors. Swatch books for this system are available from Focoltone in Stafford, England.

- **HKS**   If your client wants colors from the European HKS color system, this is the library to use. European architects and industrial designers use this system.

- **PANTONE**   InDesign provides PANTONE Coated and PANTONE Uncoated for spot colors (for the two types of paper). PANTONE Matte is for spot colors on matte paper (cheap, coated stock where colors are not nearly so bright as they are on coated stock). PANTONE Process colors are a set of standard CMYK mixes printed so you can see what they will actually look like when they are printed.

- **System (Windows)**   These are the 256 colors of the Windows default 8-bit palette, which rarely matter anymore.

- **System (Mac)**   These are the 256 colors of the MacOS default 8-bit palette, which also are of little consequence to your design work.

- **Toyo Color Finder 1050**   This system contains more than 1,000 spot colors from the most common inks used in Japan. The *TOYO Color Finder 1050 Book* is available from printers and graphic arts supply stores. This is the Japanese version of the Pantone system.

- **Trumatch** This is a process-color system that provides predictable CMYK color matching, with more than 2,000 printable colors. It is an American system that claims to scientifically provide all the colors you will ever need.

- **Web** This 216 RGB Web-safe color system is one of those things highly touted but not very useful. It has almost no yellows, tans, and soft warm colors.

Pick the Proper Color-Application Palette

InDesign's ability to apply color is masterful. All of these controls are found in the Swatches palette, which is unprecedented in power—in any application. The problem is that InDesign also has two palettes from Illustrator: the Gradient palette and the Color palette. If you are accustomed to Illustrator, you will be tempted to use these other palettes a lot. Resist the temptation!

It is tempting to use the Color palette, but colors used directly from the palette are not automatically added to the Swatches palette. It is an option to add colors to Swatches through the palette's option menu. Also, you can click the fill or stroke mixed in the Color palette and drag-and-drop the color to the Swatches palette. If you are disciplined enough to move your colors to the Swatches palette this way, that is fine. But remember that keeping the Color palette available wastes docked palette space.

The Gradient palette has the same problems and solutions. It is further hampered by its small size and difficulty of use. It's much easier to use the New Color Swatch and New Gradient Swatch dialog boxes available from the Swatches palette than to use the Color and Gradient palettes.

> NOTE *Even though InDesign has drag-and-drop color, it is implemented with no special advantages. You cannot quickly make gradients using drag-and-drop, for instance. If you do use drag-and-drop color, you need to make sure you have the proper stroke or fill icon chosen before you apply the color. Also, you really should add the color to the Swatches palette before you start the drag-and-drop application of color.*

Beware of Unnamed Colors

The true problem with both the Color and Gradient palettes is that you can easily use them to add unnamed colors to your document. In a way, these palettes produce local formatting of color. You have no way of changing these locally formatted colors globally. With the Swatches palette, if you change your mind about the dark forest green and decide to warm it up with some more yellow toward a hunter green, you can just double-click the swatch and change it. All the instances of that color throughout your document will be fixed. Locally formatted colors need to be located one by one, and you cannot tell what they are by the colors you see on the screen.

Another problem with using colors this way is that it is incredibly easy to get confused and start adding colors that are not a part of your project budget. If you are working with spot color, you can add RGB or CMYK colors that will completely blow your budget. They may all look like they are part of the two-color world you are supposed to be using. You might not even discover the problem until you get six unusable pieces of film instead of the two you had budgeted.

Take a Look at the Color Palette

The Color palette is virtually identical to the palette from Illustrator 10, but there are a couple of additions. Below the stroke and fill selectors (which you should recognize from the toolbox) are two little buttons that let you add the color you mix here to the container (frame) or the type. In the palette's option menu, you have the choice of RGB, LAB, or CMYK sliders.

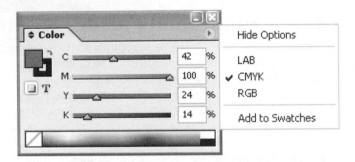

If you have a Pantone spot color selected in the Swatches palette, the Color palette will show the name of the color and give you a tint slider to make tints of that spot color. The New Swatch command in the Swatches palette's option menu is far more powerful and intuitive. The Color palette changes the color of whichever is active: stroke or fill. It does not add the color to the Swatches palette. Having unspecified colors roaming around your document is asking for disaster!

Take a Look at the Gradient Palette

The Gradient palette is much tougher to use than the dialog box that comes up when you use the new Gradient Swatch command in the Swatches palette's option menu. It's confusing to add the colors because there is no specification for them. If you drag a gradient to the Swatches palette, it is named New Gradient Swatch. You need to double-click the new swatch to open a dialog box that allows you to name it. Instead, I suggest that you use that same dialog box off the Swatches palette to create the gradient in the first place.

The Gradient palette has a reverse direction button that is nice. However, it is much easier and faster to simply press G and use the Gradient tool to control the length and direction of the gradient, as described in the next section.

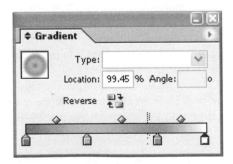

The gradient being created in the example shown here seems innocuous enough. However, that is only because the horrors are invisible. On the screen, it looks like a fairly complex radial gradient using four colors. It goes from purple, to a tint of purple, to green, to a very light tint of the purple. It is supposed to be a two-color spot project, so there appears to be no problem. However, the gradient is actually PMS 254 to C38 M39 Y6 K5 (a light purple) to PMS 348 to R235 G232 B255 (a very light purple). If you try to print this, the RGB will be converted to CMYK. This CMYK looks okay on the screen, but the tint numbers indicate that it will actually print as a very light pinkish lavender. But even worse, instead of this being a two-color job (as quoted) it is now a six-color job. And there is no visual indication of this disaster on the screen!

You can find out what the colors are by clicking the stops (the little color boxes under the gradient bar). However, if you do this in the Gradient palette, the colors show up in the Color palette. If you click in the Color palette to fix the color, the Gradient palette is deselected. If you drag-and-drop the fixed color from the Color palette, a new stop is created. It is a clumsy procedure.

Use the Gradient Tool

With the Gradient tool in the toolbox, you can control the length and direction of gradients. The length of a gradient is determined by the distance between your click and release. The direction of the gradient is determined by the direction of the drag. For radial gradients, the center of the gradient is determined by where you click, and the length is determined by how far you drag the mouse. Everything before the click is the color of the first stop of the gradient. Everything after the release is the color of the last stop. Figure 13-1 illustrates this procedure.

You can have a long starting color, with a very short gradient, followed by a long ending color, if you make a very short click-drag. This is what you see at the top of Figure 13-1. Plus,

13

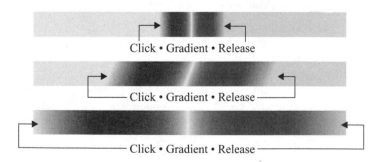

Click • Gradient • Release

Click • Gradient • Release

Click • Gradient • Release

FIGURE 13-1   Creating gradients with the Gradient tool

you can overwrite any gradient by simply applying a different gradient or by dragging over the object with the Gradient tool.

As explained in the following sections, it will save you a great deal of time in the long haul to get in the habit of adding your gradients as swatches. If you do this before you start layout and formatting, your work will go even more smoothly.

Set Up Your Swatches Palette

The Swatches palette is the queen of the color-application palettes. Basically, nothing should be done with color until you have added the color, tint, or gradient to this palette.

Plan the Colors You Will Add to the Swatches Palette

The best way to work with color in InDesign is to start your project by adding all the colors you think you will need to the Swatches palette. This means that you need to plan your color use.

In most cases, you will be using black and tints of black, black and a spot color, two spot colors, or maybe three spot colors (one of which might be black). Even with CMYK, you will do far better if you pick a color palette to use and mix those colors for the job before you start placing, formatting, designing, and so on. You may want a pastel palette, a warm palette, jewel tones, the latest fashion assortment, or whatever you need for your client.

Adding colors to the Swatches palette before you start your project gives you a set of colors to use that will greatly help the consistency of your design. It will also save you a great deal of time in production and eliminate most of your color printing problems.

Read the Swatches to Know What Colors You Are Using

The first way to make sure you have information about the colors on the Swatches palette is to always view the Swatches palette in Name view. You choose this view in the palette's option menu. You might want to use Small Name, but with high-resolution monitors, Small Name is very small. In other views, you will not be able to tell what type of color the swatches represent. In Name view, you can see at a glance what kind of color and what color space you are using.

NOTE   *You may want to go to Large Swatch or Small Swatch view after you have everything set up. However, if you do this, be very careful.*

In order to really understand what you are doing in InDesign when applying colors, you need to be able to read the Swatches palette icons that tell you the type of color you are using. If you don't keep track of the color spaces in which you are working, you will waste time and resources (assuming that you don't run yourself or your employer into bankruptcy).

Here is a Swatches palette with various colors. You will never actually use a palette with this many different color spaces, but I set this up so you could see each swatch that I will describe.

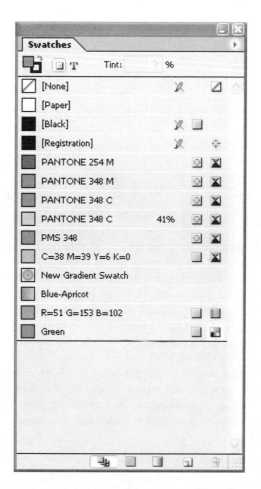

InDesign packs a lot of information into each row in the Swatches palette. It shows a swatch with the color, the color space used to display the color, whether it is a spot color, tint, or a process color, and whether you can redefine the color. Colors in brackets ([]) cannot be redefined for output (although [Paper] can be redefined for viewing on the monitor). Let's start with the top row and work our way down the list.

The [None] Swatch

The icon next to [None] is a white square with a red, diagonal line. It is to clearly warn you that there is nothing there. It means what it says: None.

As you know, we are dealing with PostScript. The PostScript descriptions have no color or dimension until you specify it. In InDesign, color defined by clicking a swatch of [None] means exactly that.

13

To the right of the name is a pencil with a red slash through it. This means that this color cannot be redefined. There is another white square with a red bar to the far right, to make sure you know nothing is there.

The [Paper] Swatch

[Paper] has a normal swatch in front of it. This is not white, as you know, or is it? Under normal use, [Paper] is an opaque knockout color with no color, which reveals the paper through the knocked-out hole.

The [Black] Swatch

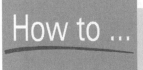

The [Black] swatch represents one of those colors you don't think about, but it actually requires some attention. The swatch color is usually black (although some color management setups show this black as its true 70 percent gray). It is in brackets, so you cannot delete it. It has the slashed pencil to show you cannot redefine it. But there is a new icon at the right edge—a tinted square. This means this is a process color.

This process icon can mean LAB, RGB, or CMYK. For any color other than [Black], there will be an additional colored icon to the right of it that tells you what process color space is used. (In earlier versions of InDesign, to the right of the swatch, you saw the four-triangle box that indicated that InDesign considers this a CMYK color.)

Even though [Black] is often treated like a spot color, this is process black. Process black is not black; it is a dark gray, because it is so transparent and weak in pigment. If you are working in CMYK, you will often need to create a separate swatch called something like Rich Black that might be 60c 60m 0y 100k. If you are printing it in spot color, remember to specify that the printing company use dense black, if it is important.

How to ... Change the Paper Color's Appearance

In InDesign, you can actually make the Paper color appear to be the color of the paper you will be using. Just double-click the Paper swatch and adjust the sliders to make the swatch look similar to the color of the paper you will be using. You can use LAB, RGB, or CMYK sliders. It doesn't matter, because the color does not actually print. Of course, you cannot imitate fiber-added stock, and you must be aware that it's still just an opaque knockout once it prints.

The [Registration] Swatch

The [Registration] row has a black swatch, brackets, a slashed pencil, and a new icon to the far right that looks like a traditional printer's registration mark.

This represents the color that prints on all plates and is used for registration marks that must print on all colors. That is all it is used for. You cannot use it for a rich black, because the amount of ink it would apply would far surpass any usable ink limit on a press or printer.

The Pantone 254 M Swatch

Here, we have a spot color from the PANTONE Solid Matte list, using the CMYK color space to spec the color on the screen.

As you can see, there are two new icons on the right. The left one (the white square with a small, gray circle in the center) means that this is a spot color. The four triangles in a square to the far right show that the color on the screen was calculated with the CMYK color space.

> NOTE
>
> *You can use any color space to specify a spot color. It does not affect how the color prints. The ink loaded in the press determines that. It will come out on its own grayscale plate and be printed in that one spot color you picked.*

The Pantone 254 M 54% Swatch

The Pantone 254 M 54% swatch is a tint of the PMS 254 color listed above it. As you can see from the swatch and icons, it is a 54 percent tint, spot color, CMYK.

The PANTONE 348 M and C Swatches

The PANTONE 348 M and PANTONE 348 C swatches represent a real problem. This is the same color from the Matte list and from the Coated list.

The color looks exactly the same on the screen, but it separates to two plates, because the names are different. At $25 to $50 a negative, it could mess up your budget. It would be even more costly if your printer trusts your artwork and uses a platesetter.

The 48%-254 & 54%-348 Swatch

This next swatch shows something new to InDesign CS. It's a mixed-ink swatch. The strange new

icon to the right of the swatch is actually two overlapping droplets. By the name, you know it is a mix of 48 percent tint of PMS 254 (purple) and 54 percent tint of PMS 348 (Christmas green).

13

However, there is a real problem here. I have printed with this ink pair before. I know that solid 254 and 348 make rich, sienna brown. I also know that this mix would be a dark tan. The swatch shows a charcoal gray, and there is no way that would result. This is always the problem with mixing PMS colors. There is no way to proof them, except on the press.

 You do not know what a mixed PMS color will look like—except with a press proof or by experience. Be very careful when mixing.

The PANTONE 348 Swatch

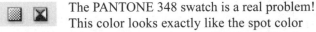 The PANTONE 348 swatch is a real problem! This color looks exactly like the spot color PANTONE 348 on the screen. However, because this is a process color, it will print on the four process plates (cyan, magenta, yellow, and black). That little tinted square is the only warning that you will get.

The 7-77 Black Swatch

 The 7-77 Black swatch is a grayscale gradient going from 7 percent black to 77 percent black. Notice that there is no indication of color space. The only way you know that is by naming the swatch accurately. (You are given the opportunity to name swatches when you create them, as described in the next section.)

You need to save gradient swatches like this if you want to use gradients for paragraph rules, underlines, or strikethroughs.

The New Gradient Swatch

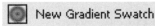 What is this New Gradient swatch? You have no way of knowing what the gradient actually is, without taking the time to look up each stop on the gradient.

Actually, this is that abomination I mentioned earlier. It goes from purple, to a tint of purple, to green, to a very light tint of the purple. It is supposed to be a two-color spot project, but it is actually a six-color mess. And there is no visual indicator on the swatch. Again, to know what a color swatch actually represents, you need to name it descriptively.

The Blue-Apricot Swatch

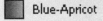 The Blue-Apricot swatch is also a mystery. It happens to be all in CMYK. This is fine if you know what you did. But there is no indicator on the screen or swatch.

The R=51 G=153 B=102 Swatch

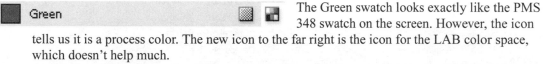

In the R=51 G=153 B=102 row, you see a new icon. This one has three vertical stripes of red, green, and blue. It is the RGB icon. This happens to be from the Web-safe color list, but there is no indicator of that.

The Green Swatch

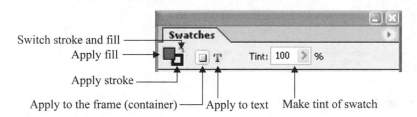

The Green swatch looks exactly like the PMS 348 swatch on the screen. However, the icon tells us it is a process color. The new icon to the far right is the icon for the LAB color space, which doesn't help much.

If you print this color, it will be converted to some unknown CMYK combination. If you export it to the Web, it will be converted to some unknown RGB combination. You might use LAB color in InDesign for very top-end calibrated-color workflows.

Apply Color from the Swatches Palette

The power of the Swatches palette lies in the row of icons across the top of the palette. Using these controls, you can choose to apply your color to the stroke or the fill, and you can apply it to the frame or type inside that frame. Plus, you can make a tint of any swatch, except a gradient or tint. If you make a tint of a tint, InDesign automatically makes that a tint of the original color.

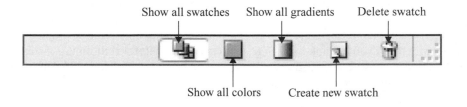

The icons at the bottom of the Swatches palette can also be useful, especially if you have a very full palette.

The easiest way to create your swatches is by using the commands on the Swatches palette's option menu. (As usual, you can make a shortcut for any or all the commands on this option menu.)

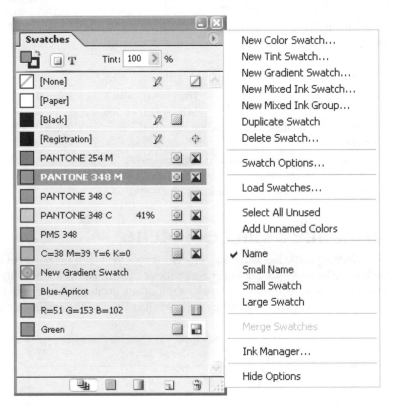

Create a New Color Swatch

The New Color Swatch command displays a dialog box that is deceptively powerful, as is the case with many of InDesign's dialog boxes. In the example shown in Figure 13-2, you see a simple CMYK process color, as yet unnamed. The New Color Swatch dialog box includes a field to name the color. As I've pointed out, naming your swatches is important. For simple CMYK color, as in this example, you should check the Name with Color Value box. Then the color will be named with its values—C=100 M=0 Y=85 K=24 in this example. This is called the *color build* of a color.

Using the color build can really help your printer locate possible printing problems. It will also gradually teach you to think in CMYK, which is a very helpful skill. In this instance, for example, printing on soft, uncalendared text paper could cause a dot gain of 20 percent of more. This will make that yellow tint go solid.

TIP   *If you select a swatch before you choose New Color Swatch or click the new swatch icon at the bottom of the Swatches palette, you start with a duplicate of that swatch. You can also copy a swatch by using the Duplicate Swatch command on the Swatches palette's option menu.*

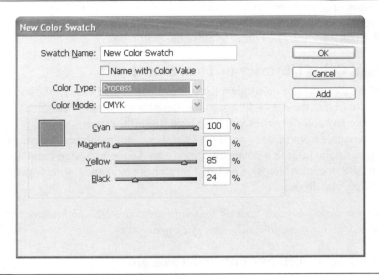

FIGURE 13-2	The New Color Swatch dialog box

Pick a Color from a Color Library

The New Color Swatch dialog box is where you find those color libraries described earlier in this chapter. The Color Mode drop-down list of all the libraries is shown here.

When you choose a library, the list of colors in that library will appear in the field where the color sliders were. If you want to choose more than one color, simply click the Add button until you are finished. Then click the OK button to close the dialog box.

Find Additional Color Libraries or Load Swatches

At the bottom of the Color Mode drop-down list is a command for Other Libraries. If you choose that, you will find yourself in the Adobe InDesign CS/Presets/Swatch Libraries/Additional Libraries folder. You can store any color libraries you have here from Illustrator.

You can also navigate from there to open the swatches used in another document. You can load colors from an Adobe InDesign document (.indd), an Adobe InDesign template (.indt), or an Adobe Illustrator EPS document (.eps). The Load Swatches command on the Swatches palette's option menu also lets you do this.

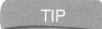

You can also drag swatches from an InDesign document's Swatches palette to an open document window of another InDesign document.

Decide Whether You Need Spot or Process Color

The Color Type option in the New Color Swatch dialog box lets you choose spot or process color. If you choose spot, the color will output to a separate negative or plate.

Remember that each additional plate costs you the same amount to print. So outside of the paper costs, a three-color job will cost about 50 percent more than a two-color job. Chapter 18 covers the different color capabilities of the various printing technologies.

Make a Tint of a Color

To make a tint swatch, first select an existing color from the swatches, and then choose New Tint Swatch from the Swatches palette's option menu. The New Tint Swatch dialog box, shown in Figure 13-3, is the same as the New Color Swatch dialog box, but everything is grayed out except for a slider and a field where you can select tints for the color that was selected. By using the Add button, you can add several tints of a color to the Swatches palette in one step.

It's true that you can make tints of any color by choosing the icon with the slider at the top of the Swatches palette, and by using an option in many of the dialog boxes. The only time you really need to add and save tints is for use as stops on the Gradient Ramp when making gradients. However, adding a selection of tints also helps you maintain consistency in your documents. It is no longer as necessary as it was in the bad old days, when you needed to have the tint in the Swatches palette before you could use that tint anywhere. But it is still a good idea.

Add a Gradient Swatch

When you choose the New Gradient Swatch command in the Swatches palette's option menu, you see the dialog box shown in Figure 13-4. The Gradient Ramp at the bottom is the same as the one in the Gradient palette, but here it is larger and easier to control. You also get the option to use Named Swatches as stops.

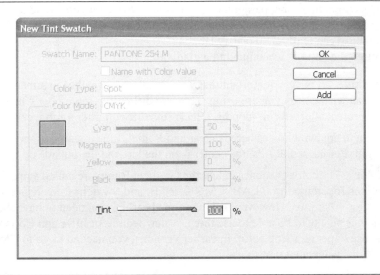

FIGURE 13-3   The New Tint Swatch dialog box

The primary advantage of creating gradients in this manner is that it adds them to the Swatches palette, and gradients must be on the Swatches palette before they become available for use in paragraph or character styles. Only named swatches can be used for paragraph rules, underlines,

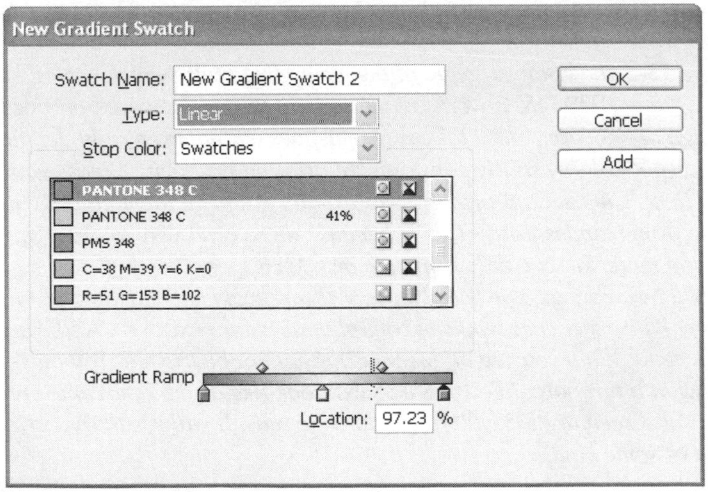

13

FIGURE 13-4   The New Gradient Swatch dialog box

and strikethroughs. A gradient line, paragraph rule, tint box stroke, or cell stroke is a nice touch in a complicated layout with many boxes, tables, rules, and lines. A gradient stroke for a callout line with an arrowhead can really help clarify labeling.

Let's go through the options when making a gradient:

- **Swatch Name**   It is very important that you name your swatches in a manner that reminds you what colors you are using. They are difficult to remember when you come back to a project after several months. (Heck, it is difficult after a fun weekend.)

- **Type**   There are two choices here: Linear and Radial. Linear starts on the left and ends on the right. For the radial fills, the center is on the left and the outside on the right.

- **Stop Color**   The color swatches below the Gradient Ramp are called stops. There are four choices for stop colors: LAB, CMYK, RGB, and Swatches. Swatches works very well for spot-color jobs. However, as I mentioned earlier, you need to have the tints in the Swatches palette to be able to use them. A new feature of InDesign CS is that you can now use Paper as a stop color. In earlier versions, you needed to go to CMYK or RGB and make a white color to use.

NEW TO InDesign CS

- **Number of Stops**   I have been able to put 50 different stops in a gradient. The documentation does not give a limit.

- **Midpoints**   The diamonds above the Gradient Ramp are midpoints. These indicate the halfway point between the two colors. You can drag the midpoints left or right to get the gradient you need.

Mix Your Colors

NEW TO InDesign CS

The New Mixed Ink Swatch option is new to InDesign CS. Everyone is really excited. Now we can mix spot colors, just like in Quark. Get yourself under control! The capability is not that wonderful.

Figure 13-5 shows an example of the New Mixed Ink Swatch dialog box, with a mix of PMS 254 and PMS 348. It works really well, in theory. However, the swatches produced by InDesign are not even close to reality. The hues are not even right, let alone the values.

Mixed spot colors usually cause severe printing problems, unless you have a very trusting client. Commercial printers will usually not print them unless you sign a waiver or release from responsibility. This is because there is no way to proof mixed spot tints. All proofing materials are either opaque or CMYK.

You will be creating color based on your theoretical understanding of what the resulting mix will be. With experience, you can control these color mixes very well, but all the proofing is in your head. What you see on the monitor cannot be trusted. You must be able to imagine what a turquoise like PMS 326 will look like as a 55 percent screen, mixed with a 35 percent screen of PMS 200 (a bright wine red). It will result in a grayed-out blue-violet tint of some kind.

The question is this: Can you get the client to trust your taste enough to authorize it? Based on my experience, this is not likely.

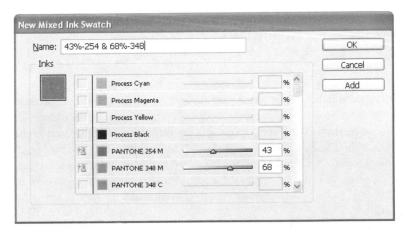

FIGURE 13-5   The New Mixed Ink Swatch dialog box

There Are No Guarantees with Mixed Spot Color

Clients and print shops usually want guaranteed color based on either a color contract proof or a printed swatch. These are simply not available for mixed spot color. Most customers get very queasy when you say, "The color is great! Trust me!" And for gosh sake, do not let the client see the screen, unless you know they absolutely understand that the screen color is not the printed color.

I learned about the dangers of mixing spot colors when it almost got me fired from one of the best jobs I ever had in a printing company. I was doing 300,000 natural organic grape juice labels for a local winery. They didn't have the budget for CMYK and had finally accepted a quote for two-color. It was about $36,000 (expensive paper). The artwork was quoted at about $300.

Their logo was a wench stomping grapes in a vat in front of a couple trees and vines. The colors in the logo were greens, tans, browns, and purples. Being the egomaniac I was in my youth, I said, "No problem! I can get your logo done two-color by using purple and green inks that will make a brown when they are mixed."

I picked PMS 348 and PMS 254, mixed up a couple tiny samples, and made some overlapping smears of the inks with my fingers. I made some educated guesses about the percentages (based on my color-mixing theory classes and practice in college) and picked several mixes I was confident would work well.

13

I made a beige blouse, tan skirt, brown tree trunks, vines, and vat, purple grapes, softer purple juice splashes, green leaves, light brown dirt, and lighter green grass using many tint combinations. This was in the early 1980s, well before digital production, so I specified the color builds on an overlay. The couple that owned the vineyard came for a press proof and loved the color. We printed the labels, and they were ecstatic.

After they left, while the press was running, the owner of the printing company came back in the art department. He told me in no uncertain terms that if I ever did anything like that again, I would be fired on the spot. What was the problem? There was no proof and there was no proof possible. I had just told the couple, "It'll look good. Trust me." And the couple had believed me. I hadn't bothered to tell the boss or the production manager. If the clients hadn't liked the color, we could have messed around for hours, with many sets of plates, and hundreds of sheets of paper, until they were happy. I could have cost the printing company thousands of dollars.

Build a Mixed Ink Group

The New Mixed Ink Group command displays a dialog box that allows you to automatically generate dozens of colors from any assortment of mixed inks. The colors start from the lightest tint and build darker in the increments you choose. The example shown in Figure 13-6 produced 36 swatches named Purple/Green Swatch 13, Purple/Green Swatch 14, and so on. These colors look good in swatches on the screen, but who knows what they will look like when they print? As you can see, you can get yourself in even more trouble than simply using the New Mixed Ink Swatch command to create one mixed-ink swatch.

Having said all that, this is certainly a wonderful tool if used with care. You could carefully build a color set with combinations that you know work well.

TIP *It is also possible to find one of the old PANTONE Two-Color specifiers that were sold in the 1970s and 1980s. They were a couple hundred dollars, but worth every penny.*

Edit Your Colors with Swatch Options

The Swatch Options command on the palette's option menu shows a dialog box that is a duplicate of the New Color swatch dialog box, with all of its power and control. You can also access this dialog box by simply double-clicking the swatch.

The problem is that as soon as you click a swatch, that color is applied to any selected objects. If you want to open the Swatch Options dialog box without applying the color, hold down CTRL-ALT-SHIFT/COMMAND-OPTION-SHIFT and double-click the swatch. The dialog box will open without applying the color.

Add Your Unnamed Colors to the Palette

If you do have unnamed colors in your documents, you can add the builds of those colors to the Swatches palette. To do this, just choose the Add Unnamed Colors option on the Swatches palette's option menu.

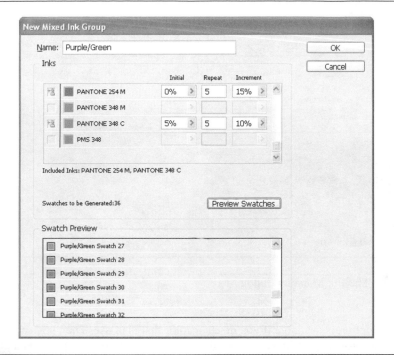

FIGURE 13-6   The New Mixed Ink Group dialog box

Depending on the color space you used when building the color, the color will be written in RGB, LAB, or CMYK. If you do use the Color palette, this is a good way to check and make sure that the colors are in the right color spaces for output.

Manage Your Colors

One of the really nice features of InDesign is that it gives you recourse if you lose control of your colors. The Ink Manager dialog box, shown in Figure 13-7, is available in four places: from the Swatches palette's option menu, the Output page of the Print dialog box, and the Advanced pages of both the Export PDF and Export EPS dialog boxes. It doesn't matter how you get to the dialog box; any changes you make will still be in effect if you access it again from another location.

As you can see, all the colors used are listed. There is a check box to convert all spot color to process. You can alias multiple spot colors to print as a single color and other things. We will look at these options in more detail in Chapter 18.

Delete Swatches

The Delete Swatch command on the Swatches palette's option menu looks simple. However, because InDesign allows you to SHIFT-select ranges and to CTRL/COMMAND-select noncontiguous swatches, you can delete whatever you like. Coupled with the Select All Unused command on the Swatches palette's option menu, you can easily clean up a cluttered Swatches palette.

13

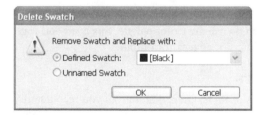

FIGURE 13-7   The Ink Manager dialog box

Another nice option is available if you delete a color that is in use. Then you see a dialog box that lets you choose from any swatch to replace the deleted color. You can replace your color with [None] or [Paper] with this option, for example. The default is black, and that is what will replace your deleted color if this dialog box does not show up.

Merge Swatches

The Merge Swatches option on the Swatches palette's option menu lets you merge multiple colors into the color you select first. If, for example, you find that you have several versions of a PMS color, you can select the color you want to keep. Then SHIFT-select or CTRL/COMMAND-select other colors you want merged into that first selected color, and choose Merge Swatches.

Know Whether Stroke or Fill Is Chosen

As you know, the stroke and fill selectors are found in many locations. Figure 13-8 shows three of these places: the toolbox, the Swatches palette, and the New Paragraph Style dialog box.

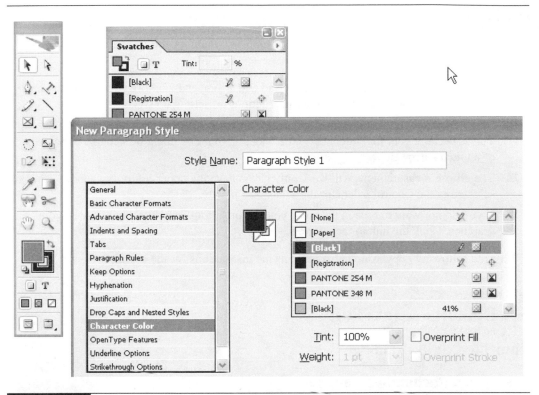

FIGURE 13-8   These are just some of the places you'll find the stroke and fill selectors.

You can also switch the colors for stroke and fill with a shortcut:

- Press D for the default colors. These are a black stroke, a fill of none for frames, and black with no stroke for type.
- Press X to switch between stroke and fill activation.
- Press SHIFT-X to switch the colors in the stroke and fill selectors.

NOTE   *The file/stroke defaults are all single letters, so they cannot be used while you are using type. However, you can make a shortcut that uses the* CTRL *and/or* ALT/COMMAND *and/or* OPTION *keys.*

You need to make a correct selection, and then watch what you are doing. It is extremely easy to apply color to the wrong object. It is also very easy to think you are applying a fill when you are actually applying a stroke. The good news is that you can undo anything you do.

Practice Your Graphics and Color Skills

Now it's time for an exercise to practice using the tools and features you've learned so far. Here are a few things to be aware of before you begin:

- You will need to make the styles 6 Subhead and 7 Subhead 2 before you can set the next style in 6 Subhead. See Chapter 8 for instructions on setting up styles.

- Some people report that they need to make the text block a little wider to make things fit. This is because your font might be a little wider or your box might be a couple hundredths of an inch narrower.

- The ellipse measurements will work only if you have the upper-left proxy handle selected in the Control palette or the Transform palette.

- If you do not want to type in the copy, you can pick it up from http://kumo.swcp.com/graphics. Click the link to the tutorials.

Type the following copy, which also contains the instructions for the exercise.

Set Defaults & Text Edit

Tutorial & Skill Exam

Step 1: Set document defaults:

Open a new document. Set page size at 10"x10", tall; set the margins at .5" with 2.5" on the left; show hidden characters; one column; optical margin alignment for 12 point.

Style palette

Here, you need to set up your Paragraph Styles palette. Start by selecting all the styles and deleting them (by using the option menu). Then make a new style and call it 2-Body. I explained the reasons for numbering the styles in Chapter 8. Each style is just a listing of specs.

2-Body: Georgia, 10/12, left justified, 1st line indent .4", tracking 0, Metrics kerning, based on No Style, 5 points before paragraph (type p5 in the field), Word spacing 85/97/115, glyph scaling 97/100/103, black shortcut Ctrl/Command-Num 2

3-Hanging: Select 2-Body in palette and choose new style, Verdana, no indents, shortcut Ctrl/Command-Num 3

5-Headline: Select no style and make new style, Trebuchet Bold, 24/auto, flush left, Metrics kerning, no indents, next style 2-Body, tracking 0, Hyphenation off, auto leading 100%, 3 points after, gradient 100-30, shortcut Ctrl/Command-Num 5

6-Subhead: Based on 5-headline, Next style 7-Subhead 2, 18/19, tracking 25, 7 points before paragraph, 1 point after paragraph, rule below paragraph, 5 point, gradient 50-7, thin-thick, offset 2 points, width of column, shortcut Ctrl/Command-Num 6

7-Subhead 2: Based on 6-Subhead, Next style 2-Body, 14/14, .6" left indent, 4 points before paragraph, 3 points after paragraph, black type, rule above paragraph, 14 point, gradient 0-77, offset -2 points, width of column, left indent .4" shortcut Ctrl/Command-Num 7

Step 2: Import type & format copy

Because this exercise is in a book, you'll need to type in the copy. Place the insertion point in the first paragraph and press Ctrl/Command-Num 5. Move the cursor down the page, pressing the appropriate shortcut in each new paragraph. The insertion point is enough to format the entire paragraph. Correct the typos.

Add ellipse   With the Ellipse tool, draw an oval with 10 pt line, 7-70 linear gradient and 7-70 radial fill. In the Transform palette, set x: .5"; y: .5"; w: 4"; h: 9". Put a .2" text wrap around the shape. Adjust the gradients to look like the sample.

Set type in the box   Click on the oval with the Text tool. Set "curved text wraps are very tricky"—centered in the oval. If it doesn't look like the sample shown in Figure 13-9, you need to examine everything to find out what you missed and fix it. So, now we need some fill copy. Mary had a little lamb—it really freaked out the doctor. Mary was sort of blasé about the whole thing, but then she is pretty jaded (plus her dolly got ripped up by the house-bound doggie with separation anxiety).

That's it! The final result should look something like Figure 13-9. If you see bold copy in Figure 13-9 that is not in your version, you can make a character style or locally format that copy to bold. If the text in the oval overflows or does not fit, pick 2-Body to make the type small enough to fit, convert it to no style, and then resize it from there. It depends on what you have set as your default style. You may need to play around with various parts, just as you would with a real job.

13

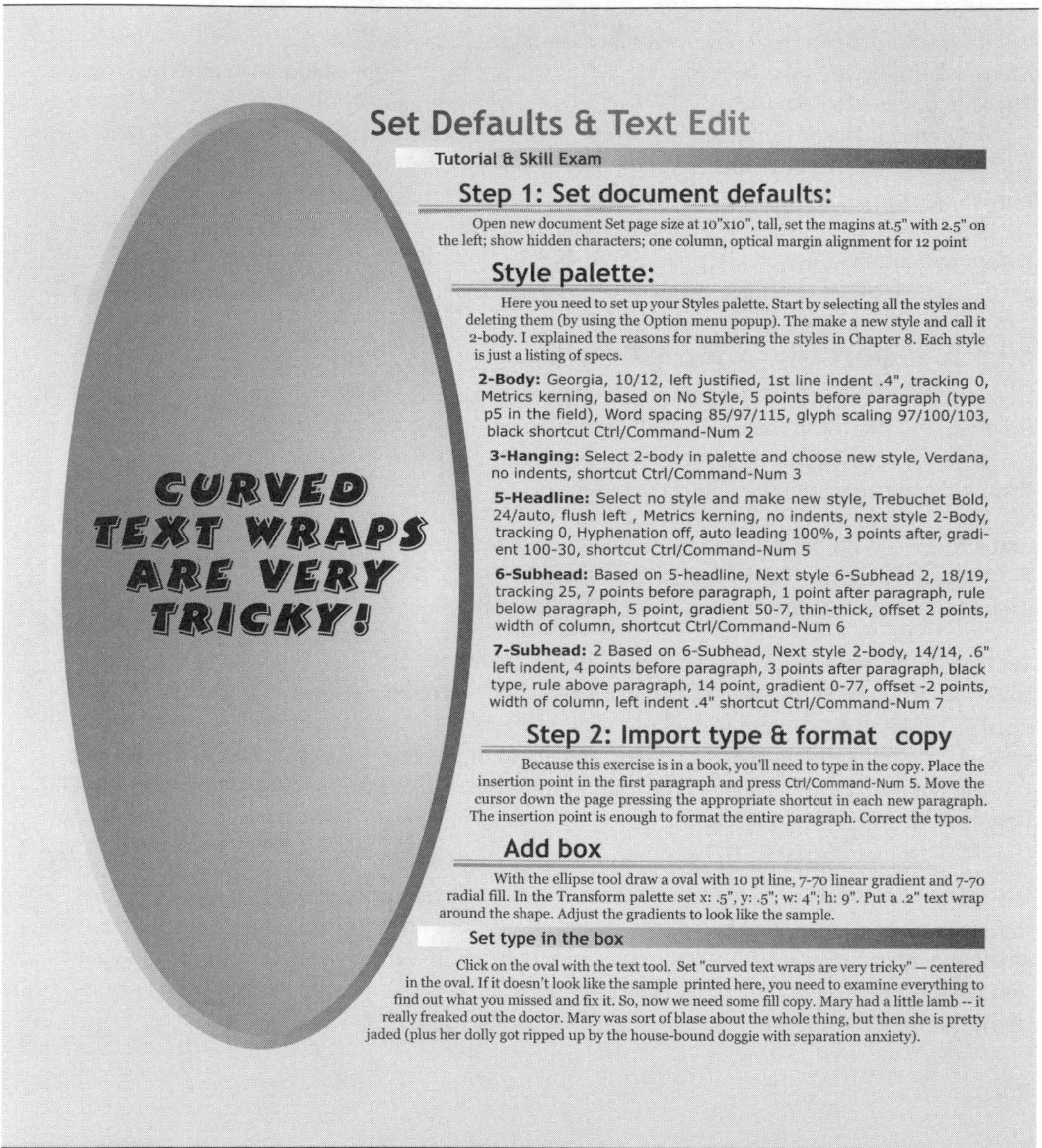

Set Defaults & Text Edit

Tutorial & Skill Exam

Step 1: Set document defaults:

Open new document Set page size at 10"x10", tall, set the magins at .5" with 2.5" on the left; show hidden characters; one column, optical margin alignment for 12 point

Style palette:

Here you need to set up your Styles palette. Start by selecting all the styles and deleting them (by using the Option menu popup). The make a new style and call it 2-body. I explained the reasons for numbering the styles in Chapter 8. Each style is just a listing of specs.

2-Body: Georgia, 10/12, left justified, 1st line indent .4", tracking 0, Metrics kerning, based on No Style, 5 points before paragraph (type p5 in the field), Word spacing 85/97/115, glyph scaling 97/100/103, black shortcut Ctrl/Command-Num 2

3-Hanging: Select 2-body in palette and choose new style, Verdana, no indents, shortcut Ctrl/Command-Num 3

5-Headline: Select no style and make new style, Trebuchet Bold, 24/auto, flush left , Metrics kerning, no indents, next style 2-Body, tracking 0, Hyphenation off, auto leading 100%, 3 points after, gradient 100-30, shortcut Ctrl/Command-Num 5

6-Subhead: Based on 5-headline, Next style 6-Subhead 2, 18/19, tracking 25, 7 points before paragraph, 1 point after paragraph, rule below paragraph, 5 point, gradient 50-7, thin-thick, offset 2 points, width of column, shortcut Ctrl/Command-Num 6

7-Subhead: 2 Based on 6-Subhead, Next style 2-body, 14/14, .6" left indent, 4 points before paragraph, 3 points after paragraph, black type, rule above paragraph, 14 point, gradient 0-77, offset -2 points, width of column, left indent .4" shortcut Ctrl/Command-Num 7

Step 2: Import type & format copy

Because this exercise is in a book, you'll need to type in the copy. Place the insertion point in the first paragraph and press Ctrl/Command-Num 5. Move the cursor down the page pressing the appropriate shortcut in each new paragraph. The insertion point is enough to format the entire paragraph. Correct the typos.

Add box

With the ellipse tool draw a oval with 10 pt line, 7-70 linear gradient and 7-70 radial fill. In the Transform palette set x: .5"; y: .5"; w: 4"; h: 9". Put a .2" text wrap around the shape. Adjust the gradients to look like the sample.

Set type in the box

Click on the oval with the text tool. Set "curved text wraps are very tricky" — centered in the oval. If it doesn't look like the sample printed here, you need to examine everything to find out what you missed and fix it. So, now we need some fill copy. Mary had a little lamb -- it really freaked out the doctor. Mary was sort of blase about the whole thing, but then she is pretty jaded (plus her dolly got ripped up by the house-bound doggie with separation anxiety).

CURVED TEXT WRAPS ARE VERY TRICKY!

FIGURE 13-9   The finished graphics and color exercise

Some Color-Handling Tips

All full-color printing is process. Sometimes, a fifth color is added to pump up the reds and purples. (Hallmark Cards has been making money using this trick for years; as far as I know, it is still their tightly held trade secret.) However, a good separator can make what is called a touch plate to beef up colors that are too weak in CMYK. What is usually needed is a fifth red plate.

Do not mix spot and process color unless you have a large budget. Process plus two spot colors is a six-color print job. This costs almost 50 percent more to print than process alone. Sometimes, you have no choice, but you can usually design around the problem. Remember that every color adds another color plate or head to the press or printer. This means that every printing cost is added again, except for the paper cost.

> **TIP** *The common procedure of adding gloss and dull varnish to a project to make the photos pop out also adds two spot colors. If you put a dull varnish on the background and a gloss varnish over the photo, it will look like it is very bright and physically lying on top of the paper.*

Limit your color palette. First of all, this is a sign of good taste and style. You might even try (horror of horrors) a coordinated color scheme. This would be especially true if you were trying to recapture the look of the 1950s and early 1960s. If you are doing two-color, black, and a spot color, use the color sparingly and dramatically. The worst thing you can do is to simply make all the heads and subheads in color. Remember that color always has less contrast than black and white. Dingbats and small emphatic graphics work well in spot color, as do hand-drawn boxes or special rules used for underlines. Color also works extremely well for tinted boxes used as sidebars, mastheads, graphics, and so on.

Approach color with fear and trepidation. Color is ridiculously easy to add on the monitor screen. However, it greatly increases printing costs. It is often not worth the money. Having said that, your clients will certainly demand it. Remember that discretion is a sure sign of refined taste. Be discreet! Do color with style and flair, not sprayed all over like a graffiti vandal.

13

Chapter 14

Control Your Color

How to...

- Check for overprinting problems
- Preview your separations
- Compensate for quickprint registration
- Use multitones
- Colorize halftones
- Build traps
- Use color management

Now that we have reviewed the procedures for applying color, we need to talk about its practical use and considerations for printing in color. The focus of this chapter is on how to control your color and how to use it wisely.

Check for Overprinting Problems

One of the more misunderstood aspects of printing is the concept of overprinting. In traditional printing, everything overprinted by default. To make color look right, we needed to spend a great deal of time creating knockouts to punch holes in underlying color. Now, digital publishing does this automatically, and we rarely think about it. Partially, this is due to the fact that most designers rarely output separations. However, you do need to be aware of overprinting, because sometimes it doesn't work properly.

NOTE *Separations are the core of process color. They have four halftones on top of each other: cyan, magenta, yellow, and black. They need to be angled to avoid moiré patterns. Separation procedures are discussed in my book,* Publishing with Photoshop *(by Onword Press, 2002), available at amazon.com or bn.com.*

CMYK images must overprint to produce the printed colors. If you have a color that is 100c 45m 0y 15k (a deep royal blue), it would be a real mess if the solid cyan plate knocked out the other colors. However, if you have type on top of that blue that is 0c 5m 20y (pastel yellow), you need to knock out the blue, yet still overprint. As I said, InDesign handles that flawlessly in most cases.

However, there are times, such as when you make changes to a design, that you will need to fix an overprint problem. You can do this by using the Attributes palette.

As you can see, the Attributes palette is very simple. There are check boxes for Overprint Fill, Overprint Stroke, Nonprinting, and Overprint Gap (which will be grayed out unless you have a stroke of multiple lines or dashes that has a gap). The Nonprinting option does just what it says: The selected item does not show up in the printed version or exported graphics. The item you made nonprinting looks normal on the page, and there is no indication that it will not print. For example, you might use this to add a note to other people who may be working on that document.

TIP *If something is missing in a proof, check the Attributes palette to see if it is set to Nonprinting.*

Check for and Fix Overprint Problems

I made a little illustration the other day. I decided that I better check out the separations. So, I printed a color proof. The result looked something like what you see here.

The rectangle is green. The seven-pointed star is purple. The words are yellow with a black stroke set outside the path. As you can see, the words do not look good.

After a quick look at the separations, the problem became clear. There was no knockout of the type in the green rectangle.

Purple star

Green rectangle

Yellow words

14

I checked out the Attributes palette with the type selected. Sure enough, the yellow fill was set to overprint.

So, I simply unchecked Overprint Fill and printed another proof. The green separation then had the knockout for the text.

The proof now showed everything was okay.

This overprint problem came about because I originally made the type black. If you remember from the discussion of the General preferences in Chapter 2, black normally overprints for many reasons. When I later decided that there was not enough contrast between the black type and the green rectangle, I made the type yellow with a black stroke. If you look at the separations shown here, you can see that the black stroke did not affect the colors at all. However, the yellow fill retained the Overprint setting of the original black fill. So, it had to be fixed using the Attributes palette.

Preview Your Separations

One new tool in InDesign CS is the Separations Preview palette, which shows your spot-color separations (that is how I produced the separations in the previous example of fixing overprinting problems).

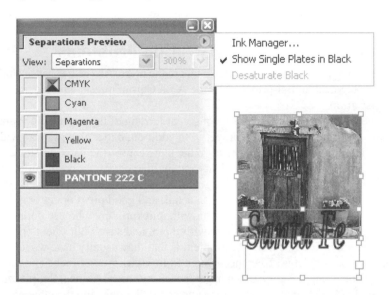

Previewing your separations can be very helpful for spotting printing problems (before you get that panicky call from the printing company). Just click each swatch in the palette to see what is printing in that color. This is certainly much faster than printing separated laser proofs; however, I still recommend printing the laser proofs for your protection. I'll talk about that in Chapter 17.

14

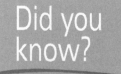

Spot Color Cannot Be Managed

There are many color standards. However, even with standards, there are still problems. Clients regularly specify a PMS color, and then get horribly upset at the results. Most commonly, they are basing their decisions on what they see on the screen.

Basically, spot color cannot be managed. All you can do is match a printed swatch. And, you can do that only on bright white paper. Beyond that, it is a matter of experience and learning the limits of the printing equipment you are using.

Compensate for Quickprint Registration

One use of overprinting is to solve registration problems with quickprinters and other suppliers using duplicators. Most people think that every time the colors do not match up perfectly, it's a registration problem. This is not true. If the plates do not line up exactly, the problem is called *fit*. This is a hardware problem. In general, fit is solved digitally, using knockouts. Some older, cheaper imagesetters and some laser printers cannot make multiple colors fit.

Understand What Causes Registration Problems

Registration refers to fit problems caused by the paper in the press. All presses have some registration issues, except for the best digital presses like the Agfa Chromapress, which can hold a half-thousandth registration.

The largest source of misregistration is inconsistent feeding of the paper. If the paper bounces at all, the various colors will not line up properly. In addition, paper changes size with humidity changes. With offset lithography, the water from the plate causes the paper to change size. This can cause fit problems. Climate-controlled plants and multicolor presses costing millions of dollars, which apply all the color in one pass, have largely solved the registration problem. All it requires is a desire for excellence in printing, attention to detail, and good press operators.

However, registration problems are common with quickprinters who use duplicators instead of presses. You can produce excellent results with them, and save your clients hundreds and thousands of dollars in printing costs. The problem is that they usually have what CMYK snobs call severe registration problems. Tolerances range from ±0.01 to ±0.1 inch. The plus or minus means that every color can move up, down, right, or left by that tolerance. So, if registration is plus or minus one-tenth inch, one color can move up and to the right and the other color can move down and to the left, producing a two-tenth-inch gap or overlap.

Obviously, registration can be a serious problem. The worst-case scenario would be a shape of one color with an outline of another color. But anyplace that colors touch can cause problems.

Solve Registration Problems

There are some easy solutions to registration problems. You can design so it does not matter if the colors move around. You can make them far enough apart, with no obvious alignments, so that movement does not affect the documents. Often this is an excellent solution.

Another solution is not so obvious. In this case, you design your project with overlapping colors set to overprint. Sure, it changes the color. If a large, blue headline on a yellow background is set to overprint, it will be slightly green, depending on the strength of the yellow. So what? Certainly, you can handle that design issue. Incorporate that into your design, so it looks like that on purpose. If the type overprints, and it is not too close to the edges, any misregistration movement will be completely unnoticeable.

A deep blue headline here — The black copy here printed over a screen of very light blue, tan, cream, or lavender. The type overprints in both cases. No problems.

NOTE

This is a place where design snobbery comes into play. The bottom line is that 1,000 flyers printed two-color spot at a commercial printer would cost around $150. The same project printed with a digital duplicator (like a Ricoh Priport) would cost between $20 and $30 to print. If designed well, they will both have the same impact. In CMYK, the cost could be $500 to nearly $1,000, depending on the process used.

Use Multitones

As mentioned, most of your design jobs will be spot color (for the next few years, at least). You may make more money on the CMYK jobs, but usually the spot-color projects have higher profit margins. Do not complain about that. Learn to design effectively within that limitation. InDesign is a great tool for this.

One of the spot-color tools at your disposal is what I call *multitones*: duotones, tritones, and quadritones. These are colored, multilayered halftones.

NOTE

Photoshop can save PSD duotones. InDesign CS can read them, but many RIPs used by printing companies cannot.

Understand Dot-Density Ranges

Multitones are a method of improving the quality of images in spot-color projects. These multilayered halftones are used to compensate for the fact that printing ink has a maximum density of around 1 on the standard density scale, running from 0 to 4. This scale is logarithmic, just like the Richter scale is for earthquakes. A density of 2 is close to ten times as dense as 1, for example. The darkest color possible is called the *dMax,* for maximum density.

Photos always have a maximum density of at least 2, and professional photos can have shadow densities far above 3. Original Ansel Adams black-and-white photos had maximum densities approaching the theoretical maximum of 4. With printing ink having a maximum density of 1, something needs to be done to get excellent reproduction quality. Duotones, tritones, and quadritones solve this by printing several layers of ink on top of each other to build up the density to something roughly approximating the original.

Duotones, tritones, and quadritones are halftones that are built in two, three, or four layers.

- A *duotone* makes a second halftone from the identical image. This second halftone contains only shadow dot information. When it is printed on top of the first halftone, the resulting duotone has shadow densities that run from 1.5 to 2.

- A *tritone* uses a third color for the highlights with the shadows being hit three times to produce densities in the 2 to 3 density range.

- A *quadritone* uses four colors for the closest approximation to photographic prints with maximum possible densities of nearly 3. If you use CMYK for this, you get a four-color separation and a printed color photo.

14

In most cases, duotone and tritones are tinted grayscale images. They are not full color. InDesign cannot produce them, but it prints those made in Photoshop well. Usually, you will be using a duotone EPS made in Photoshop. Tritones are rare.

There is one case where you must convert to a quadritone: When you have a black-and-white photo in the midst of four-color separations. If you do not make the grayscale image a CMYK quadritone, it will look very faded and weak next to the separations. Usually, with a little care, you can simply convert your grayscale image to RGB and carefully separate it.

For multitones to work well, you need exceptional photos. They should be sharp and clear, with detail in the highlights and the shadows, white whites and black blacks. Because every color adds almost as much cost as the first color, this is a quality choice, not a bottom-line option.

It is true that, if you are already using two colors, duotones are a cheap way to make your halftones look better. However, unless you understand the density-range concept, you will be disappointed with the results. The quickprinters pushing this technique rarely understand the density-range concept.

CAUTION *For years, low-quality printers have spread the lie that duotones are a cheap way to add color images to a brochure. In fact, they are an expensive way to make your black-and-white photographs richer and more beautiful. They require the same registration as CMYK images, so they must be printed at commercial printers or quickprinters with T-heads. We'll talk about these issues in Chapter 18.*

Beware of Fake Duotones

Fake duotones are not duotones at all. They are a technique sold by relatively incompetent printers as a cheap way to add color to a photo. They are pushed by Adobe in their Help guides and tutorials because they are the only technique that InDesign is capable of producing. These "duotones" are simple in concept: A tint block of color is printed under a halftone. Figure 14-1 shows an example of using this technique in grayscale.

As you can see in Figure 14-1, all the highlights are ruined with the tint of color. It is a halftone with a solid block of 20 percent color behind it. In grayscale, it is even more obvious that this is not acceptable quality. But unscrupulous printers (and software manufacturers who shall remain unnamed) still recommend these fake duotones.

Work with True Duotones

True duotone techniques are a powerful tool when you are working on two- or three-color jobs. Most duotones are made with black and a spot color. There are some good reasons to use a dark brown and a spot color (maybe a warm brown or dark tan), especially if you need the look of the old sepia tones of the late nineteenth century. The dominant halftone should always be the black one (or the darkest color). There is a tendency to make the colored (or weaker) one the stronger image, but this tints the highlights as well as the shadows.

FIGURE 14-1 The halftone on the left is ruined by the flat second color on the right. The image on the right is called a fake duotone. It should be called a ruined halftone.

> **TIP** *It is often easier to get the exact duotone effect you desire by manipulating CMYK separations, and then printing the CMYK separations in the spot colors you need.*

If your second color is green or blue, tinted highlights tend to make people in the photos look very ill. In the second halftone, all the highlights and upper midtones should be eliminated. Then all the richness is added to the shadows, without darkening or coloring the highlights.

As explained in Chapter 13, spot color proofing is almost nonexistent. This is why I have not discussed multitones done with multiple spot color. You can make beautiful designs, but it takes experience and practice. Multitones done with multiple spot colors are very hard to sell, unless the client has a lot of printing experience and has a lot of trust in your experienced designer's eye.

14

Solve Halftone Problems

Although it would be great to use only the highest quality printer, that will probably not be possible in the real world. Your job is to make your project look good when published, no matter who prints it. Often, you will be using low-resolution printers, for a variety of reasons. The most common one is money, of course. Here, we will look at some techniques for working with the available technology to handle halftones.

Use 1-Bit Dithered Halftones: Handmade Stochastic

One solution for improving halftones is a technique that can be called handmade stochastic screening. This solution works well with low-resolution technologies: 600 dpi laser printers, DocuTechs, digital mimeographs, screen printing, and so on. You will find it invaluable.

This method uses Photoshop's Diffusion Dither option. In Photoshop, you create the halftones normally. When you're satisfied, change the mode to Bitmap. One of the Bitmap conversion choices is Diffusion Dither. Common resolutions are 130 dpi to 300 dpi conversions, depending on the individual printer. (See *Publishing with Photoshop* for examples and explanations.)

Colorize Your Bitmap or Grayscale Images

One of the places where InDesign shines is in its abilities to colorize grayscale photos. It can easily do this with either 1-bit halftones or normal 8-bit halftones (grayscale).

InDesign allows you to color either TIFFs or PSDs, as long as they are bitmap or grayscale. To add color, just place the TIFF or PSD file into the document, select it with the Direct Selection tool, and click the swatch you want to use for the color. It's basically flawless. The result is a monotone in a specified color. (Monotones are just colored halftones.)

One of the real advantages of the dithered 1-bit TIFFs described in the previous section is that you can freely overlap them in varying colors, because the random dots do not produce moirés. Although two-color mixed tints are very hard to use (because of the inability to proof them), overlapping random dots providing a colored background can be very impressive, even in top-quality projects.

One reason this works so well is that the white background on 1-bit TIFFs is transparent. This means that you can get some visual reference about the color mixing before you print. You cannot get accurate color on the screen, but you can at least locate the various pieces accurately. You must set the overlapping TIFFs to overprint, so they will not knock holes in the images below them.

Remember that this is a very different paradigm from CMYK color. You never know exactly what the project is going to look like until it is printed. All you can show clients is the preprinted swatches and ask them to trust you. You can seduce them with price. Your design charges are no less; sometimes they are even a little more. But you can reduce the printing costs by a third, even for three-color jobs. For two-color projects using duplicators, you can cut the printing costs by 75 percent or more. If you can find a printer with a Priport, you may be able to do even better than that. The final result will still look great!

Build Traps

Trap building is an area it would be nice to avoid. In most cases, it is better to let the service bureau or printing establishment apply its own traps, and you should have discussed this with your output supplier before you started designing. However, if you must make your own traps, InDesign does traps much better than most applications. It has a Trap Presets palette that works well. But to use it, you must understand how traps work.

Understand How Traps Work

Let's step a little into the future. You have produced all the pieces: copy, illustrations, and photos assembled into a final InDesign document. Now you must deal with registration, as discussed earlier in this chapter.

If you are using a printing technology that can register within a few thousandths of an inch, there is a common solution to printing colors that touch. Printers use the same solution used by carpenters: They apply molding to the edges. The printer's molding is called a *trap*. Traps are created wherever two different colors touch. In other words, wherever two colors touch, the weaker color is made a little larger so it slips underneath the stronger color.

NOTE
Traditionally, traps were made photographically with chokes and spreads. The color that grows was called a spread. *A color that shrinks was called a* choke.

The Problem with Trapping

As mentioned, in digital printing, colors usually do not overlap or overprint. If you place one color on top of another, it will knock out the color underneath perfectly, edge to edge, with a "kiss fit." This would seem to be an excellent solution.

However, until relatively recently, presses have been unable to register well enough, and the kiss-fit objects always had a white line on one side or the other. This seemed intolerable to printing companies and traditional designers. (In truth, it was usually invisible without a magnifying glass.) The solution was to use traps as tiny overlap "molding," which was very tedious to build by hand with dupe film and vacuum frames. It took many layers of film or flats to construct traps.

Traps are very small. They must be wide enough to cover the registration capabilities of the press used. However, they should never be large enough to be seen easily. Modern color presses can easily handle what is called "half-dot registration." In other words, they can feed paper with a consistency equivalent to half the size of the dot in the linescreen used. Because commercial printers normally use 150-line screen, a half dot is around 0.03 inch or 0.003 inch, 0.07 millimeter, or 0.2 point. This is a tiny trap.

TIP
What is called hairline registration *is not even possible on a brand new duplicator. However, many duplicators have what is called a T-head (two plate cylinders imaging the same blanket). At most quickprint companies, all you need to do is begin talking about traps and hairline registration and carefully observe their faces. You'll know quickly whether this is a normal part of their workflow. If it seems like they can do it, ask for samples.*

14

Software has solved the problem of trapping. With relative ease, you can generate digital traps that were physically impossible before the 1990s. At this point, only operator errors—designer mistakes—create trapping problems. Designers need to understand traps well enough to create their own.

How Trapping Works in PostScript

In PostScript, traps are made with overprinting strokes. To understand that, you need to remember how a stroke relates to the path. In InDesign CS, a stroke can be inside, centered, or outside the path. Normally, it is half to one side and half to the other. You build traps with a stroke of the weaker color that overlaps the stronger color and overprints. The idea is to make the overlapping portions wide enough so that no matter how far apart the colors bounce, there will be no white gap.

You make the overprinting portion of the stroke the width of the trap you need. If you have a dark-red object in a sky-blue field, you simply make the stroke of the red object twice the size of the trap needed, make it centered on the path, color it sky blue, and set it to overprint. The blue background will touch (kiss-fit) the fill of the red object. The inside half of the stroke will overprint the red shape with a very thin, sky-blue line. You could also make the stroke the width of the trap and place it on the inside of the path.

If you reverse the colors (a sky-blue object in a deep-red area), you simply set the stroke of the blue shape to blue at the trap width outside the path, and set it to overprint. The blue shape now appears to spread under the darker red background without enlarging the blue shape.

In both of these cases, there is a thin, very dark purple line surrounding the interior shape. In the first case, it makes the red shape a little smaller. In the second situation, the purple line is outside the blue shape. Supposedly, it is so thin that it is invisible. In fact, it adds a hairline outline to all trapped shapes, unless you reduce the color of the trap by tinting it. This is a much worse problem with some colors than with others. Complementary colors tend to make a black trap. Neighbors on the color wheel will make an invisible trap.

NOTE *If it is that thin, is it necessary? Your printer will probably insist that it is. You should let the pros do what they want, unless it adversely affects the thickness of your wallet. On the other hand, do not fear kiss-fit printing. Printing companies with 2- to 6-color presses have no problem holding quarter-point registration, and often the thin, white slivers are virtually invisible. And when was the last time you put down a slick, four-color brochure because the trapping was bad? Probably about the same time you refused your burger because of ugly printing on the wrapper.*

Create Traps with InDesign

InDesign can automatically trap documents with its built-in trapping, or it can use the similar but more powerful Adobe In-RIP Trapping in RIPs that support Adobe In-RIP Trapping. Usually, In-RIP Trapping is found only in imagesetters and platesetters. Both of these automatic trapping routines can precisely calculate and apply any necessary adjustments to the edges of both type and graphics to keep those dreaded white gaps from appearing. They can apply various trapping techniques to different parts of a single object, even if that text or object overlaps several different background colors.

InDesign can trap imported vector PDFs, but not EPSs. It can trap to the edges of placed bitmaps. Internal trapping of bitmaps (if necessary) will need to be done in Photoshop. However, In-RIP Trapping is very powerful. Trapping adjustments are made automatically, and you can define trap presets to address the trapping requirements of specific page ranges.

The effects of trapping are apparent only on color separations after they are output. You cannot see the results onscreen within InDesign (or any program).

The actual production of digital traps is absurdly simple. The computer does it all. InDesign looks for contrasting color edges. It then creates traps based on the neutral densities (value or brightness) of touching colors. Normally, lighter colors spread into adjacent darker colors. The settings to control this process are in the Trap Presets palette.

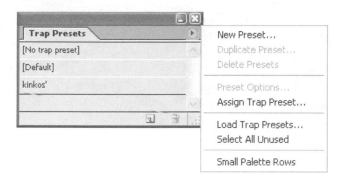

The Trap Presets palette provides a place to enter trap settings and save them as a trap preset. You can apply trap presets to any or all pages in the current document. You can also import the presets from another InDesign document. Once you turn on trapping, the entire document is trapped. If you don't apply a trap preset to a range of pages, those pages will use the default trap preset, which is a collection of typical trap settings that are applied to all pages of a new document.

You begin to appreciate the power of this when you choose to make a new preset. Take a look at the New Preset dialog box, shown in Figure 14-2.

In most cases, you can use the defaults. I could go on for pages here, but it would cause most of you to put the book down and take a nap. In general, set up your trap the way the printer tells you to set it up. If you are setting up for a printer who cannot tell you this, set the Trap Width value at twice the registration tolerance. For a T-head, I would use 0.005 inch, for example. The Trap Appearance settings are the caps and joins I talked about in Chapter 10. For the Trap Placement setting, I suggest Center (the historical norm). Then check the type of images you want trapped. Changing the Trap Thresholds settings is not a good idea.

If you like living dangerously, read the help documentation that comes with InDesign very carefully. It is exhaustive and lengthy and tedious. When you are finished, you will probably be confused and go with the defaults. Remember that these traps are so small that they are not life or death.

14

New Trap Preset

Name: Sheky's Print House

Trap Width
Default: 0.0035 ir
Black: 0.0069 ir

Trap Appearance
Join Style: Miter
End Style: Miter

OK
Cancel

Images
Trap Placement: Center
☑ Trap Objects to Images
☑ Trap Images to Images
☐ Trap Images Internally
☑ Trap 1-bit Images

Trap Thresholds
Step: 10%
Black Color: 100%
Black Density: 1.6
Sliding Trap: 70%
Trap Color Reduction: 100%

FIGURE 14-2   The New Trap Preset dialog box

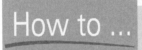

How to ... **Eliminate the Need for Trapping in CMYK**

It is not very hard to eliminate the need for trapping in process color. Remember that the concern is those tiny, white gaps. In most cases, if these gaps are even slightly colored, people do not notice them. It is easy to design a color palette that covers all spaces with some color.

All you need to do is design your swatches so that all adjoining colors have some of the same color. Let me rephrase that. If you have a purple next to a green, both of those colors need cyan. So, no matter how much the magenta bounces in the purple, or the yellow bounces in the green, the cyan will always move in union, and any gaps will be colored cyan.

There are not too many color combinations that do not have some component of common color. You do need to watch for complements. But when you look at most colors in CMYK, they usually use three of the four colors at least. Browns, grays, and jewel tones usually use all four colors. Just be sure to exercise some control when picking colors.

If you have a CMYK color that uses black, you can always convert some or most of that black to the complement of the primary hue. A brown, for example, is a magenta/yellow combination plus black. If you have 20 percent black in a brown, 30 percent cyan will probably give you the same color (or very close). The same is true of greens and purples. A magenta/yellow combination will gray out blues. However, it is the CMY color space, so black is not often needed.

Use Color Management

Color management is the latest litany from all the big boys, both authors and printing companies. "Accurate color is now easy," they say. And I've got an SUV that gets 65 miles per gallon. It is true that color management is nearly ready to go mainstream. However, accurate color is still (and will remain) a matter of long-term relationships with individuals and machines.

All monitors need to be calibrated. Color management takes calibration to the next level. Calibration involves setting a machine to the manufacturer's specifications. Color management tries to make the final output match the original art. This is done by making color profiles of all the input and output equipment. Standardized targets are scanned and compared to the actual output of the individual peripheral to produce these profiles.

InDesign has built-in color management that works reasonably well. To use it, you need a monitor profile to plug into the Color Settings dialog box in InDesign. This profile, a custom ICC (International Color Consortium) profile, is created when you use your system's calibration software: from the Displays control panel in Mac OSX or using the Windows Adobe Gamma software.

Understand the Purpose of Color Management

The purpose of color management is predictable and repeatable color. This is expensive and difficult. However, there are certainly workflows that use color management to save hundreds of thousands of dollars. These people report that they can accurately proof their projects from their monitors. This is called a *soft proof*. This is true for a very small minority of designers and is needed for a very small proportion of printing projects. The day this will be readily available to the average designer is quite a ways in the future—maybe 2005 or 2010.

The key to color management is really very simple: Ask them what they want you to do. If the company you are using to print your project uses color management, the representative will be able to tell you exactly how to set up your software. The company will have a custom profile to send you for its presses. This is one area where there is no substitute for experience.

For most designers, the solution is to learn to use swatch books and printer-supplied color proofs. You need to learn to spec colors by the book. As a result, you will be able to function with or without calibrated hardware.

Calibrate Your Monitors

Truly calibrated monitors are still rare. If you have one, that is a good thing. The best most of us have is a semi-calibrated monitor from Apple. The Apple Studio Display is really not calibrated. It adjusts the monitor's color by what it thinks will happen as the phosphors decay through time and use. A truly calibrated monitor comes with a standardized target, a densitometer or a photospectrometer, and software that enables you to adjust the colors of your monitor to match the standardized target. These monitors start at more than $1,000, and I doubt that you have one.

Recalibrate with Your System's Software

Apple's monitors are based on regular recalibration using the Displays control panel. Adobe Gamma works much the same in Windows as a separate control panel.

Mac's color management is system-wide. Open the Displays control panel and choose the Color tab, as shown in Figure 14-3. Change the default RGB to your new monitor profile.

Windows still individualizes things in each application. The default is sRGB, which does not work for designers. Change that in your Adobe Gamma control panel. Use Adobe RGB (1998) as your starting point, as shown in Figure 14-4.

Set the color temperature of your monitor for something designed for printing. Mac's monitors are very bright. Printers use 5,000°K for their light standard. Mac monitors are set at 9,300°K from the factory, and that is excessively bright and blue. Windows uses 6,500°K as the default, which is called Daylight. (It is only daylight if you live where I do—a mile above sea level.) I suggest using 6,500°K until you get used to it, and then switch to 5,000°K as soon as you can. Windows

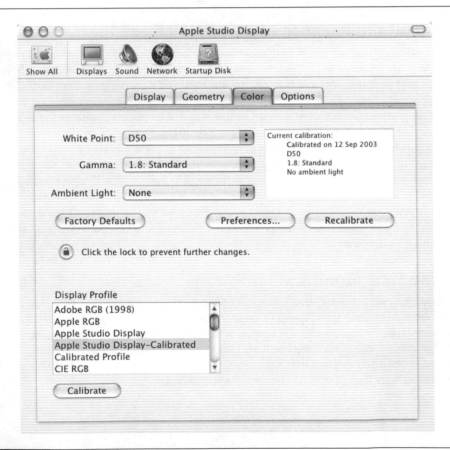

FIGURE 14-3   The Displays control panel in Mac OSX

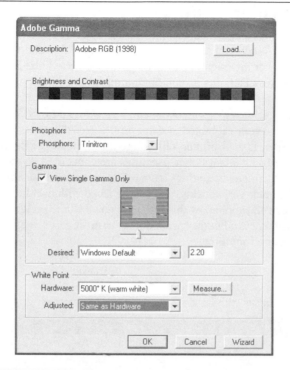

FIGURE 14-4   The Adobe Gamma control panel in Windows XP

calls this 5000°K (warm light), and Mac calls it D50. This will look very yellow to you when you first use it. But the colors on your screen will be much closer to the printed results (and you will experience less eyestrain).

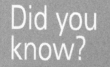

You Need to Control Your Light Environment

There is a reason why fine artists always demand a lot of light from north windows. The light is much more consistent. In the same manner, you need to make sure you get your light environment (called *ambient* light) under control. The soothing yellow of incandescent bulbs is good. Everyone agrees that normal fluorescents are the worst. That harsh, greenish glare makes everything look very strange (the pink, "warm" fluorescents are worse).

If you are in an office, at least get color-balanced 5,000K tubes. In my classes, the best I have been able to do is sit by a north window, get an incandescent studio lamp to warm things up, and remove the overhead fluorescent tubes entirely.

Use InDesign's Color Settings

InDesign has a Color Settings dialog box that looks almost exactly like Photoshop's and Illustrator's, as shown in Figure 14-5. When you start using InDesign, open this dialog box by selecting Edit | Color Settings in Windows or InDesign | Color Settings in OSX, check the Enable Color Management box, and pick U.S. PrePress Defaults as you beginning setting (unless you are not living in the United States).

As you can see, the default settings are Adobe RGB (1998) and U.S. Web Coated (SWOP) v2. Change the RGB setting to your calibrated monitor profile. Use these settings until you are certain you have something better. If your printer tells you to use something else, be obedient.

As far as the Color Management Policies settings are concerned, Preserve Embedded Profiles is best. The For Profile Mismatches settings have InDesign ask if there are any discrepancies. But now we wallow into the mud. Very quickly, you will be faced with deciding if the profile that came with the separation in that ad supplied by that little, unknown studio on the other side of town was produced by people who knew what they were doing. In most cases, a quick call will suffice, and when in doubt, don't change anything.

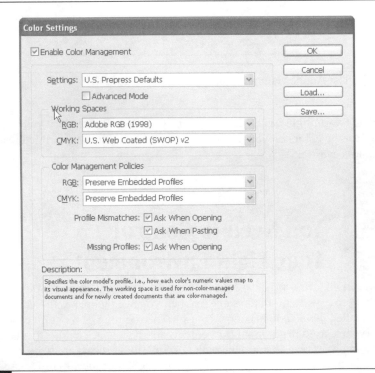

FIGURE 14-5   The Color Settings dialog box

As an example, I've played with the advanced settings and built my own profiles to use with the color presses in my lab. I managed to mess things up to the point where I had to reinstall everything: software, drivers, printer profiles, and more. This happened every year from 1993 to 2000 when InDesign came out. I've learned my lesson.

Use the defaults with your own monitor profile, unless your printer tells you different and supplies you with a profile. The point is to do it as your service bureau or printer representatives request. They need to supply you with the final output profiles, or at least tell you which ones they use. They must calibrate their equipment for consistency. You need to go with what they use.

Understand Color Printing Production

No matter what type of color you are using, always pick your printer before you begin to design. How can you possibly design within the printing capabilities of your supplier if you do not know who is going to print your project? Use cheap suppliers at your own risk. The main reason they are cheap is that they toss all the color responsibilities on you. Make sure you can handle these tasks, since someone has to do it.

Adjust for Dot Gain

Do not forget to adjust for dot gain. In process color, this is a simple setting in Photoshop. However, you need to remember that tints applied in InDesign will also gain the same amount. If you have a 10 percent dot gain, I would not recommend any screens darker than 80 to 85 percent; with a 20 percent gain, 70 to 75 percent; with a 30 percent gain, even 65 percent can be risky.

Remember that the cheaper printing processes have larger dot gain, and this means that light tints are also a problem. Commercial printing on high-gloss coated stock might hold a 3 percent dot in the highlights. Quickprinting with a 30 percent dot gain can easily have trouble holding a 10 percent highlight dot.

Printers will tell you their dot gain, if you ask, and you should ask before you start designing. Every printer has different capabilities. See Chapter 18 for more information about the different capabilities of various printing technologies.

Consider Process-Color and Spot-Color Requirements

Make sure you settle in your mind whether or not you are competent to do "magazine" quality separations. If you are not, carefully choose a service provider to handle the separation conversions. If you are providing the scans, do the best you can with RGB scans, and let the service provider or printing company do the CMYK conversions. Unless you have an excellent scanner (one that cost $1,000 or more), you are often better off letting the printer do the scans also, and merely using the 72 dpi FPO (for position only) scans they supply to show them where to insert the high-resolution CMYK.

Make sure that the costs and difficulty of process color are justified by the content of your project. Often, a one- or two-color job on gorgeous paper will look far better than a process job poorly done—at half the cost or less.

14

If you are using spot color to cut printing costs, pay special attention to the registration capabilities of your service provider. If the duplicator can handle only one-sixteenth inch plus or minus, then all of your colors must overprint, and they need to completely overlap or not get any closer than a half inch to each other. You also need to be careful of internal alignments that make any registration problems obvious.

Keep careful track of the kind of color you add. If you are quoting a straight four-color process job, adding spot colors (or even RGB colors) will add to your quoted printing costs. Always bid in a calibrated color contract proof for your process color jobs. At $50 or more per side, this can seem like an extravagance. In most cases, this contract proof will be part of the printers' quotes. A client's refusal to pay (because he does not like the color) is going to cost someone hundreds or thousands of dollars, or more. That someone will be you if you don't have a contract proof signed by both the client and the supplier. See Chapters 17 and 18 for more on proofs.

And as a last bit of color-use advice, remember that one of the surest signs of an amateur is uncontrolled color strewn about the surface of the page. Simply adding color, lines, and shapes because you can do it easily is no excuse! Add color in judicious amounts for specific reasons. Those reasons must center on improved communication about the client's products or services.

Part V

Design Web and Multimedia Documents

Chapter 15

Add HTML, XML, and Multimedia Features

How to...

- Learn the Web's limitations
- Design for the Web
- Add hyperlinks
- Create buttons
- Add multimedia
- Publish eBooks
- Package for GoLive

InDesign's Web capabilities are very impressive. You can publish an interactive Web page or eBook. You can add movies, sound, music, rollovers, and all kinds of fancy bells and whistles. However, as with all page creation on the Web, many rather harsh realities need to be considered. Adobe promotes the idea of "one document, three destinations," suggesting that you can use the same document for the Web, PDF, and full-color printing. However, using the same content for three different environments is not wise. But the truth is that you will regularly be asked to make a Web version of your printed documents.

Our rides through cyberspace are all individual searches for content. In fact, due to the present bandwidth restrictions, it may be fairly said that content is at least as important on the Web as in print. Amazing animations, glorious sound, and things like that are simply not available to many users through their modem and phone line.

So, even though InDesign can now add movies, sound, and hyperlinks to its documents, the concept of using the same document for multiple purposes is a very bad idea. The good news is that InDesign is now a very good tool for Web page and eBook production, as long as you know the limitations of the Web and design with them in mind.

Learn the Web's Limitations

This new environment is where many designers with a print history will begin having a rough time. On the Web and in multimedia, we are entering a world of coarse, crude graphics and with little formatting control, no color calibration, and no output control. The writing style necessary for onscreen reading is very different. The layout choices are very different. The available colors are very different. A relatively simple brochure in print normally requires a relatively complex, multipage document on the Web. Graphics on a Web page cause such large delays in the search for content that their use must be severely restricted in most cases. However, like all design problems, this is just another problem to solve.

Consider Bandwidth

As of early 2003, the average surfer still had modem access, with a 28.8 to 56 kilobit modem. Normal phone connections max out between 3KB and 7KB per second. Even the 56-kilobit standard is glacially slow when normal color images are dozens of megabytes in size. In reality, a 6MB file often does not make it to the surfer's computer. Even if it does, it takes well over an hour. Many ISPs time out after a half hour or less.

DSL and cable connections certainly help, but they are not available to many people who are online. All Web traffic ends up on phone lines, at this point. Even if you have access through a T1 line, download times vary vastly during the day.

Surveys consistently state that the average surfer cancels out and moves on if the entire page takes more than 30 seconds to appear. An informal study of my students over the past nine years indicates that 15 seconds is a practical limit. This means that the entire page must be under 45KB (though many agree that under 30KB is much wiser). So the sum of the limitations for the next several years is that your Web graphics must be 72 dpi, usually 8-bit, and all pages under 30KB.

Know Monitor Capabilities

The Web is severely limited by its output device: the monitor. Although it is true that the Web looks better on high-resolution monitors, less than a third of computer owners use such monitors at this time. Even when high-resolution monitors are available, most users still use 800-by-600 resolution. Even if they use monitors set at a resolution of 1280 by 1024 or higher, the graphics are still limited to 72 or 96 dpi.

Beyond low resolution is the problem of color depth, or the ability of the monitor to display enough colors to satisfy the designer's desires. Studies show that at least 80 percent of monitors are set to less than 24-bit. Even if the monitors are capable of 24-bit, most users use the Windows default of 16-bit color or less. Think about that the next time you drop in that exquisite 24-bit JPEG.

NOTE *My statistics are from Boomerang. Sadly, like many sites, that one has converted to an all-commercial, pay-for-entry site and does not offer current statistics to the general public.*

If your client's customers are mostly graphic designers or digital gamesters, you can almost count on resolutions of at least 1024 by 768 with 24-bit depth. If those customers are small business owners, caution says to design for 640 by 480 and 8-bit (although you can probably get away with 800 by 600 and 16-bit).

You also must be cognizant of the vast differences between PCs and Macs. PC monitors use a gamma of 2.2, and Macs use a gamma of 1.8. The higher the gamma, the darker the image. This means that Mac monitors are much brighter, and usually much higher resolution (Mac default is 1024 by 768). Images created on a high-resolution Mac that look great there often look very dark and dingy on a PC, not to mention that they look huge. Images created on a PC at 800 by 600 that look fine there are often far too light, with all the highlights blown out on the Mac. Often, they are

15

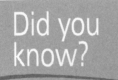

You Cannot Assume Graphics on the Web

In mid-1999, surveys said that somewhere between 15 and 30 percent of surfers browse with the graphics turned off. The best guess I have heard recently suggests it is still 10 to 25 percent. This is largely because of the speed of their connection. The average modem connection is still 33.6 to 44 kilobits, and the average person has a modem. People surf with graphics off because everything they are looking for is in the words, and it is much faster.

also much too small to read. This tends to be true, even when you set a Mac's gamma at 2.2 and lower the resolution to try to compensate.

This is also true of type. On high-resolution Mac monitors, you might use 14-point type or larger to make it legible on the screen. The type looks absolutely huge on a PC. This is also why many Web sites created on a PC are completely unreadable on a Mac, because the type is too small to be read, especially if it uses small, light type on a dark or graphic background. (Truth be told, they are probably nearly illegible on a PC also.)

Be Aware of the Lack of Typography and Formatting Options

The common necessities of typography are simply not available on the Web. Even in formats like eBooks, readability issues are very real. None of the fonts used in print are available on the Web. Most of the formatting and layout options that are normal in print do not work onscreen. The tools available for easy readability are not there on the Web.

In fact, it is worse than that. The fonts available on the Web are not used in print because they have a strong negative effect on the readers. They produce subconscious, antibureaucracy reactions, at best. Times, Times New Roman, Helvetica, and Arial are a real problem onscreen.

The Web equivalent of styles formatted with shortcuts is still a fond dream. GoLive does a little better now. When you use the Package for Web from InDesign feature (discussed in the "Use the Package for GoLive Feature" section later in this chapter), the styles of InDesign are automatically converted to Cascading Style Sheets (CSS). But, this does not mean that you can take a print document and put it on the Web.

Design for the Web

I read some excellent advice on one of the Web design sites: People do not come to your site to see the killer graphics; they come for easily accessible information.

Your customers (or your clients' customers) are not looking for amazing digital dances to amuse and pass the time. They want to know what you are offering, if it meets their needs, and how to get it. The fancy stuff does not help. It irritates! The number one irritant on the Web, in all surveys, remains looping animations.

You need to be aware of your viewers and design to communicate, not to show off. Always check your designs on both the PC and Mac platforms, and on as many different browsers as you can. For those of you designing on a PC, remember that the most common browser in Mac OSX is Safari, which comes with Jaguar and Panther.

Make It Readable

On the Web, reading is done in very short bursts. When viewers reach the data they need, their first reaction is to print the page. However, pages printed from the Web need to be carefully structured. In most cases, all the copy ends up in very wide columns with 20 to 30 words per line. This is not readable.

All of the pages need to be clear and concise, offering all the linkage options suggested by the content, so the surfer can arrive at that needed data as quickly and efficiently as possible. In most cases, subheads in print need to become links to new pages on the Web. Navigation becomes the major issue. Tables of contents and indexes are hard to pull off well on a Web site. They are far too slow and far too complex.

What we see as terse in print becomes verbose online. I find that I commonly need to eliminate half of my print copy or more.

> TIP   *When all of the copy is necessary, consider PDF delivery. That way, you can control the readability.*

Use the Same Software to Create Graphics

For all of the differences in environment, the best software applications for Web graphic creation are still FreeHand, Illustrator, and Photoshop; although I admit that I increasingly create my graphics in InDesign. Fireworks and ImageReady are more specialized, adding powerful file-size reduction capabilities, but the Save for Web command in Photoshop can do all of that. The only thing Fireworks and ImageReady are really needed for is the production of rollovers and other specialized JavaScript capabilities. As you will see later in the chapter (in the "Create Buttons" section), InDesign can do this, albeit in a limited manner.

Flash offers new and powerful animation abilities, but the download times are still very long. Also, you need a programming/scripting mentality to use it. Graphic communication is about using graphics to communicate, and the FreeHand/Illustrator/Photoshop combination is the best, no matter what the medium. The only new entry is InDesign, which can easily do things with type the others still struggle with.

15

Use Color on the Web

The Web is an environment where color has no penalty, since you can work in color at no extra cost. Although we are not talking about the impact of process color on cast-coated stock with photos popping off the page, highlighted by gloss varnish on a dull varnish background, the color available is good enough to get the reader's attention—256 colors are definitely better than black and a spot color.

The major thing to remember is that color still lessens contrast. A limited color palette is still essential to effective communication. The 216 Web-safe colors give you more than enough colors to work with in quantity. However, I do not recommend that you use Web-safe colors. They are too limited in the yellows, browns, and shades of red and orange. You need to pick colors you like and design in enough color contrast so that no matter how badly that cheap PC monitor messes up your color, the page can still be read easily.

The same color issues found in print cause problems online. For example, colored type on a colored background is still harder to read. Because color is available so easily, you must exercise restraint.

Redesign Your Page Layouts for the Web

Do not even try to mimic your incredible page layout on the Web. It is a different medium. Print projects converted directly to Web pages rarely work at all and almost never work well.

It is normally best to design your documents for print first because of the far higher resolution needed and the typographic requirements. You can always dumb down your pages for the Web. However, to make a truly usable Web site, you will need to spend a lot of time designing the site structure, and it will normally be radically different from your print documents.

InDesign has the Package for GoLive option, but it would be foolish to simply export the printed version. You are far better off to think of the conversion as a much more fundamental change. Simply exporting that gorgeous brochure with the same layout using CSS to format the type will usually result in a nonfunctional Web page or site (even though it may be visually stunning).

 *The friendliness, openness, and genuine trustworthiness of your site are primary! This needs to be your focus in Web design. The best designs are not only invisible, but they also enable the surfer to feel free, coddled, and enabled to do whatever your client needs.*

Add Interactive Content with InDesign

If you want to publish an interactive Web page, InDesign's Package for GoLive feature makes it easy for you to repurpose graphics and text from an InDesign document for use in GoLive Web pages. The details on using this feature are in the "Use the Package for GoLive Feature" section later in this chapter.

If you truly need to retain the exact look and feel of your typeset documents, the only true solution is PDF. InDesign has very strong interactive PDF production tools. Taking into account the fact that almost all reading of Web sites is done from printed copies, PDFs are really not a bad solution (except for the file-size load placed on your server). You do need to warn the surfer about the file size and the approximate download times.

However, the interactive PDF is probably the best tool for portfolios, résumés, eBooks, and presentations that need an identical printed version. If you are designing for an in-house service or intranet, PDFs work exceptionally well. Over an Ethernet connection, PDFs download quickly, print beautifully, and can be just as internally interactive as any Web site. This is also the best choice for distributed CDs.

The tools for these purposes that are built into InDesign are substantial. They allow you to make interactive PDFs from within InDesign. Let's start with basic hyperlinks.

When you print an interactive document, you can convert hyperlinks to normal text, exclude bookmarks or other interactive elements, and replace movies with high-resolution images. Chapter 18 covers printing options.

Add Hyperlinks

It is often helpful to set up the destination for a hyperlink before you create the hyperlink. Basically, we are talking about internal links within a document. InDesign's support is a lot like the linking support in Acrobat. You can certainly link to destinations outside the PDF. However, once the reader leaves, the exit can easily become permanent. Internal links let you direct people through the document to the desired decision or reaction.

You set up hyperlink destinations and hyperlink options through the Hyperlinks palette. Choose Window | Interactive | Hyperlinks to display this palette.

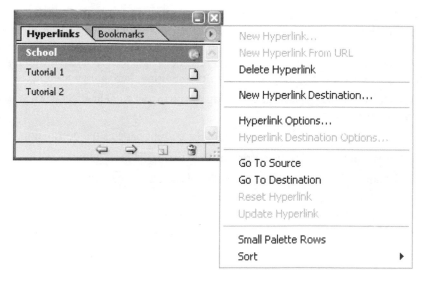

The trick with hyperlinks is to give readers the ability to return to where they started, so you do not lose control of their reading experience. Links need to be two-way streets.

Set Up Hyperlink Destinations

To set up a hyperlink destination, choose New Hyperlink Destination from the Hyperlinks palette's option menu to open the dialog box shown in Figure 15-1. For any type of hyperlink destination, enter a name for it in the Name field.

FIGURE 15-1   The New Hyperlink Destination dialog box

There are three kinds of hyperlink destinations in InDesign, which are available from the Type drop-down menu:

- **Page**   When you create a document page destination, you can also specify the zoom setting of the page you will jump to when you click the link. This works well for tables of contents and general navigation aides. To automatically use the page number as the name, check the Name with Page Number box. For Page, specify the page number you want as the hyperlink destination. For the Zoom Setting, here are your choices:

  - Fixed displays the magnification and page position that were in effect when you created the destination.

  - Fit View displays the visible portion of the current page as the destination.

  - Fit in Window displays the current page in the destination window.

  - Fit Width or Fit Height display the width or height of the current page in the destination window.

  - Fit Visible displays the page so that its text and graphics fit the width of the window. It usually eliminates the margins and white spaces around the edges of your document.

  - Inherit Zoom displays the destination window at the magnification the reader is using when the hyperlink is clicked.

- **Text Anchor**   You can specify the hyperlink destination as any selected text or insertion-point location in a document. This type of anchor works well for indexes, word definitions, and the like. To create a text anchor destination, place an insertion point or select some text where you want to make an anchor before you select the New Hyperlink Destination command.

NOTE   *Even if you only plan on using a master page once, you cannot set up an anchor destination for text on a master page.*

■ **URL**   This is what you thought when I mentioned hyperlinks. A URL indicates the location of addresses on the Internet, like a Web page, movie, or PDF. When the reader clicks a URL hyperlink, the default browser launches and goes to that URL. After you select URL as the type of hyperlink destination, type or paste a URL, such as http://kumo .swcp.com/graphics, into the dialog box. The name of a URL destination must be a valid URL address (one that would work if you typed it into your address line in your browser). You can use any valid Internet protocol: http://, file://, ftp://, or mailto://

Once you have created the destinations you think you'll need, you can establish hyperlinks between those destinations and any selection in your document. If you have not developed a set of hyperlink destinations, you can create unnamed destinations to pages within the current document or to URLs that you specify.

TIP   *To quickly add hyperlinks and edit hyperlink options, use the Interactive | New Hyperlink Destination commands in the context menu.*

To edit or delete a hyperlink destination after you've set it up, open the document in which the destination appears and choose Hyperlink Destination Options from the Hyperlinks palette's option menu. In the Destination drop-down list, select the name of the destination you want to edit. Then click the Edit or Delete button.

Create a Hyperlink

It's very easy to create a hyperlink from a URL you have typed in a document. Using the Type tool, simply select the URL (such as http://kumo.swcp.com/graphics) and choose New Hyperlink from URL in the Hyperlinks palette's option menu.

To use text or a graphic as a hyperlink source, select the text or graphic and choose New Hyperlink in the Hyperlinks palette's option menu (or click the Create New Hyperlink button at the bottom of the palette). The dialog box shown in Figure 15-2 will appear.

In the Name field, type the name of the hyperlink. This should be something that is obvious, especially if others are working with you on the same project. This name will appear in the Hyperlinks palette.

In the Destination section, set the following:

■ **Document**   Choose the document containing the destination to which you want to jump. All open documents that have been saved are listed in the pop-up menu. If it's not there, open it.

CAUTION   *Jumping around in multiple documents is something that can terminally confuse your user or reader. Be careful.*

■ **Type**   Choose from Page, Text Anchor, URL, or All Types to display the destinations you have named.

15

- **Name** Pick from your named destinations. You can also create a hyperlink to an unnamed destination, by choosing Unnamed.
- **Page and Zoom Setting** If Page is selected for Type, specify the page number and zoom setting.
- **URL** If URL is selected for Type, specify the URL. Select None to create a hyperlink with no destination (though I have to assume you will add a destination eventually).

You can also adjust the appearance of a hyperlink in InDesign and in the exported PDF file. The choices in the Appearance section are similar to the choices in Acrobat:

- **Type** Choose Visible Rectangle or Invisible Rectangle.
- **Highlight** Choose Invert, Outline, Inset, or None.
- **Color** Choose a color for the hyperlink rectangle.
- **Width** Choose Thin, Medium, or Thick to determine the thickness of the hyperlink rectangle stroke.
- **Style** Select Solid or Dashed.

NOTE *You can choose whether or not you see the hyperlinks on the page by choosing View | Show Hyperlinks.*

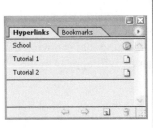
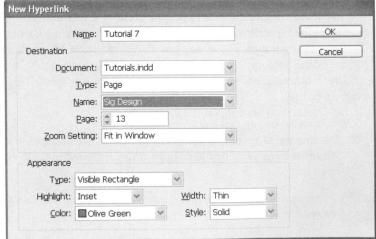

FIGURE 15-2 The New Hyperlink dialog box

Create Buttons

Another common interactive feature in Web pages and PDFs is a button. InDesign's does not provide the full power of ImageReady's capabilities. However, these buttons are intended for use as navigation aids in interactive PDFs. For that purpose, they are an excellent addition. You may want to add navigation buttons (such as Next Page or Previous Page) to a master page, for example. In the exported PDF document, the button will appear on all document pages to which the master is applied.

In InDesign, you create a button with the Button tool and then specify button properties to determine the button's behavior when it is selected. You can also set up various button states so that the button's appearance changes when it is selected or unselected.

Draw a Button

 When you create a button using the Button tool in InDesign's toolbox, you can marquee the button area with a click-drag, or you can click to specify the height and width of the button starting from the

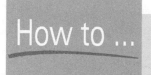 **Create a Button Hot Spot**

You can also create a button that displays a second button. This is especially useful if you want one button to act as a *hot spot* area that displays a larger image, or an image in a different area. For example, you might want to set up a hot spot so that when the user moves a pointer over a building on a city tourist map, a large detail map of the shops in that building is displayed. This detail map would disappear when the pointer moves away from the building.

To create such a hot spot, follow these steps:

1. Create the first button that will act as the hot spot.

2. Create the second button that will be displayed during rollover.

3. Place an image and then convert it to a button. To do that, use the Selection tool to select the image, shape, or text frame, and then choose Object | Interactive | Convert to Button (it's on the context menu also).

4. With the Selection tool, double-click the second button to open the Button Options dialog box. In the General tab, type **Image** for Name, and choose Hidden for the Visibility in PDF option.

5. Using the Selection tool, double-click the first button. In the Behaviors tab, choose Mouse Exit for Event, and then select Show/Hide Fields for Behavior. Click the box to the left of the Image button name twice so that the hide icon appears, and then click Add.

15

How to Do Everything with Adobe InDesign CS

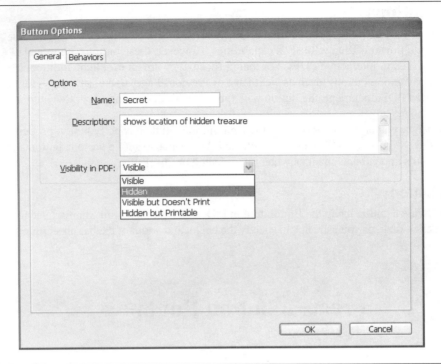

FIGURE 15-3 The Button Options dialog box

upper-left corner in a dialog box. As with all Adobe drawing tools, you can hold down ALT/OPTION to draw from the center and/or hold down SHIFT to constrain the button to a square. You can also press the SPACEBAR after you begin dragging, which enables you to move the object while drawing it.

Define Button Properties

You can use the Button Options dialog box, shown in Figure 15-3, to determine the behavior of buttons in the exported PDF. To open this dialog box, use the Selection tool to select the button, and then choose Object | Interactive | Button Options, or simply double-click the button with the Selection tool. (If the button contains text, you'll need to double-click the frame border.) The context menu also has the Button Options command.

On the General page, set button properties as follows:

- **Name** Type a descriptive name that distinguishes the button from other buttons you create.
- **Description** Type a description that will appear when the mouse pointer passes over the button in Acrobat. The description also acts as alternative text for the visually impaired.
- **Visibility in PDF** You can specify whether you want the button to be visible or invisible in the exported PDF, and whether you want the button to print. You can also hide the button so it displays only during rollover.

Next, click the Behaviors page to determine what happens when the button is acted upon. For example, you may want the button area to be invisible until the mouse pointer is moved over it. One way to achieve this effect is to apply an image to the Rollover state in the States palette, as explained in the next section. Then, in the Behaviors tab, choose Mouse Exit for Event, and choose Show/Hide Fields for Behavior. Next, click the box to the left of the Image button name twice so that the hide icon appears, and then click Add.

Another option is to show the button during mouse rollover. For this behavior, choose Mouse Enter for Event in the Behaviors tab, and choose Show/Hide Fields for Behavior. Click the box to the left of the Image button name once, so that the show icon appears, and then click Add. Then move the buttons into place, and finally, export the document to PDF (see Chapter 18 for details on exporting PDFs from InDesign).

Create a Button Rollover

A button is contained in a button frame, just as an image or text is contained in a frame. However, a button frame can have multiple objects, which Adobe calls *child states*, to apply to different states of a rollover.

Each button can have as many as three states: Up, Rollover, and Down. By default, any button you create uses the Up state. The Up state appears unless the mouse pointer moves over the button (Rollover) or the mouse is clicked on the button (Down). You can control the appearance of a button's states by using the States palette. With the Selection tool, select the button in the layout that you want to edit, and then choose Window | Interactive | States to open this palette.

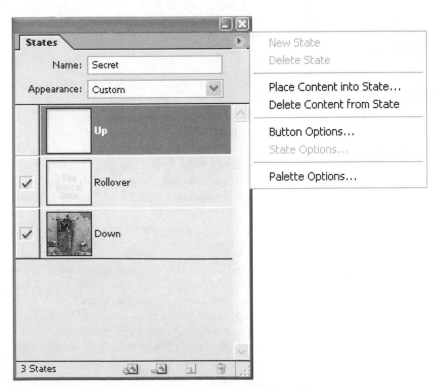

15

You have several options. You can select a preset option from the Appearance drop-down list. The preset options create slightly different button appearances for the Up, Rollover, and Down states. From the States palette's option menu, choose New State to create the Rollover state, choose New State again to create the Down state. If the Up, Down, and Rollover states exist, the New State option is dimmed. When you create a new state, the look of the currently selected state is used. To distinguish a state from the others, you can then add text or an image, or you can delete the state's contents and add new contents.

You can also change the appearance of a state in several ways:

- To place a text file or image in the state, select the state in the States palette, and then choose either File | Place or Place Content into State from the States palette's option menu. Double-click the filename of the text or graphic you want to place.

- You can also paste an image or a text frame by copying it to the Clipboard, selecting the state in the States palette, and then choosing Edit | Paste Into.

- You can type text by selecting the state in the States palette, and then choosing Delete Content from State. With the Type tool, click in the button and type the text you desire.

- To change the stroke and fill of the state, select the fill or stroke icon in the toolbox, and then select a color in the Swatches palette.

- You can use the Control palette to format the text and the Text Frame Options dialog box to center the text within the button.

You can disable a state by unchecking the box to the left of the state. Disabling means that the state will not be exported into the PDF. You can delete a state with the Delete State command on the palette's option menu.

Add Multimedia

You can add movies and sound clips to a document, or you can link to streaming video files on the Web. Although media clips cannot be played directly in the InDesign layout, they can be played when you export the document to Adobe PDF, when you export the document to XML and repurpose the tags, or when you use the Package for GoLive option. QuickTime 6.0 or later is required to work with movies in InDesign. If you embed the movie in the exported PDF document, Acrobat 6 or later is required to play the movie. You can add QuickTime, AVI, MPEG, and SWF movies, and you can add WAV, AIF, and AU sound clips.

Insert a Movie Clip or Sound File

You place a movie or sound file into a frame, and a media object (*poster*) appears. This media object links to the media file. You can resize the media object to determine the size of the play area for movies. You need to keep track of links, just as you do for graphics.

To convert a frame or shape into a media clip, select the frame and choose Object | Interactive | Movie Options or Sound Options. This creates an empty movie or sound frame. When you export to PDF, you can choose to link or embed all media files, regardless of the individual object's settings.

Change Movie Options

To set options for a movie clip, double-click the poster that appears in the frame, or select it and choose Object | Interactive | Movie Options (the context menu works, too). There are quite a few options in the dialog box that appears.

For Poster, choose the type of image that you want to appear in the play area. You can have none, the default that comes with the movie, make up one of your own, or use a still from the movie. Type a description that will appear if the movie cannot be played in Acrobat. This description also acts as alternative text for the visually impaired. To relink to a different movie clip, click the Browse button next to Choose a File, and then double-click the new filename.

To determine how the movie is played back in Acrobat or Adobe Reader, you have the following choices:

- **Mode**   Here, you determine whether the movie is played once and then closes, played once but stays open, or played in a continuous loop. (As noted earlier in the chapter, looped animations rank very high in the irritation list.)

- **Play on Page Turn**   This will play the movie when someone turns to the page of the PDF document on which the movie is located.

- **Show Controller during Play**   This will display a controller that lets users pause, start, and stop the movie.

- **Floating Window**   Use this option if you want the movie to be played in a separate window. If you select this option, specify the size ratio and position on the screen. The floating window scale is based on the size of the original movie.

Change Sound Options

The Sound Options dialog box determines which sound is played and how it is played when the document is exported to Adobe PDF. To change sound options, double-click the sound play area, or select the sound object and choose Object | Interactive | Sound Options (or use the context menu).

In the dialog box, type a description to appear if the sound cannot be played in Acrobat. The description also acts as alternative text for the visually impaired. To specify a different sound clip, click the Browse button. For Poster, choose the type of image that you want to appear in the play area. Choose Play on Page Turn to play the sound clip when someone turns to the page of the PDF document on which the sound is located.

If you do not want the poster to print in InDesign, choose Do Not Print Poster. Choose Embed Sound in PDF if you want to do that. Embedding the media file increases the file size of the PDF document, but then you do not need to send or copy the media file along with the PDF document.

Export Multimedia to PDF

When you are finished setting up your movies and sounds, export the document to Adobe PDF (choose File | Export and PDF as the format). Make sure that the Interactive Elements option is selected in the Export PDF dialog box. Exporting to PDFs is covered in detail in Chapter 18. To preview a media file, ALT/OPTION-double-click a movie or sound object with the Selection tool.

15

Publish eBooks

eBooks are relatively simple to produce with InDesign. The only difficulties are design, of course, and making sure that your images will work well in the viewing environment.

After you have finished designing your eBook, simply export it as a PDF (choose File | Export and select PDF as the export type). In the Export PDF dialog box, the top option is Preset. From that drop-down list, choose [eBook]. This preset converts colors to RGB for onscreen viewing, and it compresses and embeds movies, sound files, fonts, and images to produce a relatively small, self-contained file. Chapter 18 covers PDF exports in more detail.

> **TIP** *Regardless of which publishing format you use, the File | Preflight option helps you spot problems before output. Using it is akin to running the spell checker. It will give you a list of color spaces used, fonts used, and a lot of other helpful information about print or Web publications. Preflight procedures are covered in Chapter 17.*

Use the Package for GoLive Feature

You may want to use one design for a printed document but another layout on the Web. It is difficult to keep the same look in both your print and Web versions, because each has such different readership. The File | Package for GoLive command is designed to make it easy to repurpose graphics and text from an InDesign document for use in GoLive Web pages. You can design your Web pages in InDesign and export them to GoLive. In GoLive, you can simply drag-and-drop the pieces of your design into position in your Web site.

The idea is to allow you to set up pages in InDesign that will translate easily and exactly into GoLive. It is now possible to largely automate the procedure, assuming that you know a lot about the programming/scripting aspects of GoLive and that you are comfortable with XML.

Repurposing print documents is rarely wise and often foolish. However, this might be useful if you are going to pass your design to someone else—say, the Web production team—to implement.

Address Design Issues

To explain some of the design issues related to going from a print format to a Web format, I will go through some excerpts from the Adobe documentation on Package for GoLive and give you my ideas about the real aspects of using this feature.

With Package for GoLive, stories and graphics in InDesign can be optimized for the Web, and then dragged onto a GoLive Web page. InDesign's Package for GoLive feature lets you create a package that includes a preview of your document layout, plus the graphics and text files needed to re-create the document in GoLive. When you open the package in GoLive, the package preview displays. You can drag objects from the package preview directly onto a GoLive Web page.

As I pointed out at the beginning of this chapter, that document you are making into a Web document needs to be radically redesigned. The trick is finding ways to keep the general look and color scheme compatible in both media. The general problem concerns what happens once you get the pieces into Web page layout. Editing the pieces from InDesign in GoLive is not easy. Almost all of the powerful production shortcuts are gone. In most cases, it is still easier and faster to design in GoLive.

During packaging, stories in an InDesign document are converted to XML files with an .incd filename extension. (Threaded text frames in InDesign are saved in a single XML file.) Paragraph and character styles applied in InDesign are converted to their CSS (Cascading Style Sheet) equivalents in Adobe GoLive. Nonprinting objects and objects on hidden layers, unused master pages, or the pasteboard are not included in the package.

Notice the assumption that you have XML editing skills. It is very nice to create a CSS set automatically. But I do that only once for an entire Web site.

Placed images and graphics from an InDesign document can be converted to an optimized format, such as JPEG or GIF, for faster display on the Web. You can also save transformations (such as scaling or rotation) that you've applied to imported graphics in InDesign, so you don't have to re-create these effects in GoLive.

What a recipe for disaster this is! You want to do these conversions in a program that can handle it, like Photoshop or Illustrator. Transformations also need to be done in those applications. However, assembling those graphics in an InDesign document to send to the Web production team makes sense. Most of the work on a Web site is database management and complicated scripting. The graphic portion of a site is quite small. It makes sense to let the pros handle that, and then hand off the pieces to the Web site team for implementation.

GoLive cannot import native InDesign graphics, such as ellipses or other shapes created using InDesign's drawing tools.

This seems strange, but InDesign does type so well, you can use InDesign to make the graphics for your Web site. But this means you need to export your typographic graphics as a PDF and then open that PDF in Photoshop to rasterize it properly at the right size. The InDesign file becomes a graphic master that can be high resolution for use in print. Then you use Save for Web from Photoshop or ImageReady to make it ready for your Web site.

I am confident that for the next versions of GoLive 8 and InDesign, this will work a lot better. I find that it remains faster to do the pages the old way, by copy/pasting the text into GoLive for formatting and adding the graphics normally. For information about GoLive sites and site management, see the GoLive CS documentation. (This does not work for GoLive 6.)

Package a Document or Book for GoLive

15

The procedure for packaging an InDesign document for GoLive is simple once you have the design issues worked out. One of the major reasons for packaging is the ability to update the package and automatically update the Web site. This keeps the graphic portion under the control of the graphic designer. If the InDesign document changes, just use the File | Package for GoLive command again to repackage it.

The Package for GoLive dialog box has an Images page with a variety of image options, as shown in Figure 15-4. I do not recommend that you choose any of these options, except Original

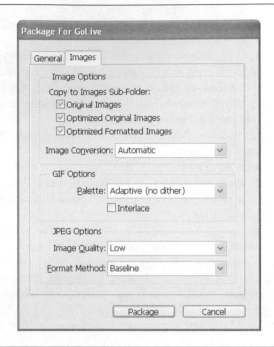

FIGURE 15-4   The Images page of the Package for GoLive dialog box

Images. You should convert your images separately in Photoshop or Illustrator and place them into the InDesign file. Or you can add them to your Web site normally in GoLive.

Design for the Web—Revisited

The completely graphic look of many contemporary designers does not translate well to the Web. This is the primary reason why Web site design and creation are still dominated by desktop publishers. It is basically the same skill set. The drawing and creative skills are almost identical, compromised only by the limitations of the formats used. The layout and design techniques and skills are still largely the same, compromised only by the limitations of viewing environment.

Software and hardware limitations are simply part of the problems we must solve as designers. Design within the medium. Do not assume that print documents can be simply converted. In another arena, think of what bridges would look like if we had a material that was so strong that a half-inch-thick plate could span a mile without twisting or collapsing while carrying a full load of cars and trucks. Your task is not to fight reality, but to use available capabilities to create beautiful solutions that communicate clearly to the targeted readership.

How to ...   **Package for GoLive**

To use the Package for GoLive feature, follow these steps:

1. Choose File | Package for GoLive.

2. Pick a name and location for the package. If you are working with a GoLive site (and you should be), it's best to save the GoLive package to the site project folder/web-data folder/web-packages folder.

3. Click Save.

4. In the General page of the Package for GoLive dialog box, select View Package Using and choose an application (it better be GoLive CS—nothing else works). For Encoding, choose UTF8, UTF16, or Shift-JIS (for Japanese characters). The encoding on the package must match the encoding of your GoLive Web page.

5. Choose your options on the Images page. If you choose to copy original images to the Images subfolder, InDesign will prompt you to relink any missing images. If you are unable to link to a source file, you have a problem.

6. Click Package to begin the packaging process.

15

Part VI

Produce Finished Documents

Chapter 16

Assemble Your Design

How to...

- Organize your work
- Correct imported copy
- Choose your paper
- Determine an economical cut
- Avoid bleed production problems
- Set professional margins
- Use columns as a design element
- Check internal alignments
- Create effective sidebars
- Understand norms for standard projects

InDesign is designed to assemble pieces, according to plan, with incredible control to shape and mold those pieces automatically. This is all hung on that innocuous word: formatting. Here, different automatic page setups can be made available for editorial copy, display ads, chapter heads, regular columns, articles, and the like. This is where illustration and photography are added to accent the typography for communication.

This chapter takes you through some of the basic steps in the assembly process, from setting up your file system and cleaning up copy to avoiding printing problems. Then we'll look at some standards, both for individual design elements and for entire projects. Basically, I am going to give you a relatively complete set of norms, along with the reasons why they became the typical solution. These will give you a place to start and a procedure to use as you put your documents together.

Get Organized

File management may be a bore, but it's the first aspect of setting up for a new project. Remember this one rule: Any person should be able to make sense of your filing system because they will need to figure it out when you call in sick. What is important is that you have a plan for your filing system that anyone can understand.

The first thing you should do for a new project is make a new folder (or directory if you are still hampered by memories of DOS). We are not stuck with 8.3 naming anymore. At this point, the only real naming restriction is intelligence and common sense. However, the Web and Windows systems have problems with spaces, punctuation, and symbols.

As an example, suppose that you have a client called D&B Glass. On your hard drive, you have a folder called Clients. Inside that folder is another folder called D&B Glass. Continuing, inside the D&B Glass Folder are several folders: one for logos; one for stationery, invoices, purchase orders, and so on; one for brochures; one for newsletters; and one for every type of normal project you do for this client. Your next project for D&B Glass is a counter brochure to be used on the checkout counters of various companies around town who recommend D&B to their customers. So where do you put your new brochure? How about a subfolder called CounterBrochure with the date on the document inside?

Every employer you work for will have a different filing setup. Sometimes these setups are very complete and complicated. At the local newspaper, you are given two days of training when you are hired—just to learn their filing system. You are not allowed to work until you have the filing system and procedures mastered. Newspapers catalog their incredible quantities of ads by client name in lettered folders: A, B, C, and so on. When they have filed all the ads for a week, they move them into the Current Month folder, then the Past Month folder, then by month and by year, and so on. Your filing system will probably not need to be so complicated.

Another important aspect of file management is where you keep your files. You should save your files on your hard drive, and also keep backup copies on a ZIP or JAZ cartridge, or a CD or DVD disc. Then you will have that backup for that inevitable day when something goes wrong with your computer.

Correct Imported Copy

Many of your jobs will come with a disk containing the copy, or the copy will be attached to an e-mail. After you've imported it into InDesign, you will find that the copy often has many errors, because it has been input by someone without any training in typesetting. It will be filled with multiple spaces and returns. Hyphens will be used instead of en or em dashes. The list goes on.

> **TIP** *Spell-check in your word processor and in InDesign. All spell checkers are a little different. Some catch initial caps on sentences, some catch double words, some catch transposed letters, some check proper names. So, you can benefit from different spell checkers by spell-checking in your word processor, and then spell-checking again in InDesign (after everything is formatted).*

Use a Quick Procedure to Eliminate Common Problems

Before you begin to work with any imported copy, you should fix as many formatting errors as possible. A quick way to do this is to immediately open the placed copy in the Story Editor (discussed in Chapter 6), although Find/Change works in regular copy, too. Use the Find/Change dialog box (select Edit | Find/Change or press CTRL-F/COMMAND-F) to eliminate the most common errors, using the basic procedure outlined here. You will need to use a special code to search for and replace many of the invisible characters.

- Change all double spaces to single spaces. Type in two spaces in the Find What field and one space in the Change To field (use the SPACEBAR), and then click the Change All button repeatedly until none remain.

- Change all double returns to single returns. Type ^p^p in the Find What field and ^p in the Change To field, and then click Change All repeatedly until none remain.

- Select the entire story. Then format everything to No Style (styles are discussed in Chapter 8).

■ With everything still selected, format everything to body copy. This way, you will be able to reformat the copy more quickly, because all that you will need to change are the heads, subheads, and special paragraphs. Plus, it will make your text as small as it will ever be to give you a clearer idea of how many pages you are going to need.

TIP   *Most of the time, that little plus will appear after the style in the Paragraph Styles palette, showing there is type selected that does not fit the specs of the style. Hold down* ALT-SHIFT/ OPTION-SHIFT *and click the style to force all the characters into the format. This will remove both character styles and local formatting.*

These procedures will eliminate most of the foreign formatting, which is probably littered with typestyles and fonts not found on your machine. Now you are ready to format everything with your style palettes. Edit your styles after eliminating all the imported styles from the palette. Often, the fastest procedure is to eliminate all styles and then copy styles from a template you have set up properly. InDesign allows you to SHIFT-select all the styles or CTRL/COMMAND-select the noncontiguous styles you need to eliminate.

Fix Other Errors

After you have the copy styled, you can fix the remaining problems. Here are some common ones:

■ **Spaces before or after paragraph returns**   Eliminating those dozens of spaces in front of the heads usually leaves a single space before the head. The easiest way to eliminate these is to find and change the return and space (type ^**p** and press the SPACEBAR in the Find What field) to a return (type just a ^**p** in the Change To field).

■ **Tab problems**   A common problem is using a tab to start a paragraph instead of a first-line indent. Find and change the return and tab (^p^t) to return (^p) to eliminate these tabs. Often, you will find many tabs in a row. Eliminate multiple tabs by finding and changing ^t^t to ^t, as many times as necessary to remove all of them. You will commonly need to replace all tabs with a space (find ^t and change it to a space) and retab everything by hand.

TIP   *If you cannot remember the code for the characters, use the pop-up menu to the right of the fields in the Find/Change dialog box.*

■ **Hyphens, em dashes, and en dashes**   You will probably need to find all double hyphens and change them to em dashes. To put en dashes in the ranges, you might need to find any digit, hyphen, any digit, and change each occurrence to any digit, en dash, any digit. You can use Find Next to locate each hyphen, and then change it to an en or em dash as needed.

NOTE   *When importing Word files, em dashes, en dashes, curly quotes, and similar characters often come in as very strange characters. You will need to use the Find/Change function to fix them.*

■ **Text copied from the Web**   If you can legally do this for your client, you will often find there is a hard return after every line. To fix this, search for return characters and change them to spaces. You will need to work your way through the entire story, eliminating all the returns except those that are actually at the end of a paragraph. In a few cases, you will want to replace the hard return with a soft return (^n). Remember that InDesign calls these forced line breaks.

■ **Smart, curly, or typographer's quotes**   Automatic typographer's quotes sound good in principle but work less than perfectly in practice. It is important that you learn how to access the characters without the smart quotes option turned on. Curly inch marks are a far worse typo than straight quotes. If you need to enter measurements, it is usually better to disable typographer's quotes and enter them by hand. InDesign has a default keyboard shortcut that toggles typographer's quotes on and off: CTRL-ALT-SHIFT-'/ COMMAND-OPTION-SHIFT-'.

Although this process may seem like a real hassle, it is much faster than other ways to correct copy. Ideally, your copy will come in properly formatted. In reality, this rarely happens, except with in-house copy or regular clients. If the copy was not keyed in by a trained typesetting professional, all formatting probably should be eliminated before you go to work, simply to save you time.

The essentials for preparing copy are simple: There must be only one return in a paragraph; there should be no styling of bold or italic; there should be nothing typed in all caps; and bold or italic words should be underlined instead (if they are emphasized at all). If the copy is typed correctly like this, you can resize and reformat it easily after importing.

Choose Your Paper

One of the first things you need to do when you get set up as a professional designer is to contact some of your local paper distributors. Get a copy of their price books and swatchbooks of the papers you intend to use. Every printing process has different paper requirements, and it is important that you pick a paper stock that will work well and easily. Also, there are tens of thousands of different papers. Picking your standard papers is as important as building your personal font list. This is an essential part of your personal style.

CAUTION   *Be careful when you find a gorgeous color or texture in your paper supplier's swatchbook. No distributor can afford to carry every color of every product line in stock. Many of the prettier colors and weights are available only as a mill order. Mill orders can require a minimum of 5 to 15 cartons and a three-month wait. You need to plan ahead to budget both the time and money necessary for a mill order.*

Another consideration is document size. Sizes for magazines and newspapers are commonly not under your control. They are limited by publisher choice or the printing presses used.

16

- If your printed product will be filed, it should be 8.5 by 11 inches (unless you are in Europe, where you need A4, which is taller and narrower).

- If it must be inserted in a standard business envelope (4.125 by 9.5 inches), it should be 4 by 9 inches for easy (or mechanical) envelope insertion.

- If it is a business card, it must be 2 by 3.5 inches.

- The dimensions of the display rack control the size and orientation of many other projects. The most common rack size takes 4-by-9-inch paper in portrait layout only.

If you have any options, make sure that you design for an economical cut of the paper stock you choose.

Know What Parent Sheet Sizes Are Available

As you will discover, most of the printing papers do not come in letter-sized reams, or even in tabloid (11 by 17 inches). These are called *cut-sheet sizes*. Only the cheapest paper comes from the mill in cut-sheet sizes. All the other papers are trimmed from *parent sheets*.

Parent sheets are the paper sizes carried in stock by your paper distributor. When you pick a paper to use, find out what parent sheet sizes are readily available in your area. The various parent sizes are sold by the carton, unwrapped, about 1,500 sheets per carton. Partial cartons are much more expensive. Multiple-carton purchases get discounted prices.

In the United States, almost every paper is available in 23 by 35 inches. This allows 8-out cutting, as shown here:

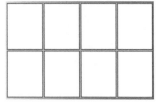

However, for projects that are not 8.5 by 11 inches, there are papers that come in 25 by 38 inches, 19 by 25 inches, 20 by 26 inches, 26 by 40 inches, and several other parent sizes. Check your paper suppliers' catalogs to find out what is available in your area.

Determine an Economical Cut

Choosing an economical cut for your paper order is very important. There is a simple way to determine economical use of paper without a lot of waste:

- Divide the length by a whole number.
- Divide the width by a whole number.

■ Check the remainder.

■ Multiply the two numbers to get the number of cut sheets you can get out of a parent sheet.

The numbers arrived at by division give you a maximum sheet size. Your projects need to be at least 0.125 inch smaller than the divided figures, on all four sides, to allow for trimming.

For example, if you have only 23-by-35-inch sheets available, 9-by-12-inch pages are a horrible cut. Instead of having eight 8.5-by-11-inch sheets, you can get only four 9-by-12-inch sheets (12 goes into 35 twice, and 9 goes into 23 twice). With 25-by-38-inch stock, however, 9 by 12 inches works well (12 goes into 25 twice, and 9 goes into 38 four times, for 8-out cuts). This means your paper costs almost double if you do not use 25-by-38-inch sheets (which are only 10 percent more expensive than 23-by-35-inch sheets).

In Figure 16-1, you can see some simple mathematical cuts of a typical 23-by-35 inch sheet of paper. The 12-out: 5.5-by-11.5-inch cut makes a beautiful 5.5-inch-square, four-page signature for a little booklet or brochure. It also makes an excellent 5.25-inch square booklet, full bleed. The 6-out: 7.5-by-16-inch cut gives an eight-page signature of that same booklet, and the full 23-by-35-inch sheet gives you a 24-page signature.

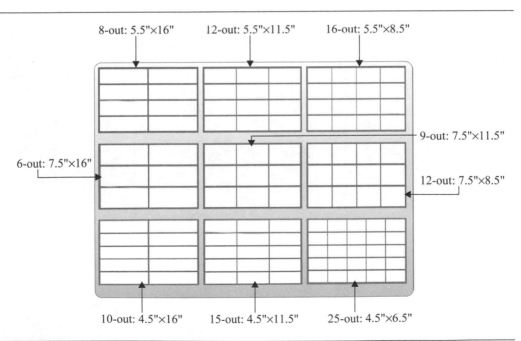

8-out: 5.5"×16"   12-out: 5.5"×11.5"   16-out: 5.5"×8.5"

9-out: 7.5"×11.5"

6-out: 7.5"×16"

12-out: 7.5"×8.5"

10-out: 4.5"×16"   15-out: 4.5"×11.5"   25-out: 4.5"×6.5"

FIGURE 16-1   Nine sample cuts of a 23-by-35-inch sheet

16

If you come up with some really wild cuts or folds, check them out with your printer or bindery before you show them to your client. It is easy to design incredible folds that need to be done by hand, but handwork costs a fortune! A quick conversation with your bindery can save you a lot of money and heartache. There are times when that custom hand-folded job is the perfect solution. Normally, forcing the bindery to do a lot of handwork is one of the quickest ways to a blown budget.

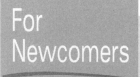 *At one of the commercial printers I worked for, we received a complicated brochure. Normal folding would have cost less than $1,000. But the client wanted an amazingly beautiful fold, which we could not do on our equipment, nor could anyone in town. We had to ship it to Mexico to be hand-folded. It cost an extra $12,000, plus an additional three weeks. This was a very determined designer with a client who had deep pockets. In most cases, it would just be a big problem and a monumental financial loss.*

For Newcomers

Plan for Signatures

A *signature* is a sheet of paper with multiple pages arranged on it so that, after it is folded and trimmed, the cut pages end up in the proper order. This is an 8-page signature and what it looks like after it is folded (on the left):

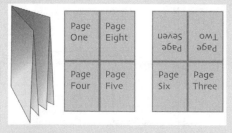

And this is a 12-page signature:

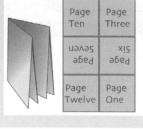

As you can see on the left, the 12-page signature has a vertical letterfold, and then it is folded in half horizontally.

Signatures need to be made up of pages in multiples of two (for perfect-bound) or four (for saddle-stitch). Perfect-bound books have a square spline and are trimmed on all four sides before binding, so you can insert a single 2-page signature, if necessary. They are commonly used for newsletters, booklets, programs, magazines, books, and newspapers. There are thousands of signatures with any even number of pages, from 2 through a 100-plus pages. Each folding machine can produce some and cannot produce others. Check this with your printing company before you start designing.

Watch Out for Bleeds and Small Margins

Two common areas of printing problems are incorrectly designed bleeds and margins that are too small. Consider how parent sheets are cut, as explained in the previous section. An eighth of a 23-by-35-inch parent gives 8.75 by 11.5 inches, which is just barely enough for a full bleed when printing eight pages at a time on a full sheet.

Design Your Bleeds Carefully

A bleed is needed when you produce a design where the ink must go exactly to the edge of the paper. To produce a bleed, you make everything that reaches to the edge of the page extend one-eighth inch (9 points, or 0.375 millimeters to be precise) beyond the edge, and then trim the piece back to finished size after printing. You must print on oversized stock and trim it. Figure 16-2 illustrates the requirements.

TIP

You may discover that the printing company you are using asks for a different bleed. For my recent books, my publisher's printer wanted a quarter-inch bleed because it fit their digital imposition better. However, that is very unusual. You will almost never go wrong in making the bleed exactly an eighth inch.

The power cutters used in the industry are the reason a bleed is necessary. These huge guillotine cutters slide their knives through stacks of paper several inches thick. They can cut 1,000 to 3,000 sheets at a time. However, due to their limitations, they are accurate only to plus or minus one-sixteenth inch. Older equipment, thicker lifts, or hungover operators can easily add another one-sixteenth inch. So, the one-eighth-inch bleed is often barely enough. You can get more accurate cuts by cutting 50 to 100 sheets of paper at a time, but you will pay a real premium for that. With better shops, and care, you can get by with the one-sixteenth inch required by the machinery. But always ask first and constantly remind your contact about the bleeds.

16

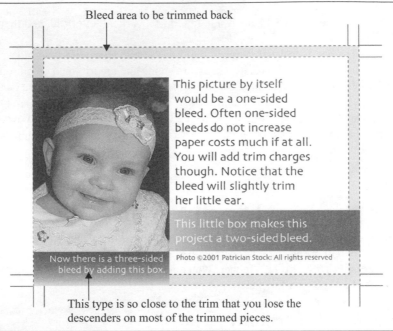

Bleed area to be trimmed back

This picture by itself would be a one-sided bleed. Often one-sided bleeds do not increase paper costs much if at all. You will add trim charges though. Notice that the bleed will slightly trim her little ear.

This little box makes this project a two-sided bleed.

Now there is a three-sided bleed by adding this box.

This type is so close to the trim that you lose the descenders on most of the trimmed pieces.

FIGURE 16-2 Bleed and trim marks showing how a bleed works with 1-, 2-, and 3-sided bleeds

The most common problem occurs when the submitted artwork goes exactly to the trim (the edge of the finished size). If you do that, you force your printer's people into four bad choices:

- They can print it as submitted, leaving little slivers of blank paper on one or two of the four sides on almost every finished piece. These are caused by the cutter variables. It will cause blank edges, just as quickprint registration does.

- They can enlarge everything by 102 percent or more, which changes the appearance and the margins. The margins at the ends become smaller than the ones on the sides. Objects that you wanted close to the edge are trimmed a little.

- They can bounce the job back to you to be fixed, which can ruin your deadlines. It also ruins your reputation with them and convinces them that they cannot trust you. Designers have problems with printers, and this is one of the reasons.

- They can fix it themselves, which can be a lot of unbudgeted expense out of your pocket. They charge $150 per hour, more or less.

The second major problem shows up when you have forgotten to tell the printer service that you plan to design with a bleed when getting your estimate or price quote. A bleed requires oversized paper to enable trimming back to size. Commonly, a bleed bumps the paper costs up 25 percent or more. For letter-sized pieces, you can cut only 6-out instead of the normal 8-out from a 23-by-35-inch sheet. The only other solution is to print it as submitted and cut it undersized. An eighth inch on all four sides means your precious 8.5 by 11 inches is cut back to 8.25 by 10.75 inches. Again, the worst scenario, as far as you are concerned, is to have the service bureau or printing company fix it for you. Not only must you pay a premium price and have your reputation damaged, but the way they will modify for bleeds will almost certainly change your design in horrifying ways.

Set Professional Margins

A common mistake is to make margins too small. All printers and presses need blank areas around the edges of the sheet. The *gripper* is that blank portion of the sheet needed for the press to physically grab the paper and pull it through. Ask the printer what their gripper is; it differs for almost every press. It's never smaller than one-quarter inch and is often nearly a one-half inch. The key is to keep your designs inside the maximum image area. All presses and printers have them, and your printing company will be happy to tell you what they are.

If you make your margins too small, not allowing for gripper and image area considerations, the printer will be forced to print it like a bleed. This will incur additional costs (often unbudgeted). Normally, this is only a problem with quickprinters when using cut sheets. But it can also arise with larger pieces, if you try to squeeze too much onto a sheet.

If you do not give enough room to pull the sheet through the printer or press, the machine will crop your image, uncontrollably. The only solution is to print on oversized paper and trim it back to size. Many digital presses cannot feed oversized paper. These problems can completely eliminate all of your profit on the project and even cause a sizable loss, if the project is large enough.

In addition, margins are often a large part of style. If you are trying for the elegant look of an old book, for example, you will need huge margins. There are many formulas, but here's one you can try: 100 percent inside, 125 percent top, 150 percent outside, and 200 percent bottom (such as 1.25-inch top, 1.5-inch outside, 2-inch bottom, and 1-inch inside margins).

Many clients will not allow the margins required for the style, "Look at all that empty paper. I can't afford to waste that space!" You might want to show them some publications with this style to help persuade them.

Conversely, if you want to convey cheap bargains—yard sale flyer, grocery store ad, and so forth—you need very small margins, gutters, and a lot of rules and boxes. You need to fill every open white space, making the page look like everything is crammed in to save money. Even if it is not strictly true, readers will think it is and assume they can find bargains.

The point to remember is that the smaller the margins, the cheaper the look. The absolute minimum, for everything other than business cards and maybe postcards, is a 0.375-inch margin. One-quarter-inch margins look terrible after printing. The variables of trimming and registration always cause those tiny margins to be off-center.

16

Finally, for individual sheets of paper and single pages seen separately, the margins are normally even all the way around. For books and booklets, you need to leave extra room at the fold. For three-ring binder sheets, you usually need to leave 0.75-inch interior margins.

Know How to Use Design Elements Effectively

Being consistent yet creative is a major virtue in digital publishing. The key is knowing how your readers will react. Then you can make specific breaks from the norm to increase their understanding and emphasize specific points.

Styles and basic format settings provide the consistent base from which the graphic devices stand out to make those important specific points. This is a very delicate balance. Too much or too little can quickly destroy the flow of communication, and clear communication is the designer's most important goal.

Use Columns As a Design Element

Be very careful with your column choices. It is easy to bore your audience to the point of reader rejection. Symmetrical layouts are the worst, unless you need to be formal and reserved. Two or four columns tend to divide in half and look like they are intended to be symmetrical. In this case, it is hard to make the spreads look like they flow as one consistent unit.

An extremely common setup is five, six, seven, or more columns. These are used as grids that can be readily divided into different column structures within the same page to keep things interesting. A seven-column grid can reserve a column for sidebars, and then have stories that are six single columns, three double columns, two triple columns, a double column, a quadruple column, and so on. Figure 16-3 shows an example of a page set up with a seven-column grid. Just set up your guides and make the text blocks as needed. Generally, the more asymmetrical and the more open you can lay out the piece, the better.

Column gutters provoke many strongly held opinions. The general rule is that a gutter should be larger than a pica (0.167 inch) and smaller than the margins of the page. For most purposes, one-quarter inch works well. The guiding principle is that gutters need to be small enough so the columns of a story hold together as a text block, yet the reader must be able to easily read down the column without jumping the gutter to the neighboring column. The reading order and visual organization need to be clear.

NOTE   *Gutter is one of those terms that means different things in different places. Sometimes it means the interior margins of a reader's spread for a book or booklet. Most often, it means the vertical gap between two columns.*

If you decide that you need narrow gutters, you should separate the columns with a thin (or lightly colored) vertical rule. The only problem with rules, boxes, and borders is their tie to cheapness and low quality because they reduce white space. In general, for readability, the use of vertical rules necessitates wider gutters than normal.

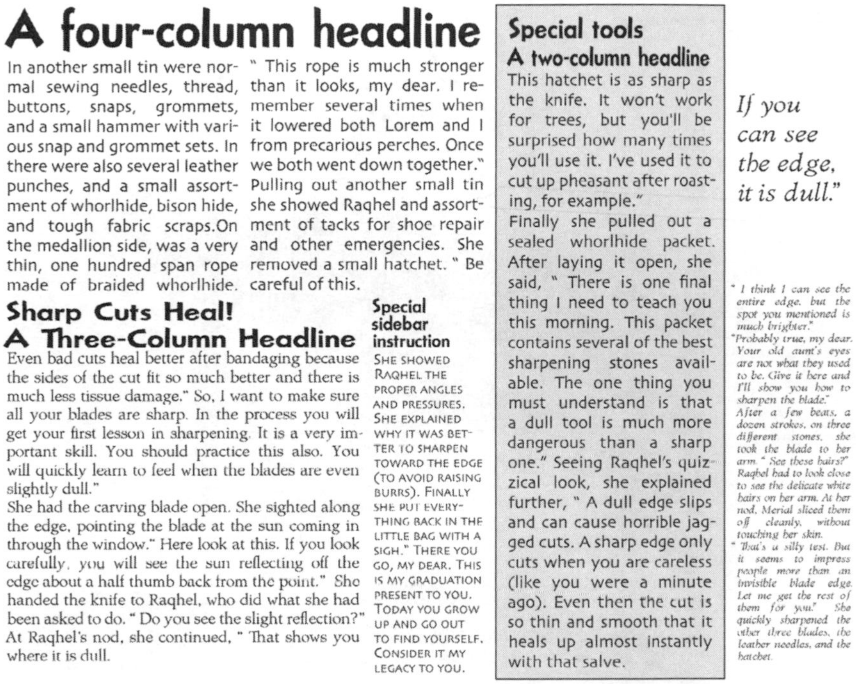

A four-column headline

In another small tin were normal sewing needles, thread, buttons, snaps, grommets, and a small hammer with various snap and grommet sets. In there were also several leather punches, and a small assortment of whorlhide, bison hide, and tough fabric scraps.On the medallion side, was a very thin, one hundred span rope made of braided whorlhide.

" This rope is much stronger than it looks, my dear. I remember several times when it lowered both Lorem and I from precarious perches. Once we both went down together." Pulling out another small tin she showed Raqhel and assortment of tacks for shoe repair and other emergencies. She removed a small hatchet. " Be careful of this.

Sharp Cuts Heal!
A Three-Column Headline

Even bad cuts heal better after bandaging because the sides of the cut fit so much better and there is much less tissue damage." So, I want to make sure all your blades are sharp. In the process you will get your first lesson in sharpening. It is a very important skill. You should practice this also. You will quickly learn to feel when the blades are even slightly dull."

She had the carving blade open. She sighted along the edge, pointing the blade at the sun coming in through the window." Here look at this. If you look carefully, you will see the sun reflecting off the edge about a half thumb back from the point." She handed the knife to Raqhel, who did what she had been asked to do. " Do you see the slight reflection?" At Raqhel's nod, she continued, " That shows you where it is dull.

Special sidebar instruction

SHE SHOWED RAQHEL THE PROPER ANGLES AND PRESSURES. SHE EXPLAINED WHY IT WAS BETTER TO SHARPEN TOWARD THE EDGE (TO AVOID RAISING BURRS). FINALLY SHE PUT EVERYTHING BACK IN THE LITTLE BAG WITH A SIGH." THERE YOU GO, MY DEAR. THIS IS MY GRADUATION PRESENT TO YOU. TODAY YOU GROW UP AND GO OUT TO FIND YOURSELF. CONSIDER IT MY LEGACY TO YOU.

Special tools
A two-column headline

This hatchet is as sharp as the knife. It won't work for trees, but you'll be surprised how many times you'll use it. I've used it to cut up pheasant after roasting, for example."

Finally she pulled out a sealed whorlhide packet. After laying it open, she said, " There is one final thing I need to teach you this morning. This packet contains several of the best sharpening stones available. The one thing you must understand is that a dull tool is much more dangerous than a sharp one." Seeing Raqhel's quizzical look, she explained further, " A dull edge slips and can cause horrible jagged cuts. A sharp edge only cuts when you are careless (like you were a minute ago). Even then the cut is so thin and smooth that it heals up almost instantly with that salve.

If you can see the edge, it is dull."

" I think I can see the entire edge, but the spot you mentioned is much brighter."
"Probably true, my dear. Your old aunt's eyes are not what they used to be. Give it here and I'll show you how to sharpen the blade."
After a few beats, a dozen strokes, on three different stones, she took the blade to her arm." See these hairs?" Raqhel had to look close to see the delicate white hairs on her arm. At her nod, Merial sliced them off cleanly, without touching her skin.
" That's a silly test. But it seems to impress people more than an invisible blade edge. Let me get the rest of them for you." She quickly sharpened the other three blades, the leather needles, and the hatchet.

FIGURE 16-3   A column setup with various stories on a seven-column grid

Check Your Internal Alignments

One of the major aspects of design excellence is internal alignment. In other words, excellent designs have countless places where type and graphics line up with each other. You need to be consciously aware of these relationships, at all times. Every time you are aware of looking at a graphic design that really pleases you, consciously check out the internal alignments. You'll be amazed.

Figure 16-4 shows an example of how internal alignments can make a design work. Notice how the *y* in *Tuesday* points at the times. The copyright information lines up with the top of the photo. The right side of the transparent prizes box lines up with the right side of the justified paragraph below it (after subtle adjustments for optical alignment). Even the baseline of the doorway headline lines up close enough to the *N* in *November* to help out.

16

Internal alignments are important to design.

You can use multiple alignments on the same page, but only if you are careful. In general, items should be all aligned left or right, or centered. Avoid reader confusion by carefully structuring your alignments.

Remember that you can use the Align palette to make selected objects align by the left, center, or right horizontally, and the top, middle, or bottom vertically. You can also produce even distribution of objects using the same locations. (See Chapter 11 for details on aligning objects.)

Many designers use snap-to guides for exact alignment. For example, if you are compulsive about vertical justification, where both the tops and the bottoms of columns line up on a grid, you can easily set up InDesign so that type baselines snap to a ruler based on your leading. However, the biggest problem with digital design is the computerized, overly perfected images. Snap-to guides are one of the main culprits. If you use snap-to guides a lot, be careful to introduce randomness in judicious quantities. Also, vertical justification adds inconsistent paragraph spacing, so you'll need to solve that problem.

If you cannot move your graphic or text block into precisely the correct position—if it keeps jumping around, out of your control—it is snapping to something. Turn off the relevant snap-to, and you will be able to move it exactly into position. If it is still jumping, try enlarging to 400 percent or more. Sometimes, you think things are jumping and you are just moving them less than a pixel. The low-resolution screen image can jump even when things are lined up perfectly.

Use Master Pages for Repeating Elements

Master pages place repeating elements automatically. Adobe suggests the idea of using a master page for a background image, for example. As explained in Chapter 3, master pages are typically used to place automatic numbering markers for page numbers.

Like all page layout software, InDesign allows for multiple master pages, plus it can have parent/child master pages where the child is based on the master (just like in Paragraph and Character Styles). The number of masters available might be important if you design a 200-page monthly magazine or a huge daily newspaper, but most of us do not. In fact, multiple master pages are helpful only to designers who work with projects that repeat monthly, such as newsletters, magazines, reports, and so forth.

Keep in mind that a 48-page booklet with 20 master pages is not going to be very consistent. You should add master pages only when the content makes them necessary.

Did you know?

Ruler Guides Can Lead to Unintended Designs

Ruler guides have replaced the nonreproducible blue lines in traditional pasteup. They are the nonprinting lines that enable designers to line up graphic pieces and text blocks to keep their designs tidy. Until you get used to the fact that these guide lines appearing in your design on the screen do not print, you will tend to leave room for them. As a result, many of your white spaces will be surprisingly large. This is a problem with programs that surround text and graphics with nonprinting lines, such as InDesign. Proofing helps a lot, but simply turning off the guides and frame edges occasionally will help keep you on track.

16

InDesign offers automatic "continued from" and "continued to" numbering (jump numbers). These are used when you are forced to continue an article in a different portion of a publication. However, you are far better off to make it a strict policy to redesign as necessary to eliminate any continued articles. Studies suggest that the vast majority of copy continued on another page is not read.

Create Tables of Contents and Indexes for Books and Magazines

Creating tables of contents and indexes are two more capabilities that are similar to master pages, in that if you need them, they are critical. InDesign can create both. In Chapter 8, you learned how to create tables of contents and lists using styles.

InDesign provides an Index palette for creating indexes. You use this palette to flag the index entries in your document, as well as to create cross-references. The Index palette shows a preview of the index, and you can edit the entries there. Similar to tables of contents, indexes use styles for the headings and levels. After you choose to generate the index, it is loaded into a text cursor, which you just click to place the index where you want it to appear. Although the process is straightforward (and InDesign provides good Help documentation for indexing), realize that creating a usable index takes a lot of editing. Indexing is a very difficult, specialized skill. In most cases, a professional indexer should write the index. A poorly written index is worse than no index. It infuriates the reader.

Both of these features are geared toward the publishing end of our industry—books and magazines. They are specialized abilities that most of you will rarely use. If every job is different, you need flexible software that makes spontaneity easy.

If most of your jobs are repetitive, you need automation and specialized features. Adobe's Web site (www.adobe.com) offers third-party plug-ins for InDesign that supply these features. Buy the plug-ins that will save you enough production time to be cost-effective.

Consider Your Table Designs

Chapter 9 covered the abilities of InDesign to make tables. Here are some table design considerations:

- **Keep it light**　Tables can very easily become cluttered with borders, colors, and tints. Tables are one place where less is almost always more. Even in the most baroque layouts, tables need to be clean and simple. Otherwise, people will not read them.

- **Watch column heads**　To make ridiculously long headers fit into narrow columns, you often need to go to 6-, 7-, or 8-point type. Many designers rotate the headers, but this causes horrible readability problems. Although it is normally bad practice, this is one place where setting the horizontal scale very low (even below 50 percent) is not a large problem. People do not really read column heads. They just quickly check to make sure that the heads are what they expect.

■ **Watch readability**   In the table cells where you regularly need to put long paragraphs, make sure that hyphenation is turned off. Set the columns flush left or centered. Use soft returns liberally to break the lines to help readability. Tables are like forms, in that readers tend to skip them if they're difficult to understand.

■ **Eliminate tints where possible**   Remember that colored backgrounds always lower contrast and make the copy harder to read. Do not make the mistake of putting colored backgrounds or tints behind your most important copy. Make the important stuff stand out by leaving blank paper as the background.

Create Effective Sidebars

In general, sidebars are a wonderful idea and add interest to a page. Here are some sidebar design considerations:

■ **Use contrast**   Sidebars need to have definite, sharp contrast to normal body copy. You can do this with different fonts, different alignment, tint boxes, borders, or all of the above. Sidebars (for all of their usefulness) must have less impact than normal body copy. It needs to be obvious that a sidebar is peripheral information. Tint boxes or background graphics lessen contrast enough to be very helpful here. Sidebars usually appear at the sides of the page. In that position, they greatly help in making newsletter or book pages asymmetric and more interesting visually.

■ **Frame the copy**   The sidebar should be the frame that shows off the normal copy. You shouldn't even see those tints, type, and graphics, but they are still working!

■ **Watch font choices**   Because sidebars often use tint blocks behind the type, this is an excellent location for easy legibility. Humanist sans serif fonts are best for this. But even styles like Gill Sans, Frutiger, Corinthian, Nördström, and the like work well in this situation.

Understand Norms for Standard Projects

One of the things you quickly discover as you begin designing is that readers have very strong ideas about what is acceptable and what is not. They are normally not conscious of these requirements, but they certainly notice when you violate their sense of propriety. These standards are what I call norms. The way to keep your designs from being boring is to break at least a couple of rules in every design, but those departures from the norms must be done intentionally and with good reason.

Here, we will take a look at the norms for some common design projects: business cards, letterhead, envelopes, and newsletters. You will find that many of them are quite rigid.

16

Use Business Card Standards

Business cards must fit into a standard business card case or they will be thrown away. Having said that, one of the nice things you can do to make a card stand out is to make it 4 by 3.5 inches, folded down to 2 by 3.5 inches. This gives you a place to present a lot of copy or even a map.

The norms for business cards are as follows:

Size	2 by 3.5 inches, with 0.25-inch margins on all sides
Logo	0.75 inch at the largest dimension
Company name	18 to 30 points
Name	8 to 11 points (often bold)
Title	6 to 8 points (often italic)
Phone number	9 to 12 points (often bold)
Address	6 to 8 points
Motto	8 to 12 points (often italic)
E-mail address	As large as possible (because of its length), but no larger than the phone number

Which items are most important? You need to be able to instantly recognize that card as belonging to the business you are looking for, but what are you looking for in that card? You keep the card for the phone number, e-mail address, and office address, in that order, usually. The most important information on the business card is the phone number (coupled with the name of the person, so you can address that person by name when he or she picks up the phone).

The e-mail address is increasingly important, and the Web site URL might generate some sales. The physical address is rarely why you keep a card. Once you have been there (if you ever go there), you can remember where it is.

Use Letterhead and Envelope Standards

A letterhead design should look empty without a letter. A letterhead is a frame to set off the letter that will be placed there. Here are the standards:

Size	8.5 by 11 inches, with 0.5-inch margins or larger (unless it bleeds)
Logo	Smaller than the business card
Company name	14 to 24 points
Address	7 to 10 points
Phone number	8 to 11 points
Motto	9 to 14 points (often italic)

It's very important to design the letterhead so a letter looks good on it. Executive letterheads are often smaller and have bleeds and a more elegant style. They are normally 7.25 by 10.5 inches, closer to the European A4 standard.

One of the major considerations for a letterhead is whether or not it will be used. You need to provide a template (and often hands-on troubleshooting) and carefully consider the needs and desires of the person who will be using the template.

For envelopes, the following standards are used:

Size	#10 business (4.125 by 9.5 inches)
Logo	12 to 18 points
Address	6 to 8 points

For executive letterheads at 7.25 by 10.5 inches, envelopes are Monarch size (3.75 by 7.5 inches) and have a smaller logo and name.

> **TIP** *You will have enough trouble getting that envelope through the gauntlet of the table and trashcan when it arrives in the mail. Make it look like personal communication, as much as possible. Hand-addressed envelopes have a far higher rate of return and are read by far more readers.*

Use Newsletter Standards

The paper size varies widely for newsletters. Just make sure that it is 8.5 by 11 inches if it will be filed. One of the most successful newsletters I ever designed was a tabloid letterfold: 11 by 17 inches, folded to 5 11/16 by 11 inches. I have designed newsletters as small as 5 inches square, and as large as 11 by 17 inches after folding.

> **NOTE** *You need to make sure the newsletter size is acceptable for mailing. If you're not sure, take a dummy to show the people at the post office.*

Because of the wide variation in size and style, the following are very approximate norms:

Flag or logo	36 to 99 points
Headlines	24 to 36 points
First subhead	14 to 21 points
Second subhead	10 to 14 points
Body copy	9 to 12 points
Masthead	8 to 12 points
Body copy	10/12, either left or justified (unless the newsletter is getting federal money for senior citizens; then the legal requirement for the body copy is 12/14)

Increasingly, newsletters are delivered via e-mail. However, online newsletters are very tricky and difficult to write well. You usually need to produce them as PDFs or in HTML.

Maintain Simplicity and Clarity

As you format type and lay out the document, consciously prioritize the copy to organize it. What is the most important copy on the page (from the reader's point of view)? What is the most important copy on the page (from the client's point of view)? Often, important information from the client's viewpoint is different from what the reader will choose to read.

For example, the executive secretary may tell you that attendance at meetings is a real problem and he wants that emphasized. However, this does not mean that people will be drawn to read the newsletter to get that information. Perhaps the reader is more interested in the background of next month's speaker. So, in a gray sidebar of trivia and required legalese, a strong little graphic splash giving the meeting time, date, and location will serve as a quick attention-getter, without competing with the main headline and photo of the speaker on the front page.

The thing to hold most dear while you are prioritizing is the need for simplicity and clarity. Too many attention-getting devices function much like the expert roundtables on CNN: That many people talking at the same time is very irritating and causes many of us to switch channels. The same is true of multitudinous headlines, subheads, and specialized headers, all competing for your attention on the same page.

Even if it is true that all of these pieces are important, the reader needs help to sort through the chaos. Sometimes, you must arbitrarily assign priorities simply to make the piece readable. Probably the most important concept to grasp at this point is consistency. Even if you do not have the best plan, if you are consistent, everyone else will understand it. Just remember that the goal of your assembled design is graphic communication (to use that dated term).

Chapter 17

Prepare Your Documents for Production

How to...

- Check for color problems
- Collect your project documents in a book
- Make proofs of your document
- Preflight your document
- Package your document

You've put together your document and it looks good on the screen. Now you've reached the next phase: getting it ready for the printer. Even Web sites should be built from graphic pieces that are printable. The first thing most surfers do when they arrive at the information they are seeking is to print it so they can read it.

Preparing for printing involves checking for problems and correcting them, collecting all the pieces, and supplying all the necessary information to the printing service. An ongoing preparation is proofing. You cannot proof too much. The good news is that InDesign offers superb tools to help you check your documents.

You also need to prepare your document according to your printer's requirements. One of the largest mistakes made by designers today is failing to realize the importance of picking the printer *before* you begin designing. As you will discover in the next chapter, different technologies have very different capabilities. As a designer, you need to design within the capabilities of your equipment. No matter what you are forced to use for output, you must be able to produce excellent designs, even if you're designing a fax cover sheet.

Check for Color Problems

One of the easiest ways to check for potential printing problems is by viewing the screen previews. As mentioned, InDesign draws its own previews. They are of much better quality than the preview produced by InDesign's competition. Also, there are the three Preview buttons at the bottom of the toolbox. But, InDesign does not stop there. As noted in Chapter 14, the Separations Preview palette is a real help for proofing spot colors and spot color overprints.

Check Overprinting and Knockouts

Figure 17-1 shows an example of checking overprints with the Separations Preview palette. As you can see, this is a quick and easy way to check and see that, indeed, the entire yellow shape overprints, and the black type does not knock out the yellow shape.

Using the Separations Preview palette, you can see the individual plates, find problems, and fix them. However, as with all spot colors, the color representation on the screen is not very close to what the colors will look like when they are printed on paper with real ink. Also, the yellow overprint is barely visible, and lighter colors like varnish will not be visible on the screen at all.

Another limitation of checking spot colors this way is that you cannot view traps on the screen. As explained in Chapter 14, trapping (or *dry trapping*) is used to compensate for registration gaps.

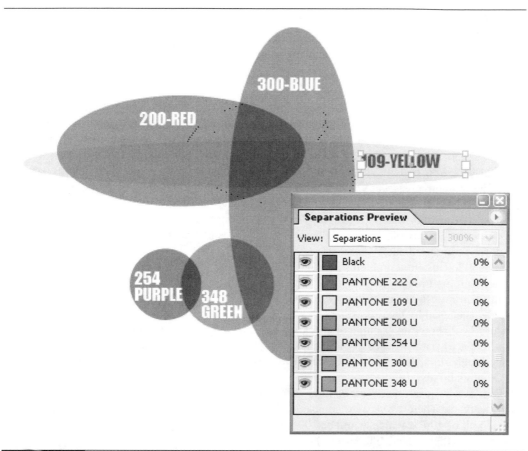

FIGURE 17-1   Five spot colors that overprint previewed on the screen

With InDesign and In-RIP Trapping, the traps are not produced until the RIP does it in the printer, imagesetter, or platesetter. (And, even if the traps were displayed, they would be incredibly small—invisible except at large enlargements.)

Watch for Ink Limit Problems

There is a real limit to how much cyan, magenta, yellow, and black can be printed on top of each other. The same is true of multiple spot color (as in Figure 17-1). If the ink pile gets too thick, colors can strip off onto the wrong ink trains, causing gray sludge and contaminated color in general. Toner has similar problems. If the toner gets too thick, it chips (or falls) off the paper. Many color laser printers and digital presses need very low ink limits. Press operators call this trapping, but others refer to it as *wet trapping*, to distinguish it from the dry trapping used to compensate for registration gaps.

17

 *If you start to see areas of dark color with spots of toner that are not adhering to the paper, fix it fast! You can quickly destroy your fuser roller. That can cost you $100 or more.*

The ink limit is the largest number allowed of the totals of the ink percentages. For CMYK, a color of 100c, 70m, 50y, 50k is 270 percent.

If you create your graphics in Photoshop, you can set the separations to CMYK with the proper ink limit. If you do that, the conversion from RGB to CMYK will automatically produce colors that do not exceed the limit set. If your placed bitmaps have problems, you can fix them in Photoshop and replace them.

In InDesign, you are left to your own devices. The Ink Limits preview in the Separations palette can flag the problem areas, but you will need to adjust the colors yourself. Sometimes this means going to the Swatches palette and changing a color build. Often, it means adjusting the tints of a color. You will need to watch this, especially if you are printing on a color laser printer in your office. For example, my old Tektronix Phaser 780 produces prints where toner chips off the paper with ink limits higher than 250 percent.

To check for ink limit problems in InDesign, choose Ink Limit from the View drop-down list in the Separations Preview palette. This view shows you places where there is simply too much ink to print. It highlights areas in varying shades of pink. The darker the pink, the more severe the problems caused by the overprint.

Figure 17-2 shows an example of checking ink limits. With the ink limit set at the default of 300%, there is a spot in the center that will have problems. Unless you fix it, that dark spot will be printed with 100% Red, 100% Blue, and 100% Yellow inks. You simply add the percentages of the ink tints involved.

InDesign's built-in choices range from 280% to 400% ink coverage. This is a general Adobe misunderstanding. There are very few companies that can print even 300% ink coverage. (Photoshop 7 uses a default of 400%, which would be 100c, 100m, 100y, 100k or any combination of process and spot colors that totaled 400 percent.)

 Adding spot colors just complicates things. Imagine that a color at 270 percent is also covered with a solid gloss varnish. The printing company will need to allow the 270 percent color time to dry—often for a couple of days. Otherwise, the varnish will become contaminated.

A 280 percent ink coverage works for the average commercial printer using coated stock. Different technologies have different limits. Here is a short list:

Commercial printers	300% to 325%, with top-quality, well-maintained presses, experienced operators, and cast-coated paper
Heat-set web (SWOP)	260% to 285%, depending on the quality standards and experience of the press operator
Cold-set web and newspapers	225% to 250%, because these presses use a very liquid ink that dries slowly
Electrostatic digital printers and presses	240% to 300%

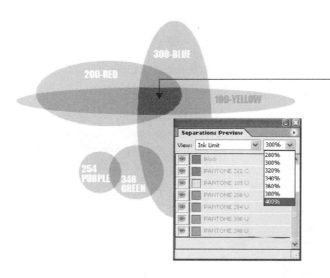

FIGURE 17-2   Use the Ink Limit view in the Separations Preview palette to check for ink limit problems.

Collect Your Project Documents in a Book

For your projects that are made up of several documents—books, annual reports, brochures using multiple types of paper, and so on—InDesign provides a handy feature for organizing those documents, checking the number of pages, and making sure that they are all using the same styles. By collecting all of the documents into a book, you get a separate book palette for managing the publication.

The first step is to choose File | New | Book. In the Save dialog box, pick an appropriate name and location to store your book. For example, when I'm working on a book with chapters, I usually use the folder that contains all the chapters (each chapter has its own folder). The book (named Piracy in this example) is saved as a file that opens in its own little palette.

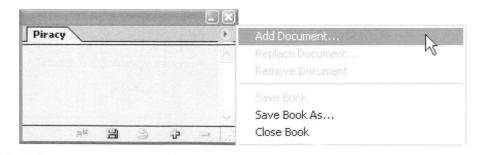

Next, add the documents that make up this book. In the book palette's option menu, choose Add Document (or click the Add Document button—with the plus sign icon—at the bottom of the book palette).

After you've added the documents to make your book, this little palette has a lot of power, as shown in Figure 17-3. You can now control your entire book from here.

First, notice the open book icon after the last chapter. That shows you that this is the document open on the screen. If you have more than one of the documents open, this icon will appear to the right of all the open documents. The icon in the column to the left of the 05SecretStashes document in Figure 17-3 shows that document will be used as the standard if you synchronize styles, as explained a bit later in this section.

The buttons at the bottom of the book palette are, from left to right, Synchronize Styles and Swatches with the Style Source (the icon is rather cryptic), Save the Book, Print the Book, Add Document, and Remove Document. These commands are also in the option menu, along with others for preparing your book for publication.

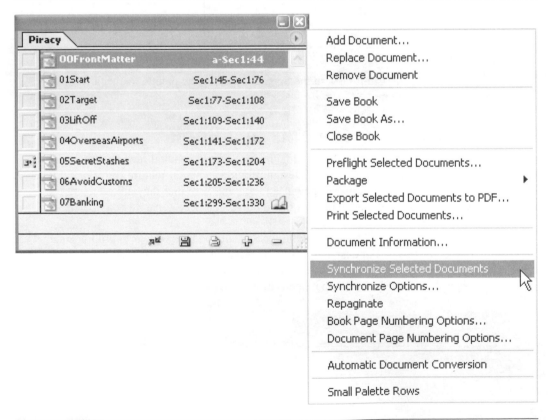

FIGURE 17-3   A book palette and its option menu

Number the Book's Pages

The page range appears beside each document name in the book palette. If you see errors, select Repaginate in the book palette's option menu, and InDesign will fix the page numbering of the entire book.

In a book file, automatic pagination is turned on by default. But this does not work if you have manually numbered the pages. The numbering style and starting page are based on each document's settings in the Document Page Numbering Options dialog box, accessed by selecting the Document Page Numbering Options command in the book palette's option menu. To turn on automatic pagination for the selected document, select Automatic Page Numbering in that dialog box, and the pages in the chapter will be renumbered automatically. (You can also do this in the Pages palette by double-clicking the section icon over the first page.) You will need to do this document by document.

NOTE *Automatic page numbering works only if you have a single section for each document. You will need to be careful with manual numbering for documents that have multiple sections with different numbering styles.*

Once you have automatic numbering turned on, you will find several options in the Book Numbering Options dialog box (opened by choosing Book Numbering Options in the book palette's option menu). For example, you can start document numbering on odd- or even-numbered pages. This is commonly done when you want to always start a new chapter on a right (odd-numbered) page. (Of course, if you were working in Hebrew or Arabic, you would want to start each chapter on a left page.) Check the Insert Blank Page box to automate inserting blank pages to accommodate a specific page order.

At any time, you can turn off automatic pagination and repaginate a book manually. You will need to do this if you have any special sections in the book with different page numbering.

Reorder Your Book

You can rearrange the order of the documents in the book by simply dragging the documents up and down in the book palette. A dark line will appear between the two documents where your reordered file will be placed.

InDesign repaginates automatically when you add or remove pages in booked documents, or when you make changes to the book file, such as reordering, adding, or removing documents. This works only if you have set each document for automatic page numbering.

If you move things around and a document is missing or cannot be opened, the page range is shown as "?" from the place where the missing document should be to the end of the book, indicating that the true page range is unknown. To fix the problem, remove or replace the missing document before you repaginate. If the In Use icon appears (it looks like a lock), someone using a different computer has opened the document; the person must close the document before you can repaginate.

Synchronize Your Book

To the left of each document listed in the book palette is a little icon. No, I do not know what it is supposed to be. I do know what it does. When you click to select that box, it makes that document the standard for styles. Once you've chosen the standard document, you can make all of the other documents in the book conform to the styles in that document, or synchronize them. In other words, you can make sure that all the chapters in your book use the same styles with the same settings.

To pick which styles you want to synchronize, choose Synchronize Options from the book palette's option menu. At the bottom of the Synchronize Options dialog box, shown in Figure 17-4, the Style Source shows the path to the document you chose to be the standard—in this example, 05SecretStashes.indd. (The fourth or fifth chapter is usually where I finalize my decisions for styles, so I chose Chapter 5 to be the style source.) The check boxes let you choose to synchronize TOC Styles, Character Styles, Paragraph Styles, Trap Presets, and Swatches to the style source of your choice.

After you've selected which styles you want to synchronize in the Synchronize Options dialog box, you can click the Synchronize button to make all the styles in the other documents in the book the same, or you can click OK to close the dialog box. If you clicked OK, you can then select the

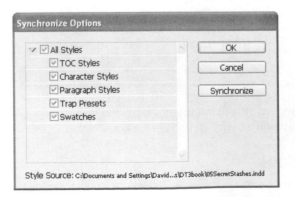

FIGURE 17-4   The Synchronize Options dialog box

documents you want synchronized in the book palette (with SHIFT-click or CTRL/COMMAND-click) and choose Synchronize Selected Documents from the palette's option menu.

Prepare Your Book for Publication

The other options on the book palette's option menu let you prepare the documents in the book for proofing or printing. You can export selected chapters as a PDF. You can print your selected chapters. You can preflight your entire book or selected chapters. You can package your book to send it off to a printer who does not use PDFs.

As we cover these proofing and preparation options in the rest of this chapter and in the next chapter, keep in mind that you can do everything for a single document, for an entire book, or for selected portions of a book. The book options are available only from the book palette.

Make Proofs of Your Documents

Along with internal proofs, three other proofs are usually necessary for documents that will be printed. (This differs a little for Web documents). In print, the first is a laser proof of the artwork. Normally this is a black-and-white PostScript laser print of each page or side. In some situations, you may want to make tissue overlays marked up to show the color break. The client must sign off on the art proof before you proceed to the expense of a color proof. After the art proof is approved, you need to supply a contract proof to your client. Printers typically produce contract proofs, and they are discussed in the next chapter.

Do Constant Internal Proofing

You need to make proofs for internal proofing as you prepare your documents. A normal workflow can require three to dozens of proofs, before the client sees a "perfect proof."

NOTE   *I cannot emphasize enough how important it is to proof the document thoroughly. Sloppy proofing is the cause of countless problems with client relationships. Three people should proof every page of every document—at a minimum. You can be one of the three, but you cannot be the only proofer. If at all possible, turn it over to a professional proofreader.*

Internal laser proofs are your best safeguard. This is where the real value of a black-and-white laser printer shows itself. The printer must be PostScript to show the screen tints and typography. Black-and-white (grayscale) prints are usually a couple of pennies or less, per print. (With a laser printer, creating color proof copies will often cost less than a quarter). With an inkjet, printing proofs could easily cost you $10 to $30 or more.

In most cases, you really want to get a good electrostatic solution to your proofing needs. If you get a laser printer with PostScript 3, these rough proofs will be all you need in most cases. The key is getting good enough resolution. There are several machines that offer true 1,200 dpi and produce excellent 100-line camera-ready copy and separations for quickprint. The key is getting PostScript 3. Genuine Adobe is always the best quality.

17

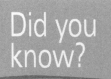

You Need a PostScript Printer

Non-PostScript printers can be used for rough proofing in black and white, but little else. Even for those proofs, they often include mistakes in rendering that can confuse your client. They cannot be used for camera-ready artwork, even by the lowest quality print shops.

When you get to color printing, you have insurmountable problems. Consumer inkjet printers are almost entirely non-PostScript. One big problem is that the color produced is not calibrated. A second huge problem is that non-PostScript printers cannot produce halftones and tints. They cannot produce printers' marks to show bleeds and such. More seriously, the proofs produced by these machines cannot be duplicated. This means that if you take your gorgeous color inkjet print to a printing company, they will probably scream at you, cut off your thumbs, or laugh hysterically. You will be upset when the documents that made your uncalibrated print are output professionally in PostScript, and converted to calibrated CMYK. The colors will change radically.

Another problem is that because inkjets are very low resolution (around 400 dpi) with the ability to make extra, tiny dots from those coarse jets, they cannot be scanned. Any image that is already printed is broken into dots. The dots used by inkjets are not reproducible. One of the worst problems in current workflows is the submission of inkjet prints as original photos. You must blur the dots out of existence before you can do anything with these monstrosities.

Everything in professional printing is done in PostScript, and probably will continue to be so for the foreseeable future. PostScript allows printers to draw their own custom bitmap of an image. The result is that PostScript documents print at whatever the resolution of the printer is. We call it resolution independence. This printer computer is called a raster image processor (RIP). A RIP takes the PostScript code and makes a custom bitmap specifically designed to use the printer to its best capabilities. This means that the same document can be proofed on a 300 dpi printer and output for plating on a 2,450 dpi platesetter. Each printer produces its own customized bitmap that works best on its own printing engine. The problem is that RIPs are not cheap. The cheapest letter-sized PostScript laser printer is still nearly $1,000 because of the RIP. You can get letter-sized USB color laser printers that have PostScript 3 for around $1,400.

TIP | *Always purchase Genuine Adobe PostScript. Currently, that means PostScript 3. There are PostScript clones, but they usually cause problems.*

If you have a color laser printer, these will even work for short-run projects. In many cases, the color is good enough for a rough proof, although for a contract proof, you will still need something that the printing company is willing to sign off on.

Make Art Proofs

The most important proofs from a legal and public relations standpoint are the customer proofs. These are sample prints or Web pages that explain what the client might not know.

An art proof is a simple presentation, but take it seriously. Never show the client an art proof that has not been proofed internally. And never show color until it is calibrated. The art proof should be black and white. You do not want to spend the time color-correcting separations if the customer has not even approved the photos yet. The basic concept of the art proof is to get approval for the layout and to correct typos.

Most companies develop a form to be attached to the art proof, as shown in Figure 17-5. As an alternative, it is now easy to make a signature line in the slug area (see Chapter 3 for details on setting up slugs). Often, this form is a rubber stamp, stamped onto the art proof. In some cases, it is better to have an artwork proof that has FPO (for position only) graphics.

It is important to make sure that the customer realizes that signing the art proof means that he or she approves of the graphics and the copy on it, including all spelling and grammar. If you do not have that signed proof, you will find it very difficult later to charge for customer alterations. Supposedly, if the client makes changes to copy or layout after signing the art proof, you charge for the time and materials it takes to make those changes. Without a signed art proof, you have no evidence that the artwork was ever approved in the first place.

Often, this art proof takes the place of what used to be called the *comprehensive*, or *comp*. The comprehensive was accurate enough to enable the client to approve the artwork (without spending any more time or money than necessary). Now, in many cases, all the budget will allow is a digital

Bergsland Art Proof
DESIGN SINCE 1967

Project Name _____

☐ OK as is: Make contract proof

☐ Changes needed: _____

_____

☐ New Art Proof needed

Client signature _____ Date_____

FIGURE 17-5   A sample art proof form to be attached to the art proof for signature

17

color print of the final artwork and the hope that the client doesn't make too many changes. Make sure it is a PostScript color print if you are forced into this scenario. It should be a print from the actual digital printer or press that will be producing the project.

 *Keep the client from the color until the contract proof. Never make a comp from inkjet prints. The client will usually fall in love with the color of the comp, and you will not be able to reproduce it.*

After you've presented the client with an art proof, everything comes to a screeching halt until the client reads, proofs, and signs off on the proof. Without a client signature on the proof, any production problems can (and probably will) be made your responsibility. You will be forced to either pay for or absorb any correction costs. These unbudgeted expenses can easily run into thousands of dollars, so be forewarned!

The signed proofs become legal contracts. You promise to produce the work as proofed. The client promises to accept and pay for the work as proofed. After the art proof is approved, the next step is to have your printer produce a contract proof, as explained in Chapter 18.

Beware of Soft Proofing

One of the worst problems facing the modern digital designer is the ability to show the client color possibilities that cannot be printed or reproduced in any fashion. I've mentioned the problem with cheap, non-PostScript inkjets. That is certainly a serious issue. However, the largest problem is showing your client something on your computer screen.

Many "experts" purport that you can calibrate your monitor to the point where you can use it for proofing. This is called a *soft proof*. It can be done, but it is expensive to get the hardware and software necessary to maintain a calibrated environment (as discussed in Chapter 14).

A monitor is a glowing light source. Colors on a monitor will always look much brighter than a printed version of those colors. The best you can hope for is a hue match, and even that is rare. Spot colors, like those found in the PMS system, are impossible to match on the screen. If you must show clients a soft proof, you need to have a swatch next to the computer to show them what it will look like when printed. Always remind them that the final print will be darker and duller. In the case of spot colors, even the hues are usually different onscreen, no matter how well you have your monitor calibrated.

Use PDF Proofs

Increasingly, you will be using PDF proofs. How does this affect your workflow? First of all, you need to know how well your clients understand color printing. In most cases, you will not want to show them a color PDF. A grayscale PDF lets them proof the copy and the layout, without getting married to a color that cannot be reproduced. Chapter 18 covers producing PDFs.

There are some real advantages with PDF proofs. Mainly, they allow proofing via e-mail. You can annotate PDFs, and each set of notes has the name of the person who made them. You will need to devise a method for your clients to use PDFs and send back a signed proof. There are many ways of doing this: snail mail, PDF forms, and so on.

Learn Standard Business Ethics

Business relationships are not social relationships. You do not have to like your clients, but you do need to respect them. In a very real way, the success of your business depends on the success of their business.

There are many lists and several books concerning business ethics and trade practices. For example, there is the excellent *Graphic Artists Guild Handbook: Pricing and Ethical Guidelines* (North Lights Books). Search the Web for other books, lists, and statements of business ethics. Ask your printing company for a copy of the guidelines they use. For example, you may be surprised to learn that business practices for printing commonly mean that they promise to produce the quantity you order, plus or minus ten percent. They reduce the price if they print less; they raise the price if they print more. Some companies always print more and raise the price accordingly.

In this day of constant litigation and adversarial relationships, it is extremely wise to have written contracts. The *Graphic Artists Guild Handbook: Pricing and Ethical Guidelines* has many of these, of almost every possible variety. You may even want to become a member of the Graphic Artists Guild (www.gag.org).

Here are some business decisions you (or your employer) need to make:

- How are roles defined?
- When will quotes and proposals be ready and what will they contain?
- What proofs will be provided?
- Who pays for which alterations?
- What are all the deadlines and delivery charges?
- Who stores the artwork and the printed materials?
- Who owns the materials: the output and the digital files?
- What is the payment schedule? Are there any late payment penalties?
- What kinds of rights are being purchased (copyright questions)?
- How will disputes be settled?
- Who is paying for production?
- Who is responsible for production?
- Who handles outside services and how are they billed and paid for?

17

Create Web Proofs

On the Web, proofs go in stages. One of the real advantages is that Web sites can be updated at any time. In fact, they should be redesigned, updated, or simply changed about once a month or so.

The standard rule is that every time a customer returns to the Web site, they should see a new offer—at least. Therefore, Web proofs tend to be ongoing e-mails with a link to the page, saying something like, "I changed [x]. What do you think?" Web graphics should just be attached to an e-mail for proofing.

Make Sure Your Documents Are Printable

A large portion of jobs submitted to printers cannot be printed as received (around 65 percent according to TrendWatch in early 2003). With an idea of the severity of the problem, it should be obvious why a new career has been birthed to handle it. Patrick White and the National Association of Printers and Lithographers (NAPL) came out with a preflight checklist in their newsletter, *Desktop for Profit* in the mid-1990s. Most people think that Patrick is the person who came up with the term *preflight*. The concept is to open the file and "see if it will fly."

When you send a job to the printer, it goes through a process called *prepress*. The jobs arrive on disk, and within an hour, they must be run through preflight. The preflight person is often an entry-level position in image assembly. In some shops, preflight is a task for the customer service representatives.

The preflight person copies the job folder to the hard drive and opens it on a computer. Supplied fonts are temporarily installed with font management software. The document files are opened. Then, most of the time, the file is checked with preflight software. Sometimes it is checked with a list, by hand. Often, both are done. The person runs the project through the checklist to make sure that everything is in place and available—fonts, graphics, color names, and so on. If the job checks out OK, it might move to the image manipulation station, the trapping station, and/or the imposition station. It depends on the complexity of the job and the abilities of the printing company you are using (see Chapter 18 for information about printing capabilities).

It is your responsibility to make sure that preflighting is done. Discuss preflight procedures with the production manager or customer service representative of the printing company you are using for the project. If you're using a quickprinter or a copy shop, you'll need to do the preflighting yourself. In fact, even if you're sending the job off to a printer, the easiest way to avoid problems is to preflight the documents before you submit them.

InDesign has a Preflight command, but it does no good unless you know what problems you need to look for, and it cannot catch every type of problem. So, first we'll look at items to check in a preflight, and then cover how InDesign's Preflight command works.

Make a Preflight Checklist

You need to make a preflight checklist. Using this checklist, you review each element of the print job for completeness and correctness. Mark any problems you find on this list, and then correct them.

Preflight must start with a clear understanding of job specifications. You will need to know and use the client name, project name, job number (if applicable), contact person, phone, e-mail address, size, number of pages, number of documents in the book file, colors used, and so on.

On the following pages, we will go through preflight checklist considerations. This is certainly not an exhaustive list. You will need to develop a checklist for every printer you use, because each has different requirements.

Are Any Required Elements Missing?

First, you need to check for items that are required for the job to be printed. The two most common problems in digital production are missing fonts and missing graphics.

Many (if not most) printers will not even accept a job unless these are supplied, if they are a part of your job:

- **Layout files**   The layout file always comes in its own folder. For the purposes of this book, this is your InDesign document.

- **Screen fonts and printer fonts**   Both of these pieces are necessary for Type 1 PostScript fonts.

- **TrueType fonts**   Older RIPs cannot handle TrueType. Most printers can, but it's wise to check.

- **Multiple Master (MM) fonts**   Adobe no longer sells these fonts, but some publications, such as larger magazines, still use them. Check with your printer before using MM fonts.

- **OpenType fonts**   This is the preferred solution, but again, you will need a current RIP. OpenType is a form of TrueType. It is true that OpenType solves many of our typographic problems. Check with your printer.

- **dfont fonts**   These are Mac system fonts for OSX. Many of these fonts come with your computer, but only Macs can read them. Be careful if you need to use a PC in any part of your workflow. The dfont format requires OSX.

- **Linked scans, graphics, and illustrations**   The assumption here is that each imported or placed graphic will be an EPS, PDF, TIFF, DCS, AI, or PSD file. However, even with the ease of use, the PSDs should be merged or flattened copies to save file size. (Merging will maintain the transparency; flattening will eliminate the transparency.)

- **PDF files**   There are good PDFs and bad PDFs. You want no downsampling, all fonts embedded instead of subset, all bitmaps 300 dpi or twice the linescreen, CMYK, bitmap, or grayscale, and so on. I'll discuss PDF settings in Chapter 18. If you can use PDFs, usually, all you will need to send to the printer is the PDFs and hardcopy proofs.

- **Hardcopy proofs**   Any discrepancies between the supplied proof and the electronic files need to be listed. Without a hardcopy proof, the printer personnel will need to make guesses about your intentions. You do not want that to happen! To avoid problems, supply a detailed, well-annotated, hardcopy proof.

17

The easiest method of determining whether all of the necessary fonts and files are present is to use the File | Preflight command in InDesign, as explained later in this chapter.

Page Considerations

Page requirements vary a lot from shop to shop. They are all items that affect imposition, and resolving page problems may involve resizing the created document, trimming smaller, or bouncing the job back to you to be fixed. (Of course, they can fix it for you, for $100 to $200 per hour.)

The following are page considerations:

- **Page size defined as final trim size**   Newcomers to printing often think that they must make their page size the size of the sheets of paper coming out of their laser printers. This is not true. The page size must be the trim size of the actual document; that is, the final size as delivered. This is the size after folding in most cases, because multiple page documents are trimmed after they are folded.

NOTE   *It is true that brochures are often set up with just a front and a back. But this page size must be the size of the brochure, after it is trimmed and before it is folded. For example, the page size of a business card is 2 by 3.5 inches, unless it is a folded card. The only time you vary from this is when you do your own setup for things like a work and turn (with the front and back of a page on the same plate) or doing business cards 10-up.*

- **Bleeds set at 1/8 inch or 9 points**   This is the norm. It is true that some printing processes, like book publishers, ask for a 1/4-inch bleed, but this bleed size is rare. It is common for beginning desktop publishers to make their bleeds stop at the trim size. See Chapter 16 for a discussion of bleeds and trim sizes.

- **Pages imposed in printer's spreads**   You rarely want to get involved with imposition. In many cases, the printing personnel will not decide which press they are using until the day they get ready to burn the plates. The number of possible pages in a signature is determined by the size of the press. Many shops have many different sizes.

- **Miscellaneous items in the pasteboard area deleted**   Never leave pieces on the pasteboard. They can cause RIP problems, take extra time and money to output, and so on. This is a common mistake.

Type-Related Problems

The practice of applying styles to fonts almost always causes printing problems. Fortunately, InDesign does not allow this. However, you need to make sure you have set your preferences to highlight substituted fonts (in the Composition page of the Preferences dialog box, accessed from the Edit menu in Windows or the InDesign menu in Mac OSX). In general, you never want to use a style applied to your type. Make the effects you need, carefully and by hand.

Here are some improper styles and other type-related issues that may cause RIP problems:

- **Underline style**   Regular underlines can be too crude and mess up the descenders. However, the new underline options in InDesign CS make it possible to make subtle underlines as a character style. Just be careful.

- **Shadows**   Here, the problem is not in the printing but in readability issues. Shadows are commonly made too dark and positioned exactly where the type is least readable. If you want a shadow, make it light and soft. You need to carefully watch the transparency settings. These soft shadows often look good on the screen yet terrible when printed. Multiple, overlapping, shadowed objects can cause printing problems with older RIPs. If you have a problem, do your soft shadows in Photoshop.

- **Widows, orphans, hyphenation, and overset problems**   If you are sending your files instead of PDFs and using the service bureau's fonts instead of sending the actual fonts you used in the document, the company's RIP might create these problems. There are many combinations where a font can be called by the same name, yet have different character widths and different tracking settings. This can add or subtract widows and orphans, change the hyphenation, and make the type longer, so the last few lines or paragraphs disappear into the overset link.

Color Definitions in Layout Files

Most color printing is two- and three-color spot. Spot colors are custom-mixed inks like those found in the PMS, or standard colors from an ink manufacturer or printer manufacturer that are only standard to that company. Regardless, you must make separations that output each color on its own plate.

Color definition considerations depend on the type of color you're using.

- **The same color names in graphics and page layout programs**   You must be careful to name the colors the same in all the programs used to make the graphics—whether those graphics are made in Quark, InDesign, FreeHand, Illustrator, or Photoshop. Otherwise, your simple two-color job could turn out to output on seven separate plates or negatives. To check for problems with different color names, open your Swatches palette in InDesign (see Chapter 13 for details).

- **CMYK colors defined as their build amounts**   This is not entirely necessary, but it will help you learn to think in CMYK. Plus, it will help people who do (like the people at your printing company or service bureau) properly visualize the color you intended.

- **Note areas where black knocks out**   Black normally overprints (does not knock out any colors underneath it) in all professional publishing programs. If you need the black to knock out, this is unusual and should be noted. Otherwise, the defaults will cause the black to overprint. Worse, your suppliers will assume the knockout black is a mistake unless you warn them, and they may try to "fix" that mistake.

NOTE   *Remember that InDesign CS overprints only solid black. Tints will knock out.*

17

- **Define CMYK values for rich black**   In pieces that are solid process color, plain 100k is a very weak black. It often appears to be an 80 percent gray or even weaker. As a result, blacks in the midst of color are often printed with an addition of 60c or even 60c, 60m. This is definitely necessary where an area of black is partially over a blank background and partially overprinting color. These undercolors should be choked, so that color does not leak around the edge of the rich black. You can set this up using InDesign's Trap Presets (see Chapter 14). You can also produce black-on-black designs with a rich black (although you must be careful not to exceed the ink limit settings required by your printer, as explained earlier in this chapter).

Image Considerations

You probably will be doing most of your image manipulation in Photoshop. You will need to know how to adjust for dot gain and dot range. Often, you will need to do your own color correction. Specialists at the service bureau or at the printing company handle these tasks in larger workflows. Large design departments have these specialists in-house.

On the proof, you should mark off each image as vector or bitmap. For vector files such as line-art illustrations, logos, or charts, mark each image on proof with the file format, software used, and version number.

When your supplier, print shop, or service bureau outputs film or plates from the files you supply, there are often problems. To help them troubleshoot, they need a map of your document, showing which graphics are which types. Vector images, PDF files, and EPS files cause the most problems. The people responsible for outputting your film or plates usually have a good idea which versions of which software cause problems. This is why they want to know what you used and where.

Along with the graphic type information, there are several other image considerations:

- **Scaled percentage in layout**   In general, you need to place your images at 100 percent. InDesign handles scaling well, but it can still cause output problems with the RIP. Scaling, rotating, or transforming a bitmap softens the image. Enlarging bitmaps pixelates them. Plus, it can increase the processing time. Normally, you can scale PDFs and EPSs as desired, unless they have an embedded bitmap. However, when you scale placed graphics to smaller than 40 percent or so in InDesign, the strokes also get smaller. If you start with a 0.5 point stroke and scale it to 25 percent, your stroke is now 0.125 point. No one can print a stroke that thin, so, it's gone.

- **Are they trapped?**   Never do any trapping without talking to the printing company first. As discussed in Chapter 14, trapping is using thin, colored lines to help colors that touch so they do not show blank paper. Obviously, scaling trapped images causes problems. However, the real problem is when you trap and the printer does not know it. Then the printer applies additional traps to your traps, and you get a snarled mess that looks bad and often chokes the RIP.

- **Mark bitmaps**   For bitmap files, mark each image as line art, grayscale, duotone or more, RGB, LAB, or CMYK. Most companies want color images supplied in CMYK, to size. In other words, they want to make you responsible for the separations. Other companies require RGB or LAB images, where they are responsible for the accuracy of the color. Duotones and tritones cause problems in many workflows. So, companies want to be forewarned.

- **File formats**   In general, printers accept only TIFF, EPS, DCS, and PDF files. Many will not believe it is possible to use the PSDs and AI files in InDesign (yet another reason for using PDFs). Duotones must be in EPS or PSD format. (Check to make sure how they handle duotones; many printers have specific handling procedures.)

■ **Transparency** TIFFs are never transparent. InDesign imports PSDs and maintains the transparency. However, if you added InDesign transparency on top of PSD transparency, there are many output glitches. Often, things look great on screen and print very strangely. Just be careful.

■ **Colors applied to line-art bitmaps** Designers frequently want to bring in grayscale (8-bit) and bitmap (1-bit) images to apply spot colors in page layout. This is no problem with 1-bit bitmaps. Just note the location. In practice, color applied to grayscale bitmaps often causes problems. Color applied to EPSs almost never works.

■ **Gray component replacement (GCR) for PhotoShop separations** GCR measures the gray component produced by complementary colors. This gray is removed from the cyan, magenta, and yellow and transferred to the black plate. It works very well and saves money on ink costs. GCR settings can be None, Light, Medium, Heavy, or Maximum. Using Medium and Heavy GCR moves so much color to the black printer that making color adjustments on the press becomes difficult. You can control only the lighter midtones and the highlights. The shadows are often all black.

An older technology is under color removal (UCR). It is rarely used because GCR is better.

■ **Black ink limit** The Photoshop Prepress defaults set the black ink limit at 100%. No one can print that correctly. The black ink limit needs to be set as the high number in your dot range for a given printer. If you are told to make your images 5-85, the black ink limit needs to be 85% (anything darker than 85% will print black). Setting this ink limit in Photoshop helps you keep shadow detail while compensating for dot gain. In InDesign, you need to make sure that you do not use any tints that are darker than 7% lighter than the ink limit. If you are not careful, your darker tints will be indistinguishable from the solid areas.

■ **Total ink limit** For colors mixed in InDesign (or in any placed graphics), you are personally responsible to add up the percentages and make sure you do not exceed the ink limit. See the "Watch for Ink Limit Problems" section earlier in this chapter for a discussion of Photoshop and InDesign settings and a short list of the limits used by different technologies.

■ **Profiles used for printing ink setup** Unless your printer tells you to use something different, use the default: SWOP. I know this stands for Standards for Web Offset Printing. However, the reality is that few printers use color management, and they assume you are using SWOP.

■ **Dot gain used** In Photoshop, use the percentage provided by the printer. For color you mix, remember that all colors get darker by the percentage of dot gain. This effect is worsened for the midtones. So, if you are told that there is a 10 percent dot gain, your lighter tints will get 10 percent darker (15 to 16.5 percent, for example). Midtones will probably get nearly 20 percent darker (45 to 54 percent, for example). And the shadows will get 10 percent darker (75 to 90 percent, for example). Multiply the tint by the percentage,

17

and then make adjustments. If the printed result is too dark, make the dot gain adjustments larger. If the images print too light, make them smaller. It is an experiential adjustment that will differ for each printer and print job.

■ **Scan resolutions**   Many companies demand that you supply 300 dpi images. The norm is twice the linescreen, so for quickprinters using 85 lines per inch (lpi) screens, 170 dpi works better. However, there are times when you do not want to use the maximum resolution. You will need to tell the supplier and give the OK to print those images as you supplied them. Otherwise, they will often bounce these images in their preflight routine.

Preflight Your Document in InDesign

After all that, I must say that InDesign has the best built-in preflighting process in page layout. It is very simple, and the command flags almost every common problem you might have, except for scaled strokes, dot range, dot gain, and similar problems. As I noted earlier, these are problems you will need to take care of yourself.

When you're ready to check your document, choose File | Preflight. InDesign will search your document, assembling information about all your fonts, graphics, and colors. When it is finished, you will see the Preflight dialog box, as shown in Figure 17-6.

In the example shown in Figure 17-6, this document passed the preflight check, except for a spot color problem. However, it didn't catch all the problems with my document. There are really three spot colors that are all the same color but have different names. It also did not catch the gradient that starts in RGB, passes through a spot color, and goes on into CMYK. There is no mention of the RGB stop at all. It does report that this is a CMYK plus spot color job though, which is another problem. It caught that from the gradient.

So, the moral is that you cannot rely on software to find all the problems with a document. I always preflight before I package. I am careful throughout production to avoid possible problems, but I still do not catch everything.

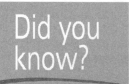

Color Name Conflicts Can Happen Even If You're Careful

You may be careful to call your dark green PMS 349. However, you might get an ad from one designer who calls it PMS349, another ad from another designer who names the same color Pantone 349 (but it is a process CMYK color), and a duotone from the scanner and image manipulator where Photoshop's default name, Pantone 349 CVU, is used. The result is that your Swatches palette shows PMS349, PMS 349, and Pantone 349 CVU listed. (The Pantone 349 is separated into cyan, magenta, yellow, and black, so you do not see it on the Swatches palette.) In this case, you need to open the original graphic files to give them the same color name for that green and make sure that all the greens are spot color.

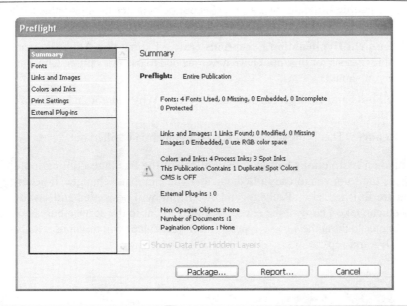

Preflight

Summary
Fonts
Links and Images
Colors and Inks
Print Settings
External Plug-ins

Summary

Preflight: Entire Publication

Fonts: 4 Fonts Used, 0 Missing, 0 Embedded, 0 Incomplete
0 Protected

Links and Images: 1 Links Found; 0 Modified, 0 Missing
Images: 0 Embedded, 0 use RGB color space

Colors and Inks: 4 Process Inks; 3 Spot Inks
This Publication Contains 1 Duplicate Spot Colors
CMS is OFF

External Plug-ins : 0

Non Opaque Objects :None
Number of Documents :1
Pagination Options : None

☑ Show Data For Hidden Layers

[Package...]   [Report...]   [Cancel]

FIGURE 17-6   The Preflight dialog box shows a summary of what InDesign checked and reports any problems.

Package Your Project

Once you're convinced that your document is ready for printing—all the problems are resolved— you can package the project. You can do this immediately after preflighting the document, by clicking the Package button in the Preflight dialog box, or you can choose File | Package.

First, you will see a dialog box that allows you to write a note for the printing company, giving names, dates, and instructions. Fill that in, and then click the Continue button. Next, the Package Publication dialog box appears. As shown in Figure 17-7, this is a modified Save dialog box. Name the new folder appropriately and navigate to an appropriate location on your hard drive.

The check boxes at the bottom of the dialog box allow you to control how your document will be packaged:

■ **Copy Fonts (roman only)**   This copies all the fonts you used to a folder called Fonts inside the new folder you made for the package. It does not copy all the fonts in the font family, only those that you used. I recommend selecting this option.

■ **Copy Linked Graphics**   This will copy all the placed graphics with links to a folder called Graphics inside you package folder. It will not copy the originals that you used (or should have used) to make those graphics. You will need to take care of that manually, especially if the printer asks you to send the originals. I recommend choosing this option.

17

■ **Update Graphic Links in Package**   This option changes the link paths to the package folder location. It's another choice that makes sense to me.

■ **Use Document Hyphenation Exceptions Only**   I know that Adobe's documentation gives some reasons for this, but I have never needed to use this option. Check it only if you are sure you should.

■ **Include Fonts and Links from Hidden Layers**   Why did you hide them if you want to include them?

■ **View Report**   This is the instructions report you already filled out.

There is also an Instructions button at the bottom of the Package Publication dialog box. Clicking it opens the form you already filled out, and you can make changes, if necessary.

When you are finished, click Package, and everything will be copied and saved to the new folder. Then you can take a copy of the entire packaged folder to the service bureau or printer.

The next chapter looks at the various types of printing services you might use. It also describes how to make PDFs and separations.

FIGURE 17-7   The Package Publication dialog box

Chapter 18

Produce Your Documents

How to...

- Compare printing capabilities
- Get a contract proof
- Print bad ink with the Ink Manager
- Export PDFs directly from InDesign
- Use PDF export presets
- Print your documents
- Make a separated PDF

In this last chapter, you'll learn how to produce your finished document. As I've emphasized throughout this book, you need to design the document for its intended output from the very beginning of the project. You need to pick your printer first, before you start designing. If you've done that, and then taken the preparatory steps described in the previous chapter, you can avoid disappointing results and costly mistakes.

Here, we'll take a look at the various printing technologies and their capabilities. Then we'll get to the details of making PDFs and printing.

Pick Your Printer First

One of the most important tasks facing designers is to make accurate quotes. These quotes must demonstrate a full understanding by you, the client, and the printer or supplier concerning what will be produced, how many copies, what colors, how many pages, and so on. Publishing is custom manufacturing. There are literally thousands of options for each project. Your task is to make sure that your client knows what the options are, how much they cost, and what limitations they place on the production schedule and budget. Additionally, you must be sure that what you are proposing can actually be printed by equipment that is currently available.

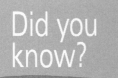

The Job Ticket Is a Communication Tool

The job ticket is the way the sales staff communicates with the rest of the shop. This is your contract with the client.

Even if you are a single-person studio, you need to have a written job ticket with all the job specs. It is extremely important that these forms be filled out accurately and *completely*. Not only are the complete job specs required, but also the complete client name and address, former job numbers, and the appropriate contact person(s) with both phone and e-mail information.

Become Familiar with Printing Technologies

For many reasons, 600 dpi PostScript is the minimum professional standard. Many hold that even this is only good enough for rough, internal proofing. Actually, the market determines the standard. There are many printing technologies that meet this standard or go far beyond it. Here, we'll review the basic technologies currently available.

Digital Printers

For digital color printing, there are many machines to choose from. Xerox is working hard to corner the market, but there is a lot of competition. The press operator shortage will ensure that most of our printing in the near future will be done on machines like this. For black-and-white work, 600 dpi machines like the DocuTech are already the standard. The linescreen is relatively crude, but the clients are usually not looking for fine art. They are just trying to get information to their customers.

PostScript Inkjets

PostScript inkjet printers are rapidly becoming the standard for art reproductions and color proofing. They are very expensive (low five figures to low six figures). They make good-quality contract proofs for around $6 a proof (actually, around $6 a square foot).

The more expensive inkjets are used for giclée fine-art prints. They are named after an Iris inkjet made by Scitex several years ago. That printer no longer exists, but the name stuck. They produce outrageously good images, at a cost of $150 per print or more. It is almost impossible to distinguish them from real watercolors, if they are printed on watercolor paper. However, even with pigmented inks, they are permanent for only around 40 years.

Large-Format and Grand-Format Inkjets

Even though the large-format machines have very high consumable costs, they have become the standard in industries where only a dozen or fewer images are required. Large-format printers come in 24-inch to 96-inch widths. The length of material on the roll usually limits the length. Grand-format machines come in 7-foot to 16-foot widths, and the rolls limit the length to about 50 yards. These printers are used for the following types of projects:

- Trade show displays are done with large-format inkjet prints on translucent substrates and backlit.
- Banners are commonly produced with large-format or grand-format prints that are laminated.
- Billboards are usually done with grand-format inkjet prints that are stretched over the billboard frame.
- Skyscraper prints are made with grand-format inkjet prints, using Mylar screen as the printing material. These long strips are then sewed together into those 100-by-300-foot (or larger) images that are hung from the sides of large buildings in the major cities.
- Truck and bus wraps are done with grand-format inkjets printing on self-adhesive vinyl, with screen covering the windows.

18

These images are not cheap, but they are much less expensive than hand-painted images. Plus they are of photographic quality with rich color. The going rate is about $6 per square foot or less. Of course, skyscraper prints and bus wraps have high installation costs on top of that. Nevertheless, in the rarefied world of large budget advertising, these prints are considered a bargain.

 Some large format printers can do HiFi printing, which adds to the standard four-color process colors. For example, they might do six or seven colors.

Paper Platesetters

Plain-paper laser printers can output plates if they are large enough. Paper and plastic plates used to be a joke from a quality viewpoint, because they stretch so badly on the press. They also could not do continuous-tone work—tints or halftones. This is no longer true. Now they can produce output with photos and screens in place. This makes them an excellent choice for single-color quickprint, because they cost much less than $2 a plate. The new plastic platesetters produce excellent plates.

Laser Printers

Printing companies also use laser printers for professional output. At the higher resolutions used professionally, toner cannot be ground fine enough to work. Even though 1,200 dpi printers can use toner, they are barely professional quality. They are used only for quickprint. The industry norm is 2,400 dpi or higher. This is necessary to make 150-line halftones of professional quality. To reach these resolutions or higher, an emulsion is needed.

Color laser printers work reasonably well for color proofing. As the calibration gets better, color laser prints become more usable. They are also used for commodity color production. The usual problem is that most of these printers are actually 300 to 600 dpi with 8-bit dots. This results in excellent color but strange halftone structures. As a result, many printers do not like to use them for proofs. However, if you are printing the final product at a company like Kinko's on a DocuColor printer, you might as well get a proof from that machine.

Imagesetters (Film Printers)

To achieve the fine detail required by commercial printing, film is usually necessary. The standard resolution is 2,400 dpi or more, and toner really has trouble in this range. The film is usually exposed with lasers. Sizes range from 12 by 18 to 24 by 36 inches or larger. A resolution of 2,400 dpi is necessary for printed process color (2,400 dpi produces only 256 levels of gray at 150 linescreen).

The 1,200 to 4,000 dpi Technologies

The 1,200 to 4,000 dpi photochemical printers have been the backbone of our industry. The problem is that photochemistry uses toxic and hazardous chemicals. You can expect these to disappear as soon as possible. In many areas, you need a license to operate a darkroom. With 55-gallon drums of spent fixer costing hundreds of dollars in disposal charges, the days of this type of chemistry are numbered. New 1,200 to 4,000 dpi technologies offer the best hope for environmental functionality.

Both the older and newer imagesetter types output composite negatives. This means that the entire image for each color on a side of a plate is output on one sheet of film.

CTP (Platesetter) Printers

Platesetter printing is usually called CTP, for computer to plate or press. Here, all the intermediate steps are done digitally and output directly on the plates to be printed. This is the only real hope for traditional printing like offset lithography. CTP is becoming common.

This is the obvious path to economically viable digital production. By directly outputting plates, all handwork is eliminated. In addition, the imposition is much more accurate. The only problem at this point is proofing, and that is rapidly being solved. As long as the same RIP is used for both proof and plate, contract proofs work well.

Platesetters are still quite expensive. However, one of the major growth areas of platesetting is in the high-quality plastic plates. The original platesetters cost hundreds of thousands of dollars. Now, there are many smaller platesetters outputting excellent-quality plastic plates for small- to medium-sized commercial printers. Because these plates cost around $3, many of the old setup charges are eliminated. These will keep the old traditional presses viable for a lot longer (*if* they can find press operators).

Thermal Wax and Dye Sublimation Printers

Thermal printers create color by melting tiny droplets of colored wax onto the paper. They provide brilliant color. Xerox was giving theirs away free if you bought the wax sticks from them. Plus, Xerox offered free black wax for the life of the printer. Those kind of desperate measures should give you a clue as to how popular these printers are. However, the people I know who have them love them.

Dye sublimation printers work much the same as thermal wax printers. The temperature is higher, so the droplets are more like a tiny spray of ink. The dots bleed more into the surrounding area. As a result, the prints look photographic. The difficulty is the lack of a halftone screen. Printers do not trust them because no dot structure is visible. They make gorgeous photographic proofs, but crude type. Plus, the prints are expensive (around $10 each for an 8-by-10-inch print).

Compare Printing Capabilities

Table 18-1 shows a comparison of printing capabilities. These are all approximate differences and averages. There are many exceptions. Production CMYK, 100-lpi screen printers do exist, but they are not common. Digital mimeographs are close to quickprint, except they can do only 71-lpi screens. In general, the figures given for screen printers are very rough because there are so many options. In addition, there are 96-inch wide presses for commercial printers and 22-inch wide webs for digital printers. However, this table gives you a good idea of the capabilities of various technologies.

18

Capabilities	Quickprint	Commercial	Digital	Large Format	Screen
Linescreen	85–100	150	N/A in Xerox, Fuji, and Canon, which use pixels instead of hard dots; 85–150 for others	12–150	25–100
Minimum stroke (points)	0.6	0.15	0.3	0.25–5	1–3
Solid area (square inches)	3–16	400+	100+	Unlimited	Unlimited
Maximum sheet size	13"×19"	26"×40"	12"×18"	3'–9' wide; almost unlimited length	6' sq. or more
Dot ranges (percent, 0 = white to 100 = black)	7–85	5–95	3–97	3–90	10–90
Raster file resolution (dpi)	170–200	300	170–300	25–300	50–200
Registration (inches)	±1/16	±0.003	0.15–0.0005	±0.01	±0.01
Color printing	Spot	CMYK/spot	CMYK/spot	CMYK/HiFi	Spot
Maximum number of colors	3	8 (unlimited)	4 CMYK/ 18 spot	4/6	Unlimited
Normal turnaround (days)	2	5	1–3	2–5	5
Letterpress (die-cuts, foil stamp, emboss)	Rare	Common	N/A	N/A	Rare
Printer (dpi)	600–1,200	1,200–2,400	400–2,880	25–400	N/A
Paper weight (maximum cover weight)	80#	120#	110# index to 80# cover	Foamcore	Unlimited
Maximum copies per hour	9,000	50,000	2,000 CMYK/ 7,200 B&W or spot	50	200
Relative cost for similar projects	$	$$$	$$	$$$$$	$$$

TABLE 18-1 Capabilities of Printing Technologies

Table 18-1 covers a lot of information and assumes that you know quite a bit about printing technologies and capabilities. In fact, you do need to know this stuff. Ask your printer for a tour.

Here are a few more comments regarding printing technologies:

- **Quickprint**   Tight registration is available for two-color spot printing if the company has a T-head on the duplicator. This allows two colors to print on one blanket for hair-line registration at quickprint prices. Quality is also greatly improved with digital plates. Just ask the printer if the equipment has a platesetter and/or a T-head.

- **Commercial printing**   Basically, this is custom manufacturing. These printing services can either do anything or get anything done for you, at a price (for example, a brochure that uses die-cut, 1/8-inch-thick aircraft aluminum for the cover). Commercial printing companies are the places to go if you need fancy letterpress options like die-cutting, foil-stamping, embossing, and the like.

- **Digital**   Most digital printing companies do not calibrate their presses often enough. Ask them how often they calibrate, and ask them to calibrate before they print your project. Also, for electrostatic digital presses, toner often chips off unless you set the ink limit to 250 percent total or less. (Chapter 17 describes how to set ink limits in InDesign.) Also, ask what the printing service prefers for a proof.

- **Large format**   Inks can fade very quickly unless they are coated with UV protection or special pigmented inks are used. Water and fingerprints are a serious problem unless you add a coating. Giclée fine-art prints need special paper, ink, and a coating in many cases, to ensure that they will last for 30 to 40 years.

- **Screen**   This process has very different requirements. It uses transparent positives instead of negatives, for example. If you are supplying film to the printing company, make sure you supply the right kind. Ask what their capabilities are. Only a few can do CMYK. Most do 50-lpi screen or even coarser.

- **Flexography**   This is letterpress using rubber plates used for packaging. Make sure you consult with the printer, because this is a very different technology. The printer may want to take a tint and make it a separate plate, for example. A single spot color may have three plates or more. Gradients are often not possible. Circles need to be designed as precise ovals that will stretch into a circle when the rubber plates are wrapped around the cylinders. The printer will handle all of this, and the quote will include these things. But you do not want to try this at home.

Get a Contract Proof

The contract proof is a full-color proof, providing an approved contract between the client (you or your employer) and the printing company. Most printing companies will not proceed with print production until they have received a signed, approved contract proof. They will not make the contract proof until they have a signed, approved art proof (discussed in Chapter 17). The art proof is between you and the client. The contract proof is between the printing company and the client. It says I (the client) will pay for this, if you (the printer) match the proof.

There are many varieties of contract proofs these days. They are all expensive. They are essential and should be part of the quote received from the printer. You need to make sure a contract proof is included in the printing price. Different varieties are Matchprints, Fujiproofs, Kodak Approval, Iris inkjet prints, and so on. Do not get involved with what type is used. It is more important that the printing company be confident in the proof. The company is guaranteeing that the finished product will match the proof.

Print In-House

You may have your own printers and even presses in your studio. This is the best solution, because you can make as many trial runs as you need to determine how to adapt to a given printer.

If you are even thinking along these lines, I highly recommend you look at a digital mimeograph, such as the Ricoh Priport. This printer will give you many of the in-house capabilities of a small quickprinter for less than $15,000. If you also have a good, tabloid, CMYK laser printer with a PostScript 3 RIP, you can handle many of your printing projects in-house.

Print Bad Color with the Ink Manager

One of the more common complaints of full-color traditional printers is the need to eliminate spot colors by converting them to PMS. As explained in Chapter 17, spot colors need to have identical names if you want them to come out on the same plate. The Ink Manager is designed to address these problems.

The important thing to realize about the Ink Manager is that it does not really fix anything. According to Adobe, "The Ink Manager provides nonbinding control over inks at output time. Changes you make using the Ink Manager affect only the output, not how the colors are defined in the document." In other words, it enables a printing company to print your document, even though you messed up. For example, if a process job includes a spot color, the Ink Manager can be used to change the spot color to equivalent CMYK process colors. If a document contains two similar spot colors when only one was in the quote, the Ink Manager can be used to create an alias to a different spot or process color.

It should also be possible to fix PDFs that you send for printing when you receive ads with bad color in them. Just remember that it is a temporary fix. The colors in the file are not actually changed.

You can find the Ink Manager button in four different locations: the Swatches palette's option menu, the Separations Preview palette's option menu, the Output page of the Print dialog box, and the Advanced page of the Export PDF or Export EPS dialog box.

In Figure 18-1, you can see that somehow PMS 301 has been put in this document with three different names. The Ink Manager dialog box allows you to alias all the spot colors to one color. It does not matter which one you choose. Remember that the colors will not be changed; they will just print on the same plate.

However, if you need to convert colors to CMYK by checking the All Spots to Process check box in the lower-left corner of the dialog box, you may have a problem. The Swatches palette to

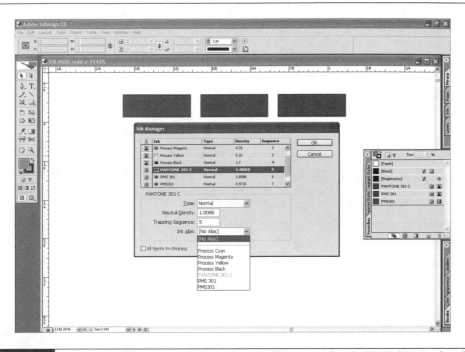

FIGURE 18-1 Three misnamed spot colors that are all supposed to be PMS 301 (a slate blue) showing the alias control

the right in Figure 18-1 shows that two of the colors were created using the CMYK model, and one was made with the RGB model. It is quite possible that the RGB color will change enough to look different when converted to CMYK, although all the colors look identical on the screen.

NOTE   *Another use of the Ink Manager's is in a wet trapping scenario. It enables you to set the ink density and the correct number and sequence of inks. If your printing service indicates that there is this type of problem with the inks, you can show the representative the Ink Manager (and maybe save your job).*

Use the PDF Solution

One of the major skills needed in digital publishing is the ability to make good-quality PDFs. Increasingly, PDFs are the prime format used for proofing. More than that, PDFs are rapidly becoming the preferred format for submission for print. PDFs have the following advantages:

- ■ Fonts can be embedded.
- ■ Graphics are embedded.
- ■ Graphics can be downsampled for excellent compression.
- ■ PDFs are relatively small for what they contain.

18

- ■ There is a free reader for virtually any computer: PC, Mac, or UNIX.
- ■ They can be viewed in a Web browser.
- ■ They can be annotated by multiple proofers.
- ■ They can be edited and color-managed.
- ■ Printers can print from them directly, avoiding the need to send fonts and graphics with the document.
- ■ There is excellent security, so others cannot even print PDFs unless you allow it.
- ■ You can add internal links, hyperlinks, movies, and sound.

But PDFs also have some disadvantages:

- ■ Their file size may be too large for the Web.
- ■ The recipient must have a compatible reader (even though it is free, many people have older versions).
- ■ You cannot annotate or edit with a reader.

You will definitely need the full version of Acrobat. Acrobat comes in several parts. The three you need to know how to use are Reader, Distiller, and Acrobat itself. You will need Distiller to generate PDFs from PostScript files. There are still a number of situations where this will be necessary, such as for PDFs with spot-color separations. Acrobat 6 Pro (which comes with the Creative Suite package) includes Distiller, under File | Create PDF | From File. (It will also process multiple files or make a PDF directly from your scanner, but those capabilities have little to do with your daily work with InDesign.)

Your clients will need Acrobat Reader, as a minimum. If they want to be able to annotate your PDF proofs, they will need the full version of Acrobat (Acrobat 6 Pro is recommended).

Producing PDFs is not nearly as easy as you might think. The assumption is that PDFs nearly make themselves. This is definitely not so. You need to be aware of version differences and final use.

Export Your PDFs Directly from InDesign

One of the best things about InDesign, as far as printing is concerned, is its ability to export PDFs directly. InDesign CS has added some nice capabilities. However, there are many types of PDFs that you will need to produce that cannot be simply exported. Separated spot-color PDFs, and separations in general, need to be printed to disk as PostScript files, and then distilled with Acrobat Distiller to make the PDF. This is often the best solution for multiple overlying transparencies, also.

Unless you have the Type tool active in an insertion point, PDF is the default export format. Choose File | Export (or press CTRL-E/COMMAND-E) to start the process. The first dialog box is a simple Save dialog box with a drop-down list to choose the exported format you need. Once you click OK, the Export PDF dialog box opens. We'll go through each of the pages in this dialog box.

Set Up General PDF Export Options

Figure 18-2 shows the General Page of the Export PDF dialog box. It contains important options for pages, compatibility, standards, and elements to include.

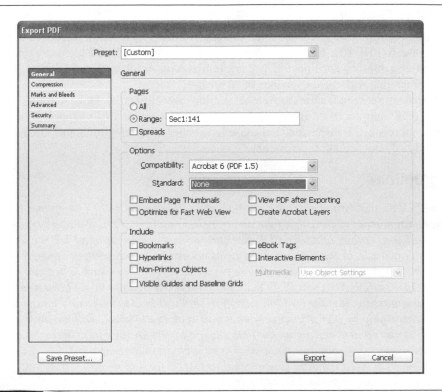

FIGURE 18-2   The General Page of the Export PDF dialog box

Like all of the other Export PDF dialog box pages, this page has a Preset drop-down list at the top and a Save Preset button at the lower left. From the Preset list, you can choose a custom or predefined set of export settings, as discussed in the "Use PDF Export Presets" section later in this chapter. The Save Preset button lets you save your current settings as a custom preset.

Page Choices

In the top section of the General page, you can choose to make a PDF of all the pages or a range of pages. You can type a range by using a hyphen, and add separate multiple pages or ranges by using commas. Ranges are not available when you're exporting books.

You can also decide whether you want to see these pages in reader's spreads. This option exports pages together, as if they were printed on the same sheet of paper. In general, do not select Spreads for commercial printing. If you do, the printer will not be able to impose your pages.

NOTE   *If you are doing your own imposition, some of the imposition scripts that are available to move the pages into printers' spreads do not actually create a double-sized page. In this case, you should choose Spreads in the General page of the Export PDF dialog box.*

18

Compatibility Choices

The Compatibility drop-down list offers three choices: Acrobat 4 (PDF 1.3), Acrobat 5 (PDF 1.4), and Acrobat 6 (PDF 1.5). For wide distribution, choose Acrobat 4 or 5 to ensure that all users can view and print the document. If you create files with Acrobat 6, the PDF files produced may not be compatible with earlier versions of Acrobat.

The differences between features in Acrobat versions are substantial. Only Acrobat 5 and 6-compatible PDFs support transparency. Only Acrobat 6-compatible PDFs support layers and JPEG 2000 compression. Transparency has caused a number of printing problems, because many of the older RIPs do not support transparency.

Standard Options

The PDF/X standard enables the creation and validation of PDF/X-compliant files by eliminating many of the color, font, and trapping problems. PDF/X doesn't replace PDF. It is a limited subset of Adobe PDF that constrains the contents of a PDF file intended for prepress use, or notifies you if any items needed for correct output are missing.

InDesign now allows you to choose two of the PDF/X standards when you create your PDFs: PDF/X-1a and PDF/X-3. These are two international ISO (International Organization for Standardization) standards that will help to make sure that your PDF files are usable by your printer in what is called blind exchange. This means that all the criteria and content making up the PDF file are in one file, and its criteria are chosen by the owner of the prepress equipment to be used for output.

The PDF/X-1a standard supports only a CMYK (and spot-color) workflow, targeted to a specific output device (for example, web offset printing according to SWOP) using the following characteristics:

- *PDF version 1.3 (Acrobat 4.0)*
- *Embedded fonts*
- *No color management allowed*
- *Specified trapped key values, output intents, and TrimBox or ArtBox, with additional keys to identify the file (the printer who asks for this standard knows what to do with this information)*

The PDF/X-3 standard differs from the PDF/X-1a standard in that it allows device-independent, CMYK, and spot colors. According to Adobe, this standard "supports a color-managed workflow, allowing the use of device-independent color (CIE L*a*b, ICC-based color spaces, CalRGB, and CalGray), in addition to CMYK and spot colors. This allows you to use ICC color profiles to specify color data later in the workflow at the output device."

NOTE *Many of these specifications are highly technical. Do what your printer asks you to do. It is not important that you know exactly what all these parameters mean. It is important to know that they will protect you by warning you if something you put in your document is not correct.*

Other General PDF Options

The check boxes in the Options section of the General page offer more choices. Some of these will cause serious problems if used in the wrong place.

- **Embed Page Thumbnails**   This causes a thumbnail preview to be created for each page or spread being exported. This thumbnail is displayed in the InDesign Open or Place dialog box (but only the first page if you are exporting multiple pages). Of course, adding thumbnails increases the PDF file size, but this is not a real concern for print-quality files.

- **Optimize for Fast Web View**   This option can pose a real problem. It reduces PDF file size by optimizing the PDF file. It restructures the file for faster viewing in a Web browser by enabling page-at-a-time downloading. However, it always compresses text and line art, regardless of what you have selected as compression settings. Make sure this one is unchecked if you are going to print the PDF.

- **View PDF after Exporting**   This opens the newly created PDF file in Acrobat, so you can check it. If it won't open there, no one else will be able to open it either. I highly recommend selecting this one.

- **Create Acrobat Layers**   This option causes each InDesign layer, including hidden layers, to be saved as an Acrobat layer within the PDF document. If you select Create Acrobat Layers and also select any printer's marks in the Marks and Bleeds page of the Export PDF dialog box, the printer's marks are exported to a separate marks and bleeds layer. Note that this requires Acrobat 6. Check with your print provider or service bureau before choosing this option, because the RIP must support it.

NOTE   *Using the Create Acrobat Layers option lets you generate multiple versions of the document from a single file. Adobe promotes this using the multiple languages example, telling you to place the text for each language in a different layer. Your printer or service provider can then show and hide the layers in Acrobat 6 to generate different versions of the document. This is probably true. However, every language has different length requirements. Spanish is often twice as long as English, for example.*

Include Options

Most of the choices for what can be included with your PDF are for interactive PDFs or eBooks. They do not affect the print version, except to make the file size larger.

- **Bookmarks**   The bookmarks are created for table of contents entries, and they preserve the table of contents levels. The information specified in the Bookmarks palette is used.

- **Hyperlinks**   This creates Adobe PDF hyperlinks for InDesign hyperlinks, table of contents entries, and index entries.

- **Nonprinting Objects**   This exports objects to which you have applied the Nonprinting option in the Attributes palette. However, my question is this: If you do not want it to print, why do you want it in the PDF? I suppose that you might use this for notes to be seen in the proof stage only. However, I recommend sending clean proofs that do not require an explanation. If an explanation is required, you have probably compromised readability.

- **Visible Guides and Baseline Grids**   This exports margin guides, ruler guides, column guides, and baseline grids in the same color used in the document, but only those currently visible in the document. Again, I really don't see any use for this choice.
- **eBook Tags**   This generates an Adobe PDF file that automatically tags elements in the story based on a subset of the Acrobat 6 tags that InDesign supports.
- **Interactive Elements**   This exports all movies, sounds, and buttons.
- **Multimedia**   This lets you specify how to embed or link movies and sounds.

I use the interactive PDF features regularly for things like digital résumés and the like. But you need to make sure that your intended reader shares your enthusiasm. Millions of dollars of sales have been lost to people who never saw a product, because they could not get through the fancy visuals.

Set Up PDF Compression

The Compression page of the Export PDF dialog box, shown in Figure 18-3, offers compression options for color, grayscale, and monochrome images.

You do not want to compress or downsample bitmaps in PDFs made for print. It lowers the quality. You need to import all your bitmap graphics at 100 percent and not transform them. So, downsampling should not be an issue. The compression options all cause damage. Compression should be set to None for printed PDFs.

For Web, multimedia, and eBook use, you will probably need to use the compression options. For Web documents, it is common to use downsampling to 72 dpi and JPEG compression set at low quality. Just remember that JPEG will add a lot of artifacts that will be very visible if you need to print the PDF. The Tile Size field is available only if you are saving for Acrobat 6 and using JPEG 2000. JPEG 2000 also allows lossless compression.

I have had printing companies demand downsampling, ZIP compression at 8-bit, and everything in between.

Set Up Your PDF Marks and Bleeds

The Marks and Bleeds page of the Export PDF dialog box, shown in Figure 18-4, lets you set up marks, bleeds, and slugs.

Your choices for marks are as follows:

- Crop marks (showing the trim size)
- Bleed marks
- Registration marks (those little targets used for hand-registration or for printing multiple colors on a single-color press)
- Color bars (very simple color bars that would not help press operators much)
- Page information (filename, date printed, and color name for separated PDFs)

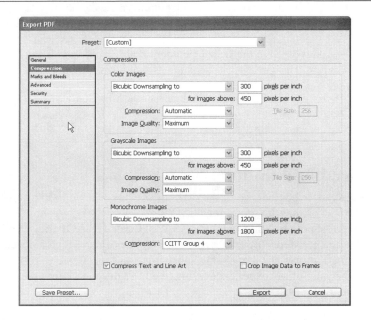

FIGURE 18-3   The Compression page of the Export PDF dialog box

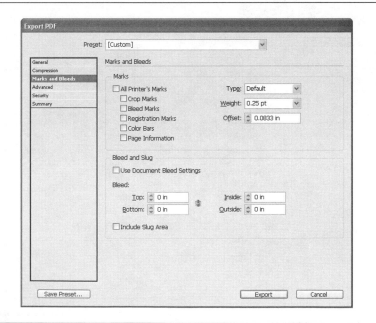

FIGURE 18-4   The Marks and Bleeds page of the Export PDF dialog box

18

In most cases, all you really need are crop marks, but check all the mark options if you do not know. If you are printing on pretrimmed paper (including letter and tabloid), you want the marks turned off.

You should have set your bleed in the New Document dialog box, so you can check the Use Document Bleed dialog box. The same is true of slugs. If you have something set in the slug area, you probably want it to show in the PDF sent to the printer.

For a proof, you want all of the marks turned off. They will just confuse your client.

Set Up Advanced PDF Options

The options on the Advanced page of the Export PDF dialog box, shown in Figure 18-5, apply to printed PDFs. Most of the options are for top-end CMYK. Set it up the way your printing supplier asks you to set it up. Most printers still expect the US Web Coated (SWOP) v2, profile, even though they are printing sheet-fed. However, you have a choice of more than a dozen profiles.

There is one setting I always change: I set to subset fonts at less than 1%. I do not want my fonts subset. This is because of my experience trying to edit PDFs and getting the "Font Not Available" alert too many times.

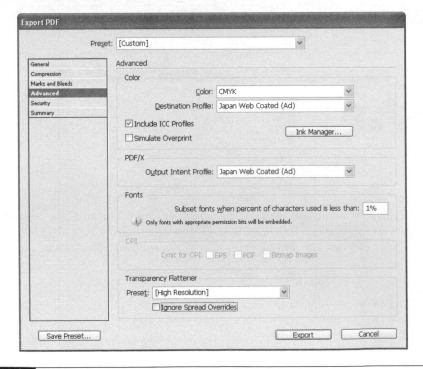

FIGURE 18-5   The Advanced page of the Export PDF dialog box

I have also found that any setting for Transparency Flattener other than High Resolution has caused problems sooner or later. Even though transparency works well on the screen, its printing is not flawless. This is especially true when using older RIPs. I have a Phaser 780 Plus from the late 1990s, for example, that often has rendering problems with transparent objects layered on top of transparent objects. Proof carefully, and do not believe what you see on the screen—either in InDesign or in the exported PDF.

Set Up PDF Security

As you can see in Figure 18-6, the Security page of the Export PDF dialog box offers powerful security for your PDFs.

These options allow you to control PDF security as follows:

- Save your PDF with 128-bit encryption.
- Require a password to open the document.
- Use a second password to restrict access to that document.
- Allow or disallow printing, or just allow low-resolution printing.
- Restrict changes to none; inserting, deleting, or rotating pages; filling in form fields and signing; commenting, filling in form fields and signing; or any except extracting pages.
- Allow or disallow copying of text, images, or pages.
- Enable access of screen readers for the visually impaired.
- Allow access to plaintext metadata.

Check Your PDF Export Settings

The final page of the Export PDF dialog box is the Summary page. You should take a look at this page to make sure you have the correct settings.

You can save your summary as a text file to send along to the printer. You can also save your PDF settings by clicking the Save Preset button. Then you will be able to select these settings from the Preset drop-down list at the top of the Export PDF dialog box. The predefined presets available here are covered in the next section.

 The Export PDF dialog box remembers your last settings and starts there. You can easily get an evolving standard, as you make small adjustments here and there. One of the easier ways to avoid this is to use a saved preset to maintain consistency.

Use PDF Export Presets

A PDF preset is a predefined set of PDF options that you can use for creating Adobe PDF files. InDesign comes with several PDF presets, and you can easily make your own by selecting Save Preset in the Export PDF dialog box. These presets are available through the Preset drop-down list in the Export PDF dialog box.

18

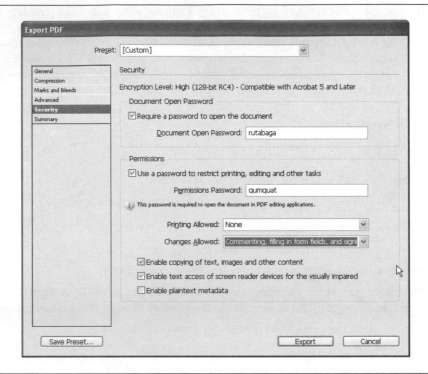

FIGURE 18-6   The Security page of the Export PDF dialog box

Here are the predefined Adobe PDF presets that are shipped with InDesign CS:

- **eBook**   This preset is used to create PDF files that will be read primarily onscreen. This set of options balances file size against image resolution to produce a relatively small, self-contained file; compresses all information; converts all colors to RGB or to Monitor RGB (if color management is enabled); and embeds subsets of all fonts used in the file (except the Base 14 fonts). PDF files created with this preset are compatible with Acrobat 5.0 and later, and Acrobat eBook Reader 2.2 and later.

- **Screen**   This preset is for PDFs that will be displayed on the Web or an intranet, or that will be distributed through an e-mail system for onscreen viewing. This set of options uses compression, downsampling, and a relatively low resolution to create a PDF file that is as small as possible; converts all colors to RGB or to Monitor RGB (if color management is enabled); embeds subsets of all fonts used in the file (except the Base 14 fonts); maintains compatibility with Acrobat 4.0 and later; and optimizes files for byte serving.

- **Print**   This preset is used to create compact PDF files that are intended for laser printers, digital copiers, and CD-ROMs. You can also send them to clients as proofs.

In this set of options, file size is still important, but it is not the only objective. This set of options uses compression and downsampling, leaves colors unchanged, embeds subsets of all fonts used in the file, and prints at low resolution to create a reasonable rendition of the original.

- **Press**   This preset is used to create PDF files that will be printed to imagesetters or platesetters as high-quality final output. In this case, file size is not a consideration. The objective is to maintain all of the information in a PDF file that a commercial printer or service provider will need to print the document correctly. This set of options converts color to CMYK, embeds all fonts used in the file, prints at a higher resolution, and uses other settings to preserve the maximum amount of information contained in the original document.

- **PDF/X-1a**   This preset is used to create PDF files that are PDF/X-1a compliant. Graphics are converted to a compliant version, if possible (or you are given a warning). The PDF/X-1a standard requires that all fonts are embedded, that appropriate PDF boxes are specified, and that color appears as either CMYK or spot colors. PDF files that meet PDF/X-1a requirements are targeted to a specific output condition and can be used only by applications that support PDF/X.

- **PDF/X-3**   This preset is used to create PDF files that are PDF/X-3 compliant. Graphics are converted to a compliant version, if possible (or you are given a warning). PDF/X-3 is like PDF/X-1a, but it supports device-independent color. It can be used only by applications that support PDF/X.

- **Acrobat 6 Layered**   This preset is used to create PDF files in which all InDesign layers, including hidden layers, are saved as Acrobat layers. This allows Acrobat 6 users to generate multiple versions of a document from a single file.

Print Your Documents

You'll frequently want to print proofs of your documents, as discussed in Chapter 17. Also, you may be producing your documents in-house.

To start the printing process, select File | Print (or press CTRL-P/COMMAND-P) to open the Print dialog box. We'll go through the eight pages in this dialog box, most of which are similar to those in the Export PDF dialog box, covered in the previous section.

Set Up General Printing Options

Figure 18-7 shows the General page of the Print dialog box. The first option is to choose a preset. You should create a preset for each printer you will use. To do this, just select Save Preset after you've completed the Print dialog box. In the next two fields, pick the printer you will be using and the correct PPD (PostScript Printer Description) file. Yes, InDesign will print to a non-PostScript printer, but as I explained in Chapter 18, you need PostScript for professional production.

18

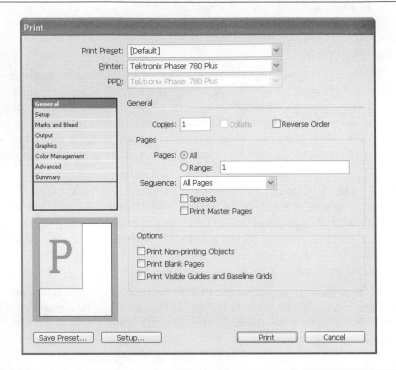

FIGURE 18-7   The General page of the Print dialog box

NOTE

This section shows the Mac version of the Print dialog box. The options are the same in both operating systems. The example is my old Tektronix Phaser 780 Plus, 400 dpi with 8-bit pixels, PostScript 3 (but a very early RIP). It has been working with few problems since 1998. I call it PaperZapper.

On this page, you set how many copies, which pages, and whether you want to collate. The Sequence choices are All Pages, Even Pages Only, or Odd Pages Only. This helps if you are hand-duplexing because you're using a machine that will not produce automatically duplexed sheets (printed on both sides). You can also choose whether to print blank pages, nonprinting objects, guides, and grids.

At the bottom of the page is a Setup button. This displays normal printer setup options. You might use this if you need to set which paper tray will be used or how the printer will treat color. Do not make changes here that conflict with your settings in the Print dialog box.

Choose Print Setup Options

The Setup page, shown in Figure 18-8, has some important items, which vary widely, depending on which printer and which PPD you are using. You pick the sheet size of the paper that you're using for printing. The page sizes available to your printer are written into your PPD.

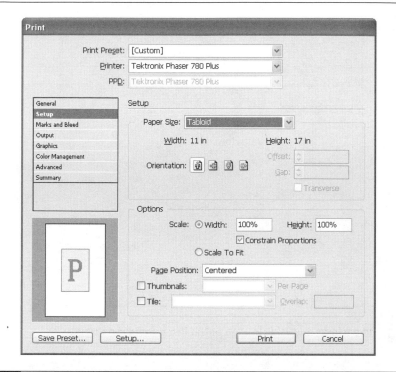

FIGURE 18-8   The Setup page of the Print dialog box

This is also where you choose the page orientation, page scaling, tiling, and the like. Again, the number of choices here depends on your PPD. On my printer, for example, Transverse is always grayed out. This is because Transverse is a choice for imagesetters, to save film.

For Page Position, Upper Left is the default setting. Unless you are tiling (printing your oversize page in sections to be taped together), you should choose Centered. This is especially true if you need to show the marks. If you do not choose Centered, the marks are often outside the printable image area.

Set Up Your Printed Marks and Bleeds

Figure 18-9 shows the Marks and Bleeds page of the Print dialog box. These are the same choices found on the Marks and Bleed page of the Export PDF dialog box (see the "Set Up Your PDF Marks and Bleeds" section earlier in the chapter).

Configure Your Printed Output

The Output page of Print dialog box, shown in Figure 18-10, is one of the most important. In most cases, your Color choice will be Composite CMYK or Composite Grayscale. These are the settings needed to make a proof.

18

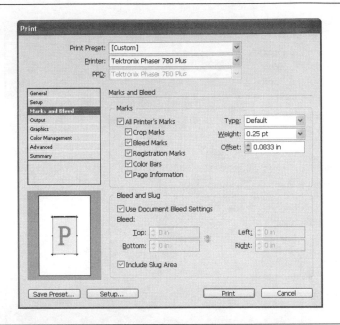

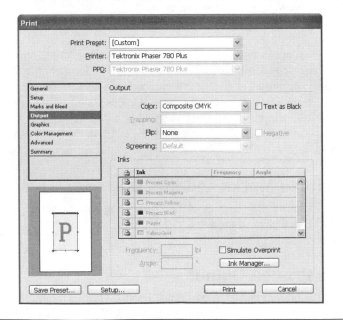

NOTE

Remember that this example shows a CMYK printer, which is not capable of printing spot color. There is no digital printer that can print spot color except for the Risograph and the Ricoh Priport. The Priport can use any PMS color, but you must make a plate and run make-readies (for each color) to use it for proofing.

There is a Text As Black check box, which you might want to check to make sure the type is easy to read. However, in my experience, this changes things too much, so I never use it. If you are outputting film, you can flip the image to make it right-reading emulsion down. However, the dot structure on a printer like the one in Figure 18-10 is strange due to the multicolored dots, so it makes lousy plates.

The Ink Manager button is here, but that is rarely needed for composite proofs.

NEW TO
**InDesign
CS**

One of the nicer features in InDesign CS is the Simulate Overprint check box. It won't show traps, but it can quickly point out color problems caused by overprinting or the lack of overprinting. The colors may not be accurate, but you can see the overprints.

Set Up Graphics Printing

The Graphics page of the Print dialog box, shown in Figure 18-11, has some important choices.

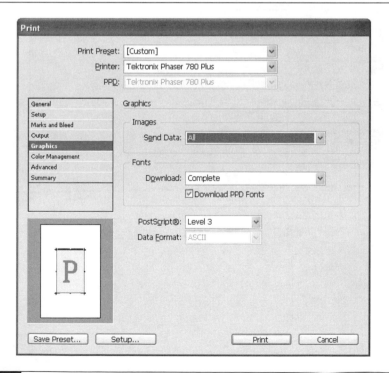

FIGURE 18-11   The Graphics page of the Print dialog box

18

The options are as follows:

■ **Send Data**   The default is Sub-sampled. This may allow faster printing, but I want to see what the graphic actually looks like, so I always choose All.

■ **Download**   This selects how you want to download your fonts. The default is Subset. This means that it sends only the characters used. This has caused some printing problems in the past, so I change that to Complete.

■ **PostScript**   This is where you choose which PostScript level your printer is using.

■ **Data Format**   This is supposed to give you the choice of ASCII or binary. Binary is faster and was always the best choice in Mac OS9 or earlier. However, OSX does not support binary, and the PC never did.

Set Up Color Management Options

The Color Management page of the Print dialog box, shown in Figure 18-12, will be entirely grayed out, unless you have turned on color management (discussed in Chapter 14). If you have enabled color management, pick the appropriate profile for your machine. I generally leave it at SWOP, because most of my printers ask for that. Set the Color Management options just as your printer or service bureau asks you to set them up.

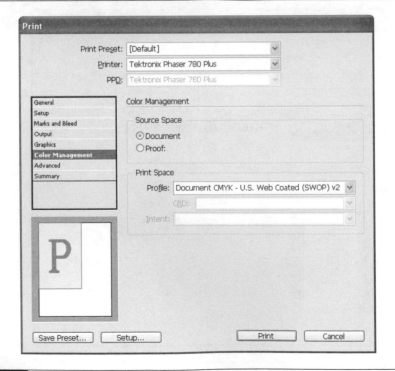

FIGURE 18-12   The Color Management page of the Print dialog box

Choose Advanced Printing Options

The Advanced page of the Print dialog box, shown in Figure 18-13, has some rarely used settings. It also has the very important transparency flattener settings.

OPI Settings

OPI stands for Open Press Interface (or Open Prepress Interface). You will use this setting when you are having your printing company or service bureau produce your high-resolution scans. They will then send you FPO (for position only), low-resolution placeholders for the images. You place those into your document. You can manipulate these placeholders any way that you find necessary. Notes will be written into your document to tell the OPI software what you did to the image. When you send the document to the service provider, the high-resolution images will be inserted in place of the FPO images, and all the changes you made will be applied to the high-resolution images.

This would be the preferred method for critical color. It puts the responsibility of the quality of the color on the shoulders of those with the experience to do it properly.

Transparency Flattener Settings

As I've noted, you cannot print transparency. The transparent portions of your document must be flattened before they can be printed. There are three settings available in the Preset drop-down list: High-Resolution, Low, and Medium. These are editable through the Transparency Presets

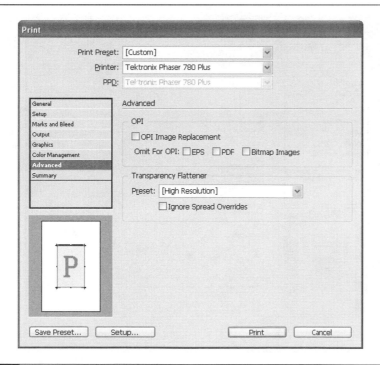

FIGURE 18-13   The Advanced page of the Print dialog box

option in the Transparency Flattener Presets dialog box (opened by choosing Edit | Transparency Flattener Presets).

Low and Medium do gradients at 144 dpi and 150 dpi, respectively. That will cause banding. These options rasterize vectors and type at 288 dpi and 300 dpi, respectively. That is very soft for line art and type, which need to be rasterized at the highest resolution you have available. The High Resolution setting does not rasterize anything. If it is vector, it remains vector.

Some people say that using the High Resolution setting can seriously slow down image processing by your imagesetter or platesetter. That's too bad. Using anything less compromises the quality of your output.

Choose the setting your service provider requests, but recognize that this choice affects the quality of your proof.

Check Your Print Settings

You need to check the Summary page of the Print dialog box regularly. As you can see in Figure 18-14, it shows all the settings you have chosen. Often, you will be surprised. If so, go back and fix your settings. Then click the Save Preset button at the bottom of the page to save a print preset for this particular printer. As noted earlier, you should have a preset saved for each printer you use.

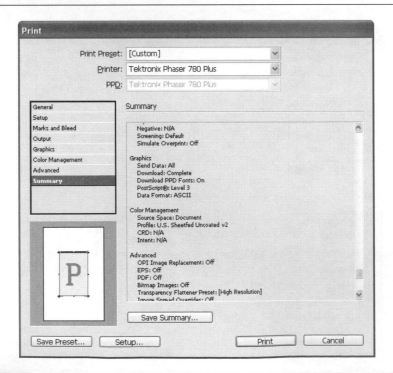

FIGURE 18-14   The Summary page of the Print dialog box

Save Summary creates a report that you should send along with the proof if your service provider asks for it.

Although the Summary page of the Print dialog box may look complicated, it is relatively simple for the complex task of printing professionally. If you just print without checking the settings, it's likely you will have problems. Every printer is a little different. You need to learn those differences and figure out how to compensate for them.

Make PDF Separations

Typically, you will not be producing the separations, because your printer usually does this for you. However, if you have your own press, you will need to print your colors separately. Every color needs its own output. If you are sending your project to a quickprinter, the workers may not have the expertise to do the separations. In most cases, the best solution is a separated PDF.

A separated PDF has each color of ink on a separate grayscale page. Each plate is grayscale, but printed in whatever color ink is needed. If you are printing a project that uses a deep red (say PMS 200) and a deep blue (say PMS 302), you will need to output one page in the grayscale that will be printed in red, and a second page that will have the grayscale image that will be printed in blue.

You cannot make a separated PDF by direct export. You must print a PostScript file to disk and then distill it. We have covered all the choices you need to make when exporting a PDF. These same choices are available when distilling a PDF in Acrobat Distiller. However, InDesign makes the separations.

In InDesign, open the Print dialog box (choose File | Print or press CTRL-P/COMMAND-P). Your first choice is the printer, and here you choose PostScript File. You are taking the PostScript file that would normally be sent to the printer when you print and saving it to your hard drive. This file contains all the code necessary for the RIP to produce each plate. Figure 18-15 shows the Output page of the Print dialog box set up for separations.

Here are the settings for creating PDF separations:

- **PPD**   Normally, you will want to pick Adobe PDF as the PPD. In this example, the Phaser 780 Plus PPD is selected, which limits the choices for linescreen. Some service providers will want you to use the PPD for the imagesetter, platesetter, or digital proofer that they supply to you.

- **Color**   In the Color drop-down list, instead of Composite CMYK or Composite Grayscale, you need to choose Separations.

- **Trapping**   For Trapping, pick whatever you need. The choices are Off, Application Built-in, and Adobe In-RIP.

- **Flip**   I have always left Flip set to None, but some providers will want you to choose a horizontal flip, vertical flip, or both.

- **Screening**   The linescreen should normally be the best offered by your output device. In the case of the Phaser, this is said to be 60 lpi/600 dpi. The Adobe PDF PPD gives these choices: 100 lpi/1200 dpi, 175 lpi/2400 dpi, 200 lpi/3600 dpi, 200 lpi/4000 dpi, 50 lpi/144 dpi, 60 lpi/300 dpi, 60 lpi/72 dpi, and 71 lpi/600 dpi. Pick the one with the resolution of your output device. If you need to guess, use 100 lpi/1200 dpi for quickprint, and 175 lpi/2400 dpi for commercial printing.

■ **Inks**   The Inks list shows the colors used in your document. Cyan, Magenta, Yellow, and Black are always there, whether you need them or not. In Figure 18-15, you can see that there are also three spot colors: Purple, YellowGold, and Green. Normally, these will be PMS numbers or whatever you use for your standardized spot colors. To the left of the color names is an icon that shows whether you are going to print that color to the PostScript file. Click it to toggle it off or on. In Figure 18-15, you can see a slash through the print icon for the Process Magenta and Process Yellow plates, indicating that will not print to the file.

■ **Frequency and Angle**   Below the Inks list are two fields for the linescreen and screen angle of the selected ink. The only screen angles usually available to a PostScript printer are 45°, 75°, 105° (or 15°), and 0°. These are the screen angles used for CMYK. The normal screen angle for any spot color will be 45 degrees, which will produce the least visible screen. However, two 45-degree screens printed on top of each other will moiré horribly. My recommendation is to use the 45-degree angle for the strongest spot color (or black) and use the 75- and 105-degree angles for the other two (if you use that many). You will need to examine the output and the finished product to see how it worked. If there are problems, try something else the next run through.

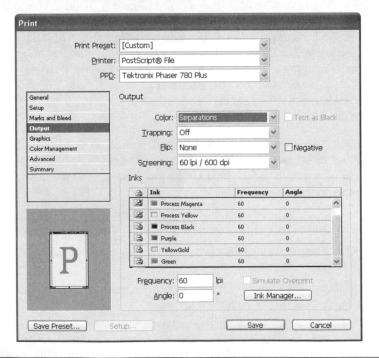

FIGURE 18-15   The Output page set up for separations

The Frequency and Angles settings are where you will get into problems if you use mixed-ink swatches. You will get bad moiré patterns and ugly screen if you use the defaults. The best advice I have is to experiment, because the proper settings vary for different printers.

You can see why it is better to pay a commercial printer who knows what to do. The problem, of course, is that if you are making separations, you have already been forced to make a different choice in the matter. With experience, you will work it out.

Always Talk to Your Printer Contact First

Always pick your printer before you start designing. Ask your contact how to set up your print job. If you contact does not know, ask to talk to the production manager or someone else who knows what is required for the company's press or duplicator.

Every setup is different. You need to adapt to the reality of the print shop you have chosen (especially if you are forced to use someone less than desired because of client choice). Have fun!

Index

INTERNATIONAL CONTACT INFORMATION

AUSTRALIA
McGraw-Hill Book Company
Australia Pty. Ltd.
TEL +61-2-9900-1800
FAX +61-2-9878-8881
http://www.mcgraw-hill.com.au
books-it_sydney@mcgraw-hill.com

CANADA
McGraw-Hill Ryerson Ltd.
TEL +905-430-5000
FAX +905-430-5020
http://www.mcgraw-hill.ca

**GREECE, MIDDLE EAST, & AFRICA
(Excluding South Africa)**
McGraw-Hill Hellas
TEL +30-210-6560-990
TEL +30-210-6560-993
TEL +30-210-6560-994
FAX +30-210-6545-525

MEXICO (Also serving Latin America)
McGraw-Hill Interamericana Editores
S.A. de C.V.
TEL +525-1500-5108
FAX +525-117-1589
http://www.mcgraw-hill.com.mx
carlos_ruiz@mcgraw-hill.com

SINGAPORE (Serving Asia)
McGraw-Hill Book Company
TEL +65-6863-1580
FAX +65-6862-3354
http://www.mcgraw-hill.com.sg
mghasia@mcgraw-hill.com

SOUTH AFRICA
McGraw-Hill South Africa
TEL +27-11-622-7512
FAX +27-11-622-9045
robyn_swanepoel@mcgraw-hill.com

SPAIN
McGraw-Hill/
Interamericana de España, S.A.U.
TEL +34-91-180-3000
FAX +34-91-372-8513
http://www.mcgraw-hill.es
professional@mcgraw-hill.es

**UNITED KINGDOM, NORTHERN,
EASTERN, & CENTRAL EUROPE**
McGraw-Hill Education Europe
TEL +44-1-628-502500
FAX +44-1-628-770224
http://www.mcgraw-hill.co.uk
emea_queries@mcgraw-hill.com

ALL OTHER INQUIRIES Contact:
McGraw-Hill/Osborne
TEL +1-510-420-7700
FAX +1-510-420-7703
http://www.osborne.com
omg_international@mcgraw-hill.com

Sound Off!

Visit us at **www.osborne.com/bookregistration** and let us know what you thought of this book. While you're online you'll have the opportunity to register for newsletters and special offers from McGraw-Hill/Osborne.

We want to hear from you!

Sneak Peek

Visit us today at **www.betabooks.com** and see what's coming from McGraw-Hill/Osborne tomorrow!

Based on the successful software paradigm, Bet@Books™ allows computing professionals to view partial and sometimes complete text versions of selected titles online. Bet@Books™ viewing is free, invites comments and feedback, and allows you to "test drive" books in progress on the subjects that interest you the most.